# Demystifying Social Finance and Social Investment

Social finance and social investment are not challenging concepts to grasp. They use commercial-style investment tools to create a social as well as a financial return. The application, however, is not always as straightforward. This book begins in the wider field of social finance but focuses primarily on social investment as a tool. The reader is helped to understand this from different angles: introducing social investment, discussing social investment and taking a "deep-dive" into it to bring it to life. This unique book takes the reader on a journey from first principles to detailed practical application.

This book examines the policy context and asks why social investment has only recently become so popular, when in reality this is a very old concept. This is linked to the agenda of making charities more "business-like", set against the changing face of investment, as charities can no longer rely on donations and grants as guaranteed income. The work they do is more important than ever and social investment, used with care, offers a new opportunity that is further explored in this text. Mark Salway, Paul Palmer, Peter Grant and Jim Clifford will help readers understand how a small amount of borrowing, or a different business model focused away from grants and donations, could be transformational for the non-profit sector.

**Mark Salway** FCA is a Chartered Accountant with over 20 years of finance experience in the charity sector. He has been Finance Director at several large charities, and also worked as a management consultant for both commercial and non-profit organisations – such as the UN, Age UK, the Wellcome Trust, and WSUP (Water and Sanitation for the Urban Poor) – and with the government. Mark was invited into Cass Business School, Centre for Charity Effectiveness (Cass CCE), to start its fledgling work on social investment and social finance. He led this successfully for five years. This eventually changed into focusing on financial sustainability and nonprofit business models. Mark currently runs the consulting services to charities at Moore Kingston Smith, a major UK accounting and advisory firm. He also runs several MSc modules at Cass Business School, where he is continuing his research work.

**Charity and Non-Profit Studies**

Series Editors: Paul Palmer and Peter Grant

**Demystifying Social Finance and Social Investment**

*By Mark Salway edited by Paul Palmer, Peter Grant and Jim Clifford*

# Demystifying Social Finance and Social Investment

By Mark Salway

Edited by Paul Palmer, Peter Grant and Jim Clifford

Routledge
Taylor & Francis Group

LONDON AND NEW YORK

First published 2021
by Routledge
2 Park Square, Milton Park, Abingdon, Oxon OX14 4RN

and by Routledge
52 Vanderbilt Avenue, New York, NY 10017

*Routledge is an imprint of the Taylor & Francis Group, an informa business*

*British Library Cataloguing-in-Publication Data*
A catalogue record for this book is available from the British Library

*Library of Congress Cataloging-in-Publication Data*
Names: Salway, Mark, editor. | Palmer, Paul, 1955- editor. | Grant, Peter, 1955 February 21- editor.
Title: Demystifying social finance and social investment / edited by Mark Salway, Paul Palmer, Peter Grant, and Jim Clifford.
Description: New York : Routledge, 2020. | Series: Charity and non-profit studies | Includes bibliographical references and index.
Identifiers: LCCN 2020024628 | ISBN 9781472481740 (hardback) | ISBN 9780367556280 (paperback) | ISBN 9781315576510 (ebook)
Subjects: LCSH: Charities–Finance. | Charities–Accounting.
Classification: LCC HF5686.C2 D456 2020 | DDC 361.7068/1–dc23
LC record available at https://lccn.loc.gov/2020024628

ISBN: 978-1-4724-8174-0 (hbk)
ISBN: 978-0-367-55628-0 (pbk)
ISBN: 978-1-315-57651-0 (ebk)

Typeset in Bembo
by Wearset Ltd, Boldon, Tyne and Wear

# Contents

# Acknowledgements

## Profound thanks

As the old African proverb goes: "If you want to go fast, go alone. If you want to go far, go together".

This book really is a product of this journey. Whereas I was able to sprint in the early stages of Cass Business School's work in social investment, I have needed to involve others to travel far.

I hope this book reflects this journey.

My profound thanks go to everyone who has travelled with me on this road:

- The Worshipful Company of Management Consultants, Denise Fellows and Professor Paul Palmer – for their initial belief
- Mr. Alexander Hoare – for his quiet sponsorship and guidance
- Paul Sizeland, my mentor and guide, who has kept prodding me to get the "blooming book done"
- Jim Clifford, who quite simply is a force of nature – with the power to keep going and see the end game
- Mark Griffiths, the consummate editor, who has kept me sane when I have struggled to see the light
- To the million and one stars who have helped me profoundly: Juliette Valdinger; Dr Peter Grant; Alex Skailes; the MSc students who have written chapters; and many others, too many to mention here
- Marcus Lees-Millais, who has read and re-read this book a thousand times, each time with a smile and positive comment; and finally
- To Ann, my partner, who is sat on a boat in Greece, editing this for me and feeling my pain. Thanks for putting up with me.

Final thanks to all those who have contributed to this book and have the dream of making social investment a powerful new force for social good.

Mark Salway FCA
Director of Sustainable Finance
Cass Business School, Centre for Charity Effectiveness (Cass CCE)
Managing Director
Moore Kingston Smith Fundraising and Management

# Editors' introduction and how to use this book

# 1 Editors' introduction

*Paul Palmer, Peter Grant and Jim Clifford*

In this first chapter, we introduce the book's three editors, its author and the book itself. We, the editors, are:

Professor **Paul Palmer** – Director of the Centre for Charity Effectiveness and Professor of Voluntary Sector Management, Cass Business School, City, University of London.

Doctor **Peter Grant** FRHistS – Senior Lecturer at Cass Business School, City, University of London.

**Jim Clifford** OBE MSc FCA – Founder and CEO of Sonnet Advisory & Impact CIC, and a Visiting Research Fellow at Cass Centre for Charity Effectiveness (Cass CCE).

## How this book came about

A look at the political and charity sector press over the last two decades would suggest that social finance and social investment are a modern phenomenon. In fact, they have a long and noble history, much of it blending charity and charitable intent with the financial structures and impetus of business.

Take Thomas Firmin's response to unemployment and destitution following the Great Fire of London in 1666 and the origins of the Building Societies in the 1840s. These are just two examples of social finance and social investment initiatives throughout history explored in this book. There are many others, yet the narrative of social finance and social investment is often seen as a very modern one, perhaps because the last two decades have seen the science, practice and policy around them change and grow beyond belief, developing a discipline that is widely acknowledged and valued at the heart of society.

## The beginning of a modern "social" renaissance

How and why did this begin? In 2000, Sir Ronald Cohen, at the invitation of HM Treasury, formed the Social Investment Taskforce (subsequently morphing into the Social Impact Investment Taskforce in 2010) to look at how this phenomenon could be developed in the UK and beyond. Bridges Ventures, blending traditional venture capital models with an overt social focus, was subsequently co-founded by him in 2002. Three years later, the Commission on Unclaimed Assets was formed in a move which ultimately resulted in the founding of Big Society Capital (BSC) in 2011. BSC was the world's first social investment institution of its kind, established by the Cabinet Office and launched as an independent organisation with a £600 million investment fund in April 2012. In short, the last two decades have seen the establishment of formal institutions whose role is to build and grow the social investment market per se.

## The impact of reduced public services

As this story unfolded, so did a crisis in the over-inflated financial markets, which collapsed in 2007–8. The response from Gordon Brown's Labour government was to bail out the banking sector to the tune of £500 billion. A move followed by the OECD and others, this was hailed as the right means to avoid the crisis escalating. As economic recession followed, the 2010 election saw a change in government to a Conservative–Liberal coalition, led by David Cameron. Where government had grown big and encountered economic recession, the Coalition promised a "Big Society" in which people and their local government would lead. Borrowing heavily to fund the bank bail-out, the Coalition promoted austerity in public services, hoping for a parallel growth in private sector trade and private sector debt to gradually rebalance and "buy back" the problem. What has partly developed from this cutting back in public services – and partly from people's wanting to move away from business where money generation is the primary driver – is a focus on social enterprise and social capital. These hybrid models recognise that both financial returns and social returns are critical.

## The Social Business Initiative in Europe

Meanwhile, in 2012, the European Commission recognised the importance of social business to economies and to individual and community wellbeing. Social business at that time encompassed 10 per cent of the EU economy (in GDP terms) and employed 11 million workers. National governments were urged to "develop eco-systems for social enterprise, to strengthen efforts at national and regional levels, and to make best use of the structural funds and other available sources of support." (Social Business Initiative of the European Commission). The Commission itself formed the Social Business Initiative to support and develop those efforts.

In the UK, the passing of the 2012 Social Value Act – originated by Chris White MP as a private member's bill – is one of many reflections of the emergence of a social and environmental awareness in public spending which has contributed to the focus on social finance and its growth.

## Charity – old-fashioned?

Against this backdrop – with an increasing focus on business solutions, blended with newly purposeful public commissioning – some suggested that charity was old-fashioned. Business had learned from 2007 and a newly emergent fusion of social businesses was seen as the way forward to deal with social issues.

New forms of finance forged out of leverage techniques borrowed from the private equity industry would be the bedrock for this new social delivery. The underlying philosophy was grounded in the age-old self-help motto of "give someone a fish and feed them for a day – show them how to fish and feed them for life". The coalition government appeared much taken by this perspective. Not only would it involve limited seed-funding from government, it was seen as sustainable and very different from the compact that had defined the previous Labour government's relationship with the sector. There was also a recognition that solving the root cause of social problems would head off growing demand for public services.

The social investment landscape evolved with UK trusts and foundations starting to earmark part of their endowment for social investment – notably the Esmée Fairbairn Foundation and Tudor Trust.

Similarly, across the world organisations started springing up focused on social investment – from pension funds, institutional funds to umbrella bodies. This has been a rapidly expanding and evolving landscape.

## Our stance, as charity academics

Grounded in history, we were quite sceptical of the claims around social investment we'd been hearing since 2008. However, when we raised our views, we were vilified in articles and at conferences that depicted us as reactionary and out of touch. Yet, as advocates, we had created the first master's degree in social investment in 2011. That said, we neither liked the hype created nor its Orwellian concept of "charity good but social enterprise and social investment better".[1] We saw that the old tools of charity – grants, donations and contracts – were just as needed as ever. We also saw that within this dynamic, social enterprise and social investment needed to be seen as tools just like any others.

## Introducing our Director of Sustainable Finance

In 2014 – with support from the Worshipful Company of Management Consultants, the co-founders of the Cass Business School Centre for Charity Effectiveness (Cass CCE) and other philanthropic supporters (most notably Hoare's Bank) – we were able to employ Mark Salway as Director of Social and Sustainable Finance.

Already teaching finance at the Business School since 2002, Mark had been behind many social finance enterprise ventures when Finance Director and joint Acting-CEO at CARE International. Our brief to Mark was first to operate within an applied business school tradition of finding out how it works; and then go further by taking a critical perspective lens to build a programme that can properly evaluate and understand what is going on; and ultimately to disseminate this knowledge.

To meet the brief, Mark has worked as a practical academic throughout with colleagues within and outside the Business School. His publications, toolkits, articles and lectures on this subject have reached thousands of charities and individuals across the world.

This book is the result of Mark's work to make sense of social investment and recognise it as an established practice; hence its title *Demystifying Social Finance and Social Investment*.

## Meeting the growing need

As Cass Business School developed its views – through Mark's action research and the operations of Cass CCE and the Charities Masters programmes at Cass Business School – much continued to change and develop, both in the charity sector and in the wider economy.

Central government's reforms of public services have continued. Privatisation programmes, such as that in the probation service, were pursued by their proponents, who seemed not to hear the ringing of warning bells. Despite the best intentions of the Social Value Act, charities and social enterprises lost contracts to private sector providers, while reduced public funding compromised their ability to deliver services of acceptable quality.

The need for investment in social provision is growing, as we learn ever more about the depth of need that people in our communities have – and what is required to meet it. The lack of public sector funding to tackle community need shows no sign of abating. The role of charity and social enterprise in supporting our society, our economy and our wellbeing is greater than ever.

## What we learned

The key thing we learned through Mark's work is that social investment is not a "silver bullet". It is, however, a powerful funding tool.

Some organisations see this through rose-coloured spectacles and want social investment to fix their broken business models. But used carefully it could be part of the solution.

Many organisations just don't realise how different using social investment can be from grants and donations; and how much time and effort it takes to engage investors, go through due diligence and deliver real value from using social investment.

Many organisations have grown using social investment and have made a great success of using it. The case studies in this book attest to this.

## Social investment is opening up new opportunities

As problems are being encountered, so too are opportunities embraced – particularly for capital funding into this field. While partly due to lower financial returns in the general investment markets, this also reflects an increasing interest in going beyond the ethical into environmental, social and governance (ESG) and socially responsible investment. Equally, crowdfunding and a focus on community provision have not been wasted efforts; innovation in areas such as social prescribing and local support networks has become established, showing future promise. All can be underpinned by social investment.

In 2020, we can see fascinating opportunities emerging. Social investment funds are building up strategic partnerships with charity and social enterprise providers, enabling funding to be better focused on impact. Indeed, there's the recognition of mixed motive investment by the Charity Commission as valid for charities, as well as a refocusing on how they can best use resources for impact.

We also see pension funds, larger investment funds and local authority pension schemes becoming more interested in this space and making their first investments. This is an exciting time.

As a result, we are seeing more charities – and not just the endowed ones – cross-investing in impact delivered by others. The corporate venturing market is also developing, with private sector corporates looking beyond investing in pure innovation and instead re-purposing existing investment models to enable mission-aligned social and environmental change. Efforts to build consensus, insight and simplicity in impact measurement are increasing, all helping with focus and transparency.

As we come right up to date, and with the Covid-19 pandemic dominating our Worlds, we need all the tools at our disposal to help create social change. Social finance and social investment also gives us hope in that context.

## The focus of this book

In this book we focus specifically on those organisations whose primary aim is to create social value. As such, we explore social investment in charities and social enterprises that are also charities.

**Overall, social finance and investment is an exciting area, one in which charities and social enterprises can and must rightly take a leading role. In this volume, we bring together many voices and views from those intimately involved. We link them together with a narrative that takes you, the reader, on a journey to understanding and rationalising social investment. We offer this to you as our contribution to your impact. We hope it helps.**

## Note

1 In *Animal Farm* the pigs, who were now running the farm and had learned to walk on two legs, introduced the mantra "Four legs good but two legs better" to distinguish themselves from their fellow animals. They had of course, lost sight of their true selves and true worth in doing so.

# 2   How to use this book

*Mark Salway, Paul Palmer, Peter Grant and Jim Clifford*

This book is designed as both a reference work and a practical guide and will be useful to anyone with an interest in the world of social investment.

With a blend of material from lead authors for each of the three sections, and a range of contributions from others giving personal views, research and case studies, we have endeavoured to give a rounded perspective of the subject so that the reader can understand it from all angles.

It is structured into three sections:

## Introducing (Chapters 3–10)

Here, we develop the interface between charities and social purpose organisations on the one hand and social investors on the other. Get to know each other's needs and motivations as the book explores the rudiments of social investment.

## Discussing (Chapters 11–19)

In this section, we give a platform to a range of business, charitable and institutional commentators who can talk about this space, historically and contemporarily, for and against: not always comfortably, but poignantly and constructively.

## Doing (Chapters 20–27)

Lastly, this part of the book takes you into the heads of charity leaders and advisors as they contemplate social investment. Not for the faint-hearted, it provides the right level of technical knowledge to set out on the journey.

Throughout, a series of **case studies** illuminates the chapters, bringing social investment to life and demystifying it for both investor and investee.

The **appendix** includes a checklist to help you ask the right questions about social investment for your own organisation; it helps you see whether all the key components are in place to start.

## Who is the book for?

We hope that many people in a variety of roles will find this book useful. A few examples are given below.

## Are you a leader of a charity or social purpose organisation today?

If you are a leader, you are going to want to take note of more than a few chapters in this book. Not everything in it will be useful or relevant; and you will want to pass some of it on to your colleagues, your trustees or your board. But some of this will be gold dust to you.

There's great experiential advice from your peers who have already set off down the road of developing and using social investment. This book will provide a foundation for you to build on.

Some of it will be like Groundhog Day. You've been concerned about disappearing income streams and worrying about what lies ahead: not just beyond 2020, but next year, next quarter.

This book is focused mainly on the UK, but also provides international case studies. It should be equally useful for those with an interest in social investment from across the world.

This first edition, launched in 2020, is for you and your determination to see your charitable or social purpose organisation succeed. In 2030, it's our hope that you'll look back, remember picking up this book and say, "Now I understand. Why did it take me so long? This is what helped me gain the courage to change and face the future differently."

## Are you a charity finance practitioner or student wanting to know more about social investment?

If you are a charity finance practitioner or student, then this book will provide a sound footing to develop a deeper understanding of social investment and how it can be used as a powerful tool to help create social impact in a sustainable way.

The book is written from a "pracademic" viewpoint – grounded in research, analysing existing literature with appropriate referencing, through to application for the practitioner to reflect and apply.

## Are you an investor wanting to know what leaders of charities and social purpose organisations really think of social investment?

If you are an investor who has made a recent commitment to social change, that's a question which you are really going to want to explore and get answers to. This book will be part of your essential pre-reading before that first meeting with leaders of charitable and social purpose organisations.

If you're an experienced social investor, you may wonder why this book is aimed at you, too. What can it tell you that you don't already know, haven't already experienced? More than anything, this book will illuminate the critical mindsets in the social and charitable organisations you have yet to encounter and with which you would seek to do business. If you are working with a charity finance director or a social enterprise CEO only just beginning to think about new financial models, this book will encourage you to use your understanding in a balanced way in helping these people develop.

Whatever your experience of charities and social purpose organisations as an investor, we hope you will see this book as the beginning of better conversations that lead to better outcomes. Having dived into this book, you'll be able to say, "At last, all the key points in one place. Now, we can start making it work."

## Are you concerned about how charities and social purpose organisations make their money and what they do with it?

You may not be involved in charitable activity, but you'll likely be a taxpayer or a student of social change. If you're interested in the role of charitable and social purpose organisations in changing the world we live in, you might want to know how the money works. You'll want to get a handle on what makes their leaders tick and what makes investors get involved.

Whilst we've seen the growth of socially focused organisations in general, charities specifically have had a hard time in the twenty-first century. They can no longer rely on donations and grants as guaranteed income streams for the future. Yet the work they do is more important than ever, leaving "problems as opportunities" to be solved by different organisations.

If all you do is dip into this book and say, "Now I get it", that's progress.

Those reading through the book in detail will note that some definitions, themes and examples appear more than once. This is deliberate and is intended to reinforce key points and illustrate the connections within social investment.

Finally, we would welcome your feedback and engagement through Cass CCE so that your own experience can contribute to the living history, community and future evolution of social investment. As part of this book launch, we will provide mechanisms to do this.

This book is the result of the efforts of many individuals – some mentioned explicitly in the text. It has proved a much harder exercise than any of us thought it would be when we embarked on the project. This reflects the fact that social investment in its current incarnation is relatively new and the "rules" are still evolving in the light of experience. Any errors of fact or interpretation are entirely ours. But we hope that you enjoy reading it and find it useful and inspiring.

Mark Salway, Jim Clifford, Peter Grant, Paul Palmer

# Introducing social investment

# 3 The purpose of this section

## Introducing social investment

*Mark Salway*

This and other *introducing social investment* chapters have been written by **Mark Salway**, Director of Sustainable Finance, Cass Centre for Charity Effectiveness (Cass CCE). They provide a practitioner and academic foundation for the remainder of this book.

## This section

We have written this book so that the reader can look at social investment and understand this from different angles: introducing social investment, discussing social investment and taking a "deep-dive" into social investment and how you bring it into life ("doing" social investment). In the appendices, we conclude by providing the reader with a toolkit (as 28 key questions) for any organisation seeking such investment. We also provide a terminology section.

**This section provides the foundations and basis for the rest of the book.** It discusses what social investment is, both from a practitioner viewpoint and from an academic standpoint.

We discuss what charities and social enterprises want from this tool, what investors want from it and how to bring the two together, including what we see as positive forces and barriers.

We also focus on definitions and terminology.

## Basic definition of social investment

In essence, social investment is an easy concept to grab hold of but hard to define. It uses more commercial-style investment tools to create a social as well as financial return to fund charities and social purpose organisations.

While there are many definitions of social investment, we start with a simple one which we believe is enough for the reader to engage in this journey. We also note that this is a contested space and discuss this more fully in Chapter 5.

Our definition:

> **Social investments have the intent and motivation of generating a social or environmental impact as well as financial return on investment. They aim to measure both the social and financial value they create and be held accountable for this.**
>
> **(Salway, 2017, p. 9)**

This book is aimed at various audiences and specifically those social purpose organisations whose primary aim is to create social value; these are typically charities and social enterprises who are also charities.

But what are social purpose organisations, and what defines them? We explore this in the next chapter.

## Reference

Salway, M. (2017), *Social investment as a new charity finance tool: using head and heart*, Cass Business School, Centre for Charity Effectiveness.

# 4 The landscape of social purpose organisations

*Mark Salway*

## Introduction

The landscape of social purpose organisations is incredibly wide and varied.

Some see these organisations as double bottom line businesses that "strive to achieve measurable social *and* financial outcomes" (Emerson and Twersky, 1996, p. 3; Clark *et al.*, 2004, p. 2; Basu and Bourke, 2016, p. 3).

Some other writers see social purpose organisations as a broad spectrum of organisations, reaching from those driven primarily by social value (such as charities), through to those managed as a traditional business, whose primary driver is to achieve financial returns but who also aim to generate social returns. They see each organisation as having a mix of social and financial outcomes to meet their individual needs and circumstances and also match the market they operate in (Ryder and Vogeley, 2017, p. 376).

**In this book we focus specifically on those organisations whose primary aim is to create social value. As such, we explore social investment in charities and social enterprises that are also charities.**

That said, it's worth spending a little time understanding the wide spectrum of social purpose organisations, shown in Figure 4.1.

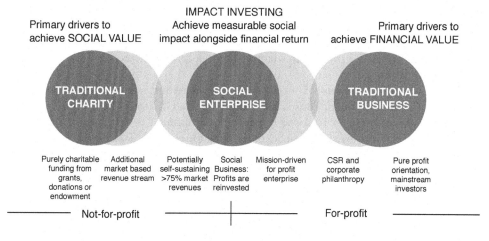

*Figure 4.1* The business model spectrum revisited.

Source: Ryder and Vogeley (2017), adapted from EVPA (2010, p. 18).

The spectrum starts on the left with traditional charity and other voluntary organisations. They typically use financial tools such as grants, donations and endowments to fund their work.

Next, many organisations generate their income from trading and selling goods and services, while at the same time creating social value. These are social enterprises which try to balance revenue generation with a social mission.

Finally, "profit-with-purpose" businesses are much more traditional businesses, focusing on revenue generation as their primary motivation, while aiming to deliver social value alongside this.

Nestled along this continuum is a variety of organisations seeing themselves as creating social value while at the same time using commercial tools to do this to varying degrees: community interest companies (CICs) and benefit corporations (B-Corps), for example.

At the commercial end of the spectrum, we are starting to see pension funds and super-ethical companies develop in this space. Corporates are starting to understand that, to remain relevant in today's markets, they must think wider than just pure profit motivation. Paul Polman, the former CEO of Unilever, questioned whether any organisation can be truly successful in future without focusing on its social value (Guardian, 2012).

We also see a new breed of enlightened for-profit entrepreneurs, like the Bangladeshi-born UK restaurateur, Iqbal Wahhab, who opened The Cinnamon Club and Roast. In his book *Charity Sucks*, Wahhab (2016) rails at the traditional charity sector for failing to evolve to meet need in the way that businesses have to. Wahhab's belief is that a new form of capitalism – socially motivated business – is in a better place to solve problems in a sustainable way than the outmoded donations model of charities, citing his own restaurants – which employ former prisoners – as an example.

Leaving these arguments aside, it's enough to see that the landscape of social purpose organisations is vast.

## Different organisational forms along the spectrum

Whilst the spectrum of social purpose organisations often overlaps, it is worth taking a look at the most common forms. As such, what is shown in Table 4.1 is not a distinct typology and should not be seen as such. For example, charities can also be social enterprises and vice versa. We provide this table to be helpful to readers and show the complexity of this landscape.

These four common forms of social purpose organisations are not mutually exclusive. For example, a social enterprise could be set up as a CIC, or as a charity.

Similarly, when it comes to social enterprises, it's enough to say that many definitions of social enterprise exist if you explore far enough. This leads Eppler (2012) to conclude that "it is the epitome of a buzzword; it is a term that means something slightly different to everyone and ultimately nothing to anyone, facilitating obfuscation and equivocation."

Many investors and philanthropists are starting to question whether charity and social purpose organisations alone are the best way to create social change. They are starting to use more commercial business-type models to change the world. We ask the reader to consider whether it matters in what vehicle social impact is created – charity or business?

*Table 4.1* Common forms of social purpose organisations

**Charities**

- Defined in the UK by the Charity Commission (2013) as organisations "set up with purposes which are exclusively charitable for the public benefit."
- Resources must be applied to charitable causes and mission within the public benefit ("mission lock").
- Assets are held in trust for those purposes alone ("asset lock").
- Mainly focused around three distinct and simple business models:
  - First, charities may receive income from fundraising, from a linked organisation, or from an endowment. They distribute what they receive on the causes they exist for.
  - Second, they may trade in goods or services, benefiting recipients from sale proceeds, or by using recipients in the work that they do.
  - Third, they may offer specific services in return for a grant or contract.

**Social enterprises**

- Defined by the trade organisation for social enterprises, Social Enterprise UK (2018), as businesses that:
  - have a clear social and/or environmental mission set out in their governing documents
  - generate the majority of their income through trade
  - reinvest the majority of their profits
  - are autonomous of the state
  - are majority-controlled in the interests of the social mission
  - are accountable and transparent.
- They reinvest the majority of profits, but not all.
- They may distribute funds to investors as they see fit (they therefore often lack both strict asset and mission lock that charities have).
- They are more able to use such tools such as the ability to distribute profits to achieve their social purpose and create value.
- Many social enterprises are registered as charities, with large cross-over in both legal and organisational forms.

**Community interest companies (CICs)**

- Defined by the Government's site on CICs (Gov.uk, 2018): "CICs are a new type of limited company for people wishing to establish businesses which trade with a social purpose …, or to carry on other activities for the benefit of the community".
- CICs limit the distribution of profits and are clear about maintaining assets for the social good in the event of a wind-up.
- As such, they are more commercial in nature, but still hold assets aside for a social purpose and only allow a certain level of funds to be distributed (up to a maximum of 35%).
- Security is provided by limited liability.
- They have access to certain forms of finance – including private donors, grants or community development finance; this allows flexibility of investment funding and profit distribution which charities lack the ability to do.
- Separately regulated by the CIC regulator
- Ongoing public compliance requirements and lack of tax breaks are among some of the perceived disadvantages of CICs.
- Many social enterprises have adopted the community interest company model.

**Benefit corporations (B-Corps)**

- Defined in *To B or not to B: An investor's guide to B Corps* (Bridges Fund Management, 2015, p. 5) as a "profit with purpose" business with a self-imposed "mission lock" plus a kind of "performance lock".
- Businesses can certify as a B Corp.
- A company must first submit to an independent assessment (conducted by a non-profit organisation called B Lab) of its social and environmental performance, accountability and transparency.
- If the company scores highly enough, it must then formally incorporate its social mission into its governance articles.
- It is subsequently reassessed every two years, to make sure it maintains the requisite standard.
- Locking in the social or environmental mission is not an "asset lock", of the kind that charities and many social enterprises have, as it can simply be reversed by the Directors and a simple vote. Instead, these companies will typically have a performance lock, whereby impact performance is somehow linked to the company's business model or commercial performance.
- In some cases, they also have a mission lock, whereby the directors choose to embed social impact into the company's governance, by amending its articles of association or otherwise.

With an idea of the landscape of social purpose organisations, let's next look at social investment today – definitions, sources and types of investment.

## Summary

The landscape of social purpose organisations is vast and varied. Therefore, we purpose-fully focus on those organisations whose primary aim is to create social value in this book.

**As such, we explore social investment in charities and social enterprises that are also charities in this book.**

In the next chapter we explore what defines social investment.

## References

Basu, R. and Bourke, A. (2016), *Social impact investing: the growing trend of financing for good*, Butterworths Journal of International Banking and Financial Law.

Bridges Fund Management (2015), *To B or not to B: an investor's guide to B Corps*, accessed 20 September 2018, www.bridgesfundmanagement.com/wp-content/uploads/2017/08/Bridges-To-B-or-Not-To-B-screen.pdf.

Charity Commission (2013), *Charitable purposes and public benefit*, accessed 22 September 2018, www.gov.uk/government/collections/charitable-purposes-and-public-benefit.

Clark, C., Rosenzweig, W., Long, D. and Olsen, S. (2004), *Double bottom line project report: assessing social impact in double bottom line ventures*, ABT Associates, Inc. and Center for Responsible Business.

Emerson, J. and Twersky, F. (1996), *New social entrepreneurs: the success, challenge, and lessons of non-profit enterprise creation*, Roberts Foundation.

Eppler, I. (2012), *The problem with social entrepreneurship*, Stanford Social Innovation Review, 13 April, accessed 22 September 2018, www.ssir.org/articles/entry/the_problem_with_social_entrepreneurship_a_students_perspective.

EVPA, European Venture Philanthropy Association (2010), *Establishing a venture philanthropy organisation in Europe: a practical guide*, accessed 22 July 2019, https://avpn.asia/wp-content/uploads/2014/12/Establishing-a-Venture-Philanthropy-Organisation.pdf.

Gov.UK (2018), *Community interest companies: guidance chapters*, Volume 1, p. 8, accessed 22 September 2018, www.gov.uk/government/publications/community-interest-companies-how-to-form-a-cic.

Guardian (2012), *Unilever's Paul Polman: challenging the corporate status quo*, The Guardian, 24 April, accessed 22 September 2018, www.theguardian.com/sustainable-business/paul-polman-unilever-sustainable-living-plan.

Ryder, P. and Vogeley, J. (2017), *Telling the impact investment story through digital media: an Indonesian case study*, Communication Research and Practice.

Social Enterprise UK (2018), *FAQs: what are social enterprises?*, accessed 22 September 2018, www.socialenterprise.org.uk/Pages/FAQs/Category/FAQs.

Wahhab, I. (2016), *Charity sucks*, Biteback Books.

# 5 What is social investment today?

## Definitions, sources and types of investment

*Mark Salway*

## The basics – definitions and context

Social investment is an easy concept to grab hold of. It uses more commercial-style investment tools to create a social as well as financial return to fund charities and similar social purpose organisations.

The Financial Conduct Authority (FCA, 2016, p. 5), considering regulatory barriers, echoes this and concludes that:

> Social investing is a broad concept which at its heart combines the idea that an investment can have a social "impact" or "return" as well as some form of financial return. This social impact or return is usually focused on a specific issue, geographic area or part of the population, for example, the rehabilitation of offenders or providing training and then employment opportunities for the long-term unemployed. This is usually done by investing in enterprises which have a specific social objective as their primary goal.

Charities are trying to solve some of society's most intractable and complex social problems: from the prevention and relief of poverty, to the advancement of education; including such diverse problems as health, sport and animal welfare (Charity Commission, 2013).

If we are to create real social change for the poorest and most disadvantaged in society, we will need to use all the tools we have at our disposal. While hard to define, social investment is one such tool.

## In search of a simple definition

We shall see in this chapter that there are many ways to describe social investment and that this is both a contested and evolving debate.

Perhaps the most important existing definition that exists is that of the Groupe d'experts de la Commission sur l'entrepreneuriat social, GECES (Clifford *et al.*, 2014) – *Proposed Approaches to Social Impact Measurement in European Commission Legislation and in Practice Relating to: EuSEFs and the EaSI*. This has been integrated into EU law.

GECES breaks down the definition of social investment into its component parts – namely investor, what constitutes "social", social outcomes and social investment (pp. 1–12):

- **Investor** – A provider of investment, that is financial or other support to or for a social enterprise for fixed capital or working capital, taking some investment risk (which may vary between cases), and expecting a return by way of interest, profit, or capital gain. In this report it is distinguished from a Funder, which is a public sector entity paying for public (social) services to be delivered by a social enterprise. An investor may provide advice, office facilities or other value in kind in addition to financial support. This, too, is investment.

- **Social** – Relating to individuals and communities, and the interaction between them; contrasted with economic and environmental.
- **Social Outcome** – Social effect (change), both long-term and short-term achieved for the target population as a result of the activity undertaken with a view to social change taking into account both positive and negative changes.
- **Social investment** – An investment (defined in "investor" above) specifically to be applied to achieve one or more social outcomes.

There are many other similar definitions of social investment which we will discuss later in this chapter, including different phrases for the idea of an investment that intentionally creates both a financial and a social return.

Cass CCE undertook research in 2017 (Salway, 2017) on social investment and concluded that a simple definition was needed. This is the basic definition of social investment that we're going to use for this book:

> Social investments have the intent and motivation of generating a social or environmental impact as well as financial return on investment. They aim to measure both the social and financial value they create and be held accountable for this.
>
> (Salway, 2017, p. 9)

In the next part of this chapter we dive into the definitions debate around what social investment is, taking the reader on the journey through this contested and evolving landscape.

## The definitions debate

The term "social investment" has only relatively recently entered the mainstream language of charity finance. But how does this differ from "social finance", "impact investment" or "social impact investment"?

> Differing interpretations of terms are at least partly responsible for "problems in the effectiveness and growth of the social investment market today."
>
> (Floyd *et al.*, 2015, p. 20)

In terms of agreed definitions, this is a contested landscape. Unsurprisingly, we have seen major debates as to what constitutes a social investment and what does not. While many terms and definitions come from an investor perspective, all highlight that the intent and motivation of generating a social as well as financial return is core to the idea of social investment.

Definitions matter because they enable a single understanding between all parties, and ultimately access to appropriate types of capital, tax regimes and other benefits.

If we want to understand and agree the term "social investment", it might be useful to consider several important questions:

1   What do practitioners and academics call this type of investment that creates a social as well as a financial return?
2   Should definitions be prescriptive about what type of institutions are making these investments?
3   Should definitions be prescriptive about the type of organisations taking these funds?
4   Should the definition talk about **"blended" value** (i.e. the need to blend financial and social returns)? And is this necessary?
5   Are measurement and accountability critical for the definition of social investment?

Taking each question in turn, we now explore the social investment definitions debate.

## Question 1: What do practitioners and academics call this type of investment?

A wide range of terms applies to investments which create a social as well as a financial return on investment. In their seminal book, *Impact Investing: Transforming How We Make Money While Making a Difference*, Bugg-Levine and Emerson (2011, p. 25) use the term **"impact investments"** for this type of financial instrument. They state that "Impact investing recognises that investments can pursue financial returns while also addressing social and environmental challenges."

Similarly, the well-respected Global Impact Investing Network (GIIN, 2018) refers to the term "Impact investments: … NOUN: Impact investments are investments made with the intention to generate positive, measurable social and environmental impact alongside a financial return".

Impact investment perhaps tends to refer to the entire universe of investments that create both financial and social returns.

The G8 Social Impact Investment Taskforce – established by the then UK Prime Minister David Cameron under the UK Presidency of the G8 – was set up to review the landscape for social investment. It refers to **"social impact investments"** as "those that intentionally target specific social objectives along with a financial return and measure the achievement of both" (G8 Social Impact Investment Taskforce, 2014, p. 1). It is worth noting that, while the Taskforce follows the definitions of GECES and EVPA, it disregards the GIIN definition, even while quoting GIIN's work throughout its own research.

Big Society Capital, the organisation established to promote these types of investments in the UK, states that "Social investment is repayable finance for charities and social enterprises that targets both financial and social returns for investors" (Big Society Capital, 2018).

In *The Landscape of Social Impact Investment Research: Trends and Opportunities* (Daggers and Nicholls, 2016), the authors suggest (p. 6) that this all sits under the umbrella term, "social finance":

> Social finance encompasses the use of a range of private financial resources to support the creation of public social and environmental value or impact … Islamic finance; mutual finance; crowdfunding; community finance; targeted socially responsible investment; and social enterprise financing.

Having defined this umbrella term, they then suggest using the term "social invest-ment" to define those investments that create both a social and financial return; they reference 73 academic papers and 261 practitioner reports (p. 3) to come to this conclu-sion. They state, "Social investment concerns providing access to repayable capital (for social sector organisations), where the providers of capital are motivated to create social or environmental impact" (p. 6).

This discourse highlights the fact that definitions of social investment are like buses. You wait for one to come along, then three come at once. This is an ongoing debate, perhaps best summarised by Daggers and Nicholls (2016, p. 6):

> Practitioners are more likely to see the "definitions debate" as a distraction from the business of actually doing deals and building the market.

## Question 2: Should the definition be prescriptive about what type of institutions are making these investments?

There appear to be no boundaries on the type of investor who is interested and/or act-ively involved in the social investment space. For example, investors can be "com-panies, organisations, and funds" (GIIN, 2018).

Equally, high-net-worth individuals (HNWIs) and family foundations are starting to make such social investments (Financial Times and Method Impact, 2015). This excel-lent report, now produced by GIST and Barclays (2019), really helps readers to under-stand the motivation as to why HNWIs and family offices are interested and how their work is progressing in this area. We provide its detail in Chapter 14 later in this book.

Finally, government, social banks and trusts as well as foundations are helping to create the landscape of social investment. This landscape is also mapped out in the gov-ernment document, *Growing a Culture of Social Impact Investing in the UK* (Gov.UK, 2017).

This is a broad landscape and we don't need to be prescriptive about the type of organisation making investments. So, what about those organisations taking on such investment?

## Question 3: Should definitions be prescriptive about the type of organisations taking these funds?

One question to ask is whether an investor can *only* claim to be using social investment if investing in a charity, social enterprise or non-profit? Or, should this be extended to commercial organisations and other corporate vehicles?

The argument goes that charities have a mission lock (i.e. resources must be applied to charitable causes and for the public benefit), asset lock (i.e. assets are held in trust for those purposes alone) and motivation to hold investment aside essentially for social pur-poses (see Chapter 4, Table 4.1 for more details on these terms). This motivation may be different from that of commercial organisations, which lack such protection to safe-guard assets for social purposes.

Therefore, can we be prescriptive about the kind of social organisation into which social investors invest?

Looking from a community viewpoint, Tan (2014) suggests that each social invest-ment should take place *only* in a commercially sustainable and profitable business. He argues that organisations should typically operate *geographically* close to the social issues they are trying to solve.

The G8 Social Impact Investment Taskforce (2014) identifies that social purpose organisations, *as well as* commercial organisations, should be able to use social investment as a force for good.

Meanwhile, the Mission Alignment Working Group (2014, p. 12) goes further and says that it is not enough to be a commercial organisation which seeks to do good as a "profit-with-purpose" business (p. 12). To classify as a social investment, it must legally commit to do good; "It binds itself to do good; has a duty to do good".

In agreement with the Mission Alignment Working Group is the report by Brown and Swersky (2012, p. 4), commissioned by Big Society Capital. This identifies five types of social investment, shown in the diagram in Figure 5.1. The authors conclude by saying that social investment is focused on Type 2 finance, but not exclusively so – socially motivated investment in socially motivated organisations.

> It is almost impossible to define the type of organisation making the investment and, equally, to define the type of organisation which is taking the investment funds. However, what clearly binds them is the motivation of the investor and the expected impact of the investee.
>
> (Brown and Swersky, 2012, p. 24)

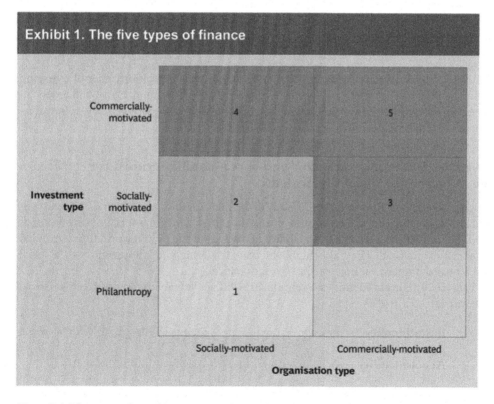

*Figure 5.1* The types of social investment versus organisation.

Source: Brown and Swersky (2012).

## Question 4: Should the definition talk about "blended" value (i.e. the need to blend financial and social returns), and is this necessary?

At the heart of each social investment is the idea of a financial return, set alongside a social return. Bugg-Levine and Emerson (2011) talk about "blended" value returns, using a definition "blending" social and financial return on investment. Their research implies, somehow, that one can be traded off against the other.

Brown and Swersky (2012) raise questions about the ability to "blend" financial and social returns – that is, to trade financial return for social impact. They put forward a model which says that the investor may be prepared to forego some interest for the social return created. However, they emphasise that commercial investors may require a full commercial return to compensate for risk. Therefore, both risk and the motivation of the investor become key components of this relationship, too. They refer to a "socially motivated" investor.

What is clear is that each investor has a decision to make about the risk–return trade-off. It is simply not enough to say that investors will accept a below-market rate of return or "blended return" (Nicholls, Paton and Emerson, 2015, p. 282).

Floyd *et al*. (2015) also highlight that any social investment must at least pay back the initial capital outlay. This gives some clarification as to what constitutes "repayable finance".

> Alignment of motivation is important in social investment. Although "blended" returns are a useful concept, they are not a prerequisite and should not be included in any definition.
>
> (Salway, 2017)

Inevitably, investors may be more likely to take one of two positions: that of requiring a full market rate of return (so-called "finance-first" investment), or willingness to invest for sub-market rates of return as a socially motivated activity (so-called "mission-driven" investment).

## Question 5: Are measurement and accountability critical for the definition of social investment?

Wagner (2002) and Emerson (2001) both make the case for a new form of "investment philanthropy" that uses the tools of investment to drive forward a social return on funds used. What they point to is accountability being key in the new relationship demanded by social investment. They also highlight that delivering and measuring both a social and a financial return on investment becomes critical.

Tan (2014) equally identifies intentionality and accountability as key facets of social investment:

1   **Intentionality** – these investments are specifically designed with a social purpose at their heart
2   **Accountability** – social investments report openly against social metrics.

In every definition, measurement of the social impact created appears as a key component of a social investment, as do being held accountable and transparent and reporting openly on the social investment.

This accountability doesn't necessarily demand an in-depth calculation, or even a socio-economic quantification, rather a sensible and audience-relevant view of the social impact created.

## Summarising the debate

Out of the confusion of terms comes a single term which is gaining traction in this investment space, "*social investment*". A single definition matters because it ensures proper understanding among all involved parties.

Social investment can take place across both socially motivated and commercial organisations. What counts is the intention to create both a social and financial return.

While it is almost impossible to define the type of organisation or individual making the investment – and equally the type of organisation taking the investment funds – Brown and Swersky do point towards the "motivation of the investor and the expected impact of the *investee*" (2012, p. 24) as critical in any social investment.

Measurement and accountability are also key, and are picked up in Chapters 26 and 27.

---

**Social investment**

- **is a powerful tool to help fund charities and other social purpose organisations**
- **harnesses the power of investment to create a social as well as a financial return**
- **aims to measure both the social and financial value it creates and be held accountable for this**

---

## Bringing social investment to life

However you define social investment, it can create social value in a multitude of different ways.

Big Society Capital (2014) and Sattar (2018) identify that social investment can be used in many ways, to:

- **finance small and medium-sized charities and other social purpose organisations** – providing working capital and operational finance to allow them to grow and develop their businesses;
- **provide capital that allows innovation in tackling social problems to quickly grow and replicate** – risk capital that allows social sector organisations to try new things, fail, pivot and try again;
- **develop mass participation in social investment** – through such mechanisms as crowd-funding and peer-to-peer lending; and
- **create greater financial scale in order to finance social issues** – providing capital that will allow social purpose organisations to leverage fundraising, for example, or grow their work directly.

Some examples will help bring this to life …

## Financing charities and other social purpose organisations

- **The Gym Group**: One of the most successful social investments to date. It provides quality, affordable gyms to local communities and has grown from one gym in Hackney in 2008 to over 80 across the UK in 2016. To grow, it used social investment from Bridges Ventures (now called Bridges Fund Management) and other investors who were positive about the health impact it created (The Gym Group, 2018).
- **Hackney Community Transport (HCT)**: A showcase project of social investment's positive impact so far – a social enterprise that helps communities get about (ClearlySo, 2018). To help develop its fleet of buses, HCT raised £17.8 million from a range of social and mainstream investors facilitated by ClearlySo.

## Providing capital that allows innovation in tackling social problems

- **Clean Team Ghana:** Water and Sanitation for the Urban Poor (WSUP) teamed up with Unilever to invest in toilets in slum areas. Local people pay for portable toilets and the waste is taken away to generate electricity and fertiliser. This innovation allowed governments and commercial organisations to see a new replicable model of delivering sanitation (see Chapter 16a for a case study).
- **Purple House:** Preston Road Women's Centre, Purple House, provides support and advice to women in Hull. This multi-purpose organisation run by women for women offers a wide range of services under one roof. Women can drop in anytime between 10 a.m. and 4 p.m. Monday to Friday to access a range of services or to meet other women in a safe environment. Social investment was used to prime this model (Purple House, 2018).

## To develop mass participation in social investment

- **www.lendwithcare.org:** A microfinance platform that allows lenders to send money to organisations in the developing world. Initial capital and investment were put up by the charity CARE International UK. It has now lent over £18 million (see Chapter 17a for a case study).

## To create greater financial scale in order to finance social issues

- **Scope:** The first charity to raise a retail bond for funds. To pay for its charity shops, Scope raised £2 million and was listed on the Euro MTF Luxembourg Stock Exchange (see Chapter 7a for a case study).

---

### Acumen – bringing electricity to the ultra-poor, Acumen (2018)

Acumen focuses on people earning less than $3.2 a day – the ultra-poor.

By using social investment, Acumen has been able to help households many times, without having to wait on more donations and grants to do further work. It also employs those it seeks to help.

> The $22.1 million invested has enabled 20 early-stage companies to provide 81 million people with high-quality, affordable light, power and improved cookstoves. These people no longer have to live in the dark after the sun goes down or use unhealthy, expensive and dangerous kerosene lanterns to read or sit together and talk into the night. This is life changing in the most basic way.

(Acumen, 2018)

# Types of investment

## *Debt versus equity*

Social investment takes in a wide range of investments and financing from loans, mortgages, bonds and simple borrowing, through to peer-to-peer lending and social impact bonds.

A great source of information is Good Finance (2018a), set up by Big Society Capital (www.goodfinance.org.uk). This provides the interested reader with the widest platform of knowledge about social investment. Equally, documents such as *Social Investment Explained* (Big Potential, 2014) provide a good source of information.

Similar to more mainstream investment, Good Finance (2018a) identifies two primary forms of investment in use, debt and equity:

1 **Debt (Borrowing):** Taking out a loan which you agree to repay over a set period of time. Most debt investments are paid back with interest – an amount you pay to the investor for the use of their money. E.g. an investor loans your organisation £10,000 and you repay a total of £11,000.
2 **Equity (Shares):** Selling shares in your organisation to an investor. Equity investors receive a share of any profits paid out by the organisation and get to have a say in how the organisation is run. E.g. an investor pays £10,000 to own 10% of your organisation.

With such a wide range of types of investment, structures through which money can flow and routes to finding an investment, any list can only be indicative.

The list in Table 5.1 provides a start. This is explored in more detail in the *doing social investment* section, Chapters 20–27.

# Social investment financial intermediaries

> A **Social investment finance intermediary (SIFI)** is an organisation that provides, facilitates or structures financial investments for social sector organisations and/or provides investment-focussed business support to social sector organisations.
>
> (Good Finance, 2018b)

In reality, the work of social investment financial intermediaries (SIFIs) breaks down into three main components:

- **Managing funds on behalf of investors.** For example, Big Society Capital has placed funds with SIFIs focused on a wide range of themes, from ex-offenders, adoption and rough-sleepers to health and ageing. This enables funds to be brought together from different sources and helps build the market between investors and social purpose organisations.
- **Facilitating transactions as intermediaries.** SIFIs will often help place investments on behalf of clients. SIFIs have links into a variety of investors from individuals to banks. For example, the SIFI ClearlySo has focused on developing investment from "angel investors" and has also released a useful guide on finding funding – *Guide for the Ambitious Social Entrepreneur* (ClearlySo, 2014).
- **Helping organisations as advisors.** Many SIFIs are focused on helping organisations to become investment-ready and understand how to use social investment funds. For instance, see Big Potential (2017).

*Table 5.1* Funding sources, structures through which money can flow and routes to finding an investor

| Funding sources | |
|---|---|
| | **Corporate funds** |
| | • **Commercial bank loans or loans from charity banks** – typically term loans, secured against property/assets or as unsecured finance. |
| | • **Investment funds and institutional funds** – established to provide social investment (including some ethical investment funds). |
| | • **Corporate organisations** – making social investments directly into charities as CSR (Corporate Social Responsibility). |
| | • **Pension funds** – starting to make initial investments, but mainly placing money into investment funds. |
| | • **SIFIs** – through Social Investment Financial Intermediaries (SIFIs) – see next section. |
| | **Charitable foundations, trusts and family offices** |
| | • **Foundations and trusts** – making direct social investments to charities, or through investing in pooled social investment funds (see Panahpur case study, Chapter 12a). Often setting aside part of their reserves or endowment specifically for this. |
| | • **Family offices** – making investments direct or through other funds. |
| | • **Community investing** – where the local community issues bonds or loans to support local community initiatives. E.g. Community development finance institutions (CDFIs). |
| | **Individuals** |
| | • **High-net-worth individuals and 'Angels'** – prepared to lend investment capital or invest in an equity stake. |
| | • **Trustee loans and existing donors** – may provide capital to develop new initiatives. |
| | • **The general public** – through such vehicles as crowdfunding. |
| | **Government** |
| | • **Local Authority pension schemes** – investing directly or indirectly in social investments. |

*continued*

*Table 5.1* continued

| Debt | Structures through which money comes in |
|---|---|
| Investment with the expectation of repayment. Debt finance usually takes the form of loans, both secured and unsecured, as well as overdrafts. Generally, these require a borrower to repay the amount borrowed, along with some form of interest and sometimes an arrangement fee:<br>• **Secured loans** – secured lending against specific assets of the charity<br>• **Unsecured loans** – lending made against the general assets of the charity<br>• **Quasi-equity** – lending where repayments are based on performance and therefore act more like equity<br>• **Charity bonds** – typically pay-back capital, along with regular payment of interest ("coupon") and often traded. | |
| **Equity**<br>An investment in exchange for a stake in an organisation, usually in the form of shares. Each share represents ownership of a proportion of the value of the company. Equity investors expect to receive dividends paid out of the organisation's earnings and/or capital gain on the sale of the organisation or on selling their shares to other investors (Good Finance, 2018). | |
| **Social impact bonds**<br>Defined by Rotheroe (2014, p. 3) as a type of outcomes-based contract:<br>• A contract between a commissioner and a separate delivery agency<br>• In which the latter delivers a specific social outcomes or outcomes, for which the commissioner will pay if it is delivered<br>• With at least one investor which is neither the delivery agency nor the commissioner<br>• With that investor taking some element of risk.<br>Social impact bonds are explored more fully in Chapter 21. | |

*continued*

*Table 5.1* Continued

| Routes to finding an investor (see also Chapter 22 for more detail) | **To existing funders and stakeholders**<br>• Going back to the audience who knows you best, by offering the right to invest before going to outsiders.<br><br>**Via direct placement**<br>• Direct approaches to a list of investors in a category. Often through an intermediary, such as a professional investment broker.<br>• Through social investment financial intermediaries (SIFIs) – see next section.<br><br>**Accessing lists**<br>• Issuing bonds on general stock markets.<br>• Accessing a wide range of investors.<br><br>**Crowdfunding**<br>• Using an online platform to collect and distribute funds.<br><br>**Microfinance**<br>• Lending small amounts of capital to non-profits and individuals. |
| --- | --- |

Naturally, SIFIs must focus on any conflict of interest which could arise. The SIFI market continues to develop and is now much more able to meet the needs of the charity sector, in terms of both capacity and understanding.

In this book we refer mainly to the role that SIFIs play when managing funds on behalf of investors and facilitating transactions as intermediaries. We do not focus on their wider advisory work.

## Summary

In this chapter, we have looked at the complexity of defining social investment. We have then explored what form an investment might take and where to find this.

We have provided some examples of social investment in action.

We have also explored social investment financial intermediaries (SIFIs) and their role in developing the social investment market.

While we explore the different dimensions of social investment in further chapters, it's important to think about the following:

- **The demand side** – how organisations taking on investment are using this; their plans for the money; how they create impact; and their readiness to use social investment as a tool.
- **The supply side and the investors** – what type of investment is being offered; the returns they expect and on what terms.
- **Alignment** – how these two organisations come together, potentially through an intermediary, to make successful use of social investment. This relies heavily on understanding culture and language.

It is the multi-faceted nature of social investment that makes it complex, but also a powerful tool in creating social value.

We'll explore the matching of supply and demand in Chapter 8. Meanwhile, in the next chapter we deal with why charities need new funding models.

## References

Acumen (2018), *Energy impact report*, accessed 20 October 2018, www.acumen.org/wp-content/uploads/2018/02/Acumen-Energy-Impact-Report.pdf.

Big Potential (2014), *Social investment explained*, accessed 20 September 2018, www.bigpotential.org.uk/resource/social-investment-guide.

Big Potential (2017), *Big Potential Grants to help win investment or challenge for contracts*, accessed 19 July 2019, www.sibgroup.org.uk/big-potential.

Big Society Capital (2014), *Our strategy for the next three years*, accessed 20 October 2018, www.bigsocietycapital.com/sites/default/files/Strategy%20v5.pdf.

Big Society Capital (2018), *What is social investment?*, accessed 20 October 2018, www.bigsociety capital.com/.

Brown, A. and Swersky, A. (2012), *The first billion: a forecast of social investment demand*, Boston Consulting Group.

Bugg-Levine, A. and Emerson, J. (2011), *Impact investing: transforming how we make money while making a difference*, Jossey-Bass (Wiley).

Charity Commission (2013), *Guidance: charitable purposes*, accessed 20 October 2018, www.gov.uk/government/publications/charitable-purposes/charitable-purposes.

ClearlySo (2014), *The ClearlySo guide for the ambitious social entrepreneur*, accessed 19 July 2019, www.clearlyso.com/wp-content/uploads/2013/03/ClearlySo-Guide-for-the-Ambitious-Social-Entrepreneur-3rd-Edition.pdf.

ClearlySo (2018), *HCT Group secures £17.8 million in funding*, accessed 20 October 2018, www.clearlyso.com/hct-group-secures-17-8-million-in-funding-to-tackle-social-isolation/.

Clifford, J., Hehenberger, L. and Fantini, M. (2014), *Proposed approaches to social impact measurement in European Commission legislation and in practice relating to EuSEFs and the EaSI*, report by GECES (Groupe d'experts de la Commission sur l'entrepreneuriat social) subgroup on impact measurement, accessed 20 October 2018, www.ec.europa.eu/social/main.jsp?catId=738&langId=en&pubId=7735&type=2&furtherPubs=yes.

Daggers, J. and Nicholls, A. (2016), *The landscape of social impact investment research: trends and opportunities*, University of Oxford.

Emerson, J. (2001), *A commitment to accountability: the coming challenge to venture philanthropy*, Community Wealth Ventures.

FCA (2016), *Call for input: regulatory barriers to social investments*, accessed 28 April 2019, www.fca.org.uk/publication/feedback/fs16-11.pdf.

Financial Times and Method Impact (2015), *Investing for global impact*, Financial Times Publishing.

Floyd *et al.* (2015), *After the gold rush: the report of the Alternative Commission on Social Investment*, accessed 20 October 2018, www.socinvalternativecommission.org.uk/wp-content/uploads/2015/03/SS_SocialInvest_WebVersion_3.pdf.

G8 Social Impact Investment Taskforce (2014), *Impact investment: the hidden heart of markets*, accessed 20 October 2018, www.gsgii.org/reports/impact-investment-the-invisible-heart-of-markets/.

GIIN (2018), *Global Impact Investment Network*, accessed 20 October 2018, www.thegiin.org/impact-investing/need-to-know/#what-is-impact-investing.

GIST and Barclays (2019), *Investing for global impact*, accessed 20 October 2018, www.gistltd.com.

Good Finance (2018a), *Types of social investment*, accessed 20 October 2018, www.goodfinance.org.uk/understanding-social-investment/types-social-investment.

Good Finance (2018b), *Good Finance glossary*, accessed 20 October 2018, www.goodfinance.org. uk/glossary.

Gov.UK (2017), *Growing a culture of social impact investing in the UK*, accessed 20 October 2018, www.gov.uk/government/publications/growing-a-culture-of-social-impact-investing-in-the-uk.

Mission Alignment Working Group (2014), *Profit with purpose businesses*, G8 report, accessed 20 October 2018, www.socialimpactinvestment.org/reports/Mission%20Alignment%20WG%20 paper%20FINAL.pdf.

Nicholls, A., Paton, R. and Emerson, J. (2015), *Social finance*, Oxford University Press.

Purple House (2018), *Welcome to Preston Road Women's Centre*, accessed 20 October 2018, www. purplehouse.co.uk/.

Rotheroe, A. (2014), *Lessons and opportunities: perspectives from providers of social impact bonds*, accessed, 24 September 2018, www.thinknpc.org/wp-content/uploads/2018/07/Lessons-and-opportunities-perspectives-from-providers-of-SIBS.pdf.

Salway, M. (2017), *Social investment as a new charity finance tool: using head and heart*, Cass Business School, Centre for Charity Effectiveness.

Sattar, D. (2018), *Four views of social investment or the resolution of Travis' moment of despair*, accessed 20 October 2018, www.bigsocietycapital.com/latest/type/blog/four-views-social-investment-or-resolution-travis-moment-despair.

Tan, Kim Dato (2014), *Impact investing: time for new terminology?*, Stanford Social Innovation Review, 1 October.

The Gym Group (2018), *The Gym's history*, accessed 20 October 2018, www.thegymgroup. com/about-the-gym/the-gyms-history/.

Wagner, L (2002), *The "new" donor: creation or evolution?*, International Journal for the Nonprofit and Voluntary Sector, issue 7, 343–352.

# 6 Why do charities need new funding models?

## The case for change

*Mark Salway*

## Why do charities, in particular, need new finance and funding models?

### Under pressure

Ten years on from the financial crisis, the charity sector continues to feel significant financial pressure.

In terms of income, there are two main trends at play. First, the stagnation in individual giving reflects in part the maturity of the UK as a generous nation, although this may have peaked in terms of traditional giving methods. Second, there is a continuing stringency in government funding, both local and central, with a contracting culture focused on price-sensitive tendering rather than grants.

Meanwhile, demand for the sector's products and services continues to grow and grow.

According to the National Council of Voluntary Organisation (NCVO) sustainability review (NCVO, 2015, p. 6), "projections point to a £4.6 billion annual shortfall in sector income over the next five years, simply to maintain current spending power." Given that the overall income of the sector is £47.8 billion (NCVO, 2018), this gap is significant.

To add to this picture, overheads are under intense pressure and scrutiny. Bridgespan (2009) warned of a starvation cycle in which charities' infrastructure is poorly funded, meaning non-profit activities cannot be scaled effectively. A recent report from Charity Futures (2018, p. 2), *To the Core*, highlights that "Infrastructure is rather more like a skeleton than scaffolding. You need it all the time and, unlike scaffolding, you can't dispense with it". It similarly highlights the pressure on overheads.

**It's important to explore how this intense pressure on infrastructure costs and overheads can be alleviated to ensure charities have sustainable platforms to deliver their work.**

The PwC report *Managing in the New Normal* (2016, p. 20) identifies "a significant increase in the number of respondents saying they were likely to use reserves to maintain services (40%) or pay for operating costs of their charity (35%)". This indicates that a number of charities are struggling to generate the income required to fund their charitable activities. However, given consistently high demand for services, this response is not unpredictable.

Given this ongoing challenge and financial pressure, how will the charity sector maintain its impact and funding for its work?

## *The figures are telling*

The breakdown of funding to the charity sector in Figure 6.1 shows that donations and government funding together make up around 80 per cent of all funding to the sector.

Looking first at donations, the *2017 UK Giving Survey* (CAF, 2017, p. 17) shows that individual donations, in absolute terms, remain steady and have been steady for some time. This is the main component of income from individuals, along with legacies. The report concludes that donation income each year "is largely consistent (and within the margins of error) at around £10 billion per annum, regardless of the economic events".

Next, looking at government funding, NCVO's *Financial Stability Review* (2015, p. 11) highlights that, in real terms, the sector's income from government has fallen since the peak seen in 2009/10, "causing serious financial difficulties for organisations that depend on government funding".

During this time, the move from government grants to contracts has been profound, changing the nature of how charities operate and fund themselves (Figure 6.2). Charities have needed to learn how to manage payment-by-results (PBR) contracts: a new way of doing business for them which moves income to payments in arrears, i.e. after services have been delivered, rather than with a grant where funding is received in advance. This has led to increased costs and pressure on working capital and reserves at a time when pressure on their funding models was already high.

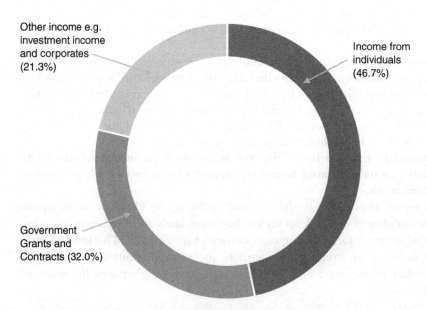

*Figure 6.1* Breakdown of charity sector funding.

Source: NCVO (2018).

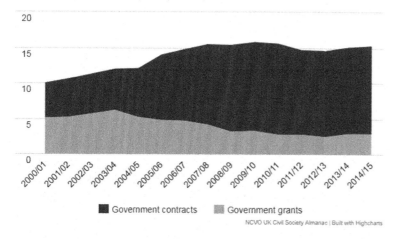

Income from government contracts and grants, 2000/01
to 2014/15 (£bn, 2014/15 prices)

*Figure 6.2* Government funding has moved away from grants and towards contracts.
Source: NCVO (2017).

## The importance of finance strategy in charities

The external funding environment is forcing many charities to evolve and change. But how are charities responding?

Finance strategy ensures alignment between operational strategy and funding, so that all resources are pulling in the same direction.

Cass CCE research (Salway, 2017, p. 19) "identifies that Charity finance is a key building block upon which all charity work is built". It provides:

- **Sustainability** – ensuring that charities are vibrant and properly funded, because their work is important
- **Impact** – identifying priorities and delivering funding (both restricted and unrestricted) to bring about social change
- **Meeting need** – ensuring that charities and nonprofits get the funding they deserve and that charity work is meeting the profound need that exists
- **Scaling up** – enabling growth and work to be taken to scale, facilitating greater impact.

However, are charities primarily focused on sustainability or impact during their strategic planning? Which drives which? Or, are the two independent of each other?

Cass CCE (Salway, 2017, p. 20) identifies that charities do consider both sustainability and impact when setting their finance strategy. That said, less than half think about the more complex factors related to their business models, such as the size of the issue they are addressing, the quality of their work or their future potential growth.

**The report further identifies that, when charities feel confident about their sustainability, they then think about other things such as impact, innovation and taking their work to scale. When charities lack sustainability they are significantly less likely to focus on any other strategic aims.**

Charities need predictable and stable funding streams to have long-term financial sustainability

While many smaller charities are focused on survival when thinking about their finances, most have a mind-set focused on sustainability first (Clifford, Markey and Malpani, 2012).

Sustainability is a constant which guides whether organisations can predict their future income or not. Those organisations with good planning, diversified income streams, large reserves and a good commercial model are the most stable.

### It depends on the size of the charity

The picture presented by a charity correlates highly to the size of the organisation.

The Cass CCE report (Salway, 2017; Figure 6.3) shows that larger organisations were significantly more positive than small and medium-sized organisations. This highlights that small organisations will need capacity building to enable them to develop funding models that can provide future sustainability.

This topic is explored in Chapter 18, where Leila Baker and Niamh Goggin from the Institute for Voluntary Action Research (IVAR) look at social investment and smaller charities.

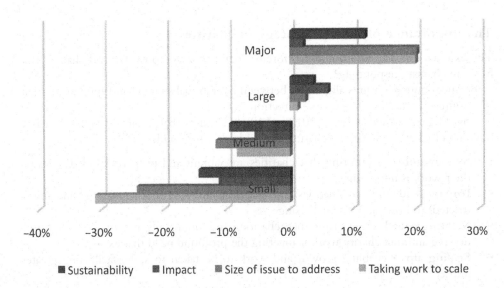

*Figure 6.3* Positivity about different aspects of finance strategy against size of organisation.
Source: Salway (2017, p. 21).

## Do charities lack the impetus to change their practice?

The Cass CCE report (Salway, 2017) showed that charities were mainly confident about their long-term financial strategy and stability:

- Most felt their reserve policy was appropriate.
- Around 23 per cent felt their reserve policy was too safe.

Given the pressure on charity finances, what are we to take from these surprising findings?

Perhaps that the non-profit sector as a whole is considerably more stable and resilient than imagined (Chapman and Robinson, 2014)? Or, that it lacks impetus to change (Salway, 2017, p. 21)?

On the other hand, maybe some charities that should be concerned about the future of their income streams are not actually recognising the change in their funding and its potential impact? When they should be exploring new models, they are becoming complacent.

## As charities grow, they need different funding models

Funding needs to be structured around a charity's objectives. However, most charities do not tend to think about the growth cycle of their work and the type of funding needed to bring this to life.

Figure 6.4 shows that the funding model should fit the strategic objectives. It does not imply growth per se. For example, a charity may focus on its strategy for "innovation", "taking-to-scale" or a mix of both.

Different funding mechanisms are more applicable at different points of a charity's growth. Where a charity has an "innovation" focus, it needs a funding model to de-risk the innovation – such as a grant. At the other end of a charity's growth trajectory – when an organisation has a focus on scale – social investment could be far more appropriate, allowing for more risk sharing, replication and growth.

Organisations also need to consider their endgame and the type of charity they aim to become (Gugelev and Stern, 2015). A simple example is to think about a charity that aims to distribute information through the internet alone, and a charity that aims to deliver physical services across the world. They will have very different infrastructure needs and consequently require very different funding models.

Charities need to think about their growth cycles and how finance can underpin growth by using the right tools at the right time to support their ambition. Charities should be able to see their strategic development and potential growth in their funding models (Gugelev and Stern, 2015).

Charities often understand technically *how to use* different sources of finance, but not strategically *why to use* each source; be that for growth, impact or innovation, for example.

Those hoping to build the social investment market will need to help charities develop strategic finance models and, specifically, to demonstrate how charities can align funding with their social impact more clearly.

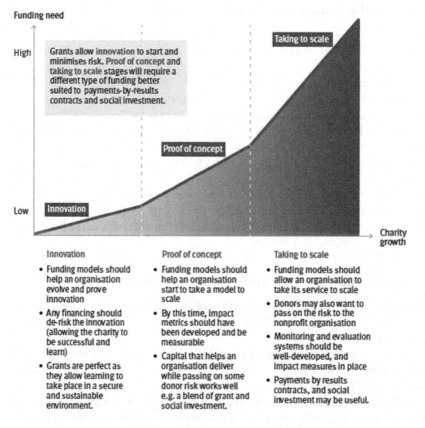

Figure 6.4 Different funding models are needed at different points of a charity's evolution.
Source: Salway (2017, p. 22).

## What about financial sustainability in social enterprises?

It is also important to understand the barriers that are holding back social enterprises.

*The Future of Business: State of Social Enterprise Survey 2017*, written by Social Enterprise UK (2017, p. 41) highlights the key barriers to sustainability as follows:

> Our survey asked all respondents to list their main three barriers to sustainability and growth. Access to finance is still the principal, most significant barrier to sustainability cited by respondents, for the fourth survey in a row: indeed, if we combine obtaining grant funding and obtaining debt or equity finance, it is at 42% (a rise from 39% in 2015).

Lack of successful funding opportunities is holding social enterprises back, too.

Social investment also has a key part to play in determining the future vibrancy and success of social enterprises.

## Summary

The funding environment is changing for charities and social purpose organisations. There is significant pressure on traditional funding streams (grants, donations and contracts), as well as intense competition for funding. It's odd, then, that many charities feel confident in their financial strategy and reserve policies. This may account for some of the reluctance to change charity funding models towards new ways of doing business, including social investment.

Second, many charities sit in a mind-set focused predominantly on sustainability. They want predictable income streams. Without this, they are extremely negative about their financial resilience and future.

Similarly, many charities are poor at considering their growth cycle and how funding can strategically underpin this to help them achieve growth. They often see the link between their financial strategy, sustainability and impact. However, they tend not to consider how they will scale their work or the size of the problem they're trying to solve. Small charities, in particular, need help developing their financial strategies, resilience and capacities.

With this understanding of charity finance and an eye on growth, how do we then use social investment to take the work of charities forward?

This is what we will explore in the following chapters, starting with history and how social investment is seen as a modern concept but is actually a very old tool.

## References

Bridgespan (2009), *The nonprofit starvation cycle*, accessed 22 September 2018, www.bridgespan.org/insights/initiatives/pay-what-it-takes-philanthropy/the-nonprofit-starvation-cycle.

CAF (2017), *UK Giving Survey 2017*, Charities Aid Foundation, accessed 22 September 2018, www.cafonline.org/about-us/publications/2017-publications/uk-giving-report-2017.

Chapman, T. and Robinson, F. (2014), *Third Sector trends in North East England and Cumbria*, www.nr-foundation.org.uk/downloads/Third_Sector_Trends_Study_Headline_Findings-Dec2014.pdf, accessed 22 September 2018.

Charity Futures (2018), *To the core*, accessed 22 September 2018, www.charityfutures.org/our-impact/.

Clifford, J., Markey, K. and Malpani, N. (2013), *Measuring social impact in social enterprise: the state of thought and practice in the UK*, accessed 24 September 2018 http://socialbusinessint.com/wp-content/uploads/Measuring-Social-Impact-in-Social-Enterprise.pdf.

Gugelev and Stern (2015), *What's your endgame?*, Stanford Social Innovation Review, Winter 2015.

NCVO (2015), *Financial stability review*, accessed 20 October 2018, www.ncvo.org.uk/images/documents/policy_and_research/funding/financial-sustainability-review-of-the-voluntary-sector-july-2015.pdf.

NCVO (2017), *UK civil society almanac 2017*, accessed 20 October 18 www.data.ncvo.org.uk/a/almanac17/income-from-government-2/ and www.data.ncvo.org.uk/a/almanac17/liabilities-and-loans-2/.

NCVO (2018), *UK civil society almanac 2018*, accessed 20 October 2018, www.data.ncvo.org.uk/.

PwC (2016), *Managing in the new normal 2016*, Institute of Fundraising, accessed 22 September 2018, www.institute-of-fundraising.org.uk/library/managing-in-the-new-normal-2016/.

Salway, M. (2017), *Social investment as a new charity finance tool: using head and heart*, Cass Business School, Centre for Charity Effectiveness.

Social Enterprise UK (2017), *The future of business: State of Social Enterprise Survey 2017*, accessed 24 September 2018, www.socialenterprise.org.uk/pages/category/state-of-social-enterprise-reports.

# 7   How did we get here?

The very fine history of social finance

*Peter Grant*

## So, what's new?

If they were around today, Thomas Firmin and Benjamin Franklin would tell us that social investment has existed for as long as there have been charities.

That said, charging interest on all loans with charitable purposes was prohibited in many religions: notably Islam and, from the first Council of Nicea in 325 onwards, Christianity. They ensured that all loans for charitable purposes were interest-free.

> God condemns usury, and blesses charities.
>
> (The Quran, n.d., Al–Baqarah 2: 276–280)

---

**Thomas Firmin – a seventeenth-century example of social finance in practice**

- A devout Unitarian born in 1632, Firmin became a successful businessman
- One of the first philanthropists to use the concept of grantmaking
- After the Great Plague and Fire of London, he became concerned at the growing numbers of unemployed in the capital
- In 1676, he established a workhouse in Little Britain, Smithfield (Sherwin, 1950, p. 38), employing as many as 1,700 people, who would obtain flax from his premises and return spun yarn
- He paid workers above the current going rate (6d for a 16-hour day), but supplemented it in various ways to reward good workers
- The finished yarn brought money back into the scheme, but never paid its way
- Both his employment scheme and that for releasing debtors from prison ensured that Firmin's personal fortune shrank from some £20,000 to a sixth of that when he died in 1697
- Yet, Firmin's scheme is the precursor of modern welfare programmes.

---

## Nineteenth-century best intentions

While across the Atlantic, in the eighteenth century, Benjamin Franklin could be described as America's first social investor (Yenawine, 2010), we now move forward some 150 years, but remain in London for the next major example of social finance.

The dramatic growth of London's population in the first half of the nineteenth century – from 959,000 in 1801 to 1,948,000 in 1841 – had brought immense problems, not least in housing. Housing legislation was "ill-conceived, uncoordinated and well-nigh useless" (Tarn, 1973, p. 7). In 1840, a Parliamentary Select Committee lamented that:

> There is no building Act to enforce the dwellings of these workmen being properly constructed; no drainage Act to enforce their being efficiently drained; no general or local regulation to enforce the commonest provision for cleanliness and comfort.
>
> (Tarn, 1973, p. 7)

Into this void stepped a number of philanthropic and quasi-philanthropic organisations, all of whom practised varying forms of social finance. The start of the building society movement.

## The Society for Improving the Conditions of the Labouring Classes (SICLC)

Founded in 1844, the SICLC was the first to actually construct housing on this principle. Limiting its annual dividend to 4 per cent – well below the rate that a Victorian investor would expect – it ensured that its supporters were those who placed social good above making a profit.

Their first development was **Bagnigge Wells, Pentonville, London**, designed by the company's architect, Henry Roberts. It provided three types of accommodation for a total of 23 families and 30 individuals: complete houses, two-storey houses divided into flats, and a lodging house for widows.

The first scheme was somewhat tentative and less than ideal. Social developments at this time were not only difficult in the absence of positive housing legislation, but also subject to antiquated forms of taxation including both window and brick tax.

Projects outside London followed, in Tunbridge Wells and Hull. In 1959, the company became the 1830 Housing Society, which was taken over in 1965 by the Peabody Trust.

---

### Streatham Street, Bloomsbury, London

- Built in 1850 by SICLC
- Its "Model Houses for Families" were well in advance of contemporary practice
- The project was less financially successful – rents were not commensurate
- Now known as Parnell House, the buildings are still standing.

---

## The Metropolitan Association for Improving Dwellings of the Industrious Classes (MAIDIC)

The earliest of these societies, founded in 1841, MAIDIC was not as directly philanthropic as the SICLC and would now be best described as a social enterprise.

It spent its four years raising £20,000 in capital and in 1845 received a Royal Charter – essential to limit the liability of shareholders to no more than their investment.

The maximum rate of return was 5 per cent, with any surplus going into a guarantee fund of £15,000.

Their first project – in **Old St Pancras Road** in 1847 – was an ambitious one: for 21 tenements of two rooms and 90 tenements of three rooms, each with its own water supply and refuse chute.

The success of this project led almost immediately to another at **Spicer Street** (now Buxton Street), Spitalfields, for a 300-person male lodging house, plus dwellings for 40 families.

Always designed for expansion, MAIDIC established affiliated associations in Brighton, Newcastle, Dudley, Ramsgate, Southampton and Torquay after 1850.

Later schemes included **Alexandra Cottages in Penge** (South London) – model houses and "the first really suburban venture of a housing society" (Tarn, 1973, p. 27). The majority of this development also still stands, now privately owned and within a much sought-after conservation area.

## George Peabody and the Five Per Cent Philanthropy Club

With the success and viability of these housing schemes proved by the end of the 1850s – with more and more people willing to invest at less than the going rate – the 1860s saw the establishment of organisations that became famous in the field. Waterlow and Peabody demonstrated the long-term viability of social housing, which has been one of the staple forms of social investment ever since.

In 1862, George Peabody established his famous Trust Fund. A year later, Sidney Waterlow founded a "commercial company which was to prove, at last, that working-class housing could produce a workable, if modest return" (Tarn, 1973, p. 43).

Peabody was a wealthy American merchant banker, who had set up operations in London. He appointed a group of trustees to administer a fund originally amounting to £150,000 (later increased to £500,000) for the benefit of the London poor. The trustees made two key decisions. First, that housing was the priority. Second, that the fund should be self-perpetuating, thus ensuring they too joined the "Five Per Cent Philanthropy" Club.

---

**The Peabody Trust**

- 1864 – the first large-scale and independent housing agency opened its first enterprise, in Commercial Street, Spitalfields, London
- 1860s – followed by four large estates in Islington, Shadwell, Westminster and Chelsea
- Not dwellings for the very poor, but for the "respectable" working class, emphasised by rents of 2s 6d for a single room, when a night in a common lodging house cost 4d
- Peabody's endowment brought financial independence – the Trust was more financially stable than other housing bodies
- A return of 3 per cent was acceptable, as opposed to the 5 per cent of less secure funds (Tarn, 1966)
- 1880s – Had the confidence of the banks, securing large loans between £265,000 and £390,000
- Achieved "a pre-eminence in the housing world which was unique" (Tarn, 1966, p. 38)
- Still retains a significant presence in the London social housing sector, with 27,000 properties under its management and assets of nearly £1 billion.

---

## Into the twentieth century

Similar schemes followed. In 1885, Nathan Mayer Rothschild founded the Four Per Cent Industrial Dwellings Company, providing homes for Jewish artisans in the very worst parts of East London (White, 2007).

By 1905, the Four Per Cent Industrial Dwellings Company had built six large blocks comprising 1,500 flats and 3,800 rooms. In 1952, the company was renamed as the Industrial Dwellings Society (1885) Limited. Today known as IDS, it manages over 1,400 properties in four London boroughs, including Tower Hamlets, as well as in Hertsmere and Barnet. Its current President is Sir Evelyn de Rothschild, a direct descendent of the founder.

As the nineteenth century moved into the twentieth, the London County Council (formed in 1889) began to build housing. After the First World War, it was councils, as opposed to private philanthropic organisations, which increasingly became the major supplier of social housing until the 1980s. However, housing associations continued in this period and again became major new social housing providers. The 1970s saw the creation of the housing corporation, followed by the reforms of the Conservative government in the 1980s, with the "right to buy" scheme and capital funding restrictions on new council house building.

Social housing schemes grew and developed from the principles of what we now know as "social finance". Charity trading shops went on a similar journey. It is this we explore next.

## The appearance of charity shops

Are today's charity shops an example of social finance? That's debatable. For over a century, they have been a feature of UK charity trading.

Many are funded through loan capital, reinvestments from trading income and, more recently, other forms of social finance (Scope, 2016; see also Scope case study, Chapter 7a).

In the late nineteenth century, the **Salvation Army** ran stalls and shops providing cheap second-hand clothing for the urban poor (Horne, 1998)

There was significant trading activity during the First World War, with the **Red Cross** leading the way. In 1918, it organised a charity sale over a period of 16 days, which brought in £150,000 (worth something like £7.5 million today) and ran a number of "gift houses".

---

**Red Cross gift houses**

- 1916 – the first gift house opened in Pall Mall, London
- It received a steady stream of gifts, including from Queen Mary, who donated her war savings certificate, which raised 50 guineas
- Also sold items on behalf of the French Red Cross
- 1918 – a second and a third gift house opened on Kensington High Street and Old Bond Street
- Even after the armistice, there was still a large demand for victory souvenirs and gifts from the Red Cross shops.

## From Oxfam to Sue Ryder

Other charities operated shops during the Second World War. Oxfam opened its first shop in Broad Street, Oxford in 1947, following overwhelming public donations to alleviate the post-war situation in Greece (Klouda, 2007).

In the early 1950s, the Sue Ryder Foundation opened premises in London, Birmingham, Hull, Manchester and Liverpool (Horne, 1998).

---

**Charity shops – yes or no?**

- 1992 – under 3,500 in the UK (Parsons, 2002)
- 2017 – over 10,000
- Greater professionalisation – better appearance; open six days a week; paid managerial staff; specialist shops for books, bridal wear, children's items, second-hand furniture and electrical, gifts, independent living and vintage and designer clothing (Klouda, 2007)
- With customers deserting them for out-of-town hypermarkets, independent high-street traders have found it harder and harder to survive, with many closing and their places taken by charity shops (Todd, 2009).

---

While some charities were growing large networks of charity shops, other charities were starting to see the need to help individuals create businesses of their own; helping people to help themselves.

## The Ford Foundation and PRIs

In the late 1960s, the Ford and Taconic Foundations began using programme-related investments (PRIs) as a means of providing much needed capital investment into black and minority-owned businesses (Bolton, 2005).

The incarnation of PRI began from the brainchild of Ford's then deputy vice president, Louis Winnick, when he realised that the Foundation could have used some form of loan mechanism rather than a grant (Ford Foundation, 1991, p. 5).

After successfully pushing for statutory recognition of PRIs in the 1969 Tax Act, Ford's trustees approved the use of up to $10 million (about one-third of 1 per cent of the Foundation's assets) for PRIs "in support of high-priority Foundation programs" (Ford Foundation, 1991, p. 7).

The early days saw significant losses. The Foundation did not have expertise in the kinds of businesses it was funding (Bolton, 2005, p. 11).

Even so, a number of notable successes included the five-year $600,000 loan, which helped launch the Harvard Community Health Plan, an experimental group practice that became a model for later health-maintenance organisations.

Between 1968 and 1978, 85 PRIs totalling $53.3 million were made, of which $34.9 million was recovered. These were predominantly in urban areas for small businesses, housing and community development corporations.

Ford's use of intermediaries to deliver many of its PRIs is an approach that other foundations have since adopted. By 1991, Ford had made 229 PRIs totalling nearly $196 million, using 2 per cent of the Foundation's then asset base. These took several forms, including:

- Direct loans, the most common, for such things as mortgage finance and predevelopment costs for both housing and businesses
- Equity investments, where the Foundation purchased stock in business ventures
- Loan guarantees, to encourage private lenders to become involved in key social projects.

Repayment terms were usually less than ten years, with an average of seven years, with any losses being funded out of the Foundation's grants budget.

Today, the total investment in PRIs by the Ford Foundation amounts to over $550 million. However, the Foundation now restricts PRIs to organisations which are also in receipt of a Foundation grant (Ford Foundation, 2018). Many other US Foundations have followed Ford's lead.

---

**Programme-related investments (PRIs)**

By 2007, education had become the top priority for American foundations. The two largest PRIs of the year included a $50 million loan to Mater Dei High School in Santa Ana, California, and a $27.3 million loan to the Diocese of San Diego, to build a new Catholic high school (Lawrence, 2010).

---

## Recent UK social finance initiatives

UK foundations have made loans for several years, though often without the establishment of a specific fund for programme-related investment. Table 7.1 shows some of these.

**The Tudor Trust** has been making loans since 1985, usually to assist in the purchase or refurbishment of property. As the housing market has changed, properties in

*Table 7.1* An analysis of social problems and related social finance solution from UK foundations

| Social problem | Social finance solution |
| --- | --- |
| Late 1980s London faced the difficulty of attracting newly qualified teachers to work in deprived parts of the capital. | In 1989/90, the Tudor Trust partnered with a housing association in equity-linked loans to buy properties in London for subsequent letting at affordable rents to teachers. |
| Voluntary organisations in the mid-1990s UK were being denied access to finance because mainstream banks did not understand voluntary sector funding models. | In 1996, the Charities Aid Foundation (CAF) launched Investors in Society for voluntary organisations with the capacity to manage a loan and with revenue streams which could service repayments. |
| Early 21st century – many historic buildings could be saved from closure and brought back into productive use. | In 2011, The Prince's Regeneration Trust (PRT) put together a private and public funding package of over £9 million, comprising both grants and loans, to purchase and develop Middleport Pottery in Stoke-on-Trent, the UK's oldest commercial pottery. |

the 1989/90 scheme have been re-valued and either sold back to the housing association or sold on the open market. Tudor received back a small financial premium on its original investment (Bolton, 2005).

**The Charities Aid Foundation (CAF)** has been involved in a number of social finance initiatives. In 2003, Investors in Society (a CAF project that became independent in 2002) became Charity Bank, the first organisation in the UK that had both charitable status and Financial Services Authority banking accreditation. In 2013, Charity Bank reported that it had lent over £177 million to more than 1,000 charities and social enterprises across the UK, as a cumulative figure. In 2018 alone, Charity Bank lent £48.6 million and continues to grow (Charity Bank, 2019, p. 18).

In 2002, CAF established **Venturesome** to provide risk finance in the space between a grant and a loan, also known as mezzanine finance. It concentrates on underwriting and unsecured lending but has also provided quasi-equity. While its main market is charities, it has also participated in social enterprise share issues. CAF Venturesome is one of the most active providers of impact-focused social investment in the UK.

> By January 2018, Venturesome had supported more than 500 social organisations with over £40m of social investment finance.
>
> (CAF, 2018)

**The Prince's Regeneration Trust (PRT)**, one of the "family" of charities established by or under the patronage of Charles, Prince of Wales, has been involved in a number of social finance initiatives.

At Middleport Pottery, home to the famous Burleigh ware, it saved 50 jobs and created another 66. Unused buildings have been converted to provide workshops for social enterprises, craft and community areas, a café, gallery and an education and heritage centre. The pottery opened to the public in 2014 and has enjoyed rising visitor numbers, winning many awards for design and conservation excellence (Middleport Pottery, 2015).

The PRT often sees projects as indicative of what can be achieved through a judicious mix of social finance from a range of private, public and philanthropic sources and as being capable of replication in many other locations.

---

### The Scottish Land Fund

- A mainly public programme for the purchase of capital assets by community trusts
- Originally conceived by the Scottish government in the late 1990s
- Funded at the beginning of the millennium through the New Opportunities Fund (the National Lottery "good cause" – now called the Big Lottery Fund)
- An initial £15 million fund provided a mixture of grant and loans to 188 projects, successfully "pioneered the community ownership model on a wide scale across rural Scotland", allowing "communities to take charge of and develop assets from which they will benefit for many years to come" (Big Lottery Fund, 2007, p. 3)
- Followed up in 2015 by a new version, again comprising a partnership between Big Lottery and the Scottish government, together with Highland and Islands Enterprise.

By 2010, the 350-year history of social finance had witnessed countless culture-changing initiatives. Yet, as we saw in the last chapter, the Credit Crash of 2008 forced many charities into thinking again. Government also started to see new ways of developing the social sector through social investment and the creation of initiatives such as Big Society Capital.

## Social finance hits the mainstream

In 2012, disability charity Scope became the first major charity to look at alternative, innovative forms of social finance. It launched a social bond programme aimed at financing 20 new shops and increasing its donor base by 100,000 (Scope, 2016).

In partnership with the social finance intermediary, Investing for Good, the bond was listed on the Luxembourg Stock Exchange. It paid a yield of 2–3 per cent to investors, including Big Society Capital (BSC) – the social investment wholesaler established with funding from dormant bank accounts – and the Esmée Fairbairn Foundation. This case study is given as Chapter 7a in this book.

In 2015, Scope repaid the £875,000 BSC loan; the first BSC investment to be repaid (Farey-Jones, 2015).

## Summary

This chapter demonstrates that, while readers may think of social investment as a fairly modern concept, in fact it has been used over hundreds of years as a tool to support social change.

Second, what this chapter highlights clearly is the need and motivation of an investor to align with that of a cause.

But what do social investors and social purpose organisations want from social investment and how can these motivations best align? It is this we explore next.

## References

Big Lottery Fund (2007), *Scottish Land Fund: Findings from our evaluation*, accessed 20 October 2018, www.biglotteryfund.org.uk/-/media/Files/Research%20Documents/Communities%20and%20places%20publications/Scottish%20Land%20Fund/Scottish%20Land%20Fund%20evaluation%20summary.pdf.

Bolton, M. (2005), *Foundations and Social Investment: Making money work harder in order to achieve more*, Esmée Fairbairn Foundation, p. 11.

CAF (2018), *Social Investment through CAF Venturesome*, accessed 20 October 2018, www.caf online.org/about-us/caf-venturesome.

Charity Bank (2019), *Money on a Mission: Charity Bank impact report 2019*, accessed 21 July 2019, https://charitybank.org/uploads/files/CharityBank_Social_Impact_Report_2019.pdf.

Farey-Jones, D. (2015), *Scope Repays the £2m It Borrowed through a Bond Issue in 2012*, Third Sector, accessed 20 October 2018, www.thirdsector.co.uk/scope-repays-2m-borrowed-bond-issue-2012/finance/article/1358245.

Ford Foundation (1991), *Investing for Social Gain: Reflections on two decades of program-related investments*, Ford Foundation, New York.

Ford Foundation (2018), *Ford Foundation – PRI Fund*, accessed 16 April 2018, https://iris.thegiin.org/users/profile/the-ford-foundation-pri-fund.

Horne, S. (1998), *Charity Shops in the UK*, International Journal of Retail and Distribution Management, 26: 4, pp. 155–161.

Klouda, L. (2007), *Charity Retailing: The future of sustainable shopping?*, European Retail Digest, 56, pp. 16–20.

Lawrence, S. (2010), *Doing Good with Foundation Assets: An updated look at program-related investments*, accessed 20 October 2018, www.foundationcenter.org/gainknowledge/research/pdf/pri_directory_excerpt.pdf.

Middleport Pottery (2015), *Middleport Pottery wins national architecture award*, accessed 20 October 2018, www.middleportpottery.org/wp-content/uploads/2016/06/Middleport-Pottery-RIBA-National-Award-draft-release.pdf.

Parsons, E. (2002), *Charity Retail: Past, present and future*, International Journal of Retail and Distribution Management, 30: 12, pp. 586–594.

Scope (2016), *The Scope Bond Programme*, accessed 20 October 2018, www.scope.org.uk/get-involved/donate/philanthropy/social-investment-bond.

Sherwin, O. (1950), *Thomas Firmin: Puritan precursor of WPA*, Journal of Modern History, 22: 1, pp. 38–41.

Tarn, J. N. (1973), *Five Per Cent Philanthropy: An account of housing in urban areas between 1840 and 1914*, Cambridge University Press.

Tarn, J. N. (1966), *The Peabody Donation Fund: The role of a housing society in the nineteenth century*, Victorian Studies, 10: 1, pp. 7–38.

Todd, D. (2009), *Are Charity Shops Harming the High Street?*, Cass and Charity Finance Group, accessed 16 April 2018, www.cfg.org.uk/resources/Document%20Library/income-generation-fundraising/donations.aspx?doc=%7BC9414F46-AA07-41D5-A148-276F1EB8AFEC%7D.

White, J. (2007), *London in the Nineteenth Century*, Vintage.

Yenawine, B. H. (2010), *Benjamin Franklin and the Invention of Microfinance*, Routledge.

# 7a  Case study

## 'Scope'

*Tom Baughan*

## Gearing up fundraising

**Tom Baughan**, Development Director, Theatre Royal Bath, explores how Scope became the first established UK charity to raise finance through the bond market. Quotes are from an interview with Tom Hall, UBS Head of Philanthropy Services, and ex-Head of Philanthropy at Scope.

This was one of the first examples of social investment in the charity space which really captured the imagination. It remains an inspiration for others who followed, and was a small but important test case.

---

### Background details

- May 2012 – national disability charity, Scope, launches a £2 million bond issue.
- Aim – to raise finance that could be invested in growing sustainable unrestricted income through new donor acquisition and an expansion of charity shops.
- Additional income used for – to support Scope's non-revenue-generating activities, including campaigns, advocacy and support services.
- Partner – to deliver the bond, Scope worked in partnership with Investing for Good (IFG, 2019) a specialist social finance intermediary.

---

## Background

The Scope bond was originally conceived as a way of upscaling a model of loan finance which the charity had used for two earlier residential projects.

Scope thought it might be rolling out residential building projects nationally and needed an efficient way of borrowing a larger sum of capital. This led to a conversation with Investing for Good, which suggested listing a corporate bond.

Mid-way through getting the bond ready, the charity had a strategic review and decided not to pursue large-scale residential care. Rather than ending the work on the bond, Scope decided to go ahead with the bond issue and use the money for something else. "We started talking about investing the money we borrowed into other forms of revenue generating activities, fundraising and charity shop".

## Bond structure

The bond issue level of £2 million was based on the amount Scope wanted to invest in fundraising and charity shops. The duration would be three years and offer investors a 2 per cent yield. The bond was listed on the Luxembourg Stock Exchange in May 2012 and the minimum investment size was £25,000.

Scope was market-led in setting the interest rate and duration of the bond. "We asked people: if you were to lend money to a charity, what would be the right interest rate? And what would be the right term? The feedback was 2% over three years".

A small return offered protection from inflation. A three-year period was the longest time people would be willing to tie up their capital without a greater market-rate return.

As it happened, by the time the bond was launched, interest rates had dropped and "the 2% yield was actually pretty competitive".

## Marketing

Marketing the bond was complicated, due to rules governing how financial products can be promoted. "Normally, only a Financial Conduct Authority (FCA) regulated entity can market a financial instrument".

Scope took legal guidance that advised the charity it could tell people it had launched the bond, but could not directly ask people to invest in it. This was the difference between giving information and making a financial promotion.

If a prospect showed interest, Scope would get a "sophisticated investor's waiver" signed, stating the prospect had investible assets of more than £250,000, or was an investment professional. Scope would then get the paperwork signed by its FCA-regulated intermediary, Investing for Good. Once Scope was comfortable with the process, the charity publicly launched the scheme.

The pioneering nature of the product garnered significant coverage within financial services publications and the national press. All used by Scope to raise public awareness of the investment opportunity and the organisation's work.

## Distribution

The target had been to try to get money "from proper financial investors, distribution into pension funds and other asset managers". This proved tricky. The bond was an unfamiliar product to the market and was also comparatively small. This meant "it wouldn't make any money for a trader, because there's not enough of it to buy and sell". It was also low yield (2 per cent) and "was never going to massively inflate [an investor's] open portfolio performance".

Ultimately, Scope did secure investment from two wealth managers via their discretionary portfolios.

It was fascinating that managers took that tiny bond, despite the low yield, because it meant they could report that they've done an impact investment.

The majority of the bond's take-up was secured from a small number of foundations and specialist social investors. These included the Esmée Fairbairn Foundation, Nesta Impact Investments, and Project Snowball (a partnership running the qualifying social investments of Panahpur and the Golden Bottle Trust; see case study in Chapter 12a).

> An incentive for foundations was that the bond provided an opportunity to use their endowment in a way that promised a financial return, but also helped to achieve their mission.
>
> (Nissan and Bolton, 2008, p. 7)

## A relationship-building opportunity

Tom Hall partly drove the Scope bond as a way of getting in front of wealthy individuals. He comments that the charity could have borrowed the money more expensively, but wouldn't have got this relationship-building opportunity.

Scope was able to use the bond to attract investment from individuals who "had never done anything significant with charity". Through its social investment initiatives, Scope "went from having three major donors giving us more than £10k in 2009, to about 40 major donors in the following four years".

The minimum investment level for the Scope bond was set at £25,000. Had it been lower, the charity might have been even more successful in attracting new donors. "I always thought it should be £10k, because I was trying to offer it as an alternative major donor product", Hall says.

The complexity of marketing and distributing the bond meant it took longer to close than anticipated. Face-to-face meetings were held with every single investor.

> In the event, about 25% of total investment came from financial institutions, 40% from organisations interested in social investment or charitable trusts, and 35% from private individuals.

## Impact for Scope

Scope invested around £400,000 of the bond's proceeds in opening new charity shops and £1.6 million in donor acquisition (Bridges Fund Management, 2014, p. 31).

It was anticipated that each new shop would generate approximately £25,000 net income per year. Also, that the 100,000 regular donors Scope acquired as a result of using this money for investment to grow fundraising, should raise around £8 million over five years (Esmée Fairbairn Foundation, 2015).

Scope's accounts in 2015 refer to a continuing growth in fundraising as a result of their decision to expand their individual giving recruitment programme in 2012 (Scope, 2015).

> The 2015 accounts also report an exceptional year for charity shops, achieving a trading surplus of £3m. It may therefore be argued that bond achieved its primary aim of boosting unrestricted income generation.

However, the charity's overall income has decreased year on year since 2012, while spend has increased. It is therefore "hard to say for definite whether it has had as much impact as we might have hoped".

The bond may have helped to maintain levels of income that might otherwise have fallen more rapidly as a consequence of the financial crisis in 2008. "It was positioned as doing more, but it might just have insulated the worst of the cuts".

## Future of the bond programme

The £2 million bond was originally positioned as the first tranche of a £20 million bond programme. While Scope acknowledged at the time that it "may not feel it necessary to issue the whole £20m" (Ribeiro, 2011), it is notable that the charity has not issued a successor bond. Perhaps, following the strategic review, it had no further need for this form of finance.

## Conclusions

Despite an early change in strategic intent, the Scope bond was successfully designed, marketed and distributed.

- It raised the target capital and appears to have triggered the desired impact in Scope's retail and fundraising.
- The bond was a pioneering initiative that brought major publicity for the charity.
- It also differentiated Scope from its competitors in attracting new support and acted as a catalyst for major donor activity.
- The Scope bond led the way for a number of charities, which have since looked to finance things in similar ways using social investment.
- One learning point to emerge from the Scope bond for other charities was to increase the scale of bond issues and put the interest rate up to ensure faster take-up in the market.
- The charity Mencap launched a bond a couple of years later. It "upped the scale to £10m and put the interest rate to 4% and so it closed down much faster".

As more charities have begun to follow Scope's example, the sector has also worked to develop a more enabling environment for social investment. The introduction of Social Investment Tax Relief (SITR) (Gov.UK, 2016) and the establishment of social investment intermediaries are just two examples of this.

The Scope bond helped to change perceptions of the sector.

It was innovative and showed that the old school part of the sector could think differently about how it could capitalise itself.

As a consequence, "borrowing and lending to charity is much more normalised than it was in 2009".

In May 2015, the Scope bonds matured and were repaid in full with interest. This all points to a highly successful and landmark programme.

# References

Bridges Fund Management (2014), *Shifting the lens: A de-risking toolkit for impact investment*, accessed 20 October 2018, www.bridgesfundmanagement.com/publications/shifting-lens-de-risking-toolkit-impact-investment/.

Esmée Fairbairn Foundation (2015), *Scope uses social bonds to increase its unrestricted long term income stream*, accessed 20 June 2018, www.esmeefairbairn.org.uk/news-andlearning/news-and-events/scope-uses-social-bonds-to-increase-its-unrestricted-long-term-incomestrea.

Gov.UK (2016), *Social Investment Tax Relief*, accessed 21 July 2019, www.gov.uk/government/publications/social-investment-tax-relief-factsheet/social-investment-tax-relief.

Investing for Good, IFG (2019), main website, accessed 21 July 2019, www.investingforgood.co.uk/.

Nissan, S. and Bolton, M. (2008), *Mission possible: Emerging opportunities for mission-connected investment*, New Economics Foundation, accessed 20 October 2018, www.neweconomics.org/2008/05/mission-possible/.

Ribeiro, C. (2011), *Scope launches £20m bond to expand fundraising and retailing*, Civil Society, accessed 20 October 2018, www.civilsociety.co.uk/news/scope-launches-20m-bond-to-expand-fundraising-and-retailing.html.

Scope (2015), *Annual report and accounts 2014/15*, accessed 20 October 2018, www.scope.org.uk/Scope/media/Documents/About%20us/Annual-Report-2015-web.pdf.

# 8 What do social purpose organisations and investors want from social investment?

## Matching supply and demand

*Mark Salway*

## What do charities and social purpose organisations really want from social investment?

In this chapter we first look at the strategic need for social investment and what charities and social purpose organisations really want social investment for.

Goggin and Baker (2013, p. 4) see that "social investment has the potential to encourage innovation, enable social impact and support income diversification at a time when the need for alternative finance is likely to rise."

These authors (Goggin and Baker 2013, p. 8) go further and identify that, "Overall, motivation to engage with social investment [falls] into two distinct but related categories: investment for strategy and investment for adaptation or survival." From their detailed interviews, the authors identified VCSE (voluntary, community and social enterprise organisations) as managing these motivations in interlocking ways:

### Where investment is for strategy:

> They [interviewees] perceived a fundamental shift in the way VCSE sector organisations are funded and thought that their organisation would need to change in order to succeed ... Second, they saw investment as more efficient and cost effective than grants. Third, a small number of participants felt that a loan enabled them to retain their independence and focus on their mission and strategy.

### Where investment was for survival:

> Some participants had sought social investment to help them finance their way through a problem such as cash flow. Investment had not necessarily been their preferred funding option and was quite explicitly linked to organisational survival.

The G8 Social Investment Taskforce (2014) similarly identifies social investment as enabling organisations to become less reliant on traditional forms of funding, such as grants and donation. They see that it gives social purpose organisations the opportunity to move towards a more financially stable funding mix (Rickey *et al.*, 2011). Similarly, Hailey and Salway (2017) identify that social investment enables and facilitates sustainability in international non-governmental organisations (INGOs).

Salamon (2014, Chapter 4) considers the demand for social investment and whether this is a "a flash in the pan or a durable trend in the financing of social-purpose activity". He looks at the demand side of social investment from a global view and considers three drivers linked to social impact:

1  **The changing environmental and human world around us:** for example, slum water and sanitation needing new solutions. The size of problems shows we need new solutions which cannot be provided by governments, corporates or charities alone.

2  **Governments and charities lack both the energy and the size to deal with problems at scale:** These interrelated environmental, economic, social, and political needs would be difficult to meet under any circumstances. But they are being confronted now by a world that has been experiencing enormous economic shocks, unsustainable governmental spending, and charitable resources that, while growing, do not come close to being able to deliver the resources needed to address the problems that exist.

3  **The rise and rise of social entrepreneurship:** spearheaded by the rise in microfinance, as changing the global dynamic and demand for social investment. He calls this the "new frontiers of philanthropy and social investment". He concludes that "there are substantial reasons to believe [social investment] has significant staying power".

## The UK government's view

In 2016, the UK government launched a large-scale strategic review called *Social Investment: a Force for Social Change.* (Gov.UK, 2016). This highlighted the then government's interest in social investment to help charities innovate and scale up to take on larger contracts.

> Social investment is a tool to help organisations increase their social impact. It helps many social sector organisations do more by providing the capital that they need to deliver their services, grow or become more sustainable.
>
> Governments around the world are increasingly recognising the potential of social investment. It is supporting economic growth, driving the innovation needed to deliver public services in the 21st century and, ultimately, tackling some of the most difficult social challenges that we face.
>
> (Gov.UK, 2016, p. 6).

The UK government sees social investment as: creating impact by providing working capital; and providing money for growth, sustainability and innovation.

Nolan (2013) acknowledges that social investment is "increasingly employed for political purposes". He sets out some serious issues and concerns in that regard, including whether social investment can credibly be presented as the paradigm most likely to underpin economic growth.

---

**Good Finance, 2018 (www.goodfinance.org.uk)**

Big Society Capital's website, Good Finance, "is a collaborative project to help improve access to information on social investment for charities and social enterprises". It identifies three main categories of social investment for charities and social enterprise:

> Charities and social enterprise can use repayable finance to help them increase their impact on society, for example by growing their business, providing working capital for contract delivery; or buying assets.

---

### Focusing on specific uses of social investment

But the discussion so far still doesn't explain what precisely charities and social purpose organisations will use social investment for.

Writing for this book in Chapters 20–27, Jim Clifford identifies four main purposes to which social investment can be applied (see Chapter 21 for more details):

- **Working capital** – borrowing to maintain cashflow
- **Fixed capital** – investment to purchase a building, property or purpose-built facility
- **Research and development** – encompassing the wider research necessary to get a business started, to develop new products and services and to establish new markets, collaborations and outreach
- **Broader risk sharing** – investment to develop social enterprise ventures to generate income. This could also be to develop new services, improve efficiency or improve an organisation's infrastructure, for example by better use of IT.

Matching the type of social investment against the four objectives here gives a thorough analysis of availability of funds versus what funds will be used for; see Figure 8.1.

| | Working Capital: General Funding (of the whole organisation) | Working Capital: Payment by Results Contracts | Fixed Capital: Capital Projects | Research and Development: Business / IP Development | Broader Risk Sharing: Project Funding | Broader Risk Sharing: Development Funding (e.g. building projects) |
|---|---|---|---|---|---|---|
| **Debt Based** Non-risk sharing (full recourse) | ✔ | ✔ | ✔ | ✔ | ✔ | ✔ |
| **Equity Based** Risk sharing (limited recourse) | ✗ Rare | ✔ | Not Applicable | ✔ | ✔ | ✗ Rare |
| **Fixed capital** e.g. for equipment and buildings (Secured) | ✔ | ✔ | ✔ | ✔ | ✔ | ✔ |

*Figure 8.1* Availability of different types of investment against what funds will be used for.
Source: Developed from Clifford (2016). Used by permission of the author.

During 2015–16, Cass Business School ran six seminars with 150 charities participating, alongside around 20 investment organisations (Salway, 2017, p. 14). The sessions were called "*Demystifying the Hype*" and the aim was to build understanding among charities and social purpose organisations about social investment.

From the seminars, Cass was better able to understand the motivations for charities potentially using social investment. This knowledge identified that social investment should be seen for what it is, a tool to help the sector, not a panacea for all.

From the seminars, the primary reasons why charities are interested in social investment are seen as follows:

### Strategic needs

- **Sustainability** – ensuring the ability to diversify income streams in a way that is self-sustaining and predictable
- **Impact** – allowing charities to identify priorities and provide funding linked to these
- **Scaling up and growth** – enabling work to be taken to scale and facilitating greater impact
- **Investing in IT or the low carbon economy** – investing in changing business models
- **Autonomy and flexibility in income streams** – rather than needing to dance to the donor's tune.

### Specific needs

- **Building internal infrastructure** – a specific example of this is contract readiness, e.g. investing in building capacity for payments-by-results contracts
- **Innovation** – to allow new ideas to flourish and charities to re-invent themselves; examples here included new technology and green tech
- **Fundraising** – Investment against fundraising, which in turn allows charities to raise more income and have greater impact
- **Assets, and developing their physical environment** – through new buildings
- **Developing a new trading activity or service** – creating new revenue-generating models of business.

However, by far and away the greatest need for charities and social purpose organisations was sustainability.

> Charities need stable and predictable income streams for long-term financial sustainability.
>
> (Salway, 2017, p. 16)

The seminar series also highlighted that charities need help understanding social investment and how it can be used, especially to develop business models that can pay back the investment. This help and support is particularly needed by small charities.

### Learnings from social enterprise

Social enterprises trade to tackle social problems and improve communities, people's life chances or the environment. They make their money from selling goods and services in the open market, but they reinvest their profits back into the business or the local community (Social Enterprise UK, 2018).

> With social enterprises, social investment is seen as a tool for growth, impact, innovation and to cater for start-ups.

In Social Enterprise UK's (2011) report, *Fight Back Britain*, the main uses of social investment were given as working capital and to help achieve growth. It also highlights a wide variety of uses of social investment practices: building social businesses; finding start-up capital; and funding innovation.

The Social Enterprise UK (2011) report dedicates a section to generating local impact from social investment, stating that "one of the key approaches used by social enterprises is the reinvestment of profit. 82% of our survey respondents stated that they reinvest the surplus or profit from contracts or trading to further their social or environmental goals locally" (Social Enterprise UK, 2011, p. 24).

## What type of funding do charities and social purpose organisations want?

Chapman (2015) discovered that, among the many factors that not-for-profits consider when seeking loans, interest rates are seen as the most significant. Charities and social purpose organisations want affordable money to match their need to demonstrate value for money to their donors and supporters.

> 80% of Third Sector Organisations (TSOs) state that interest rates are very important when considering loans … 47% of TSOs consider the ethics of a lender as being very important, and 44% say that the relationship they have with their lender is very important.
>
> (Chapman, 2015, p. 48)

CAF (2014) acknowledged that "the charity sector is facing greater demand for its services, more competition for statutory funding and increasing effort required to secure public donations" (p. 6). In its report, CAF asked how much charities would like to borrow in the future. The majority of charities provided a figure of less than £250,000, with over a third of charities stating an amount less than £50,000.

As a result of these findings, CAF concluded, "more needs to be done to increase the provision of affordable risk capital, available at lower amounts" (CAF, 2014, p. 6).

---

### General charity borrowing versus social investment

We should also not confuse general borrowing – loans for general purposes or cashflow – with social investment. General borrowing does not have an intent to create both social and financial return on investment and cannot be categorised as social investment.

The charity sector already has a recognised level of general borrowing, separate and aside from social investment. The NCVO Almanac (NCVO, 2017) reports that, in 2014/15, the voluntary sector owed around £3 billion in loans. This is not considered social investment.

In contrast, recent figures from Big Society Capital (2018) identify that social investment in the UK is worth over £2.3 billion, spread across approximately 4,000 transactions.

This again adds to the growing confusion of terminology and definitions and the complexity of what social investment is and isn't.

So, having looked at charities and social purpose organisations and the demand for social investment, what do social investors want from this new tool?

## What do investors want from social investment?

The latest figures from the World Bank, in 2018, show trillions of dollars of investment capital at work throughout the world. The force of investment markets is substantial and offers huge opportunity to do good when harnessed in the right way.

The emergence of environmental, social and governance (ESG) analysis within investment portfolios and the development of codes for responsible investment (UNPRI, 2019) have been rapid and pronounced, occurring at roughly the same time as social investment has grown. The London Stock Exchange (2018, p. 2), reflects that

> Once upon a time, environmental, social and governance (ESG) factors were a niche interest among asset owners, asset managers, banks, brokers and investment consultants. No longer. Investors now routinely analyse information on ESG performance alongside other financial and strategic information in order to gain a better understanding of companies' future prospects.

However, the growth of ESG and responsible investment is about doing business in the right way, not necessarily to create social impact.

At the same time, there's a growing wave of investors seeing their funds in a different way. They see financial and social return on investment as not mutually exclusive and that it's possible to create both by investing their money in the right way. This belief that social investment can make a positive change is being led by "profit-with-purpose" commercial companies as well as by specific individuals, such as Bill Gates and Pierre Omidyar (the founder of eBay).

We are also seeing the creation of new investment funds (e.g. Big Issue Invest, Bridges Fund Management, Impetus–PEF), focused on creating social investments.

2013 saw the creation of the Social Stock Exchange, where investments have been launched and traded. This is not an exchange per se but a form of listing and validation of social purpose, which then recognises stocks listed on various exchanges. The Golden Lane Housing bond with Mencap has been an example of this in the charity bond market (Allia, 2019).

### Mainstream banks, too

We are starting to see a wide range of mainstream and investment banks focused on social investment (e.g. Barclays, J.P. Morgan), as well as social banks (e.g. CAF, Triodos, Unity Bank) growing this market.

Pension funds are starting to invest in social investment too, but mainly through funds and not through direct investment.

Investors are becoming less hung up on the legal form of the organisation in which they are investing and are instead becoming more focused on the social impact achieved with their capital.

We saw in Chapter 5 that there's a huge variety of potential social investors, ranging from commercial banks and loans, to corporate organisations, through to individuals and crowdfunding and the government. What is it exactly that investors are looking for and what is their motivation for using social investment?

### *Technically speaking, what do investors want from social investment?*

The *doing* social investment section of this book (Chapter 21) talks about the practicalities of using social investment. It identifies what investors want from social investment, namely:

- financial returns
- aligning with the specific mission or area of social interest of the funder
- repayment of capital after a period
- placing their investment into a venture that can deliver social outcomes
- placing their money in a way that will enable an outcome that otherwise would not happen (known generally as "additionality")
- an investment which is well governed and accountable
- possibly gaining tax reliefs
- backing and developing something that will have a longer-term or system-changing social effect
- and possibly developing the investor's association with a good, and high-impact, social prospect (a form of "affinity" or brand halo)

However, to use social investment in a meaningful way, we need to develop a bridge between the investor and the recipient organisation.

### *Discussing investor motivation*

In its blog on investor motivation, *What Drives Your Social Investing Strategy?* (2016), AVPN identifies that social investors are driven by "the aspiration to build something positive". This is mirrored across most of the academic narrative.

AVPN (2016) goes further to say that

> Motivation for social investing can come in many forms – altruism and guilt seem to be the predominant themes, historically. More recently, with the advent of impact investing, even greed has started to surface as a third form of motivation, with expectations of market-rate returns for social investments …

AVPN (2016) also identifies that motivation is further influenced and changed by age, gender and education of the investor.

In Chapter 5, we saw Brown and Swersky (2012, p. 24) on behalf of Boston Consulting Group (BCG) propose a simple model whereby social investment can be categorised as "socially motivated investment in socially motivated organisations".

Caroe, writing for Allia in his paper *What Do We Mean by Social Investment?* (Caroe, 2016, p. 10), asks whether BCG's analysis is really that easy:

Can we really infer motivation [for social investment] simply by looking at the terms of a deal? Couldn't some investors be both socially and commercially motivated? And just how socially motivated do you need to be to cross over the magic line into "social investment"?

Caroe (2016, p. 15) then goes further.

> The BCG proposition, as described previously … implies this binary distinction between social-motivation (or "social intent") and commercial-motivation (or "no social intent") … the concept of social intent as an on-off switch seems to me to be an over-simplification.

This author sees on the one hand people who want to manage an investment portfolio but who also want to create positive impact. On the other hand, he sees a range of foundations, specialist funds and individual investors who recognise that mainstream finance may not be appropriate or even accessible for some social purpose organisations. They care about creating impact and see investment as an extension of philanthropy that enables money to make a change while being preserved and recycled.

Writing for Third Sector, Rodney Schwartz (2014), Chief Executive of ClearlySo (a finance intermediary and convenor of an Angel network) identified that, "Deep-seated individual motivations play a vital role."

Schwartz said, "The importance of social impact means that values play a big part in the investment decision-making process: values shift and are challenging to measure and the trade-offs investors are prepared to make change constantly." He continued,

> Individuals might be willing to accept even a negative return to achieve a social impact they value – such as educating young girls in Africa – but seek market returns on the rest of their portfolio. Then they might have been inspired by a health-sector social entrepreneur and are investing a substantial sum with a relatively low return. These ever-changing desires make social finance fun and are part of the self-discovery process in which we are collectively engaged.
>
> (Schwartz, 2014)

This is a complex area.

### Viewing the spectrum of financial returns

To really understand social investment from an investor's perspective, we need to consider investor motivation in terms of financial return.

In Chapter 5, we started with a simple definition of social investment: "Social investments have the intent and motivation of generating a social or environmental impact as well as financial return on investment. They aim to measure both the social and financial value they create and be held accountable for this." (Salway, 2017, p. 9)

But within this definition, investors' expectations of returns are diverse. They range from mission-driven investors who are focused on the social returns and willing to provide funding for organisations unable to generate market returns (so-called sub-market rates of return), through to finance-first investors who are interested in having a social impact *as well as* a market rate of return.

The Social Economy Data Lab (2016–17) identifies that "[social investment] differs from conventional investment in that it is anticipated that a social benefit will be realised through the use of the money. It also differs from philanthropically motivated grant-making, as an economic return is also expected."

This spectrum of financial returns is explained by Bridges Fund Management (2015, p. 3) in the report, *The Bridges Spectrum of Capital: How We Define the Sustainable and Impact Investment Market*, seen by many as the de facto classification for social and responsible investment.

Bridges Fund Management (2015, p. 3; Figure 8.2) sees capital as having the following motivation as a spectrum from most financially motivated, to most social impact focused:

- Delivering competitive financial returns
- Mitigating ESG risks
- Pursuing ESG opportunities
- Focusing on measurable high-impact solutions.

We are also starting to see the evolution of more complex forms of capital, mixing philanthropy, impact-focused money and investment seeking a commercial rate of return.

> Even though investors who are focusing on maximising return can unintentionally generate impact, only investors striving for impact will be motivated to actively seek out and fund the appropriate opportunities. Besides these two categories, there is a third one which results from combining impact first, financial first capital *and* eventually philanthropy as well. Derived from the Chinese term "Yin-Yang" these deals blend different types of capital, requirements and motivations with the aim of creating sophisticated investment structures generating the highest leverage of social and financial return.
>
> (Brandstetter and Lehner, 2014, p. 33)

Spectrum of Capital

| Financial-only | Responsible | Sustainable | Impact | | | Impact-only |
|---|---|---|---|---|---|---|
| Delivering competitive financial returns | | | | | | |
| | Mitigating Environmental, Social and Governance (ESG) risks | | | | | |
| | | Pursuing Environmental, Social and Governance opportunities | | | | |
| | | | Focusing on measurable high-impact solutions | | | |
| Focus: Limited or no regard for environmental, social or governance (ESG) practices | Mitigate risky ESG practices in order to protect value | Adopt progressive ESG practices that may enhance value | Address societal challenges that generate competitive financial returns for investors | Address societal challenges where returns are as yet unproven | Address societal challenges that require a below-market financial return for investors | Address societal challenges that cannot generate a financial return for investors |

*Figure 8.2* Bridges Fund Management classification spectrum of sustainable and impact investment market.

Source: Bridges Fund Management (2015, p. 3).

### What about family offices?

It is interesting to consider family offices and high-net-worth individuals as wanting to use their capital for the future and in a responsible way.

The Financial Times and Global Impact Solutions Today (GIST) report (2017, p10) highlights that family offices have moved forward in their exploration of social investment:

- 32 per cent are active, with multiple impact investments across asset classes or causes
- 34 per cent have made their first impact investment and are considering further impact opportunities
- 11 per cent are actively researching impact investment opportunities but have made no investment yet
- 15 per cent consider impact investing to be their primary approach to the portfolio
- 9 per cent are exploring impact investing, with no investment opportunities identified.

The social investment world is moving rapidly and where family offices move, others follow.

The authors of the Financial Times and Method Impact report (2015, p. 19, chart 28) – the forerunner of the GIST report – identified family office motivation for social investment as follows:

- Contribution to sustainable development – 70 per cent
- Responsibility to society/community – 55 per cent
- Values of family – 32 per cent
- Giving back – 23 per cent
- Financial opportunity – 22 per cent.

The landscape of family offices as social investors is explored fully in Chapter 14 of this book.

### Meanwhile corporate entities are keen on effecting change in a few key areas

Similar to individuals, corporates are approaching social investment for a wide range of reasons. Some companies purely want to "do good"; others want to use an investing approach to help them find "the next big business idea".

Oliver Wyman (2016), completing research for Big Society Capital (2015), sees primary drivers for corporate interest in social investment as follows:

- The "corporate conscience" appears to be the primary driver of general corporate impact initiatives (including grant making, volunteering, etc.).

> Companies are increasingly feeling compelled to have a clear set of social impact activities. Whether they are managed by the "Corporate Social Responsibility" teams or the business units themselves, many large companies feel the need to have a portfolio of activities that reinforce a strong public image.

- However, "corporates' interests tend to cluster around a few social issues within education, sustainability and health";
- Additionally, "corporates appear to be more motivated by the prospects of finding new growth opportunities or scaling innovative business models; at times, they also use social investment tools as a response to external stakeholder pressure".

This implies that, for corporates the first-ranked motivation is the commitment as a responsible investor; the second reason why investors choose social investments is because they are an effective way to meet their impact goals; and the third motivation indicates that investors are responding to client demand.

### Government has a huge role to play

Last but by no means least, government has a huge role to play in promoting and developing the social investment market. The UK government document, *Social Investment: A Force for Social Change, 2016 Strategy*, was clear in its ambition and motivation (Gov. UK, 2016).

In Chapter 1 (p. 6), it is straightforward and to the point, laying out "Why Government supports social investment":

1.1 Social investment is a tool to help organisations increase their social impact. It helps many social sector organisations do more by providing the capital that they need to deliver their services, grow or become more sustainable.
1.2 Governments around the world are increasingly recognising the potential of social investment. It is supporting economic growth, driving the innovation needed to deliver public services in the 21st century and, ultimately, tackling some of the most difficult social challenges that we face.
1.3 This itself is part of a wider trend. Consumers, employers and investors are increasingly focusing on the social and environmental impact of their spending decisions, places of work and investments. Evidence suggests a new generation for whom doing good and doing well are not seen as being incompatible. Given the leading role that the UK has played in driving this field, we are in a unique position to be a world leader as it reaches the mainstream.
1.4 As a government, we have an interest in both helping the social investment market grow and in partnering with this market to deliver better services to the public. Social investment does not relieve governments of their responsibilities. But it can help to fulfil them more effectively. By financing innovative approaches, social investment also has the potential to help deliver public services more efficiently and, in some cases, tackle the underlying causes of growing demand for services instead of just trying to cope with their consequences.

There is also the argument that social investment could help take pressure off the public purse.

As an aside, local government pension schemes (LGPS) are starting to make their first social investments.

*Institutional investors*

As we shall see in Chapter 19, there is one final thought for the future. That is to open up the opportunities for social investment to retail investors. What needs to be made to work is how this can deliver both serious impact and decent financial returns for investors. That will be the future, one where Big Society Capital will no longer be the biggest investor in the social investment space, but a catalyst for much larger flows of capital for positive social impact.

So, the future requires other investors to join in – pension funds and banks. To get to scale, we need to bring in institutional investment and, if possible, retail, i.e. mass involvement. Most people's savings go via institutions and retail investors. People need their pensions to live on into old age – they need financial returns. This all needs to be figured out if social investment is to grow (further explored in Chapter 12).

Some of the recent work on going "beyond the trade-offs" is useful in this space. It highlights that gains in momentum and impact investing's potential are hindered by this debate on trade-offs.

> The reality, however, is far more nuanced. Even as the field continues to debate whether impact investing does or does not achieve market-rate returns at the sacrifice of social impact, we have found that leading practitioners have moved past this conversation to create highly nuanced and sophisticated portfolios of impact investments that target different levels of financial returns, different types of social impact, and a broad spectrum of risk profiles. This disconnect between the public debate and the actual diversity of investment opportunities available is creating confusion among existing, new, or potential impact investors, and may impede the healthy development of this market.
>
> (FSG, 2018)

FSG partnered with the Omidyar Network to curate a new series, *Beyond Trade-offs: Investor Perspectives from across the Continuum of Impact Investing* (FSG, 2018), showcasing a set of examples from leading impact investors that illustrate the diversity of investment approaches helping to shift the debate and bringing new investors to the table.

Watch this space …

*Big Society Capital*

As a wholesaler of investment funds, Big Society Capital (BSC) does not invest directly, but places capital with social investment financial intermediaries (SIFIs) to build the social investment market on their behalf.

> There are around 4,000 separate social investments across the UK with an aggregate value of £2.3bn.
>
> (Big Society Capital, 2018)

BSC has placed funds with SIFIs covering a wide range of themes, from ex-offenders, child adoption and rough-sleepers to health and ageing. Figure 8.3 gives an indication of some funds and their impact

| Investor | Motivation |
|---|---|
| **Impact Ventures** UK | Impact Ventures UK (LGT)<br>Growth capital for social enterprises that will improve the lives of disadvantaged people in the UK. |
| **adviza** brighter futures | Energise SIB<br>Social impact bond programme run by Adviza, to build resilience and aspiration, delivering better education and achievement for young people. |
| **SiS** social investment scotland | Social Growth Fund<br>Finance for charities and social enterprises, principally in Scotland, looking for growth funds. |
| **Cheyne** Capital | Cheyne Social Property Impact Fund<br>Provides properties to increase the capacity of social sector organisations for people with housing and support needs. |
| **leapfrog** | Pure Leapfrog Bridge Loan<br>Finance for communities wanting to participate in large, professionally managed solar farm developments, to then use the profits to fund local projects. |
| **ANANDA** SOCIAL VENTURE FUND | Ananda Social Venture<br>Investing in growth stage social ventures working in educational technology, sustainable consumption, impactful health and employment. |

*Figure 8.3* Big Society Capital Funds and their social impact.

Source: Big Society Capital (2019), by permission.

## Summarising social investment supply and demand

Much of the social investment landscape to date has been dominated by the supply of money from investors, rather than the demand that charities may have for capital. This is changing.

In this chapter, we have considered the supply and demand for social investment and how this is coming together now with a much more aligned motivation between investor and investee.

There's a world of interested social investors out there. They are looking to receive a financial return on their investment, while having the aspiration to build something positive.

Social investment has come to a tipping point. It is gaining a momentum and traction to move into the mainstream and away from being seen only as a "niche" product.

The market for social investment is also growing (Big Society Capital, 2018). The average size of *individual* investments and loans is coming down; which is better suiting the demand for smaller loans within the sector.

As a key factor identified in existing research, the cost of borrowing will also impact the success of the social investment market and its growth.

So, what about business models? We explore that subject next.

## References

Allia (2019), *Retail charity bonds*, accessed 6 May 2019, www.retailcharitybonds.co.uk/bonds/golden-lane-housing/.

AVPN (2016), *What drives your social investing strategy?*, accessed 20 October 2018, www.avpn.asia/blog/what-drives-your-social-investing-strategy-and-how-can-you-make-it-sustainable/.

Big Society Capital (2015), *What motivates corporates to do social impact investing?*, accessed 20 October 2018, www.bigsocietycapital.com/latest/type/blog/what-motivates-corporates-do-social-impact-investing.

Big Society Capital (2018), *Size of the social investment market*, accessed 20 October 2018, www.bigsocietycapital.com/home/about-us/size-social-investment-market.

Big Society Capital (2019), https://bigsocietycapital.com/portfolio/.

Brandstetter, L. and Lehner, O. (2014), *Impact investment portfolios: including social risks and returns*, accessed 20 October 2018, www.ssrn.com/abstract=2519671, ACRN Oxford Publishing House.

Bridges Fund Management (2015), *The Bridges spectrum of capital: how we define the sustainable and impact investment market*, accessed 20 October 2018, www.bridgesfundmanagement.com/wp-content/uploads/2017/08/Bridges-Spectrum-of-Capital-screen.pdf.

Brown, A. and Swersky, A. (2012), *The first billion: a forecast of social investment demand*, Boston Consulting Group.

CAF (2014), *In demand: the changing need for repayable finance in the charity sector*, accessed 20 October 2018, www.cafonline.org/about-us/publications/2014-publications/in-demand.

Caroe (2016), *What do we mean by social investment?*, accessed 6 May 2019, www.allia.org.uk/wp-content/uploads/2016/05/What-do-we-mean-by-Social-Investment.pdf.

Chapman, T. (2015), *An assessment of the willingness of organisations to borrow money in the Third Sector: Findings from studies in Yorkshire, North East England and Cumbria*, Durham University.

Clifford, J. (2016), *Advanced social impact measurement and payment by results: social investment and SIBs*, Lecture for Cass Charities and NGOs MSc Programme, July 2018.

Financial Times and GIST (2017), *Investing for global impact 2017*, accessed 20 October 2018, www.gistltd.com/investing-for-global-impact-report.

Financial Times and Method Impact (2015), *Investing for global impact 2015*, accessed 20 October 2018, www.gistltd.com/investing-for-global-impact-report.

FSG (2018), *Moving beyond trade-offs in impact investing*, accessed 6 August 2019, www.fsg.org/blog/moving-beyond-trade-offs-impact-investing.

G8 Social Impact Investment Taskforce (2014), *Impact investment: the hidden heart of markets*, accessed 20 October 2018, www.gsgii.org/reports/impact-investment-the-invisible-heart-of-markets/.

Goggin, N. and Baker, L. (2013), *Charities and social investment: a research report for the Charity Commission*, IVAR, accessed 16 April 2018, www.gov.uk/government/uploads/system/uploads/attachment_data/file/284706/social_investment.pdf.

Good Finance (2018), *Big Society Capital*, accessed 20 October 2018, www.goodfinance.org.uk.

Gov.UK (2016), *Social investment: a force for social change, 2016 strategy*, accessed 20 October 2018, www.gov.uk/government/publications/social-investment-a-force-for-social-change-uk-strategy-2016.

Hailey, J. and Salway, M. (2017), *New routes to CSO sustainability: the strategic shift to social enterprise and social investment*, Routledge.

London Stock Exchange (2018), *Your guide to ESG reporting*, accessed 6 May 2019, www.lseg.com/sites/default/files/content/images/Green_Finance/ESG/2018/February/LSEG_ESG_report_January_2018.pdf.

NCVO (2017), *UK civil society almanac 2017*, accessed 20 October 2018, www.data.ncvo.org.uk/almanac17/.

Nolan, B. (2013), *What use is social investment?*, Journal of European Social Policy 23(5), 459–468.

Oliver Wyman (2016), *Corporate social investment: gaining traction*, accessed 21 July 2019, www.oliverwyman.com/content/dam/oliver-wyman/global/en/2016/feb/OW_Corporate_Social_Investment_Final.pdf.

Rickey, B., Joy, I. and Hedley, S. (2011), *Best to borrow? A charity guide to social investment*, NPC, accessed 20 October 2018, www.thinknpc.org/resource-hub/best-to-borrow/.

Salamon, Lester M. (2014), *Leverage for good: an introduction to the new frontiers of philanthropy and social investment*, Oxford University Press.

Salway, M. (2017), *Social investment as a new charity finance tool: using head and heart*, Cass Business School, Centre for Charity Effectiveness.

Schwartz, R. (2014), *Investors' motivations are not what you might expect*, accessed 20 October 2018, www.thirdsector.co.uk/investors-motivations-not-expect/finance/article/1281107.

Social Economy Data Lab (2016–17), *What is social investment?*, accessed 20 October 2018, www.socialeconomydatalab.org/.

Social Enterprise UK (2018), accessed 20 October 2018, www.socialenterprise.org.uk/.

Social Enterprise UK (2011), *Fight Back Britain report*, accessed 20 October 2018, www.socialenterprise.org.uk/fightback-britain-2011.

UNPRI (2019), *Principles of responsible investment*, accessed 26 May 2019, www.unpri.org/.

# 8a Case study

## Bridges Evergreen Holdings

*Scott Greenhalgh*

## A new kind of investment vehicle

Bridges Fund Management's Evergreen is a new form of impact investment vehicle, offering a new source of long-term capital. Executive chairman **Scott Greenhalgh** explains how it works.

## Background

> **Bridges Fund Management**
>
> - Bridges Fund Management (formerly Bridges Ventures) is a specialist sustainable and impact investor.
> - Founded in 2002, it has raised over £1 billion across 14 funds.
> - Funds support investible solutions to pressing social and environmental challenges within four impact themes: health and wellbeing, education and skills, underserved areas and sustainable living.

## Launching a dedicated fund in the social sector

In 2012, Bridges launched its first fund dedicated to investing in high-impact social sector organisations. The Bridges Social Entrepreneurs Fund (SEF) provided subordinated debt or quasi-equity to scalable enterprises with sustainable models and ambitions for growth – including HCT, the social enterprise bus operator, and CASA, the employee-owned social care provider.

In 2016, Bridges Evergreen Holdings (Evergreen) was launched as a successor to SEF. Evergreen is a new kind of social investment vehicle, designed to provide long-term patient capital as well as hands-on support to ambitious mission-driven organisations. Structured as a holding company rather than as a typical private equity fund (the latter typically have a ten-year fixed "life", meaning that most investments will be exited within five to seven years), it aims to generate returns to investors through ongoing yield, rather than purely through capital gains on exit.

> Evergreen is a new kind of social investment vehicle, designed to provide long-term patient capital as well as hands-on support to ambitious mission-driven organisations ... it aims to generate returns to investors through ongoing yield rather than purely through capital gains on exit.

## Responding to a clear market need

The Evergreen model came about as a direct result of the challenges Bridges faced when investing the Social Entrepreneurs Fund (SEF).

On the one hand, SEF was undoubtedly a success. Its portfolio of investments helped to:

- deliver 2.2m hours of quality, at-home care
- support 3,400 qualifications gained by young people at risk of being NEET
- support 4,500 direct jobs
- move 4,700 previously unemployed people back into work
- provide over 1.1m passenger trips to disadvantaged individuals.

(Bridges Fund Management, 2015)

By pioneering an investment model that other managers have since emulated, Evergreen also played an important role in catalysing the social investment market.

However, in the course of investing the fund – and talking to other impact-focused organisations with growth aspirations – it became clear that the SEF model placed **certain constraints** on the kind of organisations Bridges was able to back; and thus the kind of impact it was able to achieve:

- there was sometimes a tension between the funding needs of investee companies and the investment timeframe of the fund
- creating positive, sustainable social change – and building the organisational infrastructure necessary to scale – takes time
- a five to seven year exit timetable (which is standard for a ten-year closed-end fund) can be sub-optimal for a mission-led organisation and lead to lower investment and social returns
- some mission-led organisations would prefer a longer-term partnership, rather than a time-limited one

## Finding the right partner

In addition, the range of organisations committed to achieving social change has increased markedly during the last few years.

When SEF was launched, most high-impact organisations operated in the social sector. Today, there's a growing number of mission-led private businesses outside the social sector seeking to balance profits with purpose.

Indeed, there's a growing recognition that purpose-driven business is more attractive to customers, suppliers and potential employees. The rise of the B-Corp movement, providing accreditation for businesses of this type (B-Corp, 2018), highlights this trend.

As these organisations look to scale and grow, it's difficult for them to find an investment partner who, in addition to supplying capital, also shares their values and supports their long-term mission.

## A solution: Bridges Evergreen Holdings

Bridges Evergreen Holdings was incorporated in 2016 as a mission-locked investment company (i.e. its mission to combine impact and financial returns was written into its articles of association, along with a commitment to measure its impact). Initial equity commitments were £22.5 million, with BSC acting as the cornerstone investor, and the balance coming from a range of pension funds, foundations and trusts.

In June 2018, Evergreen successfully increased its committed capital to just over £50 million.

Since Evergreen is structured as a holding company, it doesn't have the same time constraints as a standard private equity fund, with a typical ten-year fixed life. In fact, Evergreen can theoretically support its investees over an indefinite period – enabling Bridges to offer its investees a long-term partnership with no exit requirement. The hope is that this combination of patient capital and operational support will be attractive to mission-driven enterprises looking to scale their operations and their impact in a sensible, sustainable way (although it may be less appropriate for management teams actually wanting to exit within five to seven years; in this case a normal private equity fund may be a better fit).

---

**Key benefits**

- As Evergreen is structured as a holding company, it doesn't have the same time constraints as a closed-end fund
- It can theoretically support its investees over an indefinite period – offering them a long-term partnership with no exit requirement
- This combination of patient capital and operational support could be attractive to mission-driven enterprises looking to scale their operations and impact in a sensible, sustainable way
- With a slightly broader and more flexible investment remit than the Social Entrepreneurs Fund (SEF), it is able to invest in mission-led businesses as well as social sector organisations, via equity, quasi-equity or debt (taking either majority or minority positions).

---

## What type of investees will it attract?

Bridges expects investees to fall into one of three categories:

- **'Take-social' acquisitions of private businesses**, helping them to measure and articulate their impact, increase alignment with key stakeholders, better engage with key customers, and (where necessary) change their culture or structure
- **Supporting employee-owned businesses, mutuals and spin-outs**, to build a sustainable business model, better engage and support employees and win new contracts
- **Helping social sector organisations scale** by supporting them to attract talent, build capacity and secure long-term finance.

---

**New Reflexions**

New Reflexions is an excellent example of the kind of organisation Evergreen is looking to back. Its management team is highly mission-driven and wants to scale the business over the long term.

Evergreen's first investment, New Reflexions provides children's care services. It operates 17 children's care homes, 4 "rapid response" services and 1 special school across England, Wales and Scotland (New Reflexions, 2018).

Evergreen invested £6.1 million to acquire a 56 per cent stake, backing the existing management team to grow the business.

## Challenges and opportunities

- Since this kind of model is relatively unusual in the UK, there's still some work to be done to explain the concept to financial intermediaries and interested management teams.
- Until Evergreen has been able to build up a more substantial portfolio of assets, the "running yield" return model will remain largely unproven – although Evergreen has recently paid its first dividend to investors.
- Enabling ambitious, mission-driven organisations to access long-term financial, strategic and operational support from a values-aligned, patient capital vehicle can help them scale their impact.
- Validating this new investment model within the sector could act as a catalyst, drawing in additional capital that can support these organisations.

There's a growing sense that a commitment to mission can serve as a competitive commercial advantage, while also driving better outcomes for vulnerable people. That is particularly true for organisations providing services that are predominantly public-funded, since social value is becoming an increasingly influential aspect of all local and central government commissioning.

## References

B-Corp (2018), *Certified (B) Corp*, accessed 20 October 2018, www.bcorporation.uk.

Bridges Fund Management (2015), *Annual impact report 2015: the value of impact*, accessed 20 October 2018, www.bridgesfundmanagement.com/wp-content/uploads/2017/08/Bridges-2015-Impact-Report-UK-print.pdf.

New Reflexions (2018), *New Reflexions: where every child matters*, accessed 20 October 2018, www.newreflexions.co.uk.

# 9 Are we ready for social investment?

## Re-imagining charity business and operating models and governance principles

*Mark Salway*

## Introduction

There are 168,000 charities in the UK (Gov.UK, 2018b), each with its own object-ives and reasons for existence. From animal welfare organisations to international development, fundraising charities to those contracting. This is a vast and varied landscape.

In addition, the umbrella body Social Enterprise UK (2018, p. 3), identifies that "most recent Government estimates have suggested there are 99,000 social enterprises that collectively employ just over 1 million people"; many of these are charities.

Add to this a large number of informal charities and volunteer groups not registered with the Charity Commission, and, in reality, there probably exist around 471,000 social purpose organisations in the UK (Civil Society, 2017).

While it may seem likely that many of these could use social investment, the majority are small, volunteer-led organisations with limited turnover and often no staff. Realistically, only the largest of these will be able to take on social investment and have the scope and infrastructure necessary for it. Big Society Capital (2016) sug-gests, "it is not a stretch to imagine that the universe of investible organisations may be in the low tens of thousands – perhaps between 15,000 and 26,000 organisations currently".

The previous chapter examined what social investors and investees want from social investment. But which charities and social purpose organisations are most likely to use social investment and how? And which of those are most likely to succeed?

To answer these questions, we now turn to exploring the business models of char-ities and social purpose organisations.

Let's use the following Oxford Dictionaries definition of a business model:

> A plan for the successful operation of a business, identifying sources of revenue, the intended customer base, products, and details of financing.
>
> (Oxford Dictionaries, 2018)

We first consider charity business models conceptually. In the second half of the chapter we then consider how an organisation can get ready for, and plan for, social investment and we provide practical steps on how to do this.

## Section one – looking at charity business models

*How can we define and categorise charity business models? Which fit social investment best?*

Taking the definition of a business model above and mapping this on to charities, we can see that the business models of charities are driven in three main ways:

- **By customer, beneficiary and "theme"** – focusing on different causes and why charities exist, e.g. to stop homelessness or to provide work to the unemployed. *This is a social lens on a charity's business model.*
- **By "endgame"** – focusing on what a charity wants to achieve strategically and its operational model, e.g. by asking government to adopt its services, or through distributing specific information in an open source way to the general public. *This is a strategic lens on a charity's business model.*
- **By considering income generation** – focusing on how a charity makes its money and how it spends it on its good causes. *This is a financial lens on a charity's business model.*

Each charity is also underpinned by its **infrastructure**. It uses this to support its work.

We next consider social investment in the context of each of these four areas.

*Area 1: Considering customer, beneficiary and "theme"*

We look first at whether social investment works as a tool across all thematic areas or if certain areas are better candidates for social investment than others.

In the UK, the definition of a charity is based on the public benefit in a number of specific areas (Gov.UK, 2018a):

> relieving poverty, education, religion, health, saving lives, citizenship or community development, the arts, amateur sport, human rights, religious or racial harmony, the protection of the environment, animal welfare and the efficiency of the armed forces, police, fire or ambulance services.

Good Finance (2018, 2019) – www.goodfinance.org.uk – has been set up by Big Society Capital to promote social investment and offers many case studies. It has a wide range of examples of social investment across different thematic areas and identifies a wide range of social investment instruments being used.

Similarly, the case studies in this book highlight the broad range of charities and social enterprises using social investment, including Scope (mental health, Chapter 7a); WSUP (water and sanitation in the developing world, Chapter 16a); and St Mungo's (rough sleeping, Chapter 14a).

> Almost every thematic area listed above has taken on and used social investment. The diversity of organisations using social investment is huge.

To back this up, Big Society Capital began releasing its data on types of social investment and their scope and scale (Big Society Capital, 2018). An indicative list of the top areas where social investment has been made by Big Society Capital is as follows:

- *Housing and accommodation*: affordable housing, transitional accommodation, social lettings, supported living
- *Energy*: community energy, renewable energy
- *Employment and apprenticeships*
- *Community sport and affordable leisure*

**In conclusion:** Social investment can be used broadly across the entire universe of charities and social purpose organisations. Thematic focus areas, customer types and beneficiaries do not define it.

### Area 2: Analysis by "endgame"

Work by Gugelev and Stern (2015), *What's Your Endgame?*, postulated that business models for non-profit organisations could be categorised by the ultimate aim of the organisation.

They defined six "endgame" states:

- **Open source** – where a charity creates knowledge or an idea that others find easy to use in their own organisations; relying on developing a knowledge hub to disseminate the information. Money is spent on conducting research and the development and sharing of knowledge. An example would be a gender or diversity charity hoping to influence others with the broad application of the work and learning.
- **Replication** – where a charity develops a product, training services or a centre of excellence, allowing other organisations to use it. Money is spent on developing a replicable operating model, demonstrating impact and demonstrating its efficacy.
- **Government adoption** – a model with focus on integration into government sector programmes. Money is spent on delivering services for government and undertaking research and advocacy efforts around this.
- **Commercial adoption** – a model focused on integration into the commercial sector. It must have revenue-generating potential that solves a market failure or reduces market risk. Money is spent on delivering services for government and undertaking research and advocacy efforts around this.
- **Mission achievement** – money is spent on targeted interventions to solve a discrete problem, e.g. the eradication of smallpox or malaria.
- **Sustained service** – continued provision of a core service at an ever-increasing level of efficiency. Money is spent on delivering and growing this service, including developing a solid infrastructure to do so.

Gugelev and Stern (2015) subsequently look at the start-up capital cycle and ongoing budget implications of various endgames (Figure 9.1). They show that different types of financing and funding are needed at each level.

Invariably grants will be needed to start an organisation. Thereafter, each of these models could use social investment to grow its work and achieve its strategic ambition.

Big Society Capital (2014, pp. 10–11), in its *Vision, Mission and Activities* document, identifies four main areas where social investment will be most successful. We adapt this for our discussion and identify uses of social investment within this.

BSC sees these four areas (set out in Table 9.1) as most likely to use social investment: those that trade, those that deliver public services through contracts, those that

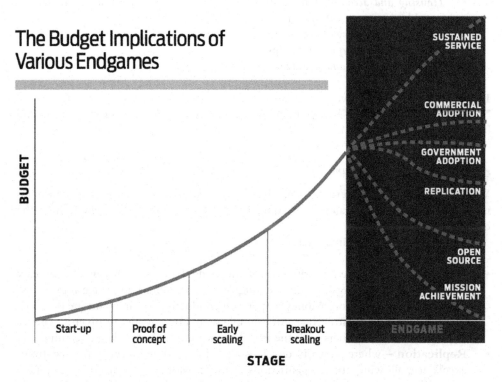

*Figure 9.1* Different budget implications of various endgames.
Source: Gugelev and Stern (2015).

provide services to vulnerable and excluded groups, and those that provide financial services.

**In conclusion:** Within this landscape the scope for social investment remains huge. Social investment does not appear to be defined by the organisation's business model or strategic endgame.

### Area 3: Analysis by income generation

In Chapter 5 of this book we saw that charity business models typically cluster around three distinct and simple business models:

- First, charities receive income from fundraising, from a linked organisation or from an endowment. They then distribute what they receive on the causes they exist for.
- Second, they may trade in goods or services, benefiting recipients from sale proceeds or by using recipients in the work that they do.
- Third are those charities who offer specific services in return for a grant or contract.

Murphy and Saxton (2017) show that this analysis of income leads to six basic "archetypes" of charities when viewed through an income-based lens. Adapting their analysis

*Table 9.1* Four main areas where social investment could be most successful

| Type of charity or social purpose organisation | Revenue-generating activity and potential to use social investment |
| --- | --- |
| **Trading for social purposes** – typically take a social enterprise approach, making money through trading. (p. 10) | **Revenue-generating activity?** Earned income from sales to customers. **Potential use of social investment?** • Product/service development • Development capital to fund people, stock and marketing costs, ahead of break-even • Working capital. |
| **Delivering public services** – social sector organisations enter into contracts and grant agreements with the public sector for specific outputs or outcomes. (p. 10) | **Revenue-generating activity?** Earned income from contract payments. **Potential use of social investment?** • Product/service development • Working capital • Capital to manage delivery risk, e.g. not delivering social outcomes as expected • Development of fixed assets. |
| **Providing support and services to vulnerable and excluded groups** – while public spending and trading may fund some of this activity, philanthropic funding is still vital to the majority of social sector organisations in this category. (p. 11) | **Revenue-generating activity?** Grants, donations and fundraising. **Potential use of social investment?** • Product/service development • Working capital to smooth fluctuations in income, allow retention of staff and continued provision of services • Development of fixed assets. |
| **Providing financial services** – some social purpose organisations exist to provide affordable financial services to individuals, groups and organisations excluded from mainstream finance. (p. 11) | **Revenue-generating activity?** Earned income from interest payments and fees. **Revenue-generating activity?** • Organisational capacity-building • On-lending • Core capital (to protect against default risk) • Equity to strengthen and grow balance sheet. |

Source: Mark Salway, adapted from Big Society Capital (2014, pp. 10–11). Page references come from the same report.

and aligning social investment alongside these different areas could give us an idea how social investment might be used. This is set out in Table 9.2.

In reality, this analysis is oversimplified. Many organisations and charities operate to a mixed model – for example, they often deliver services and in addition fundraise for money to undertake advocacy on behalf of the cause they exist for.

**In conclusion:** There are no types of charity defined by income generation that cannot use social investment. While trading and service delivery charities are most likely to use social investment, this is a broad environment.

*Table 9.2* Income categorisation of charities and how social investment could be used in each

| Type of charity | Defining characteristics | How social investment could be relevant |
| --- | --- | --- |
| **Linked trusts** | Tend to either be the charitable trusts of large organisations, such as the Shell Foundation; or vehicles for donating large sums of private money, such as the Sigrid Rausing Trust. (p. 7) | These organisations could provide social investment funds. Examples are the Shell Foundation, which lends to businesses established to help the poor. Equally, they could help create new social businesses through partnering with charities or social enterprises. |
| **Contracts and service providers** | Provide government contracts or paid-for services. Examples are Leonard Cheshire Disability and Mencap. (p. 9) | Social investment could help develop new services (by innovation), or could provide the infrastructure money to take on contracts by improving impact measurement and finance capacity, for example. |
| **Fundraisers** | Generate their funding mainly from fundraising and events. They tend to have a reasonably high profile with the general public and raise money through a wide range of different fundraising methods. Examples are CLIC Sargent and Battersea Dogs and Cats Homes. (p. 9) | Social investment could help leverage fundraising, or help create new fundraising ideas. For example, social investment could help develop digital platforms for improved fundraising. |
| **Traders** | Tend to be heavily reliant on charity shops or other forms of trading for their income. Examples are Sue Ryder and British Heart Foundation. (p. 11) | Social investment could be used to invest in assets and infrastructure, or provide working capital to develop work in progress for onward sale. Social investment here acts like more mainstream investment to help develop a trading business. |
| **Legacy fundraisers** | This group is made up of fundraising charities that rely heavily on legacy income, such as Cats Protection. (p. 12) | Limited perceived scope for social investment use, but could help leverage fundraising, or help create new fundraising ideas. |
| **Invested trustees** | These are generally charities with an independent endowment, or fund of their own, e.g. Joseph Rowntree or the Wellcome Trust. (p. 12) | These organisations could provide social investment funds. Examples include the Wellcome Trust. Equally, they could help create new social businesses through partnering with charities or social enterprises. |

Source: Mark Salway, adapted from Murphy and Saxton (2017). Page references come from the same report.

### *Area 4: Infrastructure – providing an operating platform*

The final part of developing an appropriate business model is to establish the right infrastructure, be that finance, IT, HR or the establishment of impact measurement tools. Equally, it could be the right operational infrastructure to deliver services and activities.

The Cass CCE Cost Recovery Toolkit (Cass CCE, 2018) explains what overheads are and what how to define "core" capacity. It builds on the CFG (2007) report, *Know Your Cost Base, Know Your Charity*.

Social investment could be used "for contract readiness … [and to allow] charities to build their infrastructure" (Salway, 2017, p. 29). This will rely heavily on investment which can deliver demonstrable savings. For example, it can lead to setting up a better IT infrastructure, or investing in automation in finance (Salway and Boughtflower, 2018).

However, both Charity Futures (2018) and Charity Finance (2018) consider the mind-set of charities to be a real block on using social investment to invest in infrastructure. Most charities believe they should spend on the end cause not on overheads. This is a cultural consideration which will need to be addressed before social investment can become more helpful in developing more sustainable organisations.

**In conclusion:** There appears a broad application for social investment in developing infrastructure.

## Summary

When looking at social investment and its application, it does not appear to be defined by customer, beneficiary and "theme", by strategic endgame or business model, by income generation or by its use in infrastructure.

It appears to be a tool which has many applications and a potentially large impact for an organisation in a wide variety of ways.

While not a silver bullet, used thoughtfully it can be a powerful tool to help develop sustainability and innovation.

## Section two – getting ready and planning for inward investment

The main chapters on *doing* social investment are later in this book, Chapters 20–27.

This section focuses on steps and suggestions for how to develop a simple revenue-generating idea and how social investment can be used to underpin this. It is taken from the Cass CCE Social Investment Toolkit (Cass CCE, 2016) – a basic toolkit to help readers plan for – and use – social investment.

While social investment could be used for a wide variety of purposes, any organisation using it must be confident it can pay back the capital and any interest payment. Or alternatively the organisation must be happy to share equity with an investor.

### *Engaging with and preparing for social investment*

To attract social investment, organisations need to look for opportunities that will deliver both a social and a financial return. These opportunities will need to have a measurable impact, and organisations will need to be confident they can produce a reliable income stream. Alternatively, in the case of infrastructure development, the social impact investment must be able to provide demonstrable savings.

Organisations can develop propositions from either a mission-focused or a commercial perspective, according to Cass CCE Social Investment Toolkit (Cass CCE, 2016, p. 9):

> **Developing a mission-focused proposition:** A good way to develop a social investment proposition is by looking at an organisation's vision and mission and at the activities required to achieve these. A theory of change model could help establish a proposition by linking vision and mission to outcomes and activities. … Ideal candidates for social investment are activities identified through a theory of change process that create both revenue and a social return.
>
> **The commercial perspective:** Organisations can take a commercial approach to developing a social investment proposition by looking at those areas of work that can be commercialised in some way. You could, for example, start charging for services that were previously given for free. Remember that, as charging for certain things could exclude those who can't pay from accessing vital services, it's important to take real care to balance the commercial income flow and the needs of beneficiaries. You could "segment" products or services, so that those who could pay a little more underpin the social provision for those who can't afford it. Nurseries are a good example of this segmentation system in action.

Activities that are suitable for social investment include (p. 10):

- Those already making money through, for example, a social enterprise, where investment could help grow them faster
- Those currently paid for through grants and donations, but which could be paid for by charging people for goods and services in future
- New activities that are aligned to the organisation's mission and which can be set up to generate income for the charity.

Social investment is not just about social enterprise. It could be used to build capacity to take on new contracts or to purchase a building. It could pay to build a shared administration facility among small charities to help grow capacity while keeping the costs down. It could also underpin an expansion in fundraising. While a social investment model does not work for every situation, the range of possibilities is wide, as we saw earlier in this chapter.

---

### Example: A charity helping female ex-offenders

Previously, the charity paid for female ex-offenders to be housed and gave them training to learn a skill to be able to find a job. The charity used grants and donations to pay for this service.

By changing their model, the charity found local businesses that were willing to take on ex-offenders as staff. The businesses got a dedicated member of staff and the wage allowed the ex-offender to pay for their own housing and living costs, giving them dignity.

Social investment was used to prime the model. It paid for the recruitment scheme to be set up and for the identification of businesses that would take the ex-offenders.

---

### The social entrepreneur mind-set

Many charities and social purpose organisations may have become locked into a certain way of working or thinking. Staff with the entrepreneurial flair to deliver the new social investment idea will be important for success. Without this change in approach, the idea may fail.

Do not under-estimate how culturally different this may feel. The new venture will need to focus on making money, which can be hard if your mind-set is "non-profit". Accounting may also look different, moving from income and expenditure to more of a profit-and-loss format.

While subtle, these changes sit at the heart of why social investment sometimes fails. Thinking through the cultural and process changes in advance will improve the chances of success.

### Taking a proposition to market

Organisations will need a plan that demonstrates how to take its proposition to market, typically involving selling to customers or users. There are three aspects to this plan (see Figure 9.2):

- **Customers: who will use the product or service?**
  The more you can learn about each market you intend to serve and how the different customers in those markets will buy and benefit from what you are offering, the better able you will be to develop a suitable value proposition.
- **Value proposition: why would they choose you?**
  Before a customer will buy or use your offering, they need to know it exists, have a sense of what they will gain from it and have a reason to choose it over alternatives.

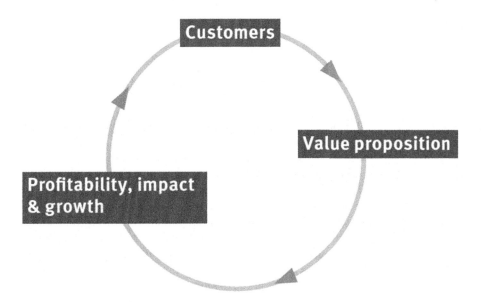

*Figure 9.2* Taking a proposition to market.
Source: Cass CCE (2016).

- **Profitability, impact and growth: making money and impact**
  Initial forecasts should provide answers to these questions, but both income and impact are inevitably based on many assumptions. There is a need to research these and test with potential customers to ensure your ideas are viable and appropriately targeted.

The level of development of an idea will dictate how much evidence is needed to assure social investors that it is a sound proposition. It is generally easier to obtain funding when an initiative has been proven and requires funding to scale up, compared with seed funding for new start-ups.

### The business plan

Consolidate all of the information about your idea into a business plan, which then needs to be agreed by both management and trustees.

The business plan will look at customer needs, competitors, opportunities and risks, as well as the financial and non-financial impacts of each. The business plan is different from the investment pack, which you will use to negotiate with funders. The tools for "doing" this are considered in Chapters 20–27 of this book.

Be aware that a business plan using social investment may change the risk profile of your organisation or bring new risks. Always consider and manage risk appropriately.

### Governance – what needs to be considered?

A fuller discourse on governance is provided in the *doing* section later in this book – Chapter 27.

Investors will want to look at your organisation's governance. They will specifically consider:

- Structure
- Key personnel
- Internal processes
- How the board considers the social impact of their work and quality mechanisms.

Investors will often request to see terms of reference, agendas, lists of actions and minutes and also to meet the chair and vice-chair.

Investors may request a seat on the board to oversee their investment. This can either be seen as bringing new skills and resource to the board, or as intrusive. In either case, it requires careful thought and discussion with potential investors.

The essence of good governance is setting time aside regularly to share all the relevant information in an organised way, enabling clear actions and decisions to be made and recorded, to direct your organisation. The cadence of good governance is about setting up and embedding that rhythm, those processes and functional behaviours, as the norm within an organisation. Any investor will expect this.

Governance of social investment activities can require more frequent attention to risks and to monitoring social and financial impact. If not already present, you may need to set up an "investment" board or sub-committee to oversee and report back to the main board.

## Legal and tax issues

Certain tax reliefs and benefits are available to investors who want to invest, specifically Social Investment Tax Relief (SITR) (Gov.UK, 2016).

When considering social investment, you should always take appropriate legal and tax advice. Good advisors and social investment finance intermediaries (SIFIs) should be able to help.

## Doing it differently

There has been considerable interest in how social investment could help stimulate intrapreneurship and start internal new social businesses within existing organisations (Salway, 2017, p. 34), "Existing staff can often act as 'intrapreneurs' – effective and dynamic internal social entrepreneurs empowered to drive impact forward."

Social investment could also help prime new social businesses and partnerships created by bringing commercial organisations, governments, charities and social purpose organisations together in new, innovative vehicles, solving complex problems. Salamon (2014, Chapter 4, p. 53) highlights that, without this change to new ways of working, we simply won't solve many of the world's most intractable problems:

> These inter-related environmental, economic, social, and political needs would be difficult to meet under any circumstances. But they are being confronted now by a world that has been experiencing enormous economic shocks, unsustainable governmental spending and charitable resources that, while growing, do not come close to being able to deliver the resources needed to address the problems that exist.

The WSUP case study on water and sanitation in the developing world (Chapter 16a) is an example of Unilever in partnership with NGOs, commercial organisations and academic institutions. It shows how they are working together to solve the future need around global water and sanitation for the urban poor.

## All RISE!

We saw in Chapter 8 that "Sustainability came out very strongly as the main reason that charities are interested in social investment as a new tool to help their funding" (Salway, 2017, p. 29).

However, charities and social purpose organisations of all sizes could choose to use social investment in other ways (Salway and Ramsey, 2018) – for example using the RISE model:

- **Re-imagine:** to create new solutions or new products and services – using technology, or getting small and large charities to work together, for example.
- **Impact:** to measure the social outputs and outcomes created and underpin social investment.
- **Sustainability:** to develop robust business models, with well-funded infrastructure at their heart.
- **Efficiency:** to focus on doing things more efficiently and effectively, so organisations are using their scarce resources in the best way.

The RISE framework (Re-imagine, Impact, Sustainability and Efficiency) can help you consider how social investment can change your organisation. This is shown in Figure 9.3.

---

**Thinking beyond sustainability, Salway and Ramsey (2018)**

One good application of the RISE framework is a woman's centre and refuge against sexual violence, which spent three years developing a social impact bond.

As the organisation went on the journey, its leaders realised that sustainability was its core problem. They mapped out their different services and the impact of each and stopped a service which neither made money nor created the type of impact they wanted. Today, they have one service which makes money, but they want it to create more impact and are working out how to do this.

Although the organisation now realises that a social impact bond isn't right for it, the process has led to developing an online tool which will help to focus on the needs of the beneficiary. They may now think about social investment to build this, or use grants and donations. But overall, they have focused what they are doing much more tightly.

---

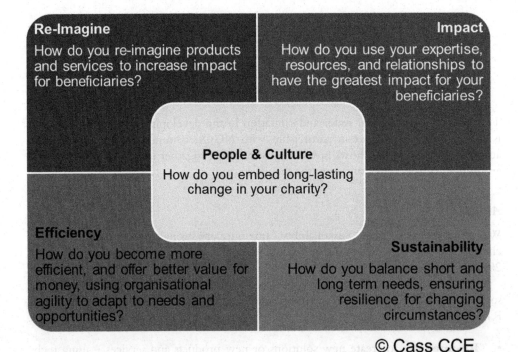

*Figure 9.3* The RISE framework.

Source: Cass CCE; Salway and Ramsey (2018).

## Conclusion

Thinking about business models is central to the success of using social investment.

To do this, charities and social purpose organisations must understand how to create social impact and how their finances support this through their business models.

Besides being used to develop a sound infrastructure or purchase a building, social investment could also be used for re-imaging your organisation, innovation, to develop impact, for sustainability or to develop greater efficiency (the RISE model). It can also release intrapreneurs within your own organisation to develop new models.

While the range of uses is huge, it all revolves around a revenue-generating model.

## References

Big Society Capital (2014), *Big Society Capital: vision, mission and activities*, accessed 11 May 2019, www.bigsocietycapital.com/sites/default/files/pdf/BSC Vision, mission and activities.pdf.

Big Society Capital (2016), *UK social investment: opportunities, challenges and the "critical" questions*, accessed 20 October 2018, www.bigsocietycapital.com/sites/default/files/UK Social Investment – Opportunities, Challenges, and Critical Questions.pdf.

Big Society Capital (2018), *Data Dives into social investment* and *Data Dives No. 3: but what's the business model?*, data blogs, accessed 20 October 2018, www.bigsocietycapital.com/latest/type/blog/data-dives-social-investment and www.bigsocietycapital.com/latest/type/blog/data-dives-no3-%E2%80%9C-what%E2%80%99s-business-model%E2%80%9D.

Cass CCE (2016), *Social investment tools for success: doing the right things and doing them right*, accessed 20 October 2018, www.cass.city.ac.uk/faculties-and-research/centres/cce/resources/tools-for-success.

Cass CCE (2018), *Cost recovery tools for success: doing the right things and doing them right*, accessed 20.10.2018, www.cass.city.ac.uk/faculties-and-research/centres/cce/resources/tools-for-success.

CFG (2007), *Know your cost base, know your charity*, accessed 20 June 2018, www.cfg.org.uk.

Charity Finance (2018), *Because you are worth it: the case for investment*, Charity Finance Magazine, September 2018, Civil Society Media.

Charity Futures (2018), *To the core*, accessed 20 October 2018, www.charityfutures.org/our-impact/.

Civil Society (2017), *There are 471,000 social enterprises in the UK, government report finds*, accessed 20 October 2018, www.civilsociety.co.uk/news/there-are-471-000-social-enterprises-in-the-uk-government-report-finds.html.

Good Finance (2018), *Case studies*, accessed 20 October 2018, www.goodfinance.org.uk/case-studies.

Good Finance (2019), main webpage, accessed 20 October 2018, www.goodfinance.org.uk/.

Gov.UK (2016), *Social Investment Tax Relief*, accessed 21 July 2019, www.gov.uk/government/publications/social-investment-tax-relief-factsheet/social-investment-tax-relief.

Gov.UK (2018a), *Charitable purposes*, accessed 20 October 2018, www.gov.uk/setting-up-charity/charitable-purposes.

Gov.UK (2018b), *Recent charity register statistics: Charity Commission*, accessed 20 October 2018, www.gov.uk/government/publications/charity-register-statistics/recent-charity-register-statistics-charity-commission.

Gugelev and Stern (2015), What's your endgame?, *Stanford Social Innovation Review*, Winter 2015.

Murphy, C. and Saxton, J. (2017), *Just my type: an archetype analysis of charity finances*, accessed online at https://nfpsynergy.net/free-report/just-my-type-archetype-analysis-charity-finances, 20 October 2018.

Oxford Dictionaries (2018), *Business model*, accessed 20 October 2018, https://en.oxforddictionaries.com/definition/business_model.

Salamon, L. (2014), *New frontiers of philanthropy: a guide to the new tools and actors reshaping global philanthropy and social investing*, Oxford University Press.

Salway, M. (2017), *Social investment as a new charity finance tool: using head and heart*, Cass Business School, Centre for Charity Effectiveness.

Salway and Boughtflower (2018), *How is the role of the finance function changing?*, accessed 21 July 2019, www.civilsociety.co.uk/finance/how-is-the-role-of-the-finance-function-changing.html.

Salway and Ramsey (2018), *All RISE! How charities can reimagine their organisations*, Charity Finance Magazine April 2018, Civil Society Media.

Social Enterprise UK (2018), *Size and scale of social enterprise in 2018*, accessed 20 October 2018, www.socialenterprise.org.uk/Handlers/Download.ashx?IDMF=4284a743-4846-4084-b625-ccbc7967bf09.

# 9a  Case study

## Southmead Development Trust

### *Big Society Capital*

Southmead Development Trust serves the local community of Southmead, one of the most deprived areas of Bristol. They provide training courses for job seekers, fitness classes, as well as facilities for local groups and start-ups.

Big Society Capital placed funds with Pure Leapfrog which in turn was approached by Southmead Development Trust. This allowed the Southmead Development Trust to use social investment to buy solar panels to reduce its costs.

> "Social investment has enabled us to reduce our overheads so we can do more good things."
> Alex Kittow, General Manager, Greenway Centre

CITIZENSHIP AND COMMUNITY

# SOUTHMEAD DEVELOPMENT TRUST

### Problem
Southmead is one of the most deprived areas of Bristol, with life expectancy more than nine years lower than other parts of the city.

### Solution
The Greenway Centre, run by Southmead Development Trust, serves the local community, providing training courses for job seekers, fitness classes for referrals from local GPs and Southmead Development Trust, facilities for local groups and a business centre for local start-ups.

### Revenue Model
The loan enabled the centre to install 207 solar panels. Regular income from the feed-in tariff is used to repay the loan.

### Impact
The solar panels have reduced overheads at the centre, so that they can host a play scheme without charge and offer reduced gym membership and low rents to community businesses that will bring money into the local economy.

| | | | |
|---|---|---|---|
|  Invested | £50,000 | Cost of capital | 4% |
| Turnover | Not Disclosed | Duration of investment | 7 years |

**Organisational form**
Charity

**Investors**
Pure Leapfrog

**Other supporters**
Ethical Energy, Centre for Sustainable Energy

**www.southmead.org**

# PURE LEAPFROG

Pure Leapfrog provides affordable finance for community-led projects across the UK to help fund the capital costs of installing renewable energy technologies and energy efficiency measures.

## Approach to investing

Pure Leapfrog's goal is to be the financial partner of choice for community groups, helping to provide financial support for those undertaking their first project, or those looking to expand the pioneering work they already do.

The Community Energy Fund is designed to help community groups deliver their renewable and energy efficiency projects. To date, dozens of groups have accessed funding to help address issues of fuel poverty, take ownership of community assets, and deliver community led initiatives.

## Why the investment was made into the Greenway Centre

The Greenway Centre approached us for a loan because they wanted to put solar panels on the roof and couldn't afford it. Somebody else was going to do it for them, but then all of the financial value would have stayed with that organisation. Our loan enabled the Greenway Centre to pay for the panels themselves and keep all of the financial benefit.
**Robert Rabinowitz, CEO, Pure Leapfrog**

## Key fund terms

| | | | |
|---|---|---|---|
| Liquidity | NA | Social issue | Community energy |
| Duration | 10 years | Investment from Big Society Capital | £1 million |
| Size | £1 million | Big Society Capital strategy element | Small and medium-sized charity finance |
| Product type | Revolving credit facility | Other investors | Credit facility supported by grants from British Airways, Barclays, Bank of America Merrill Lynch, Simmons & Simmons, Esmée Fairbairn |

**Accessible to**

| | |
|---|---|
| Institutional investors | ✔ |
| Professional individual investors | ✘ |
| Retail investors/depositors | ✘ |

**www.pureleapfrog.org**

# 10 How do we begin thinking about social investment?

## The nine components of social investment. A model

*Mark Salway*

### Introducing the nine components of social investment

In the *introducing social investment* chapters so far, we have introduced social investment and the complexity of bringing investors and charities together. This final chapter in the *introducing* section puts forward an holistic model for social investment, with nine components which any organisations should think about before embarking on the social investment journey.

Cass Business School's practitioner research into social investment (Salway, 2017, p. 32) sees social investment as developing around nine different components. This is shown in Figure 10.1.

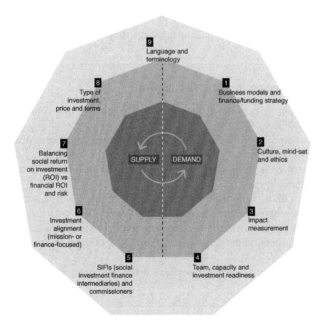

*Figure 10.1* The nine components of social investment.

Source: Salway (2017, p. 32).

## Component 1: developing business models and appropriate funding strategies for social investment

We explored business models in the last chapter – Chapter 9. We now also consider business planning to make sure that any use of social investment is robust, signed off by the trustees and management, and properly thought through.

First, and most important, a charity's business model must be aligned with the use of social investment. The business case must:

- clearly identify the revenue-generating activities, organisational savings or savings to the public purse
- show how investment capital will be paid back, including any risk premium and interest
- be flexible, to ensure that the model is sustainable, even if income and expenditure vary against expectations.

All charities see a future shift towards social investment and borrowing and away from grants and donations. As business models are key, taking the time to understand how social investment can be deployed effectively is critical.

In previous chapters, we highlighted the need to evolve charity funding models to relieve the pressure on government grants, contracts income and donations. A model which is replicable and scalable through social investment plays well to most charities with ambitions of growth.

Interest rates in the market have been historically low. However, charities should be careful to ensure that any social investment taken is sustainable in the future even if interest rates rise. Ultimately, the charity will need to pay back the money it has borrowed, plus interest, if using debt. This may depend on future interest rate levels.

---

### Using existing charity reserves as investment capital

- Of charity respondents, 23 per cent feel that they have surplus reserves that could be used to do more (Salway, 2017, p. 27)
- Using reserves is an exciting proposition that could help other social projects, either within the same charity or externally
- A charity could use its reserves as security for external borrowing to leverage fundraising or start a new social enterprise
- It can encourage existing staff to become "intrapreneurs" – effective and dynamic internal social entrepreneurs empowered to drive impact forward
- Investing internally can help intrapreneurs to come up with business ideas based around a social investment model, aligning powerfully with the existing business of the charity
- Alternatively it could invest to create new partnerships with corporates, other charities or the government.

## Component 2: culture, mind-set and ethics

### Tackling cultural resistance

There's a considerable *cultural resistance* towards using investment tools in the charity sector. The mind-set of charities is focused on grants, donations and delivering social change. Charities often feel conflicted about commercial tools such as "investment" when they think about "charity" and cannot see the link between the two.

Following from this, charities that will consider borrowing are generally positive about social investment. Those that will not consider borrowing are almost wholly negative about social investment.

As many organisations (both commercial and charitable) grow organically and without borrowing of any kind, we should also factor this into our thinking.

### Ethics and equity

Ethics is often at the heart of why some charities feel uncomfortable with social investment – viewing it as wrong to profit from social issues unless all profits are reinvested back into the charity.

There's a demand for specific "social" capital, separate from mainstream investments and banks, avoiding such perceived conflicts of interest.

Different funders have different motivations, too. Some may be financially motivated, e.g. mainstream banks. Others may be socially motivated, such as trusts, foundations and angel investors. What is important is that a range of investors exist to meet different charities' needs and motivations.

However, the clear divide in the sector lies around understanding what social investment is and how it can deliver impact for charities.

> If organisations understand social investment, they are more likely to use it and think positively about it (+20%). If they do not understand it, they are less likely to use it and think less positively about it (−24%).
>
> (Salway, 2017, p. 12)

To help build understanding of social investment, we need more sector money focused on training and mentoring charities through this change.

Cass CCE has launched a simple, free-to-download toolkit on social investment as part of its Tools for Success guide series – the *Cass CCE Social Investment Toolkit* (Cass CCE, 2016). Initiatives such as Big Society Capital's *Get Informed* (Get Informed, 2018) are also helping to build understanding.

## Component 3: impact measurement

The measurement of social impact is critical in social investment. We explore this in depth in later sections of the book (Chapter 16 and Chapter 26 in particular).

In this section, we just provide the absolute basics. Any aspiring student of social investment will want to delve much deeper to really understand the complexities.

## Inputs, activities, outputs, outcomes and impact

Perhaps the most important definitions that exist are those of GECES (Clifford *et al.*, 2014, p. 6). This series of definitions has been integrated into EU law and maps out the following chain of outputs, outcomes and impact (pp. 12–13):

- **Inputs:** what resources are used in the delivery of the intervention
- **Activity:** what is being done with those resources by the social purpose organisation (the intervention)
- **Output:** how that activity touches the intended beneficiaries
- **Outcome:** the change arising in the lives of beneficiaries and others
- **Impact:** the extent to which that change arises from the intervention.

The ability to evaluate the measurable social impact achieved for a given financial return is key to the success of social investment. A charity needs to be able to measure its outputs, outcomes and impact effectively to achieve this. A more detailed explanation of the impact value chain is given in Figure 10.2.

Salway (2017, p. 37) takes a deep-dive into charity's ability to measure social investment. He finds the following:

## What's holding back charities from measuring impact?

- concerns about the cost and time implications of measuring social impact
- difficulties of measuring social impact and social outcomes
- small charities finding it considerably more difficult to measure outcomes and impact than larger organisations
- poor measurement practices.

## Ways forward

- sharing measures openly across the sector
- helping organisations to plan and measure their social impact, e.g. The Good Finance Impact and Outcomes Matrix (Good Finance, 2018)
- better handling and management of data.

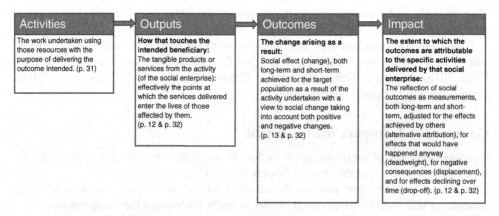

*Figure 10.2* The EU Social Impact Framework, GECES.

Source: Clifford *et al.* (2014). Page references come from that report.

While 72% of charities say they can measure outputs and 65% can measure outcomes, only 49% can measure impact.

(Salway, 2017, p. 37)

---

**Is social impact measurement becoming too complex?**

The whole area of measurement is at the heart of social investment and still in its infancy. There's a growing feeling that measuring social impact has potentially become too complicated. What's needed? Good conversations. Training to build understanding. Simplification. And reducing the cost of the measurement process.

---

## Component 4: the team, capacity and "investment readiness" of the charity

### A social investment champion

Where organisations have a social investment champion, this person can help take forward social investment and help others to see the potential. "It is highly correlated that those organisations where no champion exists typically do not even consider social investment" (Salway, 2017, p. 12).

The question then becomes how to identify a champion within a charity and give that person a voice.

Many trustees have great knowledge of mainstream investment tools and can use their skills as the champion to rally around. However, they can be very negative towards social investment, often being risk averse, even feeling that they cannot influence the charity's funding model.

### Forward-thinking trustees

Most trustees have a good understanding of charity finance and many have built professional careers and businesses using commercial investment tools.

Unfortunately, many trustees have become locked in a stewardship mind-set, in which survival and financial viability alone become the de facto standards by which to judge the organisation's vibrancy.

Trustees need to look past fiduciary duties and be able to take appropriate and well thought-through risks, as well as adopt a generative mind-set.

Addressing trustees' risk aversion towards social investment will be critical if social investment is to be successful. Initiatives such as Big Society Capital's "Get Informed" (2018) campaign, which helps trustees understand social investment, should be welcomed.

*The evolving finance director*

Charities need help building commercial propositions and taking these to market effect-ively, as well as with building capacity so they understand how to use investment tools.

Culturally, this may feel quite different to a "traditional" way of doing charity with donations and grants. The new venture will need to focus on revenue generation. This can be hard if one's mind-set is "non-profit".

Specifically, charity finance directors will need to change and evolve and gain new skills to deliver social investment. Building their capacity to handle these new tools will be critical to future demand.

While subtle, these changes sit at the heart of why social investment sometimes fails. Thinking through the cultural and process changes in advance will improve the chances of success.

> The cost, complexity and time required to take on social investment should not be under-estimated.

---

**Why the sector needs to build cross-over skills**

How can the private sector become part of the charity and non-profit sector and build motivation for both sectors to work together? While building these long-term relation-ships takes time, a new commercial DNA is needed if social investment is to succeed.

Investors often lack knowledge of social impact and rue the lack of "real cross-over talent" from those that have worked in the commercial sector, but also have a good understanding of charities.

Bringing cross-over skills into charities will be critical for the future growth of social investment.

---

## Component 5: social investment finance intermediaries and government commissioners of services

A key part of social investment for your charity or social purpose organisation is likely to be working with a social investment finance intermediary, in either a broking or an advisory capacity. They will help develop the proposition and find funds.

### Social investment finance intermediaries (SIFIs)

In Chapter 5 we took time to explore the role and work of SIFIs. This identified that they play three key roles in developing the social investment market through:

- Managing funds on behalf of investors
- Facilitating transactions as intermediaries
- Helping organisations as advisors.

### Funding models in the SIFI market

The SIFI market is quite complex and various funding models and products have developed.

Many SIFIs focused on the Big Potential Fund (Big Potential, 2017), helping organisations to become investment-ready and understand how to use social investment funds. SIFIs have links into a variety of investors, from individuals to banks.

> While many SIFIs are effective in helping to the build the market, some have come under criticism for both providing advice and finding investments. As such, they may have a clear conflict of interest acting both for the investor and charity. Similarly, to regulated markets, there needs to be a much clearer divide between those finding funds and those giving advice.

### Looking ahead

On the whole, SIFIs are seen as a vital part of the social investment ecosystem as it develops.

While most SIFIs provide a good standard of advice, it will be critical to uphold the quality of their work and ethical standards for the future trust and integrity of the social investment market.

---

### Government commissioners

Another area of funding to the sector as social investment comes from central and local government and other commissioners of services.

To focus on social value created and to build on the leadership shown to date:

- commissioners need to be trained and better understanding of social investment built
- the policy environment needs to be further enabled
- risk-sharing approaches need to develop further.

Latest government policy and thinking can be found at Gov.UK (2018) – *Growing a Culture of Social Impact Investment in the UK.*

---

## Component 6: alignment of purpose behind the investment

### Investment motivation: mission-alignment or finance-first

While social investment has the intent to create both a social and financial return, investor motivation seems to divide squarely between those who are making investments led primarily by their social mission, versus those motivated primarily by a financial return.

Mission-motivated investors tend to target their investments towards specific causes and take on greater risk for a lower financial return to compensate for this. Finance-first investors are motivated by the financial return on investment they will generate and aim for a market rate of return.

> Charities need to work in partnership with the investor to define investment motivation. Aligning this effectively is critical to building trust, enabling investors to engage meaningfully with charities.

## Hands-on or hands-off

Investors also consider the level of involvement they require with their investment – "hands-on" or "hands-off".

Those with a hands-on approach may ask for a seat on the board or to work closely with the management team and CEO to shape delivery. This can be challenging, but it can also bring new skills and capacities to charities.

The most powerful investments are those where motivation has been clearly and effectively discussed and both charity and investor understand what they each get from the investment. They are also careful to work together to create trust and a bond in a long-term partnering arrangement. Good SIFIs are also working with charities to build this trust.

The diagram in Figure 10.3 highlights the different investors in the social market and their primary motivation and approach to lending.

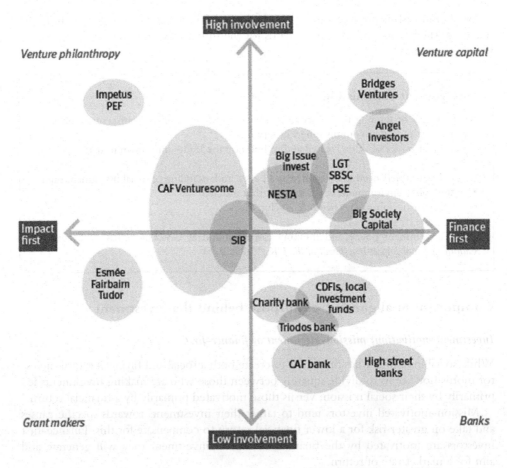

*Source: CAF (Charities Aid Foundation)*

*Figure 10.3* Different investors in the social market and their primary motivation and approach to lending.

Source: Salway (2017, p. 42); recreated with permission from CAF.

Many charities simply do not realise that different investors have different motivations

Many charities also feel more relieved when they understand that not all funding comes from mainstream banks.

This enables them to address some of the ethical concerns they may have and see that not all funders are just looking to make a financial return from social issues – which is far from the truth.

The majority of investors in this new social investment space – such as Big Issue Invest – take ethical and sector issues very seriously.

---

### The undeniable force of investment

At the same time as grants and donations are reducing in size and volume, the social investment market and "revenue-generating activities" are growing. As social investment continues to grow, it will exert a strong force on the sector.

The push and pull on the charity sector is profound. With trillions of pounds of investments available, there's an undeniable "gravitational force" of investment at play (see also Figure 10.4).

Responsible investment practices and ESG (environmental, social and governance) practices are also moving mainstream money towards the social (London Stock Exchange, 2018).

---

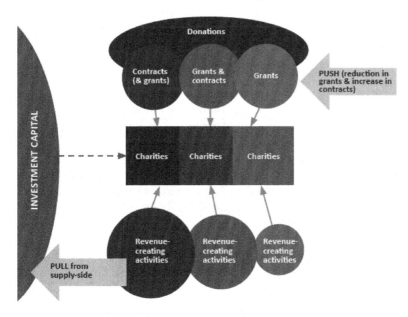

*Darker colours show change over time*

*Figure 10.4* The undeniable "gravitational" force of investment as grants and donations shrink and social investment grows.

Source: Salway (2017, p. 43).

## Component 7: balancing three forces – measurable social impact, financial return and risk

### Balancing three forces

When considering a commercial investment, investors typically weigh up the financial return on investment against the risk of that investment, to come to an acceptable return. The greater the risk, the higher return investors need to compensate for the risk.

Social investment adds a further dimension to this, namely the generation of social impact and the risk associated with its delivery.

**The balance of three forces – measurable social impact, financial return and the associated risk – is the critical conversation that charities need to have with investors.**

### The changes we're seeing

We're starting to see various ways of pricing the social impact, as well as a range of different investment tools:

- equities and quasi-equities
- bonds, social impact bonds
- crowdfunding and loans to handle this.

Some investors are asking if interest rates can be incentivised to generate greater social returns.

This is further explored in Chapters 20 to 27 in this book – *doing* social investment.

### Theory versus reality

The theory is that investors will trade off risk and return and look towards a return on investment which blends the social and financial return on investment (Bugg-Levine and Emerson, 2011).

The reality is that different investors have different motivations. As we're at the start of a journey of how to price social impact, both charities and investors lack sophistication in this conversation. Investors are concerned about risk and the costs of assessing social impact measures, while charities are concerned about paying high rates of interest.

In the eyes of the investor, charities want access to high risk capital at low cost. In the eyes of the charity, investors can be an expensive form of capital.

### Research opportunities

Charities have complained about both the length of time and the person hours that the due diligence required by an investor takes. This whole area is worthy of considerable further research.

Equally, many investors suggest that the deal size is too small. It's complex and costly to put in place social investments. Therefore, one of the key issues is how to capitalise small deals to allow smaller charities and social purpose organisations into the market space.

The Access Foundation (2018) is the latest initiative to wrestle with this problem. To address this, it focuses on blending social investment capital with grants, as well as deploying small amounts of capital and innovation.

### What do investors consider?

Investors often go through a screening and mapping process when considering a portfolio of investments – screening to identify investments that fit their criteria; and mapping to ensure they can identify where those investments will fit in their portfolio.

However, investors are frustrated by the legal "form" of charity and how they get money into a charity and exit successfully.

For example, this may mean they are more pre-disposed to invest in a social enterprise or another "profit-with-purpose" company. They are also surprised at how slow the decision-making process is within charities.

All that said, investors are, on the whole, excited about the possibilities that social investment brings.

The GIST *Investing for Global Impact* report (2015) shows that family offices and foundations have moved from thinking about this and gaining specialist knowledge, to making their first fledgling investments. Mainstream banks – such as UBS, Barclays and JP Morgan – have also set up teams to start focusing on action in the social investment marketplace.

Investors are fully aware of the effort it will take to bridge the gap between investors and charities, but see this as something that their clients want. This shift towards using money-for-good is a growing trend across the world.

If, eventually, social purpose organisations do not make use of social investment, then investors will go elsewhere in the long term.

## Component 8: the type of investment, prices and terms

### Different investments, different terms

Often, social investment occurs between a single investor and a single charity. Equally, some of the investments made to date have multiple lenders to spread the risk away from any one investor.

Therefore, the critical question becomes: Who is going to take on the "first-loss position"?

If a charity is able to put up some reserves to underpin this "first-loss position", it can de-risk the investment and lead to a significant reduction in costs through better negotiations. It could do this by using its unrestricted reserves. Equally, if a charity can offer security, e.g. borrow against its building, then it can command lower rates.

## Different charities, different business models, different demands for social investment

One size doesn't fit all. SIFIs and the intermediary market will be critical to help charities understand the breadth and depth of products available. Training and mentoring will also be important.

Several years ago, most social investments were made against asset-backed models to provide security to the investor. This is now changing with more unsecured funding becoming available.

> The *First Billion* report (Brown and Swersky, 2012, p. 15), identified that, in 2011, 84% of investments were secured. And that, in 2015, they expected 73% to be unsecured or quasi-equity and risk-taking. The market is changing.

### Keep innovating

Charity models do not allow equity sharing and many investment models are focused on equity, not debt. This creates a problem for social investment.

The social investment world will need to keep innovating to provide a wide range of investment products to meet all demand and supply requirements.

It's interesting to note that crowdfunding has been growing faster than social investment in recent years. This is allowing different models to develop, giving communities a chance to lend capital through community development finance institutions (CDFIs) on a local basis. The rise in pubs purchased from community bond issues gives a real example of this.

We are also starting to see long-term patient capital evolving as well as evergreen funds (see the Bridges Evergreen case study in Chapter 8a for more information).

> What is needed is long-term, patient capital, with varying time horizons – capital that stays with a charity as it develops.

---

**Win-win financial arrangements**

There's an exciting opportunity for corporate organisations to provide funds, to go beyond CSR (corporate social responsibility) and produce a win-win arrangement by building new social businesses. Corporates need to provide funding to projects that align with their mission.

WSUP, an NGO, and Unilever, a commercial organisation, team up to provide water sanitation in Africa. The NGO is happy to meet the water and sanitation needs of slum dwellers. The commercial organisation brings know-how and commercial skills, while focusing on profit-making endeavours for its shareholders. This case study is explored in Chapter 16a.

---

## Component 9: language and terminology

### Stating the problem

There's a considerable cultural barrier towards using investment tools in the charity sector.

Part of this barrier is language and terminology. In particular, two language barriers are beginning to hold back the development of the social investment market:

1 Confusion around the proliferation of terms – *social investment, social finance, social impact investing* (See Chapter 5 for a full discussion of this debate)
2 Charities and investment providers speak different languages. One speaks the language of head and investment, the other speaks the language of heart and social value.

### *Working on it*

SIFIs are helping to bridge this communication gap and build from both sides; they have a critical role to play.

Much more work will be needed to bridge the terminology divide, not least to enable academics and practitioners to understand clearly the range of different social investment vehicles and be able to talk about these with real clarity.

## References and bibliography

Access Foundation (2018), *Access the Foundation for Social Investment*, accessed 20 October 2018, www.access-socialinvestment.org.uk/.

Big Potential (2017), *Big Potential*, accessed 20 October 2018, www.bigpotential.org.uk.

Brown, A. and Swersky, A. (2012), *The first billion: a forecast of social investment demand*, Boston Consulting Group, accessed 16 April 2018, www.bcg.com/documents/file115598.pdf.

Bugg-Levine, A. and Emerson, J. (2011), *Impact investing: transforming how we make money while making a difference*, Jossey-Bass (Wiley).

Cass CCE (2016), *Social investment tools for success: doing the right things and doing them right*, accessed 20 October 2018, www.cass.city.ac.uk/faculties-and-research/centres/cce/resources/tools-for-success.

ClearlySo (2014), *The ClearlySo guide for the ambitious social entrepreneur*, accessed 20 October 2018, www.clearlyso.com/wp-content/uploads/2013/03/ClearlySo-Guide-for-the-Ambitious-Social-Entrepreneur-3rd-Edition.pdf.

Clifford, J., Hehenberger, L. and Fantini, M. (2014). *Proposed approaches to social impact measurement in European Commission legislation and in practice relating to EuSEFs and the EaSI*, report by GECES (Groupe d'experts de la Commission sur l'entrepreneuriat social) subgroup on impact measurement, accessed 20 October 2018, www.ec.europa.eu/social/main.jsp?catId=738&langId=en&pubId=7735&type=2&furtherPubs=yes.

Get Informed (2018), *Social investment for boards*, accessed 20 October 2018, www.bigsocietycapital.com/get-informed.

GIST (2015), *Investing for global impact*, accessed 20 October 2018, www.gistltd.com/investing-for-global-impact-report.

Good Finance (2018) *Impact and Outcomes Matrix: Start to plan and measure your impact using the Outcomes Matrix*, accessed 20 October 2018, www.goodfinance.org.uk/impact-matrix.

Gov.UK (2018), *Growing a culture of social impact investing in the UK*, accessed 20 October 2018, www.gov.uk/government/publications/growing-a-culture-of-social-impact-investing-in-the-uk.

London Stock Exchange (2018), *Your guide to ESG reporting*, accessed 20 October 2018, www.lseg.com/esg.

Salway, M. (2017), *Social investment as a new charity finance tool: using head and heart*, Cass Business School, Centre for Charity Effectiveness.

# 10a Case study

## Big White Wall

*Big Society Capital*

Big White Wall is an innovative online service developed to offer people experiencing mental health issues with a space to talk about their problems and self-manage their own mental health and wellbeing.

Through LGT Venture Philanthropy, funded by Big Society Capital, and other social investors, they received £2million of capital which has enabled them to scale their social business in a way that would not have been possible without social investment.

While not a charity, this is a Private Limited Company, focused on social issues, growing through social investment.

**MENTAL HEALTH AND WELLBEING**

## BIG WHITE WALL

### Problem
People with mental health issues, or experiencing emotional or psychological distress, may avoid sharing their feelings with friends, family or healthcare professionals due to stigma. Of the one in four who experience a mental health problem, the majority will not receive treatment.

### Solution
Big White Wall is an anonymous digital mental health and wellbeing service where people who are experiencing mild to moderate mental health issues can talk freely about their problems and self-manage their own mental health.

### Revenue Model
Big White Wall is a subscription service. The investment is repaid through subscribing organisations, including NHS providers, government departments, the armed forces and universities, as well as individuals.

### Impact
Big White Wall members get instant access to 24/7 support, are supported to self-manage their mental health without recourse to further help, with 95% of users reporting improvements in their wellbeing.

| | | | |
|---|---|---|---|
| **Invested** | £2 million | **Cost of capital** | Equity |
| **Turnover** | Not Disclosed | **Duration of investment** | Equity |

**Organisational form**
Private Limited Company

**Investors**
LGT Venture Philanthropy, the Whittemore Collection

**Other supporters**
A number of charitable trusts and foundations

**www.bigwhitewall.com**

# LGT VENTURE PHILANTHROPY

LGT Venture Philanthropy (LGT VP) is an impact investor supporting organisations with outstanding social and environmental impact. The LGT VP Impact Ventures UK fund can invest through equity, quasi-equity and debt-like instruments between half a million and £5 million.

## Approach to investing

Impact Ventures UK will support social ventures which have a clear social mission, addressing key social challenges in the UK, improving the lives of our disadvantaged communities. Key social themes within its scope include education, employment and skills, health, housing and shelter, communities and social inclusion.

LGT VP is an impact-first investor. Whilst LGT VP examines social ventures for financial sustainability and aims to deliver a financial return to fund investors, social ventures are first examined on their social performance. LGT VP assesses ventures for reach, how many people a social venture impacts; and depth, how fundamentally the social venture improves the lives of those it impacts.

## Why the investment was made into Big White Wall

Big White Wall is transforming mental health services in the UK, improving the wellbeing of thousands of people. We invested in the organisation so that it can scale up its activity and bring its innovative solutions to even more people.
**Raf Goovaerts, LGT Venture Philanthropy**

## Key fund terms

| | | | |
|---|---|---|---|
| Liquidity | NA | Social issue | General |
| Duration | 10 years | Investment from Big Society Capital | £10 million |
| Size | £30–£40 million (target) | Big Society Capital strategy element | Innovation |
| Product type | Growth capital fund | Other investors | London Borough of Waltham Forest Pension Fund |

**Accessible to**

| | |
|---|---|
| Institutional investors | ✔ |
| Professional individual investors | ✔ |
| Retail investors/depositors | ✘ |

Other investors:
London Borough of Waltham Forest Pension Fund
Deutsche Bank Impact Investment fund
Golden Bottle Trust

**www.impactventuresuk.com**

# Discussing social investment

# 11 The purpose of this section

## Discussing social investment

*Mark Salway*

This and the other *discussing social investment* chapters have been written by various authors. They offer their thoughts and wisdom on social investment. Some of these chapters are wide-ranging thought pieces, while others are very technical in nature.

Readers will learn from these experts and commentators as they explore the nature and complexity of social investment.

### This section

The discussing social investment section allows the reader to dive into and explore different elements of social investment.

- It starts by looking at the case for social investment and explores how we can democratise capital such that social investment principles can be used across an entire investment portfolio.
- The discussion then looks at charity and non-profit culture and how this can be quite conflicted when we talk about "investment" tools working in "social" businesses.
- We then touch on what family offices (as investors) want from social investment. Where they lead, other investors typically follow.
- We next look at a critique of social investment from Northampton University, before deep-diving into impact measurement and the technical knowledge needed to deliver this.
- We ask if social investment can develop a market space sufficient to become sustainable from a government and investor perspective.
- We next explore small charities and how their needs differ from large charities with regards to social investment.
- Finally, we look to the future of social investment and what may be in store.

In between each of these practitioner-led articles sits a case study. These case studies seek to highlight certain aspects of social investment and bring the topic to life.

We hope the reader will enjoy the discussions and depth of practitioner thought – sometimes inspiring and always thought provoking – in these chapters.

# 12 The case for social investment, and how to "democratise" capital

*Mark Salway and Nigel Kershaw*

**Mark Salway** draws inspiration from a conversation with **Nigel Kershaw**, Chair of Big Issue Invest and The Big Exchange.

## The starting point for social finance

Within the vast spectrum of social purpose organisations there is an ever-present cultural difference between those organisations who focus on philanthropy for their funding, versus those who trade.

A more traditional charity model might ask a third party for money which is subsequently spent on the cause. Once this funding has been spent, the charity must return to the donor for more funds to distribute. Meanwhile, social businesses and social enterprise aim to deliver social change in a more sustainable way through trading.

Of course, there are many areas of charity in which trading just won't work; for example, in a humanitarian crisis you just need grants and donations to save lives. However, there are equally many examples where social business could well work better, or certainly more efficiently, as a model to create social value.

Social businesses need social capital ("social finance") to help them grow. It is this which we explore now.

## Making social finance mainstream

Some commentators feel there has perhaps been too much discussion in the past about whether the intention behind social finance is to gain either financial return or social return in a binary way. As Nigel Kershaw suggests,

> If you're delivering both a financial and social return from both markets, it's the bit where they overlap in the middle that you're creating, it's neither one nor the other. It's something new; a contradiction in some ways but also a synthesis of the two.

Similarly, labelling the returns of social organisations as "sub-market return" is also the wrong perspective.

> Most social entrepreneurs are addressing a market failure. Both a social-market failure and a financial-market failure. So, how can solutions be 'sub-market', when we are actually creating solutions?

Social entrepreneurs are creating something different that is not easy to categorise. As the goal is to bring about much needed social benefits, social finance and social investment need to become part of the mainstream narrative.

> With social businesses, we need to move away from referring to them as "not-for-profit" organisations. To be sustainable using trading, any organisation has to be for-profit or for-surplus. The way you make that profit and how you re-invest these in your mission is the question.

Many business leaders believe they are creating social value simply through creating jobs. However, to get corporates consistently focused on creating social value calls for a profound change of mind-set and system. Although some CEOs are really committed to social change, often their business decisions are guided by the shareholder value and corporate reporting systems.

Trading within social businesses creates profit which need to be reinvested into social causes *at the same time as* creating financial returns for investors. In social enterprises, for example, the majority of the dividends or surpluses are reinvested to further the social mission (Social Enterprise UK, 2018).

---

**There is no sacrifice of financial returns**

"The [Big Issue] mission encouraged us to be ambitious", Mr Kershaw says. Although he likes to joke that people were surprised when they received money back, he insists that socially responsible investing does not come at the cost of financial returns. "There is no sacrifice of financial returns" (FT, December 2018).

---

## Impact matters

Social investment is a powerful tool within this dynamic. It enables you to really look at need first, and focus more on mission; this enables you to systematically address social problems more effectively.

Nigel Kershaw explains that

> We, as social investors, need to be able to see the social changes we are creating – good and bad. We need to enable people to help themselves not in top-down way; feeling somehow that we know best, when we often don't understand or have the experience or don't ask people and communities what they want.

Looking at outcomes and impact systematically is a very important exercise. Organisations need to measure the social value they create, not just focus on financial returns.

Narrative can be qualitative, quantitative or both. That said, some outcomes are difficult to quantify and care must be taken not to enforce measurements which may end up being inaccurate or over-complex.

## Across the world – enterprise not aid

Other commentators are focusing on the need to develop enterprise not aid, again challenging the traditional notion of charity. Kim Tan Dato and Sir Brian Griffiths, writing for the Transformational Business Network (Tan and Griffiths, 2017, p. 23) express their thoughts. They mirror those of Henry Ford: "A business that only makes money is a poor kind of business".

They argue that it makes sense to invest in aid through enterprise. Investing in sustainable businesses creates employment in low-income countries. Real employment gives people the dignity and self-determination to transform their own communities. This is in contrast to the dependency culture which may have been engendered by aid.

They further add (p. 23): "An ecosystem to facilitate SME [social business] development is needed. Incubator and accelerator hubs, government business grants, angel networks and venture capital providers are all components of this enabling environment."

Many businesses exist solely to make a profit for their shareholders: that is the financial bottom line. Social investment doesn't necessarily require the same high rate of financial return because it also seeks social and environmental returns. In other words, it is not investing purely for a financial return. That is not to say that it loses money. In order for businesses to be sustainable, they have to be profitable.

> A "hand-up not a hand-out" to alleviate poverty.

## The Big Exchange

Nigel Kershaw and Big Issue Invest want to go further: "We have come to see that core to The Big Issue's mission of dismantling poverty is how we impact the mainstream by 'democratising' capital" (Nigel Kershaw, Good with Money, 2019).

Big Issue Invest sees that it's all about giving ordinary people, such as readers of The Big Issue, a choice in how they invest, how they save, and also where their ISA and pension goes, in a way that will give them a financial return that benefits their families and communities and helps create a more fair, inclusive and balanced economy. This, in turn, will help towards Big Issue Invest's mission of dismantling and preventing poverty.

It was in response to these issues that The Big Exchange was set up. It sees the creation of a blockchain-powered platform that offers impact funds to retail investors. It will invest in impact investments – those that generate a positive social return.

To measure impact, The Big Exchange have created a methodology whereby they look in detail at each investment and see how much positive impact it has. Mr Kershaw says that

> funds are assessed against a robust criteria to make sure they help achieve real change for People and Planet. We have awarded Medals acknowledging those funds that really go the extra mile in contributing to the UN Sustainable Development Goals (SDGs).

This is a fledgling initiative that will help organisations in the social sector work together to develop the "social pound". "The Big Exchange, will offer 30 to 40 social and environmental impact funds … The Big Exchange believes it can attract about £3bn of assets within five years" (FT, November 2018).

Social finance needs to grow its own market, with organisations buying from each other, procuring from each other and taking investment and lending between each other; all provided that price and quality are the same or comparable to a similar commercial organisation. Only in this way can it develop, grow and meet customer need.

## In conclusion

There is a significant case for a new type of capital for social issues. Social investment and social finance are fresh, vibrant and energetic.

The launch of The Big Exchange as a new Social Exchange platform will allow people to invest in a wide range of investments; all with a positive social benefit, which is very exciting for the sector.

## References

FT, Financial Times (November 2018), *Big Issue works with fund managers on impact investing push*, accessed 24.6.2019, www.ft.com/content/b51e7623-c28d-3a81-95d2-9f137c86f2b2.

FT, Financial Times (December 2018), *Nigel Kershaw: people want much more than a financial return*, accessed 24 June 2019, www.ft.com/content/73d1aae6-51e4-34b7-975e-33997dc53203.

Good with Money (2019), *The Big Issue's Nigel Kershaw sets out to democratise capital*, accessed 24 June 2019, https://good-with-money.com/2019/02/07/the-big-issues-nigel-kershaw-sets-out-to-democratise-capital/.

Social Enterprise UK (2018), *FAQs: what are social enterprises?*, accessed 22 September 2018, www.socialenterprise.org.uk/Pages/FAQs/Category/FAQs.

Tan and Griffiths (2017), *Social impact investing: new agenda in fighting poverty*, Transformational Business Network.

# 12a  Case study

## Panahpur

*James Perry*

**James Perry** is Co-Founder of COOK and, through his B-Lab work, understands the needs and nature of social business. Here, he talks about how the charity Panahpur used its capital to become a social investor.

## How does a charity change its focus and become a social investor?

### Social capital for social solutions

Whilst environmental, social and governance (ESG) screening for investment portfolios is growing in importance, it is inherently a screening mechanism which removes negative aspects of portfolio performance (FTSE Group, 2019).

Social investment is different from this. It's the purposeful use of repayable capital to charities and social enterprises to create social change. So, what we are talking about with social investment is a positive, measurable and attributable impact.

When Sir Ronald Cohen came up with the idea of social investment, he envisioned a market where charities and social enterprises could access capital at scale.

Panahpur was supportive of this agenda, whilst also seeing an opportunity to put all of its assets to work to support, rather than detract from, its charitable purpose.

### What led you to the idea of using social investment?

Panahpur is a UK charitable foundation that dates from 1907. It has an open mandate as to its charitable activities.

Back in 2006, much of Panahpur's capital was tied up in property. The trustees elected to sell their property and were faced with the challenge of how to invest their endowment. We went to asset managers for advice on what to do, in order to invest our capital in a way that was consistent with – and not at odds with – our charitable purpose. We were told that the purpose of our endowment was to maximise our financial returns, and that the asset managers could not tell us what the social and environmental impact of that activity was, on the grounds that it was not their concern. We didn't want to do this as we saw it as contradictory in a world that was so clearly suffering from profit maximising corporate activity. Asset managers didn't get "positive investing" and so couldn't help us.

Panahpur understood ESG investing, but this was a negative screening process rather than positive. Early social investment pioneers, such as Social Finance and Big Issue

Invest, were starting to create positive investment products which interested us. After some experimentation, we realised that, if we were to deploy all of our assets into social and impact investments, we would need to embrace portfolio theory and apply an asset class lens to our investments. We began to see that it was possible to have a positive social and environmental impact from a portfolio view.

Since then, people have begun to wake up. They are coming to realise that the purpose of business is not purely to maximise shareholder wealth.

### How did we chance upon this space? Was it thoughtful or reactive?

It all started with the idea that our investments must align with our purpose. Investment managers weren't considering social and environmental impact, so we needed to do it ourselves. We wanted to ensure that we were compliant, given that the prevailing culture suggested that our fiduciary duty was to maximise the financial return of our investments and, in turn, to maximise the grant value for our beneficiaries; this was the Charity Commission's guidance following the Bishop of Oxford case law, and Charity Commission CC14 guidance (CC14, p. 11).

The Charity Commission and legal guidance at that time saw that the best interests of charities were "served by the trustees seeking to obtain the maximum return, whether by way of income or capital growth which is consistent with commercial prudence" (Charity Commission, 2014).

This led us to the Cabinet Office, who were writing the government social investment strategy. We had to comply with our fiduciary duty under CC14 and felt that the guidance of the time was unhelpful and constraining. A number of charity leaders were campaigning for a change to the CC14 guidance, which we supported. This guidance ended up being changed (in about 2012); and programme-related investment and mixed motive investments were introduced to the CC14 guidance (CC14, 2017).

### What type of organisations are you investing in directly and how do you do your due diligence?

Panahpur found it really onerous to invest directly well. One example is a business in Bangladesh that we have an equity investment in. The business employs women to support them into better lives.

We have been in that business for ten years and have made a moderate return of 2–3 per cent internal rate of return (IRR). However, this is not a risk-adjusted return and we haven't managed to exit yet.

We see the Bangladesh investment as high social impact, but very hands on and needing a lot of input. It is a better way of achieving impact and transformation for disadvantaged people, but it is onerous and difficult to manage directly.

Our experience of going through investment managers is that they are better at it than we are. They have better focus, better niche knowledge and more time. So, we have moved to an approach of going through managers, rather than direct investments.

### Project Snowball

Initially, Panahpur moved into direct social investment during the early 2010s. However, we also saw that this was bigger than just charities and was about all businesses. In a world where the purpose of business had come to be understood as maximising profits for share-holders, we saw that a better form of capitalism would be one where social and environmental impact was also considered in portfolios. This is impact investment. Project Snowball LLP (Snowball) is the expression of that thinking.

Snowball is where the idea of social and impact investment meets a whole portfolio approach; it is seeking to have the most possible social impact for a solid investment return. It is a separate investment vehicle with an independent investment manager.

> Snowball is a partnership running the qualifying social investments of Panahpur and the Golden Bottle Trust. It seeks to expand with other partners with a view to offering an institutional-quality, diversified, social investment fund accessible to the ordinary retail investor by way of a listing on a public market. Early investments included the likes of Big Issue Invest and Bridges Ventures, both of which now have new vehicles fundraising.
>
> (Big Society Capital, 2019)

Panahpur has about £3.5 million of investments, of which £3 million is invested into Snowball; it is a diversified portfolio that is mission aligned.

Some of our investments in Panahpur are still directly managed, with the remainder being in Rathbones' ethical fund to give Panahpur the liquidity that Snowball, initially, couldn't offer.

### Do social investment ventures always have to make a positive return?

As we explore this market space, there are social and impact investment opportunities that will make a market rate of return, those that will make a sub-market return and those that may ultimately lose money but have a significant social impact. What matters is that we use the right kind of investment (whether that be mixed purpose, programme related or grants) for the right task.

We still need to address how to value and exit social investments. In private equity, value is traditionally driven by a multiple of earnings before interest tax and deductions (EBITDA); and so, why would investors do anything other than try to drive up EBITDA? We have no comparable social EBITDA measures.

### What next?

We stopped undertaking impact investing at Panahpur as soon as Snowball was created; now that our assets are aligned with our charitable purpose, we focus on our charitable activities. We hope that, through Snowball, we can have an influence by creating something that has a broader relevance in the form of an asset management company based on this idea. Snowball is a holistic portfolio focused on social, as well as financial, return.

### Could any charity do this?

All charitable endowments are investment companies, they just happen to have a charitable purpose for their investment profits. Conventional investment companies pay their returns out to shareholders or savers, whereas charitable endowments pay their investment returns to their beneficiaries. Panahpur is a charitable endowment that has evolved to recognise this reality and therefore bring its investments into line with its charitable purpose. Now, through Snowball, we have a portfolio that we hope is contributing towards building and supporting social and impact investment and the social and impact investment markets.

## References

Big Society Capital (2019), *Alexander S Hoare*, accessed 27 June 2019, www.bigsocietycapital.com/alexander-s-hoare.

CC14, Charity Commission (2017), *Charities and investment matters: a guide for trustees (CC14)*, accessed 25 June 2019, https://assets.publishing.service.gov.uk/government/uploads/system/uploads/attachment_data/file/581814/CC14_new.pdf.

Charity Commission (2014), *Changing attitudes to ethical investment?*, accessed 25 June 2019, www.gov.uk/government/speeches/changing-attitudes-to-ethical-investment.

FTSE Group (2019), *Your guide to ESG reporting*, accessed 25 June 2019, www.lseg.com/esg.

# 13 It's all about the culture

*Jonathan Jenkins*

**Jonathan Jenkins**, Chief Executive Officer at London's Air Ambulance and Previous Chief Executive of Social Investment Business, takes us on a personal journey.

## Back in the 1980s

I remember the late 1980s, when no-one had even heard or talked about "social business" or "social investment". I grew up as a third generation "man in the City" and there was no discourse about social enterprises or anything to do with funding social issues at all. It was all about Wall Street and the Gordon Gecko character, all about making money. Capitalism was going to change the world for the better and my peers and I were going to be part of it.

---

### Nights out in the City

I remember going to charity functions in the City in the 90s, which were basically big nights out with after dinner speakers (normally comedians), with a charity raffle or auctions.

Although we knew it was for a good cause, we never thought too much about the reason behind it. There was no presentation from the charity, no beneficiary to embody its impact. We were simply part of a big fundraising machine that was raising money and we were not involved in choosing or even understanding where that money was going or what effects it would have on others.

---

Most people's perceptions of their need for a pure financial reward set the framework of everyone's attitudes and formed the baseline for communication strategies between different individuals and groups. There was nothing else to consider other than how to maximise the financial return we received; both for our employer and ourselves.

Most of my graduate trainee peers were from private schools and/or Oxbridge and I can't believe any of us had ever experienced (or even witnessed) much hardship in life, let alone poverty. If we did, we never talked about it. When Band Aid was at the forefront of the press, it was the concept that interested us and engaged us but we never reached out to really understand what was lying beneath it and its root causes.

I do not know if it was our age, our backgrounds or if it was because it was a very consumer-led environment that surrounded us. Perhaps it was just me.

We were – certainly I was – living in a Square Mile bubble.

## Closer to impact

As my career developed, having worked on the trading floor – where it's all about maximising financial gain and moving money from A to B with no discernible social impact – I started to work in our family business and so unintentionally moved closer and closer to impact.

It was our responsibility to provide a platform to get equity investment into start-up or early-stage companies. It was in that role that I began to see people building on the monetary value to create products and services that other people were buying and signing up to. I began to meet entrepreneurs who were driven by particular industries and striving to find their niche area in the economy and in society.

> I recognised that my role in life was to be their navigator, to help them raise the money and help them achieve their hopes and dreams.

## Into the Third Sector

When I moved from the financial world to the Third Sector, I worked for an organisation that generates start-up funds for social entrepreneurs. But I had no real idea what a "social enterprise" actually was or how it functioned. Although I had got the job, I wasn't sure whether my future lay in the social world. I'd just got to the stage where I ejected from the City and that was where I landed. It was to change my life, my understanding of the world I live in, and instilled a passion to help create a better future for my children who were born right at this career crossroads. But I didn't realise that at the outset.

In fact, I spent the first six months struggling quite hard. I was the only formally financially trained and "City institutionalised" person working with social entrepreneurs. I discovered that, although they had similar issues to the people I had worked with before, their motivations could not have been more different.

In the commercial world, it was really easy to help an organisation go forward, because everyone had the same denominator goal – they were all trying to achieve financial value for the business. I discovered that, when you're working for a socially driven organisation, it is not necessarily the same common purpose that founder and their employees share, for example. In addition the multitude of stakeholders made the decision making complex.

> I found this clash of identities quite a struggle to manage, because you lose the sole purpose goal of "money, money, money". You have to try different ways to achieve the organisation's diverse range of targeted goals, not to let them conflict against each other (which they often did) and to focus on growth for its work to become sustainable.

I worked for UnLTd then, so my first exposure to this market was giving out grants. It was there that I met people right at the start of their journey, incubating social ideas. After three years there, getting some of my capitalist edges knocked off me, I then moved to Social Investment Business, much more focused on distributing and using investment capital.

## With a cultural hat on

There is an inherent contradiction within social investment – you are not only a financial investor but you also striving to achieve your desired social impact. However, your stakeholders on each side will punish you if you get unbalanced and push one side and negatively affect the other side. It is those tensions you live with day-to-day.

So, with a "cultural hat" on, social investment was originally seen as binary. You were either one or the other: you either focused on financial return or social return.

---

**A binary decision**

If one is asking "how do you make a decision on a social investment opportunity?" through a cultural lens, there are two ways that could be approached:

1   Is this **the social impact** we want to scale up, grow or support and if we do invest in it, what is our likely rate of return?
2   Is **gaining a financial return** from this project our primary concern? If we are offered a range of financial options that will bring this to us, which of them fulfil our expectations of social return to an acceptable level?

Anybody coming from mainstream finance will be much more comfortable with choosing option 2.

---

## Investors are changing

One challenge I've faced since I left the financially motivated sector is trying to explain to my peers what I am doing.

Although a few of them have also moved over to roles which have more of a social purpose, some of them are still high-flyers in the City. I'm looking forward to the day when they realise how powerful and exciting that feeling is when your work is positively affecting others – and how you want it to grow and grow.

There is an acceptance of a spectrum of financial returns and social impact trade-offs. I think the "blended return" (Bugg-Levine and Emerson, 2011, p. 25 and p. 28) is happening, but you need to find the point in the spectrum where you feel comfortable as an individual investor. There is no "right" place that everyone should be. There are different people with different attitudes to the financial returns and different attitudes to the level and degree to which they assess and manage the levels of social impact.

I ended up in the sector rather accidentally, but I am so pleased that accident happened. It is becoming more and more evident that the cohort of individuals who are starting to work in the finance sector are more values-driven. They will be the ones who really change the big institutions and bring big systemic change to how both society and the economy function.

Some of the most successful funding programmes in this space so far have been more commercial. If you look at the Bridges Ventures funds, for example, they have been very commercially successful, but they have been focused on more profit-focused investments.

I feel the optimal return came in some funds where when we actually lost 10 to 20 per cent of our capital, but the social impact of the work is deep. That is the best possible financial return we should expect to receive if we want to support the Third Sector at scale. The scope for "market rate" commercial returns is not what many of us, including me, imagined ten years ago.

## Addressing failures

If you look at social investment failures in the market to date, most of them were saveable if we had worked with those organisations earlier and more closely:

> *Timely information.* We had one example where we were struggling to get information out of an organisation. By the time that we got it, it was almost too late to save the organisation. We should have intervened much faster to support the organisation, rather than rely on the board level governance for timely information. Successful examples of social investment have often relied quite heavily on the level of support received from the board to drive it.
>
> *Supporting individuals.* I also saw that, with the board and CEO, the board is either in denial when things go wrong or the CEO is afraid to take issues to them. You just see some very lonely, very good natured, very committed people that get themselves in a downward spiral. If the performance is going off the rails, they are just working harder and harder but not being helped. We need better mechanisms to identify and help these individuals and share the burden they feel.
>
> *Better relationships.* Most businesses go bust because of a lack of governance or help for the CEO in the early stages of failure before it becomes fatal. We need to work harder at our relationships to:
>
> * make sure that both board and CEO feel confident in the investment they are using
> * believe that applying and using social investment is a positive call to make
> * have people proactively responding when things are starting to go wrong, rather than when they have gone too far down the failure pathway.

In essence, we need to become more responsible investors.

Four to five years ago, social purpose organisations were expected to just go where the social investment market was sat; it was very one-sided. Build it and they will come. Charities and social enterprises were also expected to change their language and speak financial jargon.

> However, it is the investor (supply-side) that is serving the front-line organisations and not the other way round. We need to find a way to take on, and shoulder, greater responsibility for failure.

It's also time for us to recognise that there's a space for both a quasi-commercial money market in this environment, including using equity, and venture philanthropy.

Social investment is in for a tricky few years ahead, unless we can show positive case studies and demonstrate that it works, and decide what is the best way to achieve scale of impact, not just flow of funds. We must also look at which areas have not been successful, and ask why.

## Concerns for the future

Some of the concerns I have for the future social investment market are as follows:

*Large overtaking small.* I can see that not many small charities or start-up social enterprises have the space and time to learn and consider social investment opportunities. It is the bigger institutions who have the wherewithal to accommodate this change. We must help smaller charities to learn and evolve using social investment.

*Risk aversion.* Following the Kids Company scandal (House of Commons, 2016), and recent Oxfam safeguarding issues, there has been a concerted push to improve trustee education and for improved governance processes to be established. However, both of these cases have been widely publicised and have increased the conservative and risk-averse approach many are taking to governance across the sector. I wonder how much this will affect the innovative new approaches which social investment has brought.

*Rural deprivation.* Social investment programmes have been primarily urban-centric. Social investment is not really helping rural areas, because you cannot get the financial economies of scale. It is not that there is a lack of social need in these areas, but it is a challenge to see ideas that are strong and sustainable enough to take on investment. The real basics of investment numbers just do not seem to work in the rural areas, and grants become a much more powerful tool.

What we have not understood, is the work on the ground and the needs and wishes of the smaller organisations in smaller cities and rural areas. We cannot just sit in London assuming we understand the issues at hand. There is a trade-off in local knowledge and, if investors do not take the time to go through that process, they will gravitate to what looks financially stronger and continue to view it from a distance, and from London.

*Not listening.* Even when we have tried to use the right language, inadvertently we are talking in market terms, about financial returns, profits, product etc. "Product" is probably the word that has been used too much.

Rather than trying more nuanced language, people actually need to listen more carefully. Even though most of us thought we were being careful and simple with our language, we may have been inadvertently not careful enough, even patronising.

### *Above anything else, we have been in broadcast mode rather than listening*

Within charities, there can often be a tension between the board and the executive team regarding risk. The executive team can be more tolerant of risk and want to move forward faster than the board is comfortable with. When debt or external investment is taken in, there's ultra-conservatism, on the whole. When there's a lack of intervention, when things do not go well, it starts to spiral downwards.

Heavy governance at the start can lead to lack of governance down the road. I think we will all privately admit that most social investments go wrong, not because the business model is not right, but because they hit a few bumps in the road. For example, because the CEO hasn't got the breadth or depth of management team in place, or because they are small organisations living on very restricted means.

We need to improve governance and confidence around social investment.

## In conclusion … the intention is there

When people are looking at social investment, we expect integrity from investors, to be respectful of others, and be realistic in expectations. We're not looking at values as a de minimis set of behaviours. We should support those with a more entrepreneurial character: people who are curious, restless, want to try new things, are brave and authentic.

We should connect with these individuals and align our journeys.

We also need to move away from this being seen as an investor-led market. We cannot assume that if we build it "they will come". We need to develop bridges so we can reach each other.

> There has been a lot of success in this market space, because there's a lot of great people plugging away to make it work. On the whole it is getting far better than what it was because of these efforts. But, I think now is the time that we pause, reflect and readjust before we go on to the next stage.

If we miss out on the benefits of social investment and what it can bring, this will be such a lost opportunity. If social investment processes are to succeed:

- The different cultures on the supply and demand sides need to be acknowledged and addressed
- The language needs to speak more easily to both sides
- The expectations need to become more honest and realistic
- We need to support those failing much more quickly and with greater integrity, and finally
- We need to build more bridges so capital can flow.

## References

Bugg-Levine, A. and Emerson, J (2011), *Impact investing: transforming how we make money while making a difference*, Jossey-Bass (Wiley).

House of Commons (2016), *The collapse of Kids Company: lessons for charity trustees, professional firms, the Charity Commission, and Whitehall*, accessed 20 October 2018, www.publications. parliament.uk/pa/cm201516/cmselect/cmpubadm/433/433.pdf.

# 13a Case study

## Inqo Investments Ltd

*Jim Tan*

From social start-up to a listed social impact company: creating a new asset class and investments in low-income countries. **Jim Tan** provides an overview of the ongoing work and ambition of Inqo.

---

**Background details (Inqo, 2019)**

- Inqo was incorporated in the Republic of South Africa in 1998. Its primary investment focus is sub-Saharan Africa.
- Inqo believes that enterprise is the best way to tackle poverty through creating sustainable employment that empowers the poor and transforms communities.
- As a social venture investment company, Inqo invests in businesses that create jobs and provide services and products for the poor as well as tackle environmental issues.
- Inqo invests in small medium size enterprises (SMEs) that are scalable and have potential for growth and asset appreciation.
- In addition to the financial returns, each investment is monitored for its measurable social and environmental impact.

---

## Where it all began: jobs in the bush

Inqo's story began deep in the bush of South Africa's Eastern Cape back in 1998. Founder, Dr Kim Tan, became disillusioned with his personal donations to charities as a means of poverty alleviation. After ten years in the biotechnology venture capital (VC) industry, Dr Tan began looking for ways to apply his skills in a more meaningful way.

Having seen first-hand the transformative effects of business in his home country, Malaysia, he was drawn towards the social impact space – at that time still in its infancy. With his past experience and passion for the poor, Dr Tan embarked on a journey into what he calls "social venture capital".

And what better place to put the theory to the test than the Eastern Cape, one of the poorest regions in South Africa? Unemployment in some towns exceeds 70 per cent, with a high prevalence of HIV, accounting for 30 per cent of deaths within the district where Inqo's first investment project, Kuzuko game reserve, is based. In Somerset East, the closest town to Kuzuko, more than 50 per cent of the total local population, or 70 per cent of the black population, was classified as living in poverty in 2004 (Global Insight Southern Africa, 2004).

## Eastern Cape – a tough challenge

The first step was to analyse the possible enterprise opportunities in the region. However, these proved to be thin on the ground. The Eastern Cape is historically an agricultural region famous for its Karoo lamb – but it is a tough place to make a living. The semi-arid climate supports very low stocking densities, often too low for a commercially viable operation. Sheep farming only employs a relatively small number of farm labourers. Wages are low and conditions are tough, with no prospect for progression. Years of overgrazing have severely degraded much of the region's farmland, further reducing the limited employment prospects. The rural towns of the Eastern Cape are many miles along dirt roads from the major cities and transport hubs, so opportunities for other industries are limited.

## Creating Kuzuko

After a visit to a private game lodge in Kruger National Park, Dr Tan was inspired by South Africa's eco-tourism potential. At the time, there were very few game reserves in the Eastern Cape, yet its position at the end of the "Garden Route" and the absence of malaria made it an ideal location.

With the right investment, the vast tracts of unproductive farmland could generate far more jobs and, more importantly, relatively well-paid jobs with the opportunity for progression, as a game reserve. And so, the vision for a 5-star "Big Five" game reserve called Kuzuko was born.

In 2000, the long process of acquiring land began, resulting in the consolidation of 22 separate farms into one 39,000-acre property. To restore the land, 20 tonnes of metal and alien vegetation were cleared, 230 km of internal fencing was taken down and numerous old farm buildings were removed. Over a 10-month period, a team of 70 men erected over 70 km of elephant-proof fencing. Kuzuko was now ready for the re-introduction of wildlife. In 2005, elephants once again roamed in areas that they had been absent from for 150 years. The full range of the Big Five can now be found on the reserve alongside countless other species; and Kuzuko now runs successful conservation programmes for elephants, cheetahs, Cape Mountain zebras and black rhinos.

## The social impact

Even more exciting than the wildlife is the social impact that Kuzuko has facilitated. Kuzuko employs more than 80 full-time staff alongside a number of other part-time and casual positions working in the five-star lodge and on the reserve. This is more than three times as many jobs as when the land was operated as farms. It's not just the number of jobs, but the quality of the jobs that counts. Kuzuko pays 5.7 times more than the regional average, provides extensive training for its employees and genuine opportunities for progression.

Whereas farm labourers previously lived in "cottages" – that, in reality, were little more than shacks with no facilities – Kuzuko's staff live in properly built houses with electricity, solar panels, running water and flush toilets. The tourist dollars spent by the predominantly international clientele provide a much-needed injection of cash for the district. The income enters the local economy in the form of wages for Kuzuko staff and revenue for the local enterprises that supply Kuzuko. It is estimated that for every ten tourists that visit, one new job is created in the region.

## The importance of SMEs

Kuzuko has demonstrated the transformative impact that intentional social investment can make. Inqo believes that private enterprise has a crucial role to play in the alleviation of poverty in developing nations. SMEs are the backbone of the economy in low-income countries.

In 2018, more than 99 per cent of the 5.7 million private businesses found in the UK were SMEs, accounting for 60 per cent of private sector employment and 52 per cent of private sector turnover (Rhodes, 2018). Similarly, in the less developed nations, it is crucial that the SME sector develops into a significant part of the formal economy. SMEs not only provide stable jobs but also generate the tax revenue that governments of low-income countries so desperately need to fund education, health and infrastructure improvements. By contrast, many of the micro businesses funded by the micro-finance sector remain in the informal economy, generating no tax revenue.

The single biggest obstacle for SMEs in sub-Saharan Africa is access to finance. The World Bank's 2007 report, *Making Finance Work for Africa*, states (p. 30), "Given the importance of private sector credit for economic growth, finding effective ways of ensuring the banks channel more of their resources to the domestic private sector is crucial for financial sector development."

The World Bank report found that African banks intermediated a lower proportion of their deposits into private sector finance than other regions, preferring liquid assets and lending to governments. The report shows a link between private sector credit and GDP, highlighting the importance of access to finance. Senbet and Otchere (2006, p. 83), note that Africa is now the only region in the world where development assistance exceeds private capital funding. Even where finance can be found for the private sector, the interest rates charged often exceed 20 per cent, adding a debilitating cost that very few start-ups are able to afford.

## A new asset class

Inqo believes that, in order for widespread and rapid change in sub-Saharan Africa to be possible, we need to find ways for social businesses to access patient capital beyond the philanthropic sector. In November 2015, Inqo became the first social impact company to be listed on the ISDX Growth Market in London. Inqo's aim is to help create a new asset class to meet the growing demand for social investments that offer both a social and a financial return.

Triodos Bank (2018) research suggests that the socially responsible investment market is set to grow by 173 per cent to £48 billion by 2027. Much of the change is being driven by a young generation disenfranchised by the current financial markets and looking for an ethical home for their pensions and investments. But there is still a paucity of truly positive social investment options available in the market. A large number of the social investment alternatives currently being promoted by pension funds would best be described as "least harm" rather than truly ethical or social.

Being listed as a public company allows retail investors to participate as shareholders in Inqo's transformational work. The social impact space undeniably carries a higher risk for investors than many traditional investment arenas. But recent trends have shown that investors are willing to risk a portion of their capital in pursuit of positive change. Even a small percentage of the total funds under management could help drive a meaningful reduction in poverty.

## An evergreen fund

Operating as a listed company gives Inqo other benefits besides access to capital. Many social impact funds are modelled on traditional VC funds with a ten-year lifespan. After ten years, the fund will exit the businesses it has invested in and return capital plus any profit made to its investors. This life cycle limits the companies that the funds can invest in, counting out many worthwhile opportunities that do not show potential for rapid growth. Inqo operates as a holding company, essentially an "evergreen fund", so is able to offer patient capital and invest in a diverse portfolio of businesses, including those that offer a significant social return but limited financial return.

Once a company is established, an entrepreneur may want to access some or all of the capital they have created. Most social enterprises are unlikely to ever reach a scale where a public listing is feasible. As a public listed company, Inqo is in a position to offer an exit, or partial exit, for entrepreneurs by exchanging equity in the social enterprise for shares in Inqo.

## Inqo's investment rationale

Inqo is now in the process of building a diverse portfolio of investments that offers shareholders a strong social and financial return. Inqo currently holds investments in South Africa, Zambia, Kenya and Uganda, covering a range of sectors from micro pensions to honey production, with pipeline investments across an even wider range of countries in agriculture, healthcare and biotechnology awaiting due diligence.

In seeking out and assessing new investments, Inqo follows the following investment rationale:

1 **Investments must be profitable**
  Profitability means sustainability. A business dependent on grants will not survive in the long run and continue to generate the impact Inqo seeks. In order to pioneer a new asset class and attract mainstream investment, Inqo must also provide a close-to-market-rate financial return for its shareholders. As a rule of thumb, Inqo looks for businesses that are three to four years from profitability and have the potential to achieve at least three times growth. Inevitably, some businesses in the portfolio will fail, so the other investments must achieve enough returns to compensate for these losses.
2 **Investments must provide a social return**
  All Inqo's investments must provide a social return, but the nature of this return can take different forms. For some investments, this may simply be the creation of jobs in a region of endemic unemployment. Other investments may provide basic goods and services at affordable prices, or bring an innovative solution to a problem faced by the poor without necessarily creating many jobs. As an evergreen fund, Inqo is able to support a diverse range of investments, balancing trade-offs between financial and social returns across the portfolio.

3　**Investments must be environmentally sustainable**

Whilst environmental benefits are not a prerequisite for investment, any investee enterprises must at least be environmentally sustainable and do as little harm as possible. Inqo also actively seeks out investments that proactively achieve an environmental or conservation benefit. We strongly believe that the enterprise and conservation must work together – if we are to have a sustainable future with development for all.

4　**Inqo invests in entrepreneurs**

Even the best ideas will fail without the right people to make them happen. The management team at the investee company is one of the most important considerations prior to investment. We expect competence, hard work, integrity and modesty from all the entrepreneurs we work with and promise to offer the same in return.

5　**Inqo is sector-neutral**

Several philanthropic funds are tied to a single sector by their donor base. At Inqo, we have the freedom to pursue any investment that provides a meaningful social return whilst also generating a financial return. Each individual investment can therefore be assessed entirely on its own merits.

6　**Inqo invests for equity**

At Inqo, we want to go beyond simply providing capital and travel along the journey with our investee companies. We believe that the best way to do this is by becoming equity partners in a position to influence the business, share in the risk and earn our right to share in the rewards. Our investee companies have a wide range of business experience from experienced serial entrepreneurs to those that have never created a cash flow. A key benefit for investee companies is the advice, expertise and network that Inqo is able to offer – something that would not come with a commercial loan. Each investment provides a valuable learning experience both for the investee and for the investor.

## Measuring social returns

There is an increasing interest in the measurement of social returns. Traditional economic models rely heavily on the measurement of financial metrics; and, as the saying goes, "what gets measured, gets managed", so this interest is understandable. Unfortunately, social factors do not always fit into neatly measurable and directly comparable metrics in the same way that economic factors do.

Of course, Inqo must have some way of measuring social returns – otherwise how do we know if we are achieving our core aim of social transformation? The measurements Inqo chooses are investment specific and pragmatic with regard to the availability and sensitivity of information. It is important that the measures we choose are not too onerous for the investee company and so distracting from their primary function as a viable business.

Inqo believes that simple, easily collected employee metrics – such as gender, average salaries, standard of housing, number of children in education and number of meals per day – offer a reasonable snapshot of standard of living for those businesses where job creation is the primary social return. For those businesses meeting an important social need for the poor, such as the provision of pensions, then number of people served acts as a good indication of social value delivered. Where possible, we also seek to undertake a more in-depth analysis of impact, but this is not on a routine basis.

## The future

Many exciting things are happening in the wider social investment space, with many traditionally philanthropic and grant-based institutions starting to rethink their approach to tackling social issues. At present, there is a shortage of individuals with the right skill set and experience to successfully manage social investments. We are confident that this will change, as those with philanthropic experience learn the skills of investment and those from a commercial investing background learn to account for social returns.

Impact investing in developing nations is not easy. Cultural differences, educational differences, political instability, lack of infrastructure, volatile currencies and a challenging regulatory environment all create additional challenges. However, it is an immensely rewarding experience and, as we have already seen, it can be a powerful catalyst for change.

Inqo is working towards paying its first dividend to shareholders and so realising Dr Tan's vision of a public-listed investment fund, open to all, offering a meaningful social return whilst generating a close-to-market-rate financial return.

## References

Global Insight Southern Africa (2004), *Regional Economic Explorer*, Rican (Pty) Ltd: Johannesburg.

Inqo (2019), *Inqo: innovative social investments*, accessed 22 July 2019, https://inqo.co.za/.

Rhodes, C. (2018), *Business statistics*, briefing paper 06152, House of Commons Library, accessed on 09.05.2019, https://researchbriefings.parliament.uk/ResearchBriefing/Summary/SN06152.

Senbet, L. W. and Otchere, I. (2006), *Financial sector reforms in Africa: perspectives on issues and policies*, In F. Bourguignon and B. Pleskovic (eds), *Annual World Bank conference on development economics 2006: growth and integration*, World Bank: Washington, DC (pp. 81–120).

The World Bank (2007), *Making finance work for Africa*, accessed on 09 May 2019, http://documents.worldbank.org/curated/en/254441468009032125/pdf/388960Making0f10082136909101PUBLIC1.pdf.

Triodos Bank (2018), *A tipping point for ethical investing?*, www.triodos.co.uk/articles/2018/a-tipping-point-for-ethical-investing.

# 14 What do family offices and foundations want from social investment?

*Megan Preston and Gamil de Chadarevian*

In this chapter, **Megan Preston** (Director at RISE Beyond, a global consultancy platform) and **Gamil de Chadarevian** (founder and Director of GIST, and co-author of the Financial Times report), discuss social investment from the point of view of family offices and foundations.

## Introduction

In Chapter 8, we started to understand what social investors want from social investment and what their motivations for using it are. We also highlighted that family offices, trusts and foundations are often "first movers", using new investment tools and innovating way before the mainstream.

This previous chapter highlighted the Financial Times and GIST report (2017), *Investing for Global Impact*, as the premier survey on how family offices, and related trusts and foundations see social investment. It shows that, whereas three years ago family offices and high-net-worth individuals (HNWIs) were learning and taking advice, they are now making their first social investments in their portfolios.

This chapter provides a unique snapshot of social investment and family offices' motivation for using it.

## Wealth is not new, neither is charity

> Wealth is not new. Neither is charity. But the idea of using private wealth imaginatively, constructively and systematically to attack the fundamental problems of mankind is new.
>
> (John Gardner, Carnegie Corporation, quoted in Stanford Social Innovation Review, 2017)

Until recently, high-net-worth individuals spent the majority of their lives acquiring and amassing wealth and only considered giving back to society at the point of retirement or through philanthropy at their death. This is changing.

Chuck Feeney, an Irish-American businessman and philanthropist, advocates that "giving whilst alive is a lot more fun than giving when you're dead" (Atlantic Philanthropies, 2018).

This attitude to giving is picking up momentum. We're seeing the next generation with a heightened social conscience actively initiating family offices' and foundations' first forays into impact investing.

Social investment is seen as a particularly strong proposition for philanthropists as rather than just giving their money away, they can create blended returns on investment which mix both financial and social returns (Bugg-Levine and Emerson, 2011). Whereas philanthropy takes place once and the money has been spent, social investment allows capital to be reused. Family offices find the proposition of reinvesting and reusing their capital compelling.

The 2017 Financial Times and GIST report, *Investing for Global Impact* (2017, p. 6) saw a huge spike in the number of family offices and foundations considering that "the next generation of families is likely to apply a greater focus on social entrepreneurship and impact investing. 90 per cent, the highest level in the four-year history of this survey".

These are exciting times.

## The evolution of giving

The last few years have seen a profound shift in the way family offices are applying their investment wealth and how they are using their philanthropic giving. High-net-worth individuals, family offices and their organisations are experimenting with new hybrid investment models and private–public partnerships to tackle the current global challenges and meet the expectations of a growing population.

This evolution of giving – from philanthropy to the many innovative ways of social investing today – has inspired more active ownership and personal responsibility for the allocation of money. This shift is enhanced by a deeper sense of purpose and an increased understanding that new models for social investment can provide significant social, environmental and financial return.

Major events of the last century caused philanthropy to evolve and become more professionalised and global. "The growth of new nation states, coupled with global economic downturn prompted increased government involvement in social welfare resulting in the redefinition of the role of private philanthropy" (A history of modern philanthropy, 2017).

In more recent years, advancements in technology have enabled instant, global exchanges. Philanthropy and social investment have found new ways of reaching people, engaging and inspiring them to act.

High-net-worth individuals, family offices and foundations are known for their strong hold on the philanthropic world. Their engagement in philanthropy emerges out of their desire to give back and use their financial capital to support and impact a particular interest or passion through grants and donations.

However, these wealth holders are starting to recognise that philanthropy alone will not meet the needs of our twenty-first-century global challenges. The growth of social business and innovative business models offering scalable solutions to large-scale issues is attracting the interests of a range of investors including private wealth holders.

What are the new expectations? What really motivates family office investors and foundations? What do they think about social investments? It's this that we explore next.

> Impact investing offers an alternative to philanthropists who are looking to go beyond traditional grant-making and leverage the power of markets to create change.
>
> (Bridgespan, 2017)

**The most precious form of capital**

Daniel Madhavan, CEO of Impact Investing Australia, spoke in 2016 at the Philanthropy Australia Conference of "philanthropy being the most precious form of capital. However, for most funders, it's just 5% of their wealth. Imagine what could be done if 100% of available wealth is used to generate positive social impact?" Madhavan challenged those that fundamentally separated how they make money and how they then give it away, with the question: "How do we begin to express our values through our investment port-folios?" (Alliance Magazine, 2017).

## The opportunity for impact investing

In a relatively new industry, terms such as impact investing, social investing and responsible investing are thrown around without clarity and understanding. So, it's important to define how family offices and foundations see social investment.

Social entrepreneurs and investors engage for the primary purpose of supporting an organisation to have **positive social impact and often to innovate**. To be a social investment, some degree of financial return is essential, yet investors in this space often make some concession regarding return, to support the investee's mission.

To focus on the social, we use Brown and Swersky's (2012, p. 6) definition of social investment as most appropriate to family offices that are

> able to take risks on innovations with primarily social, rather than financial returns … This is especially the case of innovative social enterprise start-ups with untested business models … Social Investors may, therefore, be willing to invest in these organisations to support greater experimentation, and therefore, innovation in the social sector.

For wealth holders in this new industry, impact investing offers a unique opportunity, a chance to pioneer the way forward and catalyse sustainable change. If wealth holders were to focus their attention "on the 'sweet spot' between philanthropic grants that have no financial return and impact investments seeking market-rate returns", we might see significant advancement on some of the most financially underserved social issues (Stanford Social Innovation Review, 2015).

Family offices as social investors are attracted to organisations where they can build strong relationships and a shared vision.

Brown and Swersky (2012, p. 6) report that

> social investors share with their investees an overall desire to create social impact. By taking on social capital, organisations can align their mission with that of their finan-ciers. Where trade-offs emerge between financial and social returns, commercial investors are likely to force a resolution in favour of profit, whereas social investors would have a more balanced view.

## Revelations from *Investing for Global Impact 2017*

The *Investing for Global Impact 2017* report is a partnership between the Financial Times and GIST Initiatives, with the support and collaboration of Barclays (Financial Times and GIST, 2017).

The fourth edition attracted 246 respondents from 45 countries, representing a mixture of family office representatives, foundations and high-net-worth individuals.

This latest edition explores how these groups approach impact investing and identifies key trends and changes between previous reports and 2017.

## Key findings from the report

The 2017 "cohort of wealthy families" believed overwhelmingly that impact investing is "a more efficient use of funds than philanthropy" (p. 7). While the desire to see an appropriate financial return is also a driving factor, the focus is on exceeding the expected balance of social and financial returns (p. 6).

> What has been revealing is that key barriers preventing these family offices from allocating to impact investments – notably, scepticism around proving that positive social outcomes can be achieved without depleting financial returns – are, in fact, being proven by the reported experience of family offices and foundations from around the world who are engaged in impact investing.
>
> (p. 2)

In terms of performance, 75 per cent of respondents stated that the financial performance of their impact investments "met or exceeded their expectations" and 88 per cent reported this for their social returns. Great news for the future.

> 90% of responding family offices and foundations reported achieving a positive financial return from their impact investments over the past three years, with a typical average annual financial return of around 5%. This single digit overall financial performance is in line with returns provided by traditional asset classes.
>
> (Financial Times and GIST, 2017, p. 3)

Barriers include "lack of awareness of opportunities" and "lack of qualified advice", and insufficiently robust social impact measurements remain a key perceived barrier, preventing an increase in impact investment allocations.

The report highlights that more role models are needed to raise awareness of impact investing (p. 3) and 90 per cent said they expect the next generation of family members to "bring a greater focus on social entrepreneurship and impact investing" (p. 6).

The report comes to a positive conclusion that as large, well known foundations – such as Rockefeller Brothers Fund – increasingly choose to go public about their mission-aligned investing strategies, we are likely to see barriers being overcome and impact investment becoming more popular.

Figures 14.1, 14.2 and 14.3 are taken from the report and highlight successful attributes of impact investments in the mind of family offices, identify comparative average annual returns and consider the key barriers to the impact investing market (Financial Times and GIST, 2017).

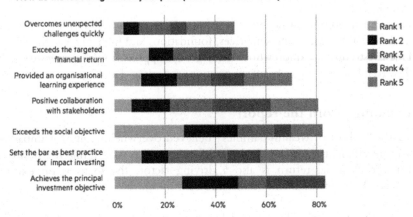

Figure 14.1 Successful attributes of social investments.

Source: Financial Times and GIST (2017).

Note
The last bar, *achieves the principal investment objective*, is focused on the expected blend of financial and social returns.

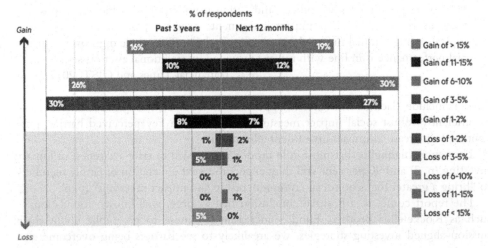

Figure 14.2 Average annual financial returns from impact investment: achieved (left) and expected (right).

Source: Financial Times and GIST (2017).

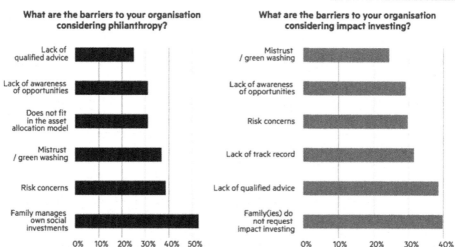

Base: Those not active in either impact investing or philanthropy

*Figure 14.3* Barriers to philanthropy and impact investing.
Source: Financial Times and GIST (2017).

## 2008 was a game changer

Following the financial crash, a movement has been sparked in which wealth is seen as a potential force for good.

In comparison with the environment just after the 2008 financial crisis, the emergent impact investment economy is driven by asset owners, entrepreneurs and investors seeking a positive impact with their investments. The financial crisis served as a wake-up call; it highlighted how greed and profit alone were not a path to fulfilment and success, particularly from a holistic social perspective.

In parallel, the "tough economic climate has left its mark on the psyche of the working wealthy, with a lack of confidence impacting their perceptions of wealth and appetite for risk" (Langan, 2009).

The consequence of the 2008 financial crisis has been a shift in our conventional financial wisdom, in the investment ecosystem and in the types of investments people are seeking. Equally, the upshot of a very low interest environment has meant a growing number of forward-looking investors willingly focusing on blended social and financial returns for their capital.

The average annual financial return for survey participants was 5%; …. this return is in line with traditional asset classes. This refutes the common preconception of a trade-off between a positive social return and a below market financial return.

(Financial Times and GIST, 2017, p. 3)

As more investors step into experimenting with this new form of investing, they start to see how they could match the financial returns they expect, and do good with their capital.

> Impact investing is no fad: 90% of responding family offices and foundations reported achieving a positive financial return from their impact investments over the past three years, with a typical average annual financial return of around 5%. This single digit overall financial performance is in line with returns provided by traditional asset classes. This survey clearly also refutes the common preconception that in order to generate positive social return, a below-market financial return (if any) must be accepted. Family offices and foundations are entering a "scaling-up" phase: one-third report being "active" in the space, holding multiple impact investments across asset classes or causes and 15% consider impact investing to be their "primary portfolio approach".
>
> (Financial Times and GIST, 2017, p. 3).

Family offices, foundations and individuals are setting the example for the future. In particular, social investment champions have redefined the meaning of wealth, the responsibility it brings and how it can be managed and deployed during one wealthy person's lifetime to generate social as well as financial returns. Their experimentation with pilot initiatives has started to inspire and encourage peers around the globe to engage in more productive philanthropy.

> In the period of global financial crisis, social investment was established as an alternative form of finance that aimed to fill gaps left by conventional finance.
>
> (Lyon, 2016, p. 187)

A stronger sense of shared responsibility is emerging. The remaining worry is that, once central banks begin raising interest rates and the prospect of greater and easier financial returns re-emerges, will investors revert to an investment strategy that favours financial returns over social outcomes?

We must continue to encourage experimentation and provide real case studies to support the success of impact investing. The change in mind-set for the expectations of investments will fundamentally shift the sense of responsibility investors have and take for their capital.

## Driving forces

Other important external driving forces are stimulating changes in investor behaviour. Technology and initiatives such as the United Nations Sustainable Development Goals are all helping to move the impact investment conversation forwards. Governments also have an important role in stimulating this nascent market. Table 14.1 shows some of the factors at play.

*Table 14.1* Driving forces in the impact investment market

| The United Nations | • 2015: launched the Sustainable Development Goals, to track progress against vast social and environmental challenges, like extreme poverty, inequality and climate change<br>• "Achieving the ambitious targets of the 2030 Agenda requires a revitalised and enhanced global partnership that brings together Governments, civil society, the private sector, the United Nations system and other actors" (United Nations, 2016)<br>• UN studies report that more than half of the impact-investing industry is intent on tracking returns directly against SDG-related targets. |
|---|---|
| Technology | • Advances in technology and open data are helping to push social investment forward<br>• The scalability of technology – and the ability to access it even in the most rural parts of the world – mean tech initiatives with a focus on social good have major potential impact<br>• Companies like M-Pesa – a mobile-based money transfer and microfinancing system in Kenya and Tanzania – are having profound social impact. Over 50% of the adult population in Kenya currently uses the M-Pesa service to send money and receive money (BBC News, 2010)<br>• That said, "there's currently a growing dissatisfaction with the way in which we're using, and developing, digital technologies for social good" (Shift Design, 2014)<br>• Technology continues to penetrate every element of our lives, yet we are still seeing only a proportion of this influence harnessed for social good. |
| Government | • In the UK, the government has supported social investment under the leadership of the G8; in other countries, the government has less will or ability to influence the fledgling investment market<br>• As public sector austerity results in cuts in funding, governments are facing increasing delays and difficulties in meeting the expectations of people and responding to the accelerating pace of change as well as the demand for social services<br>• Are we witnessing a transition from a welfare state to a welfare society? Wealth holders are taking back control and responsibility for their investments and social giving; they are stepping up and leading the way in the world of social investment. |

## Changing attitudes

The motivations and investment priorities of family offices and foundations have shifted.

(Financial Times and GIST, 2017, p. 15)

Investor motivation and changing attitudes were reviewed in the survey by Financial Times and GIST (p. 15). It highlighted that

This year, both the motivations and the investment priorities of family offices and foundations have shifted. A sense of "responsibility to make the world a better place" was top-ranked (at 25% of respondents) as the major motivation for allocating to impact investments, with "contribution to sustainable development" sliding into the second-highest ranking (20%) from top-ranking in last year's survey.

Figure 14.4 outlines the areas respondents had invested in or planned to invest in over the next 12 months.

The investment themes of "clean energy/green tech" and "education and skills" dominate portfolios, with a wide variety of themes making up the remainder. This may not be surprising. Global focus is on the impending consequences of climate change. The correlation between education and skill building in the workforce and wider economy and lower instances of poverty has been widely accepted. Both issues are pressing hard.

Money is beginning to move away from socially irresponsible companies. The fossil fuel divestment campaigns are an example of how society is beginning to request accountability for those companies that are doing more harm than good.

This change in focus helps to motivate other companies to recognise the market advantages of a more responsible and positive impact approach, thus creating the opportunity for more social investment.

> In several decades, I think we'll look back and say, "I can't believe we used to think companies should only be held account for their risk-adjusted return." Patently they all have an impact on society, we should be holding them to account for that and they should be reporting on it. That is the direction of travel and the more families that get involved and the more advisers that are asked to help, they can all be a part of "changing the world" in the direction we need.
>
> (Michele Giddins in Financial Times and GIST, 2017, p. 14)

## What do investors really want?

Figure 14.4 shows us what areas investors want to invest in, but it does not illuminate what those investors actually want from their investments.

The traditional view is that investors fall into two categories: impact-first or finance-first. Impact-first investors are viewed as "those who have a specific social or environmental return expectation, above a minimum level of impact, but can accept a lower rate of financial return" (Nicholls, Paton and Emerson, 2015, p. 226). At the other end of the spectrum sits the finance-first investor who has a minimum acceptable financial return with the social impact being seen as a secondary goal.

This view is being seen as less and less applicable as investors are less frequently having to choose between financial and social impact but are increasingly seeing the opportunity to achieve a social return alongside a financial one with neither return being marginalised. As Clarke *et al.* (2014) demonstrate, with 12 different examples ranging from microfinance in India to sustainable property in the UK, the idea that there must be a trade-off between social and financial returns is no longer such a valid viewpoint.

Despite this rosy outlook, the vast majority of investors still want to make a market-driven financial return from their social investments. Ninety per cent of the 2017 *Investing for Global Impact* survey respondents said that they achieved a positive financial return from their impact investments over the past three years. The fact that this figure is so high shows us that financial return is still a large factor for investors when considering social investment. Indeed, 72 per cent of respondents said that their due diligence process for social investment was no different than for any other investment (Financial Times and GIST, 2017, p. 6), highlighting that social investment is no longer something to be done on the side but is now treated as just another investment.

CHART 4

**Which themes are you invested in /
do you plan to invest in? (%)**

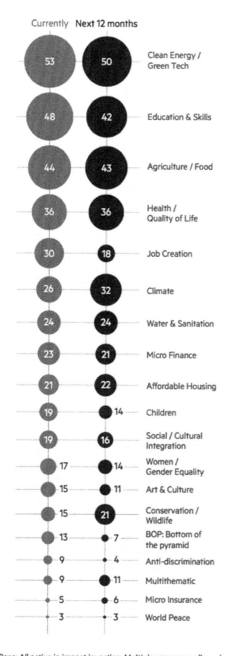

Currently   Next 12 months

| | | |
|---|---|---|
| 53 | 50 | Clean Energy / Green Tech |
| 48 | 42 | Education & Skills |
| 44 | 43 | Agriculture / Food |
| 36 | 36 | Health / Quality of Life |
| 30 | 18 | Job Creation |
| 26 | 32 | Climate |
| 24 | 24 | Water & Sanitation |
| 23 | 21 | Micro Finance |
| 21 | 22 | Affordable Housing |
| 19 | 14 | Children |
| 19 | 16 | Social / Cultural Integration |
| 17 | 14 | Women / Gender Equality |
| 15 | 11 | Art & Culture |
| 15 | 21 | Conservation / Wildlife |
| 13 | 7 | BOP: Bottom of the pyramid |
| 9 | 4 | Anti-discrimination |
| 9 | 11 | Multithematic |
| 5 | 6 | Micro Insurance |
| 3 | 3 | World Peace |

Base: All active in impact investing. Multiple responses allowed.

*Figure 14.4* Which themes are you invested in or do you plan to invest in?
Source: Financial Times and GIST (2017).

Investors are using a wide range of different investment types to achieve social impact. This shows us that it is the financial and social returns that are important to investors, rather than the vehicle or tool for achieving this. Investors are also being innovative in how they create this impact.

Ultimately, the best way to know what an investor really wants is to have good communication and to be open and honest with them about what both parties are hoping to achieve.

## Vision for the future

Globalisation means that, now more than ever, people are working across borders, cultures, religions, races and genders.

To prepare for the challenges ahead of us, we can no longer separate how we make our money and how we give it away. It needs to be acknowledged that all investments have impact: some positive, some negative.

We are moving in the right direction. There are many successful examples of social investment having significant positive impact with acceptable financial returns. By way of example, Unilever's products address sanitation issues in the slums of India, yet also generate good profits for corporate stakeholders. Advancements in the methods for sustainable farming, social housing, clean technology and financial products all help to showcase the promise of this process of investing.

A social finance vision for the future needs to call for some key developments:

**A joint and coordinated effort:** Only a joint and coordinated effort between governments, civil society, the private sector and other stakeholders will catalyse the change in our world that is so desperately needed.

**Focused and intentional investment:** For much of our existence on this planet, transformation has been a steady process. Today, we experience increasing disruptive innovation across all sectors. In order to deal with this pace of change and prepare for the potential consequences of development, we need focused and intentional investment.

**Deeper sense of responsibility:** We can gain confidence from the stories and case studies highlighting that humanity is beginning to feel and acknowledge a deeper sense of responsibility. As well as from the "we're in it together" attitude that's needed if we are to effect change.

**Unlocking new capital sources:** The massive scale of our problems far exceeds the resources currently available to us. We need innovative business models to unlock new capital sources that will complement government funds and deliver new solutions.

**Change in mind-set:** It's time for a more holistic approach, one where positive impact starts at the beginning of the supply chain and generates an inclusive and sustainable product or service. One which meets the social and environmental needs of our planet, as well as generating reasonable financial returns. This anticipated change in mind-set championed by social entrepreneurs will contribute to improving the quality of life of communities.

We need to adapt our horizon and expectations to a world in the near future with a growing population of eight billion people. There has never been a better time to accelerate progress and have a profound impact on and around the world.

> We must continually remind ourselves, as Pope Francis did to an audience at Davos, "Ensure humanity is served by wealth, not ruled by it."

(The Independent, 2014)

## References and bibliography

A History of Modern Philanthropy (2017), *Global Outlook of Giving*, accessed 20 October 2018, www.historyofgiving.org/1930-1980/.

Alliance Magazine (2017), *Impacting Investing: The Future of Philanthropy?*, accessed 20 October 2018, www.alliancemagazine.org/blog/impacting-investing-future-philanthropy/.

Atlantic Philanthropies (2018), *Giving while Living. Engage Now. Give Today. Change Tomorrow*, accessed 20 October 2018, www.atlanticphilanthropies.org/giving-while-living.

BBC News (2010), *M-Pesa: Kenya's Mobile Wallet Revolution*, accessed 20 October 2018, www.bbc.co.uk/news/business-11793290.

Bridgespan (2017), *What Is Impact Investing and Why Should or Shouldn't Philanthropists Consider It?*, accessed 20 October 2018, www.bridgespan.org/insights/library/philanthropy/frequently-asked-questions-about-philanthropy/what-is-impact-investing-and-why-should-or-shouldn.

Brown, A. and Swersky, A. (2012), *The First Billion: A Forecast of Social Investment Demand*, Boston Consulting Group, accessed 20 October 2018, www.bcg.com/documents/file115598.pdf.

Bugg-Levine, A. and Emerson, J. (2011), *Impact Investing: Transforming How We Make Money While Making a Difference*, Jossey-Bass (Wiley).

Clarke, C., Emerson, J. and Thornley, B. (2014), *The Impact Investor: Lessons in Leadership and Strategy for Collaborative Capitalism*, Jossey-Bass.

Financial Times and GIST (2017), *Investing for Global Impact 2017*, Financial Times, accessed 20 October 2017, www.gistltd.com/uploads/global-impact/investing-for-global-impact-report-2017/investing-for-global-impact-final-report-2017.pdf.

Langan, S. (2009), *Has the Recession Changed Today's Perception of Wealth?*, Personal Finance TV Show Interview, accessed 20 October 2018, www.broadcastexchange.tv/live/has_the_recession_changed_todays_perception_of_wealth.

Lyon, F. (2016), Lending to Social Ventures. In Lehner, O. M.. (Ed.), *Routledge Handbook of Social And Sustainable Finance*, London, Routledge.

Nicholls, A., Paton, R. and Emerson, J. (2015), *Social Finance*, Oxford University Press.

Shift Design (2014), *The 3 Strands of Value Vital to Social Tech Ventures*, accessed 20 October 2018, www. shiftdesign.org.uk/the-3-strands-of-value-vital-to-social-tech-ventures/.

Stanford Social Innovation Review (2015), *Philanthropy's New Frontier: Impact Investing*, accessed 20 October 2018, www.ssir.org/articles/entry/philanthropys_new_frontierimpact_investing.

Stanford Social Innovation Review (2017), *Innovating Philanthropy*, accessed 20 October 2018, www.ssir.org/articles/entry/innovating_philanthropy.

The Independent (2014), *Pope Francis Tells Davos: "Ensure Humanity Is Served by Wealth, not Ruled by it"*, accessed 20 October 2018, www.independent.co.uk/news/world/politics/pope-francis-tells-davos-business-leaders-ensure-humanity-is-served-by-wealth-not-ruled-by-it-9076618.html.

United Nations (2016), *Goal 17: Partnerships for the Goals*, accessed 20 October 2018, www.unstats.un.org/sdgs/report/2016/goal-17/.

# 14a  Case study

## Charities Aid Foundation and St Mungo's

*Holly Piper*

This case study is written by **Holly Piper**, Head of CAF Venturesome, which since 2002 has made more than 570 social investments totalling £46 million to a wide range of social enterprises and charities.

---

### Social impact bonds (SIBs)

- A social impact bond (SIB) is a contract to pay for an improvement in social welfare.
- SIBs rely on attracting initial investor funding, usually from social funds or philanthropists, which will be repaid by a commissioner (often the government) on delivery of a successful outcome.
- A service provider, often a charity, undertakes to deliver an intervention to a group within a community, funded by working capital supplied by investors.
- SIBs operate on a payment-by-results (PBR) model, meaning that the service provider must meet predetermined social targets in order to secure repayment, typically outcomes.
- If the intervention does not meet expectations, the commissioner doesn't pay, or partly pays, meaning the investor can lose money.

---

The SIB model has given us more opportunity to work with clients in a personalised and holistic way and we have been able to deliver the service faster and more effectively. I believe that this approach and the creativeness of our team has made things happen for our clients.

(Dobrochna Zajas, St Mungo's Street Impact Outreach Worker, in St Mungo's Broadway, 2015, p. 56)

### Mayor of London Social Impact Bond

In 2012, CAF Venturesome was approached by St Mungo's Broadway (then St Mungo's) regarding a new SIB backed by the Greater London Authority.

Formed by the merger of two long-standing homelessness charities in 2014, St Mungo's Broadway had almost 50 years' experience in helping rough sleepers off the streets.

In November 2012, the coalition government officially launched the GLA (Greater London Authority) Rough Sleeping Social Impact Bond, developed in partnership with the Mayor of London, St Mungo's Broadway and Thames Reach, another London-based homelessness charity.

This SIB aimed to reduce rough sleeping and help people get into stable accommodation, find employment and manage their health better.

The interventions aimed to reduce long-term dependency on the state, thereby saving taxpayer funds on emergency care and short-term solutions. A target cohort of around 800 identified rough sleepers was equally divided between the two providers, St Mungo's Broadway and Thames Reach.

> The payment-by-results approach has allowed the providers flexibility to innovate. In particular, by not issuing a service specification and instead focusing on outcomes, providers have been able to develop approaches that respond to the needs of service users.
>
> (Cabinet Office, 2012)

## The SIB met CAF Venturesome's criteria for social investment

CAF Venturesome was interested in becoming an investor in the SIB scheme. It used three key criteria to assess the viability of the investment:

1   social impact
2   financial risk
3   strategic impact.

The **social impact** was evident; St Mungo's was assigned a target of assisting around 400 rough sleepers to move off the streets by the end of the project. Additional targets sought to move clients into secure accommodation, place some into volunteering or employment and reconnect others with their home countries.

**Financial risk** was mitigated by the fact that St Mungo's took on the role of equity partner. If the project could exceed expectations, it would reap the rewards; however, if it proved ineffective, St Mungo's would have been the first to lose its stake. This had the dual benefit of minimising risk for the lenders and providing further incentives for St Mungo's to succeed.

The potential **strategic impact** was also assessed to be high, given the relative newness of the SIB model and the implications it could have for future outcome-oriented initiatives.

CAF Venturesome, Triodos Corporate Finance and several individual social investors raised the £650,000 upfront working capital required by the charity. St Mungo's Broadway contributed an equity stake of around £200,000, giving the project £850,000 investment, to be repaid by the Greater London Authority on delivery of results.

Figure 14a.1 shows the structure used to deliver the SIB, including a special purpose vehicle (SPV) established for this.

## How did they do it?

In putting together the plan for the SIB, St Mungo's was able to build upon lessons and feedback from decades of successful work with the homeless.

*Figure 14a.1* St Mungo's Broadway investment structure.

After identifying the limitations of existing provisions, they settled on four essential factors that could enhance the project's effect:

1   **Extra time for staff** to spend with clients in order to provide in-depth, personalised assessment and to focus on sustained outcomes.
2   **Greater choice for clients** in terms of the staff, service and housing that best suited their recovery. Also giving them dignity by respecting what they actually wanted in terms of support.
3   **Comprehensive care and support** to ensure interventions encompassed all aspects of a client's recovery.
4   **Personal budgets** to be spent on tailoring support to clients' needs.

Many of the St Mungo's street impact outreach workers expressed a frustration with the general awareness of the need to act holistically being undermined by time and budget constraints – a complaint that was effectively addressed in this model.

> Many clients' lives do not fit into a support plan or risk assessment … support should not be restricted to the transfer of knowledge from worker to client, but collaboration between the two.
>
> (Harry Smith, Street Impact Outreach Worker, St Mungo's Broadway, 2015, p. 25)

In this project, outreach workers were given full flexibility to act in the best interests of the individual client, allowing them to go above and beyond the usual steps taken to persuade a rough sleeper to move off the streets.

Every outreach worker was assigned a client list, which they maintained for the project duration. This was engineered to provide each client with a sense of stability, avoiding the sense of being shunted from one service to another. "What was crucial for the success of SIB was that clients had the same worker available to support them throughout the project, no matter that their other support networks may have been in a state of flux" (St Mungo's Broadway, 2015, p. 43).

The unusual time and budget allocated to the project allowed it to empower street impact outreach workers and put trust in them to act independently and creatively in solving each individual case:

> After 18 months of the project, more and more clients were in their own flats and the importance of encouraging meaningful activity ... became more apparent, in order to foster confidence and self-worth and prevent clients becoming bored, isolated and potentially returning to the streets.
>
> (Shayeena Mamujee, Street Impact Outcomes Officer in St Mungo's Broadway, 2015, p. 67)

## Personal stories

In March 2015, St Mungo's Broadway published *Street Impact: Stories from the Street*, documenting a selection of case studies from the SIB so far (St Mungo's Broadway, 2015).

The stories provided compelling support for the long-term, personalised help enabled by the SIB model. In some cases, this innovative approach allowed the team to put an end to decades of addiction, insecurity and sleeping rough.

> Eric is in his late 70s. Homeless for the majority of his adult life, he had abandoned social housing on several occasions. His Street Outreach Worker, Michael, worked closely with Eric to help him find accommodation he was happy with, accepting his determination to avoid hostels, where he had previously had bad experiences. Eric now lives in his own flat by the sea in Cornwall, where he has two cats, is connected to local support services and enjoys long walks.
>
> (St Mungo's Broadway, 2015, p. 44)

For other clients, employment had been crucial to rediscovering a sense of worth and removing inducements to return to rough sleeping.

> Petr, who came to the UK from Latvia in search of work, became homeless after losing his construction job, which had already paid less than minimum wage. Alcohol dependency and shame at his circumstances prevented Petr from contacting his family. After a sustained intervention from Street Outreach Worker, Svetlana Lopotenco, Petr was able to move into accommodation and resume communications with his family. He had held down a part-time job for six months so far at the time of Street Impact's publication.
>
> (St Mungo's Broadway, 2015, p. 68)

## Back home

The 2015 government survey also found that in London, 43 per cent of people sleeping rough are from the UK while 36 per cent are from Central and Eastern Europe, with 18 per cent of the total from Romania (Department for Communities and Local Government, 2015, p. 6).

This had particular significance for the "reconnect" arm of the SIB, which successfully assisted 49 homeless people back to their home countries.

It's important to make a distinction between involuntary deportation and the practice of St Mungo's, which offered this option only to those who desired to return home but needed financial and practical help to do so. Outreach workers able to speak the native languages of their clients played a crucial role in facilitating these voluntary reconnections.

The flexible budget allocated to caseworkers enabled one street outreach worker to purchase a wheelchair for a client who had been hospitalised due to a car accident in the weeks preceding his reconnection. She was also able to accompany him on his journey home, ensuring that he suffered as little distress as possible and arranging for accommodation with family members to begin as soon as the client left the local hospital.

## Impact

Throughout the three years of the SIB, homeless rates rose steadily across the UK, but most acutely in the capital.

Government figures showed a 27 per cent rise in the number of rough sleepers in London between autumn 2014 and 2015, based on a one-night snapshot count.

The number of rough sleepers with an identified mental health support need has more than tripled in recent years, rising from 711 in 2009–10 to 2,343 in 2014–15.

Against this challenging backdrop, the SIB achieved mixed success in meeting its targets, with over-performance in sustained accommodation offsetting under-performance in reducing rough sleeping, reconnection and employment outcomes (DCLG, 2015).

Against a target of assisting 168 people to move into accommodation, St Mungo's Broadway concluded the project with 184 formerly homeless people in accommodation. This was a remarkable achievement, particularly given that the initial target was thought of as ambitious.

The main work of intervention finished in 2015, although street impact outreach workers continued to monitor and support many of the clients who were still adjusting to life indoors or were not yet in secure accommodation.

Investors were repaid in full and on time.

## The organisation's wider practices

The SIB had an impact on the organisation's wider practices. It challenged its standard narratives about what it was possible to achieve with clients who are rough sleeping and how budgets are designed to support staff teams in achieving outcomes.

> The notion of investment became part our team conversations: investing time with our Clients to help them rebuild their sense of self-worth whilst investing financially

in deposits, training courses, transport etc. to remove the many practical barriers that came in the way. The SIB gave us the autonomy and the means to achieve the right balance between the two. It changed people's lives.

(Kathleen Sims, former SIB co-manager, now St Mungo's Head of Outreach)

## Conclusion

The SIB model provided funding for an innovative, well-structured social initiative, which has had a demonstrative effect on the lives of many individuals.

While there are still refinements and improvements to be made, the evidence thus far suggests that SIBs could play a crucial role in widening access to working capital for charities, enabling them to deliver effective social interventions.

## References

Cabinet Office (2012), *New boost to help Britain's most vulnerable young adults and the homeless.* Accessed 24 June 2019, www.gov.uk/government/news/new-boost-to-help-britain-s-most-vulnerable-young-adults-and-the-homeless.

DCLG, Department for Communities and Local Government (2015), *Qualitative evaluation of the London homelessness social impact bond, second interim report.* Accessed 24 June 2019, www.gov.uk/government/uploads/system/uploads/attachment_data/file/414787/Qualitative_evaluation_of_the_London_homelessness_SIB.pdf.

Department for Communities and Local Government (2015), *Rough sleeping statistics online.* Accessed 24 June 2019, www.gov.uk/government/uploads/system/uploads/attachment_data/file/503015/Rough_Sleeping_Autumn_2015_statistical_release.pdf.

St Mungo's Broadway (2015), *Street Impact: stories from the street – holistic approaches to lasting recovery.* Accessed 9 June 2020, https://www.mungos.org/app/uploads/2018/05/SIB_Booklet_Final_June_2015.pdf [St Mungo's Broadway became St Mungo's again from 2016].

# 15 Critiquing social finance

## Are there alternative models?

*Richard Hazenberg and Simon Denny*

Dr **Richard Hazenberg** and Professor **Simon Denny** of the Institute for Social Innovation & Impact, University of Northampton, share their learnings from the Investment Readiness Support Programme, a good indicator of the readiness of the sector to take on social investment and the inherent barriers.

## Introduction

The social investment market in the UK is often held up as a world leading sector due to its depth of social purpose organisations, its strong financial sector (Evenett and Richter, 2011) and the strong political support for the "social investment market" that has come from successive UK governments (Nicholls, 2010a, 2010b).

Indeed, Robinson (March 2016) estimated that the social investment market in the UK is worth approximately £1.5 billion and involves over 3,500 individual investment deals. This scale and scope, when combined with the significant policy support that has existed for the social investment market (Nicholls, 2010a, 2010b), has created a momentum within the UK towards a focus on investment as the main means to drive scale and growth in the Third Sector.

This can be viewed as part of the wider "marketisation" of the Third Sector that academic research has identified as the normative policy narrative (McKay *et al.*, 2015). These policies have included:

- the creation of Big Society Capital (Cabinet Office, March 2012);
- the introduction of Social Investment Tax Relief (HM Treasury, November 2016);
- and the revisions to the state-aid "de minimis" European rules that the UK government engaged in (Department for Business, Innovation and Skills, July 2015).

This rapid growth has left academic research behind, as practitioners have accelerated their development of new products and extended the scope and number of investment deals in the UK Third Sector (Dagger and Nicholls, 2016). This has led to a paucity of (much needed) academic critique within the field of social investment, particularly in relation to the UK model.

Indeed, while some academic papers are now seeking to explore alternatives to the Anglo-Saxon model of social investment (see Michelucci, 2016 for a good exploration of the alternatives to the Anglo-Saxon paradigm), there remains an acute need for further research that seeks to theoretically critique the social investment market and also provide empirical data on the impact that social investment has upon the sustainability and growth of the Third Sector in the UK.

> Sustainability should be the main focus of government policy. Social investment is merely one element in this wider policy strategy.

## The UK Third Sector and social investment

The prominence of the Third Sector in UK policy narratives has grown significantly over the last 20 years, as it has been increasingly viewed as a legitimate deliverer of public services and as a panacea for social problems that can unburden the welfare state (Austin *et al.*, 2006; Amin, 2009; Haugh and Kitson, 2007).

This shift in how government interacts with the Third Sector has seen the state overtly promote an idealised vision of a sector that is more business-like, entrepreneurial and better governed (Macmillan, 2011; Wells, 2012). The UK Third Sector includes over 160,000 "voluntary, community and social" (VCSE) organisations, which contribute an estimated £43.8 billion to the UK economy and employ over 827,000 people (NCVO, 2016).

The UK government defines VCSEs as including "small local community and voluntary groups, registered charities both large and small, foundations, trusts and the growing number of social enterprises and co-operatives" (Department of Health, July 2011).

However, the rise of the Big Society policy narrative over the last six years has led to an increasing focus on marketising the VCSE sector (McKay *et al.*, 2015), particularly through the continued encouragement to focus on commercial revenue generation that has existed for the last 30 years (Eikenberry, 2009).

That said, there has been a shift in the focus of this commercial revenue generation, towards a model that encourages VCSEs to focus on investment as a means to achieve sustainability, scale the business, and achieve greater impact (Wells, 2012; Hazenberg, Seddon and Denny, 2014; Moore *et al.*, 2012).

This policy shift has seen increased policy support for social investment, including programmes such as Futurebuilders, the Social Enterprise Investment Fund and most recently the establishment of Big Society Capital. It has also led to the emergence of a network of intermediary social investment organisations that have become known as "social investment finance intermediaries" (SIFIs) (Hazenberg *et al.*, 2014).

This growth in the social investment market has in large part been driven by the state. Indeed, UK government policy has sought to encourage the growth of the social investment market through:

- the capitalisation of the marketplace (e.g. Big Society Capital, Bridges Ventures, Big Issue Invest) (Michelucci, 2016);
- the encouragement of public sector investment and contracting with VCSEs through changes in procurement and purchasing legislation (the 2012 Social Value Act) (Spear *et al.*, 2015);
- support for public service mutuals (spin-outs) that has resulted in whole public services becoming VCSE organisations (Hall, Alcock and Millar, 2012; Hazenberg and Hall, 2016); and
- regulatory framework changes such as the Social Investment Tax Relief (HM Treasury, November 2016).

These policy frameworks have also been supported by other network stakeholders including foundations, investors and large Third Sector funders (Michelucci, 2016). These include specialist network facilitators who bring together investors, business consultants and other key stakeholders as a means to support VCSEs to become "investment ready" (for more on this concept see the next section).

This has led to numerous programmes being launched in the last seven years including:

• Big Issue Invest Corporate Social Venturing Fund (https://bigissueinvest.com/corporate-social-venturing-programme/);
• the Big Lottery Fund Big Potential Programme (www.sibgroup.org.uk/big-potential#:~:text=What%20is%20the%20fund%3F,to%20deliver%20greater%20social%20impact);
• the Access Foundation Reach Fund (www.reachfund.org.uk/);
• and the Investment and Contract Readiness Fund (ICRF) (Ronicle and Fox, 2015).

Despite operational differences between these programmes, they all share the same strategic focus – that is to increase the investment readiness of VCSEs and increase the "deal flow" of social investments in the UK (or at least in England and Wales).

However, this focus on social investment as the main means of driving VCSE sector growth and sustainability is reflective of the dominant neo-liberal paradigm that exists in Third Sector policy in the UK, and which has led to the aforementioned wider focus on the marketisation of the sector (Dey and Teasdale, 2016; McKay *et al.*, 2015).

It is important that academic research seeks to critique this narrative where applicable, in order to understand whether a focus on investment readiness and social investment is really the best means for delivering scale and sustainability in the VCSE sector.

## Investment readiness and sustainability

Gregory *et al.* (2012, p. 6) define "investment readiness" as "an investee being perceived to possess the attributes, which makes them an investible proposition by an appropriate investor for the finance they are seeking".

The process of seeking investment and becoming "investment ready" begins at the point that an organisation realises that its resources are insufficient for its start-up, growth or sustainability needs (Silver *et al.*, 2010).

While, historically, there has been a lack of academic focus on "investment readiness" in the Third Sector, this has changed in recent years as researchers have sought to identify what investment readiness means to social investors and policy-makers (McWade, 2012; Hazenberg *et al.*, 2014).

This research has identified that within the supply and intermediary sectors of the "social investment market", investment readiness is seen as constituting:

• financial sustainability;
• robust governance structures;
• broad management skill sets;
• an ability to increase social impact alongside the growth of the business; and
• a willingness to seek investment (McWade, 2012; Hazenberg *et al.*, 2014).

However, these conceptions of investment readiness are investor focused and fail to take into account the perceptions (and more importantly the needs) of VCSEs.

In addition, the prior research fails to identify whether the marketisation of the VCSE sector through social investment is really the best way to drive the growth and sustainability of the sector. Indeed, while the development of demand-led capacity building in markets is to be welcomed, there is the possibility that such schemes can favour the already well-resourced organisations within a market (Macmillan, 2013) and hence overlook those that have greatest need. Although it could be argued that this is the aim of such policies.

Nevertheless, it is important to also acknowledge that developing investment readiness and securing social investment can be very beneficial for VCSEs, as it builds organisational independence and resilience (Sakarya *et al.*, 2012).

Investment readiness support can allow VCSEs to:

- strengthen their business model;
- improve their financial forecasting;
- identify new (or better understand existing) market opportunities;
- improve staff and management skills and capacity; and
- diversify their income streams.

However, these changes to the VCSE's core model of mission delivery provide challenges to management teams (Bugg-Levine and Emerson, 2011) that often require restructuring or skill-set injections at board level. An inability to successfully undertake these changes often causes problems for VCSEs seeking finance from social investors, as they do not have robust governance structures, skilled management teams and detailed business plans in place (Hines, 2005; Hill, 2011; Howard, 2012).

Through this analytical lens, it can be argued in many ways that investment readiness and sustainability are effectively the same concept, as the latter is also based upon organisational resilience through the development of robust organisational structures, enhanced marketing strategies, network and partnership formation, and increased commercial revenue (Jenner, 2016).

Indeed, Sharir, Lerner and Yitshaki identify social venture sustainability as being dependent on the ability to "gain resources and legitimacy, create co-operation between institutions and develop internal managerial and organisational capabilities" (2009, p. 90).

As Jenner (2016) notes, the development of social venture sustainability occurs through the facilitation of access to the most appropriate resources and networks that allow the VCSE to grow commercially and deliver greater social impact (and hence increase legitimacy).

While investment readiness and sustainability support for the VCSE sector are to be welcomed, the wider policy narrative around social investment ignores the needs of the majority of VCSEs in a way that can be dangerous to the future sustainability of the sector.

## The Investment Readiness Support Programme

The rest of this chapter now considers results and learnings from a major national investment readiness programme.

The programme seeks to improve the sustainability, capacity and scale of VCSE organisations, to enable them to deliver greater social impact in their communities and beyond.

The programme also seeks to specifically support organisations looking to grow through securing repayable investment, as well as to buy in specialist support from a range of expert "providers" to improve their investment readiness. It offers grant funding of between £20,000 and £75,000 to VCSEs towards these aims so that they can undertake in-depth investment readiness work with approved providers.

As the focus of the programme is on the smaller-end of the VCSE sector – those seeking less than £500,000 of investment – the sample in this research is inherently biased. However, given the focus on sustainability issues and investment readiness, this is potentially a strength, as it allows the research to focus on the elements of the sector often overlooked by traditional interventions, namely the less well-resourced VCSEs (Macmillan, 2013).

The programme has **seven distinct phases**:

- **Online registration:** Through the programme web portal
- **Online diagnostic tool:** Completed by the VCSE, this online tool automatically assesses investment readiness
- **1:1 support advisor session:** Carried out by a specialist programme advisor to further assess investment readiness
- **Selection of a "support provider":** The VCSE selects from a list of "approved providers"
- **Submission of a grant application:** Detailing the investment readiness work to be completed and the grant funding required
- **Assessment of grant application:** Applications can be rejected, accepted or asked for revisions and resubmission
- **Post-grant work:** Completed with the support provider to develop investment readiness (if successful).

### VCSE investment readiness

Given the focus of the programme on the smaller-scale element of the VCSE sector, the survey data contained in Tables 15.1 and 15.2 – especially in relation to turnover and investment need – is not surprising.

The research highlighted the following challenges the VCSE sector faces in becoming investment ready and sustainable, especially in relation to the low profitability of the sector:

- VCSEs are relatively reliant on just two income sources for over two-thirds of their income and over half of their income comes from public sector sources
- There are also issues with VCSE reliance on volunteers, with their ratio of total staff to volunteers being 1:4
- VCSEs are much better capitalised, having on average a debt to asset ratio of only 25.9 per cent

*Table 15.1* VCSE demographic data

| Demographic variable | | N | Mean | Median | SD | Min | Max |
|---|---|---|---|---|---|---|---|
| VCSE age (years) | | 507 | 14.09 | 7.81 | 16.72 | <1 | 112 |
| Turnover | | 506 | £1.18m | £277,500 | £3.15m | £0 | £41.3m |
| Net profitability | | 357 | £30,194 | £3,000 | £85,495 | £−79,924 | £997,637 |
| Total assets | | 503 | £927,668 | £109,079 | £4.05m | £0 | £60.64m |
| Total debt | | 454 | £240,386 | £17,025 | £776,123 | £0 | £10.84m |
| Investment needs | | 511 | £599,555 | £250,000 | £4.15m | £0 | £90m |
| Income diversity (% of income from top 2 customers) | | 480 | 66.3% | 70% | 26.5% | 1% | 100% |
| Public sector reliance (% of income from public sector) | | 410 | 51.4% | 50% | 31.8% | 0% | 100% |
| Staffing | FT | 518 | 14 | 3 | 48 | 0 | 847 |
| | PT | 516 | 15 | 3 | 49 | 0 | 847 |
| | Volunteers | 513 | 127 | 10 | 1,605 | 0 | 35,000 |

Note
N < 527 as some organisations did not complete all parts of the diagnostic tool.

*Table 15.2* VCSE investment readiness diagnostic tool (DT) scores

| VCSE DT scores | | | |
|---|---|---|---|
| Factor | N | IR score | SD |
| Investment readiness score | 467 | 53.7% | 18.8% |

Note
N < 527 for the overall data as some organisations did not complete all parts of the diagnostic tool.

- VCSEs are poorly placed to secure investment, or to be classed as investment ready, as they do not have the requisite financial sustainability
- The VCSE sector is far from meeting the investment readiness expectations of the social investment sector
- The median investment need of the VCSEs is nearly 100 per cent of their turnover, a relatively significant amount in investment terms
- In relation to investment readiness, the VCSE sector struggles with leadership and governance, as many smaller organisations do not have managers with the requisite skills or the formalised process in place to provide effective governance.

When looking at the figures presented in Tables 15.1 and 15.2, it is unsurprising that the vast majority of social investment still involves secured lending (77.5 per cent of all lending to VCSEs and 51.3 per cent of all social investment deals excluding "profit-with-purpose" deals) (Robinson, March 2016).

The sector as a whole has the assets to provide security, if not the financial performance to give investors confidence on unsecured or equity investments.

In addition, as many VCSEs are charitable organisations (54.4 per cent of this sample), the skills and capabilities of trustees are also important. These were issues that were identified both in the diagnostic tool (DT) and also in the qualitative data, with DT respondents identifying sub-optimal performance in relation to:

- Board cohesion
- Board financial skills
- Leadership skills
- Board strategic control
- Senior staff experience

This is shown in Figure 15.1.

> We haven't really paid that much attention to our governance systems and how we manage ourselves over the years because we've just been two blokes doing what we do.
> (Participant 17 – Unsuccessful VCSE – Theme "Investment Readiness and Sustainability")

## Social impact delivered by VCSEs

The data gathered identifies that social impact measurement is another area that the VCSE participants do not perform well in, as they rate themselves at between 46 and 49 per cent for their performance management, social impact measurement fairness and dissemination of social impact data, again against an investment ready threshold of 70 per cent (see Figure 15.2).

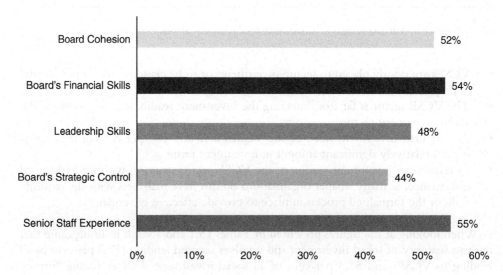

*Figure 15.1* Survey responses identify sub-optimal experience in governance and leadership in specific areas.

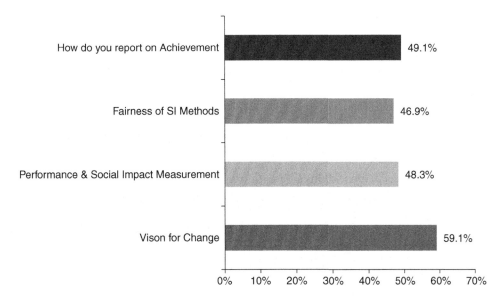

*Figure 15.2* Responses highlight sub-optimal social impact measurement practices against a benchmark of 70%.

As prior research has identified the ability to be able to measure and report social impact as a key feature of investment readiness in the social investment sector (Hazenberg *et al.*, 2014), this skill gap in the VCSE sample identifies further issues for the sector in securing social investment. Indeed, this was also an issue articulated within the qualitative data, with interviewees discussing the lack of robust social impact measurement frameworks as an issue. As one programme provider noted:

> I think with [VCSE], they came in and they were kind of like, "Social Impact, what's that?" you know. And so, I think what we managed to do in that six months was to create a framework for them … to help them understand what their social impact might be. So, what we were trying to do was to pull out what the social impact, to get them to understand what the social impact of them as individual [centres] was and then actually how the consortium, the impact in terms of the consortium worked alongside that.
> (Participant 13 – Provider – Theme "Investment Readiness and Sustainability")

## Sustainability focus and social investment

Investment readiness and sustainability are closely intertwined concepts (Sharir, Lerner and Yitshaki, 2009; Jenner, 2016). When exploring the investment readiness problems facing the VCSEs on this programme, it's clear that the sector is still lacking in areas including:

- robust governance and management structures/skillsets (Hines, 2005; Hill, 2011; Howard, 2012; Hazenberg *et al.*, 2014);
- financial performance (McWade, 2012; Hazenberg *et al.*, 2014);
- and social impact measurement and reporting (McWade, 2012; Hazenberg *et al.*, 2014).

However, dealing with these issues has a wider importance than just investment readiness, as these are also factors that relate to sustainability. Indeed, issues related to governance and management skill sets are directly related to "legitimacy" and the development of "internal capabilities" (Sharir, Lerner and Yitshaki, 2009). Improved financial performance and resource acquisition, on the other hand, are related to co-operation/co-production, network formation and social impact delivery (Sharir, Lerner and Yitshaki, 2009; Jenner, 2016).

These are all areas that are required for any organisation to grow and even more critical for VCSEs that have to balance commercial and social missions (Bugg-Levine and Emerson, 2011).

> We have quite a forward-thinking board of trustees of the charity, they had rightly recognised that the income streams were changing and that we needed to move with the times, and we needed to be proactive.
>
> (Participant 20 – Successful VCSE – Theme
> "Investment Readiness and Sustainability")

The awarding of grants on the programme in question (of which 124 have been awarded in the first two years) have unsurprisingly tended to fund VCSEs to develop their social impact measurement, increase income diversification and improve organisational/governance structures (58.1 per cent of all grant awards).

VCSE motives for seeking grant funding and wanting social investment include:

- social/commercial scaling
- consolidation of previous growth
- organisational independence/flexibility.

If the overall *sustainability* of the sector is to be improved, there's a clear need for programmes offering this type of support to the VCSE sector. However, this is very different to a sole focus on securing social investment, which is not suitable for all VCSEs. Indeed, it is about finding the most appropriate mechanisms and resource types to facilitate sustainability and growth (Jenner, 2016), rather than presupposing that social investment is the panacea for all of the VCSE sector's problems.

> I think also it's just worth pointing out that, in my experience at least, any organisation that embarks on an investment readiness journey gets lots of added value on that journey. It's not just about becoming investment ready. Yes, that is the focus of the programme but actually there's a whole lot of spin-offs in terms of the capacity building and strengthening and the culture change within the organisation which is a bi-product of the investment readiness journey.
>
> (Participant 15 – Provider – Theme
> "Investment Readiness and Sustainability")

## Social investment uptake

The actual uptake of social investment – and VCSE attitudes to it – also provides interesting data. This is perhaps the most telling area when offering a critique of both the social investment narrative and VCSE investment readiness.

To date, only five of the 124 VCSE grant awardees have gone on to secure social investment (of the 124, 32 are at least 12 months' post-grant). This suggests a number of possible factors:

1   VCSEs are still not investment ready even after the grant support
2   VCSEs do not see social investment as viable having explored it or see alternative routes to sustainability (through existing models of grants and donations)
3   12 months' post-grant is still not enough time for the VCSEs to have developed sufficiently to become investment ready.

> Some of the data suggests that it is a lack of desire to engage with social investment from the VCSE sector rather than the other way around.

Some of the VCSE participants who completed (or almost completed) the post-grant phase said:

• a growth model based around social investment was not right for them
• social investment and deal flow should not necessarily be the way to judge such grant programmes, as the key was to identify relevant routes to sustainability

They had an improvement in their investment readiness score to 73 per cent, above the threshold considered to be investment ready.

> So, the conclusion we came to … was that the model that we're actually working [describes business model] was probably better at this moment in time than [describes alternative business model], which was a bit of a shock to us, but I think we felt going through the process as well that it was too early for us to look at social investments.
> 
> (Participant 10 – Successful VCSE – Theme "Social Investment")

## Scaling up

Finally, the research data also revealed an interesting theme in relation to the idea of the scaling and growth of VCSEs.

The dominant policy paradigm – characterised by neo-liberal attitudes to the marketisation of the Third Sector (Dey and Teasdale, 2016; McKay *et al.*, 2015) – is that the growth of VCSEs is inherently good, as it will lead to more social impact. Indeed, growth for the sake of it, outside of a wider framework of strategic planning, could have detrimental effects on VCSEs (Dees, Anderson and Wei-Skillern, 2004).

> It's not always about scaling up, actually. It's about working in different ways … It's about creating the opportunity for generating a mixed portfolio of income rather than just relying on grant funding … So, for some organisations, it's not about increasing your turnover, it's about becoming more profitable. And I know that's a dirty word for a lot of voluntary organisations so you can call it a surplus, call it what you like, ultimately it's money that gets recycled back into the organisation to help it develop and deliver better in the future.
> 
> (Participant 16 – Provider – Theme "Social Investment")

This idea is one that needs to be challenged, as the focus for the sector should be on sustainability delivered through the most appropriate means (Sharir, Lerner and Yitshaki, 2009; Jenner, 2016).

> While social investment has much to offer and is clearly relevant for some organisations, it is dangerous to assert that this should be the dominant means of supporting the VCSE sector.

## Summary

The growth in the social investment market and the increase in deal flow over the last five years (20 per cent per annum) demonstrate that the need is there (Robinson, March 2016).

However, the dominance of social investment in policy and the focus of grant funding programmes on increasing social investment deal flow fail to recognise the serious sustainability issues of the VCSE sector (particularly at the lower end of the market).

They also provide a dangerous focus on pushing social investment to a sector where clearly a significant number of organisations either aren't ready for it or are not interested in the products offered.

Instead, support that focuses on driving sustainability within organisations – whether to scale or simply survive – should become the aim for policy-makers, with social investment being merely one tool in this process.

The rhetoric around the social investment market at the moment means that this is seemingly not the case. Policy-makers should reassess whether the mechanisms they are putting in place will really achieve the aims that they are looking for.

## References

Amin, A. (2009), *Extraordinarily ordinary: Working in the extraordinary economy*, Social Enterprise Journal, 5(1), pp. 30–49.

Austin, J. E., Stevenson, H. and Wei-Skillern, J. (2006), *Social entrepreneurship and commercial entrepreneurship: Same, different, or both?*, Entrepreneurship Theory and Practice, 30(1), pp. 1–22.

Bugg-Levine, A. and Emerson, J. (2011), *Impact investing: Transforming how we make money while making a difference*, San Francisco, Jossey-Bass (Wiley).

Cabinet Office (March, 2012), www.gov.uk/government/news/launch-of-big-society-capital-the-world-s-first-ever-social-investment-market-builder.

Dagger, J. and Nicholls, A. (March 2016), *The landscape of social investment research: Trends and opportunities*, Macarthur Foundation, www.sbs.ox.ac.uk/sites/default/files/research-projects/CRESSI/docs/the-landscape-of-social-impact-investment-research.pdf.

Dees, G., Battle-Anderson, B. and Wei-Skillern, J. (2004), *Scaling social impact: Strategies for spreading social innovations*, Stanford Social Innovation Review, 1(4), pp. 24–32.

Department for Business, Innovation and Skills (DfBIS) (May 2015), *State aid: The basics guide*, www.gov.uk/government/uploads/system/uploads/attachment_data/file/443686/BIS-15-417-state-aid-the-basics-guide.pdf.

Department of Health (July 2011), *The voluntary, community and social enterprise sector*, Department of Health and Cabinet Office Overview, 12 July 2011, available online at http://webarchive.nationalarchives.gov.uk/+/www.dh.gov.uk/en/Aboutus/OrganisationsthatworkwithDH/Workingwithstakeholders/DH_128070.

Dey, P. and Teasdale, S. (2016), *The tactical mimicry of social enterprise strategies: Acting "as if" in the everyday life of third sector organisations*, Organization, 23(4), pp. 485–504.

Eikenberry, A. (2009), *Refusing the market: A democratic discourse for voluntary and nonprofit organisations*, Non-profit and Voluntary Sector Quarterly, 38(4), pp. 582–596.

Evenett, R. and Richter, K., (2011), *Making good in social impact investment: Opportunities in an emerging asset-class*, Social Investment Business & the City, London.

Gregory, D., Hill, K., Joy, I. and Keen, S. (2012), *Investment readiness in the UK*, Big Lottery Fund, July 2012, London, available online at (www.biglotteryfund.org.uk/er_invest_ready.pdf).

Hall, K., Alcock, P. and Millar, R. (2012), *Start up and sustainability: Marketisation and the Social Enterprise Investment Fund in England*, Journal of Social Policy, 41(4), pp. 733–749.

Haugh, H. and Kitson, M. (2007), *The third way and the Third Sector: New Labour's economic policy and the social economy*, Cambridge Journal of Economics, 31(6), pp. 973–994.

Hazenberg, R., Seddon, F. and Denny, S. (2014), *Intermediary perceptions of investment readiness in the social investment market*, Voluntas, 26, pp. 847–871.

Hazenberg, R. and Hall, K. (2016), *Public service mutuals: Towards a theoretical understanding of the spin-out process*, policy & politics, 44(3), pp. 441–463.

Hill, K. (2011), *Investor perspectives on social enterprise financing*, City of London/Big Lottery Fund/ ClearlySo Report, July 2011, London, available online at www.cityoflondon.gov.uk/business/ economic-research-and-information/research-publications/Documents/research-2011/ Investor%20 Perspectives%20on%20Social%20Enterprise%20Financing.pdf.

Hines, F. (2005), *Viable social enterprise: An evaluation of business support to social enterprises*, Social Enterprise Journal, 1(1), pp. 13–28.

HM Treasury (November 2016), *Social Investment Tax Relief fact sheet*, www.gov.uk/government/ publications/social-investment-tax-relief-factsheet/social-investment-tax-relief.

Howard, E. (2012), *Challenges and opportunities in social finance in the UK*, Cicero Group, October 2012.

Jenner, P. (2016), *Social enterprise sustainability revisited: An international perspective*, Social Enterprise Journal, 12(1), pp. 42–60.

Macmillan, R. (2011), *"Supporting" the voluntary sector in an age of austerity: The UK government's consultation on improving support for frontline civil society organisations in England*, Voluntary Sector Review, 2(1), pp. 115–124.

Macmillan, R. (2013), *Demand-led capacity building, the Big Lottery Fund and market-making in third sector support services*, Voluntary Sector Review, 4(3), pp. 385–394.

McKay, S., Moro, D., Teasdale, S. and Clifford, D. (2015), *The marketisation of charities in England and Wales*, Voluntas, 26(1), pp. 336–354.

McWade, W. (2012), *The role for social enterprises and social investors in the development struggle*, Journal of Social Entrepreneurship, 3(2), pp. 96–112.

Michelucci, F. V. (2016), *Social impact investments: Does an alternative to the Anglo-Saxon paradigm exist?*, Voluntas, Online article, DOI 10.1007/s11266-016-9783-3.

Moore, L. M., Westley, F. R. and Brodhead, T. (2012), *Social finance intermediaries and social innovation*, Journal of Social Entrepreneurship, 3(2), pp. 184–205.

NCVO (2016), *Size and scope: UK civil society almanac 2016*, available online at https://data.ncvo. org.uk/a/almanac16/size-and-scope/.

Nicholls, A. (2010a), *The institutionalization of social investment: The interplay of investment logics and investor rationalities*, Journal of Social Entrepreneurship, 1(1), pp. 70–100.

Nicholls, A. (2010b), *The landscape of social investment in the UK*, SIFI Evaluation Paper, TSRC and HSMC – University of Birmingham, December 2010.

Robinson, M. (March 2016), *The size and composition of social investment in the UK*, Social Investment Insight Series: Big Society Capital, available online at www.bigsocietycapital.com/latest/ type/research/size-and-composition-social-investment-uk.

Ronicle, J. and Fox, T. (2015), *In pursuit of readiness: Evaluation of the Investment & Contract Readiness Fund*, Ecorys Research Report, Social Investment Business October 2015, available online at www.sibgroup.org.uk/icrf-evaluation/.

Sakarya, S., Bodur, M., Yilidirim-Öktem, Ö. and Selekler-Göksen, N. (2012), *Social alliances: Business and social enterprise collaboration for social transformation*, Journal of Business Research, 65(12), pp. 1710–1720.

Sharir, M., Lerner, M. and Yitshaki, R. (2009), *Long-term survivability of social ventures: Qualitative analysis of external and internal explanations*, in Robinson, J., Mair, J. and Hockerts, K., (eds.), *International perspectives of social entrepreneurship*, Palgrave Macmillan, Basingstoke.

Silver, S., Berggren, L. and Vegholm, F. (2010), *The impact of investment readiness on investor commitment and market accessibility in SMEs*, Journal of Small Business & Entrepreneurship, 23(1), pp. 81–95.

Spear, R., Paton, R., and Nicholls, A. (2015), *Public policy for social finance in context*, in A. Nicholls, R. Paton, and J. Emerson (eds.), *Social finance*, Oxford University Press, Oxford.

Wells, P. (2012), *Understanding social investment policy: Evidence from the evaluation of Futurebuilders in England*, Voluntary Sector Review, 3(2), pp. 157–177.

# 15a  Case study

## SASC (Social and Sustainable Capital)

*Ben Rick*

In May 2019, SASC (Social and Sustainable Capital) launched the Social and Sustainable Housing Fund with £26 million of commitments from 19 investors. The fund aims to support 30 organisations to house 10,000 vulnerable people over the next ten years.

In this section, **Ben Rick**, SASC's Managing Director, explains how the fund came into being and its plans for the future.

### Housing – a problem for charities

Since SASC (Social and Sustainable Capital) launched its first two funds in 2014, it has met dozens of great charities and social enterprises all facing a common problem: a lack of access to safe, high quality housing for the vulnerable people they support. These include adults with learning difficulties; people with drug and alcohol problems or mental health issues; children leaving care; ex-offenders; refugees; and victims of domestic violence.

Many of the organisations had thought about buying property, but decided that traditional mortgages were not a realistic option. For some, it was a challenge to find the deposit (typically 30 per cent of a property's purchase cost). Others were concerned about the risks. For many, it was both. Often, they ended up relying on the private rental sector. But, finding landlords with high quality properties who were prepared to accept society's most vulnerable is challenging.

Then a meeting in 2017 with Lisa Hilder, trustee of Hull Women's Network (HWN; see Hull Women's Network, 2019), made us focus on finding a better way. For 14 years, this dynamic charity had been supporting women fleeing domestic violence. Statistics show that women return to their abusers on average seven times before they finally break free. HWN had found that if a woman had access to safe, stable and appropriate housing, she would leave on her first attempt and never return.

HWN had built up a portfolio of 99 houses. It leased some of them from private landlords and owned others thanks to grants it had received to bring empty homes in Hull back into use.

But HWN had almost 200 women on its waiting list, some suffering violence on a daily basis. As we discussed in that meeting with Lisa the best way to address HWN's housing challenge, the story of the Social and Sustainable Housing fund (SASH, 2019) began.

## Recognising the need for co-design

Our first proposal to HWN was that SASC would provide mortgages for the full amount required to purchase more homes. We thought this was an unbeatable offer, because it removed the need for a deposit. But HWN turned us down. They were concerned about committing to fixed loan repayments and the unpredictability of house prices. Add in the uncertainty around housing benefit and a traditional mortgage loan structure just felt too risky to HWN.

Lisa's response was a turning point. With residential housing as the underlying asset, we saw an opportunity to co-design a product that would work for both investees and investors (see Figure 15a.1). The SASC team caught the train back to Hull and began discussing this in detail with Lisa.

## The solution – impact-led

The new loan to HWN covered the entire cost of purchasing the new housing, including the properties themselves, renovation, adaptation and professional fees. Since internal capacity is often an issue for charities and social enterprises, the loan also funded a member of staff to manage the roll-out of the new activity.

The key innovation in the new structure is the way risk is shared. Instead of making fixed repayments, HWN passes on the net rent it receives after deducting property management costs. These costs include ongoing repairs, maintenance and insurance. This payment structure insulates HWN from risks such as voids, reductions in housing benefit or the non-payment of rent.

HWN purchased 33 additional houses with the funding made available by SASC. Over a ten-year period, these houses will allow more than 300 women and children to flee violent relationships.

THE SOLUTION: CO-DESIGNED WITH CHARITIES FOR CHARITIES

*Figure 15a.1* The solution.

Source: SASH (2019).

## Maximising our impact – creating a new housing fund

SASC's experience with HWN – and then with Homes for Good (based in Glasgow) and Caring for Communities and People (based in Cheltenham) – led us to see the potential for a fund dedicated to loans like this.

The Social and Sustainable Housing fund (SASH) reflects the desire to put the control of housing in the hands of exceptional charities and social enterprises across the UK. Control will enhance the quality of support they can offer to vulnerable tenants (see Figure 15a.2).

These investors' desire to see innovation in social investment provided a powerful endorsement for others, some of whom were new to the sector. As SASC moves into the next phase of SASH, we acknowledge the vital role played by early adopters.

A critical part of the design of SASH has been to recognise the different ways that borrowers and investors think about property. A small-to-medium-sized charity that works with vulnerable people may recognise that lack of control over housing can limit its ability to provide support to its service users. But buying property may seem either too risky or simply out of reach.

Investors welcomed the decision to focus on small-to-medium-sized, locally rooted charities and social enterprises. Organisations with deep local knowledge see it as a priority to be able to buy homes in areas they identify as appropriate for their beneficiaries. Homes in the right locations can prevent vulnerable clients feeling isolated, magnifying the impact of the support provided.

By supporting property ownership as opposed to rental, SASH seeks to build each charity's asset base and its ability to plan for the long term. The fund offers organisations a 15 per cent discount to market value after ten years. This is designed to help borrowers re-finance and retain ownership for the long term, thus increasing the chances that properties will remain in the sector beyond the life of the fund.

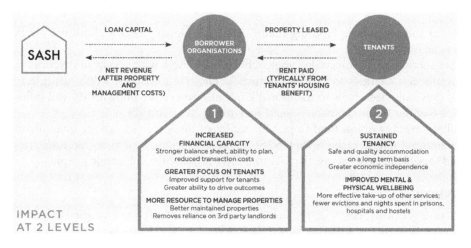

*Figure 15a.2* Impact at two levels.

Source: SASH (2019).

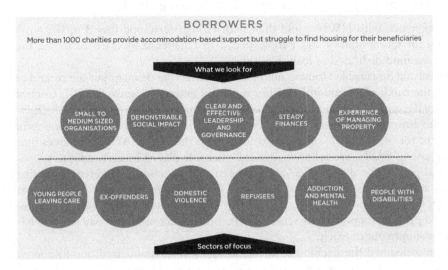

*Figure 15a.3* What SASH is looking for and what SASH is focused on.
Source: SASH (2019).

In delivering this new fund, SASC aims to see a number of key outcomes:

- Small and medium-sized charities and social enterprises getting stronger and becoming key players in the delivery of housing for vulnerable people (see Figure 15a.3)
- 1,000 additional homes made available to deliver safe, stable and appropriate housing for vulnerable people over the long term
- Increased understanding of how secure access to housing helps to deliver long-term social outcomes
- A new precedent for further social investment funds.

## Ahead ...

The Social and Sustainable Housing fund (SASH) has clearly struck a chord with both investors and investees.

SASH shows that an impact-led approach can mobilise a wide group of investors to support effective charities and social enterprises. These organisations would struggle to grow if they only had access to traditional kinds of finance. We hope SASH will influence the way the sector approaches social investment more broadly.

Finding investors in our fund to provide sufficient funds to start making investments was a significant milestone for SASH. SASC are now working hard with inspiring charities and social enterprises across the UK to deliver housing for vulnerable people.

## References

Hull Women's Network, HWN (2019), website, accessed 22 July 2019, www.socialandsustainable. com/cases/hull-woment-network and www.purplehouse.co.uk/.
SASH, Social and Sustainable Housing (2019), *SASC launches ground breaking housing fund*, accessed 22 July 2019, www.socialandsustainable.com/news/sasc-launches-ground-breaking-housing-fund.

# 16 Impact measurement in social investment

*Abigail Rotheroe*

This chapter, written by **Abigail Rotheroe**, Head of Impact at Project Snowball and previous Head of Social Investment at NPC, focuses on impact measurement. It uses the ground-breaking report from Ní Ógáin, Pritchard and Lumley, *Making an impact: Impact measurement among charities and social enterprises in the UK*, NPC (2012) as its base.

## Introduction

Social investment and impact measurement have emerged, grown and reached adolescence (if not yet full adulthood) hand in hand with each other over a similar time period in the UK.

The creation of the first Social Investment Taskforce in 2000 initiated the development of the UK's social investment market at a time when the then nascent field of impact measurement was still yet to significantly emerge. Some social sector organisations were beginning to engage in evaluations of their services. However, this represented only a small minority.

The next decade was a period in which the social investment market saw the creation of Charity Bank, funds such as Bridges Fund Management (previously Bridges Ventures), and social investment finance intermediaries (SIFIs), including such organisations as Social Finance.

---

*Making an Impact*, **NPC (2012)**

- Published by New Philanthropy Capital in 2012
- Study of evaluation and measurement practices across the UK voluntary sector
- Found that impact practice had developed at an encouraging rate, with three-quarters of charities now saying they measured some or all or their work
- The same proportion said they had invested more in measurement and evaluation over the previous five years.

---

## Impact measurement is integral to social investment

An understanding of the blend of social and financial returns expected from social investment requires a quantification of both. But, despite the seemingly interlinked intentions of social investment and impact measurement, developments in both fields have sometimes occurred in parallel rather than together.

One reason has been the focus on expanding the social investment market, which has meant that the desire to understand social return has often been eclipsed by the need to "get money out of the door" and understand how much financial return has been achieved. Even this has been limited to an aggregate level analysis (Social Investment Research Council, 2015).

*Making an Impact*, NPC (2012) found that only around half of social organisations that received their main funding from "other sources" – including investment income – measured their impact. In contrast, for charities funded primarily by government contracts, that figure was 96 per cent (NPC, 2012, p. 15)

However, as the social investment market has matured, investors, intermediaries and delivery organisations have – albeit often in isolation – begun to develop frameworks and tools to evidence social change. Social investment financial intermediaries (SIFIs) are developing proprietary systems for assessing impact risk when making investment decisions. New products have also emerged, particularly social impact bonds, which put measuring social outcomes at the centre of the finance model. Impact measurement is, therefore, increasingly recognised as a key component for monitoring the success of any investment.

## The terminology of impact measurement

The terms "impact measurement", "monitoring" and "evaluation" are often used interchangeably. However, impact measurement refers to the set of practices through which an organisation establishes what difference its work makes. This can range from service planning to delivery to communication and campaigning.

In this sense, monitoring and evaluation are important components of a broader impact measurement process. Such a process can be challenging to apply to charities and social enterprises. With funders, whose social impact is achieved indirectly, the challenges of measurement are even greater.

**Monitoring**: A systematic way of collecting and recording information to check progress against plans and enable evaluation.

**Evaluation**: The use of information from monitoring and elsewhere to judge and understand the performance of an organisation or project.

The key propositions of impact measurement are:

- communicate clearly what you are trying to achieve
- explain how you are working to achieve it
- report on progress.

Whether aiming to reduce homelessness, eradicate malaria or improve educational attainment, your social impact is the progress you make towards achieving that goal.

Some core definitions are set out in Table 16.1.

*Table 16.1* Core definitions focused on impact measurement

| | |
|---|---|
| **Outputs** | The products, services or facilities that result from an organisation's or project's activities.<br>E.g. In a programme to improve mental health in young people, outputs might include the number of counselling sessions attended. But attending counselling sessions alone might not result in a young person feeling better; the desired outcome from those sessions has not been achieved. This is where outcomes come in. |
| **Outcomes** | The changes, benefits, learning or other effects that result from what the project or organisation makes, offers or provides.<br>E.g. For the same counselling programme, outcomes might be improvements in clients' emotional health, which should lead to a longer-term impact on that person's life. |
| **Impact** | The broad and/or long-term effects of a project's or organisation's activities, outputs and outcomes, after taking into consideration an estimate of what would likely have happened anyway (i.e. the outcomes that can be reasonably attributed to a project or organisation).<br>E.g. Not only may there be a longer-term impact on the client, but also a change in the way counselling is delivered. Or mental health policy may have been influenced at a local or wider level. |
| **Counterfactual** | An estimate of what would have happened in the absence of the intervention, service, or organisation. |

## New Philanthropy Capital (NPC)'s four pillar approach

NPC's four pillar approach (Kazimirski and Prichard, 2014; see also Figure 16.1) outlines an effective measurement framework to help organisations measure the right things in the right way.

It aims to provide results that can be used to understand and improve charities' services, as well as report on their progress. The approach is simple in theory but can be tricky to implement well.

## Why measure?

> Having social impact measurement baked into an organisation's DNA from the start, even if this involves extra upfront cost, is likely to help it be far more effective in the long run in achieving its social mission.
>
> (Social Impact Investment Taskforce, 2014i, p. 30)

With greater focus on impact measurement from government, funders, advisors and the general public, many charities and social enterprises now seek to measure the difference they make as a matter of course.

The risk, however, is that the increasing "business" of measurement activity is distracting organisations from their social objectives and removing resources from this. It is argued measurement and evaluation now represents a means to its own ends (Siddiqi, 2013).

For social investors and investees, any measurement system should always be in service to generating greater impact. Thinking about the reasons why we measure – and how the resulting data can be used to make organisations more effective – can therefore guide the choice of a suitable evaluative framework.

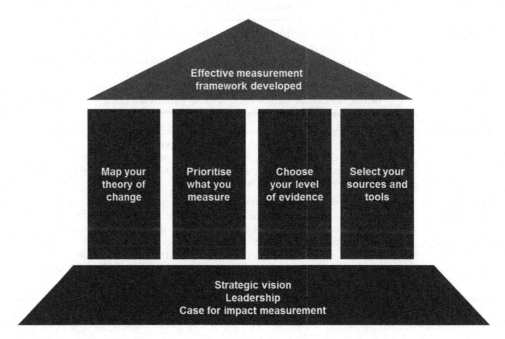

*Figure 16.1* NPC's four pillar approach.

## The four key drivers for impact measurement in social investment

The four key drivers for impact measurement in social investment are shown in Table 16.2.

> Better evidence and practice will help both investors and social sector organisations understand which social investment approaches and products can best deliver real social outcomes, and ultimately drive more positive and lasting change in society.
> (Marcus Hulme, BSC and Caroline Mason, Esmée Fairbairn Foundation 2015, in Moreau and Hornsby, 2015, p. 4)

## How to measure

As impact practice has developed over the last decade it has been accompanied by an array of guidelines, frameworks and tools (Vo *et al.*, 2015) – a diversity reflective of the varied contexts in which measurement may be applied:

- types/stages of investment
- levels of distance/proximity to beneficiaries, e.g. between investors and delivery organisations
- intervention model
- social and/or environmental settings.

This diversity also reflects organisational differences, with some funds developing their own proprietary systems and other ecosystem actors and advisors keen to establish their approach as the industry standard.

*Table 16.2* The four key drivers for impact measurement in social investment

| **Measuring progress against mission – focusing on beneficiaries** | Are we effective at delivering against our stated goals for the people we aim to serve? |
|---|---|

**Measuring progress against mission – focusing on beneficiaries**

Are we effective at delivering against our stated goals for the people we aim to serve?

This question is beneficiary-focused and should be uppermost in the "mind" of any charity, social enterprise or social investor and continually revisited.

Answering this question requires going beyond the anecdote and developing a deeper understanding of the changes that an organisation is creating for the people it aims to support.

The primary use of impact measurement should be as a tool for learning and continual improvement.

By using data from regular monitoring and one-off evaluations, or contributing to wider evidence on what works, social sector organisations can learn and reflect on activities; adapt services; allocate resources; review strategies; and ultimately provide better services and programmes for beneficiaries.

The measurement of outcomes can also influence other actors, contributing to the knowledge base of their sector and even influence government policy.

**Learning and improving**

**Calculating the level of social return**

Social investment has an implicit need to evidence the social value it creates.

Investors may have different expectations regarding social and financial return and different appetites for risk; however, understanding social impact is important across the investor spectrum.

For impact-first investors, measuring impact is central to evidencing their success.

While finance-first investors may focus less on the precise social impact of each investment, they still expect their investment to support social goals in exchange for lower financial return and/or higher risk. In these cases, the social investment market needs to offer a reasonable articulation of the social value that increased risks or lower returns have bought.

Understanding the social impact of investments – as a successful and sustainable mechanism for generating social change – is important for giving credibility to the market as a whole.

Big Society Capital has been tasked with developing the UK social investment market, through significant investment from Government and other stakeholders.

While a growing number of SIFIs and investment products point to a developing market, evidence of the social progress generated is central to securing its legitimacy in the eyes of Government and other socially-minded investors.

A growing evidence base on social impact can help develop knowledge of what works, not just in terms of interventions, but also in which types and structures of investment lend themselves well to tackling particular social problems.

**Increasing market credibility**

The choice on offer could, paradoxically, present a problem for the continued development of impact practice, putting off the inexperienced and preventing those using different approaches from communicating with each other and comparing results.

The Social Impact Investment Taskforce was established to start to address this issue and review opportunities in the social investment market (Social Impact Investment Taskforce: measuring impact, 2014ii).

---

**The Social Impact Investment Taskforce**

- Set up under the UK's presidency of the G8 in 2013 to consolidate different approaches to social impact measurement
- Its Impact Measurement Working Group distilled the multitude of frameworks into a simple four step process: Plan, Do, Assess and Review
- Through these four phases, an investor establishes their aims and goals (in partnership with investees) and chooses an appropriate framework for tracking progress (Kazimirski and Prichard, 2014)
- This one approach encourages collecting data in a robust and validated way, analysing data to assess the level of impact and reviewing evidence to determine future strategic priorities.

---

Figure 16.2 and Table 16.3 show the four phases of impact measurement determined by the Social Impact Investment Taskforce (2014ii): Plan, Do, Assess, Review. This gives a framework for how investors and social organisations can measure impact, hold and use data and learn from this to drive future work.

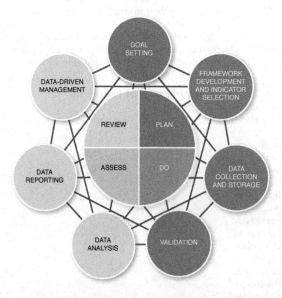

*Figure 16.2* The four phases of impact measurement.

Source: Social Impact Investment Taskforce (2014ii).

*Table 16.3* The four phases of impact measurement in a narrative review

| Phase | Stage | Description |
|---|---|---|
| **Plan** | Goal-setting | • Articulate the desired impact of the investments<br>• Establish a clear investment thesis, theory of change (ToC) or theory of value creation (ToVC), to form the basis of strategic planning and ongoing decision-making; and to serve as a reference point for investment performance |
| | Framework development and indicator selection | • Determine metrics to be used for assessing the performance of the investments<br>• Develop an effective impact measurement framework that integrates metrics and outlines how specific data is captured and used; utilise metrics that align with existing standards |
| **Do** | Data collection and storage | • Capture and store data in a timely and organised fashion<br>• Ensure the proper functioning of the information technology, tools, resources, human capital and methods used to obtain and track data from investees |
| | Validation | • Validate data to ensure sufficient quality<br>• Verify that impact data is complete and transparent by cross-checking calculations and assumptions against known data sources, where applicable |
| **Assess** | Data analysis | • Distil insights from the data collected<br>• Review and analyse data to understand how investments are progressing against impact goals |
| **Review** | Reporting data | • Share progress with key stakeholders<br>• Distribute impact data coherently, credibly and reliably to effectively inform decisions by all stakeholders |
| | Making data-driven investment management decisions | • Identify and implement mechanisms to strengthen the rigour of investment process and outcomes<br>• Assess stakeholder feedback on reported data and address recommendations to make changes to the investment thesis, ToC or ToVC |

Source: taken from Rotheroe (2014).

The adoption of these principles in the sector has resulted in an increase in planning – developing theories of change and measurement frameworks – data collection and data reporting. However, the extent to which this data is feeding back into decisions on strategy, practices and pricing is unclear.

In their 2015 report on impact measurement practices in UK SIFIs, Sarah Moreau and Adrian Hornsby conclude that "if the expectations and rhetoric around impact data outrun the operational use of impact data, there is a significant risk of datawash" (Moreau and Hornsby, 2015, p. 33).

While the initial stages of this impact cycle are vital, it is the review stage which is most crucial, as without this the primary purpose of impact measurement – learning to improve – will never take place.

## Quantitative or qualitative?

The Taskforce framework shown in Figure 16.2 and Table 16.3 is not prescriptive about the type of data collection or method of data analysis. A social investor will want to know the impact of their investment and be in a position to understand or evaluate any financial trade-off that might have been taken. An investee will want to use impact measurement for learning and improvement within the organisation.

Therefore, both quantitative and qualitative data have a role within social investment. While quantitative methods can help provide clear numbers to evidence trends and compare sub-groups, qualitative data is important for understanding the complexities of social change and giving voice to differing opinions and subjectivities.

Within the two broad churches of measurement there are a multitude of techniques to choose from, with that choice influenced by the research context, the type of intervention and the level of available resources. Table 16.4 summarises the most common types of data.

Research by Vo *et al.* (2015, p. 12) into impact measurement practices in social investment (based on a sample of 160 members of the Social Impact Analysts Association) found that a range of data collection methods were used by analysts. Perhaps unsurprisingly, by far the most popular among impact professionals measuring outcomes targeted by investors were surveys and individual interviews: 92 per cent reported using the former and 85 per cent the latter. The use of observation and cognitive/behavioural tests was found to be less common—used in 68 per cent and 20 per cent of cases, respectively.

> By far the most popular among impact professionals measuring outcomes targeted by investors were surveys and individual interviews … use of observation and cognitive/behavioural tests were found to be less common.
>
> (Vo. et al., 2015, p. 12)

## Evidence standards

A key consideration in any measurement framework is deciding what sort of evidence will enable an investor to credibly demonstrate and analyse the impact of an investment. A lot of attention has been placed on so-called "evidence standards" as a route to doing this.

As with other evidence standards, the Nesta scale places experimental approaches such as randomised controlled trials (RCTs) at the top of the hierarchy, as these are regarded as the best at reducing bias. The highest levels of the scale are reserved for replicable experimental studies that have provided consistent findings.

Evidence standards imply a need to move up the scale.

However, not all social scientists and evaluators agree that such hierarchies are useful or that experimental approaches provide the best evidence.

Experimental studies work best for clearly defined programmes where there are many cases (individuals, groups of people, places), but are less suitable for programmes with one or a few cases in complex and changing environments.

*Table 16.4* The most common forms of data for impact measurement

|  | Type of data | Guidance and recommendations |
| --- | --- | --- |
| Quantitative data | Monitoring data is data you collect routinely, through staff and volunteers | • Look at your theory of change and work out what consistent measures you need to implement<br>• Use modern customer relationship management systems to help you manage the data |
|  | Secondary data is information that other organisations collect, (while everything that you collect yourself is "'primary") | • Identify any secondary data that might exist and look for opportunities to access and analyse it |
|  | Surveys (online or paper questionnaires) provide quantitative data on attitudes, opinions, knowledge and behaviours from a sample of a population | • Think about whether the group you survey – likely to be a sample of your beneficiaries – accurately represents your wider service users<br>• Consider commercial panels and omnibus surveys – regular surveys conducted by research companies that organisations can buy questions from |
| Qualitative data | Interviews allow the interviewees to expand their answers and accounts of their experiences and feelings. They are often one-to-one, follow a rough guide and take place face-to-face, or over the phone | • Interview a range of service users to ensure your data is representative<br>• Avoid cherry-picking the service users who have most benefited; talk to failures as well as successes<br>• Practise, or get training where possible – interviewing style is a skill which is often developed over time and involves careful listening |
|  | Focus groups are group discussions which allow researchers to understand how groups of people might describe their experience of a service | • Involve a range of service users, which is broadly representative of your wider beneficiaries<br>• Be aware that focus groups can intimidate more hesitant service users and are not appropriate when sensitive or personal issues are being discussed |
|  | Ethnography means observing the subject matter you wish to understand (e.g. a charity's workshops or support groups). It bridges the gap between stated and actual behaviour, allowing you to understand the reasons underlying this behaviour | • Consider what training may be necessary for undertaking this type of data collection; the quality of data and analysis depends on the skills of the researcher |

Source: taken from Thorne and Noble (2016).

Perhaps reflective of the range of impact measurement approaches, there are also numerous evidence "standards" or "levels", such as the Nesta Standards of Evidence (Puttick and Ludlow, 2013; see Table 16.5) – which were primarily developed for impact investing.

*Table 16.5* Nesta Standards of Evidence

| Nesta Standards of Evidence | |
| --- | --- |
| Level 1 | You can describe what you do and why it matters logically, coherently and convincingly |
| Level 2 | You capture data that shows positive change, but you cannot confirm you caused this |
| Level 3 | You can demonstrate causality using a control or comparison group, e.g. from randomised control trials |
| Level 4 | You have one or more independent replication evaluations that confirms these conclusions |
| Level 5 | You have manuals, systems and procedures to ensure consistent replication and positive impact |

Source: taken from Puttick and Ludlow (2013).

Ultimately, there is no hard and fast rule as to which approach is best – context will dictate. For instance, for the social impact bond (SIB) model using a targeted, clearly defined intervention lends itself well to control group studies. By contrast, measuring impact at a fund-level would not suit experimental approaches, as it would be unfeasible to set up comparison groups. Here, statistical methods such as trend analysis are more effective at understanding impact at an aggregate level.

## Impact measurement for charities in the health sector

Next we consider an adapted version of the Nesta Standards of Evidence to review evaluations of, or by, charities in the health sector (Bull *et al.*, 2016).

It focuses on the first three levels of the Nesta scale. It is rare to see evaluations of Level 4 or 5, given that these levels of evidence are unlikely to be achieved by the charity sector alone. Level 4 requires "one or more independent replication evaluations that confirm your conclusions" and Level 5 means that "you have manuals, systems and procedures to ensure consistent replication and positive impact".

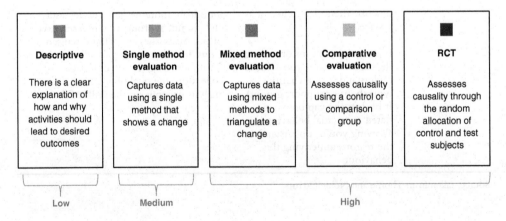

*Figure 16.3* The NPC scale developed to review evaluations in the health sector, *Doing the Right Thing* project.

Source: Bull *et al.* (2016).

Note

Low, Medium and High reflect the level of confidence in the measurement of social impact.

The scale shown in Figure 16.3, developed by NPC, therefore adds additional layers to better differentiate between approaches that would have sat at Levels 2 and 3 in the Nesta Standards. At Nesta Level 2, the scale differentiates between single and mixed-method studies, and at Level 3 between a non-randomised comparison group and an RCT.

## SROI and economic evaluation

Social return on investment (SROI) was developed by REDF (formerly the Roberts Enterprise Development Fund), a San Francisco–based philanthropic fund, as a way to help assess the impact of charities and social enterprises (REDF, 2018).

This and other types of economic evaluation (Figure 16.4) – such as cost–benefit analysis – can help organisations and their funders compare the value of the impact created by an organisation with the cost of creating that impact – in a way that's easy to understand, particularly to those unfamiliar with the subject matter.

> There are some risks surrounding the incorrect use of economic evaluation – it can misrepresent value, take up scarce resources and produce something of little relevance.

In SROI, social, environmental and economic outcomes are assigned monetary values. Challenges to this arise when organisations are unclear about the difference they make, or if the monetary value of the difference is not relevant or difficult to ascertain.

However, the end figure can be less important than the actual process used to achieve it, since the rigour of the SROI process itself helps organisations to better understand and report their outcomes.

Charities report a number of additional benefits of conducting economic evaluations including getting feedback about what they do and helping to secure funding.

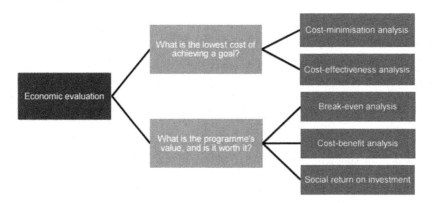

*Figure 16.4* Types of economic evaluation.
Source: Svistak and Pritchard (2014, p. 10).

The seven principles that underpin any SROI analysis (Social Value International, 2015) are:

- involve stakeholders
- understand what changes
- value the outcomes that matter
- only include what is material
- do not over-claim
- be transparent and
- verify the result

## Challenges for measuring the impact of social investment across the entire market (including investors and their portfolios)

While impact practice among social investors is evolving, significant challenges remain in embedding effective measurement across the social investment market as a whole.

Some of these challenges are linked to the intrinsic difficulties of measuring social impact, while others relate to organisational and resource barriers to ensuring that measuring social value is seen as both feasible and necessary by social investors and intermediaries.

The combination of these two factors means that at present there are no commonly accepted standardised systems for measuring social return.

## Intrinsic difficulties: measuring the impact of investors

The difficulty for social investors in measuring their impact and that of their investees is similar to the challenges faced by traditional grant funders.

As both investors and grant-makers occupy a more detached position than that of delivery organisations, they have a harder time linking investment with impact outcomes. Doubly so when their investment forms only part of a wider funding portfolio.

---

### Articulating additionality (Rotheroe and Joy, 2014)

Articulating the additionality of an investor's funding needs to happen more if the market is to be persuasive as to its impact. What is the "counterfactual" – what would have happened without the social investment, and what value does the investment add?

To fully understand their impact, investors need to ask themselves questions such as these:

- What would have happened if investment had not been made available?
- How bleak is the counterfactual? Would people not have received services at all?
- Are there other options? Are they as good, nearly as good or no good? When a repayable offer is the only option on the table, is this better than no funding at all?
- Does a social investment instrument achieve more than a grant? Does it unlock extra potential or leverage by expanding funding options?
- Does the discipline required of social investment enhance organisational performance? Does market participation enhance profile?

In considering these questions, investors will get a clearer sense of their own objectives and, therefore, what they need to measure.

---

These challenges mean that current measurement practice, particularly at an aggregate level, focuses predominantly on monitoring outputs as proxies for impact.

Measuring and aggregating outcome data is less widespread, although progress is being made.

As Moreau and Hornsby in their report, *Oranges and Lemons* (2015), explain, "While SIFIs would generally favour information on outcomes, the majority recognise this is difficult to obtain, and rely mostly on outputs. This is regarded as 'better than no information', and does provide useful figures regarding the organisation's reach" (2015, p. 18).

## Organisational and resource barriers: embedding measurement

The second challenge – one that cuts across the whole of the social sector – is inspiring and enabling organisations to develop their impact practice in a meaningful and useful way.

Clearly, great strides have been made around increasing awareness of impact measurement and encouraging organisations to collect data, but it is still unclear if this has fed through to driving continuous improvement.

For social investment, like grant-making, this challenge of embedding impact practice occurs at two levels:

* encouraging social investors to think about their aggregate impact; and
* supporting investees to measure the outcomes they support.

While grant-makers have often been reluctant to aggregate impact and impose prescriptive measurement requirements on grantees (Baumgartner *et al.*, 2013), some social investors are taking a more systematic approach – specifying certain metrics for investees to report on.

Here we find a trade-off between developing prescriptive measurement practices that may attract larger pools of capital, and developing investee-driven measurement practices that may be fragmented and less attractive to investors used to metrics and ratings.

Ultimately, any measurement system should help investors and investees improve and increase their capacity to drive positive social change.

This does not mean measuring everything or developing incredibly complex frameworks – for impact measurement, quality is definitely more important than quantity.

## Understanding the social value of the market

While individual investors may be making strides to more effectively monitor their impact and that of their investees, the social investment market is still far from developing a standardised approach.

Without some standardisation, investors cannot compare results and this limits our understanding of the social value generated at a market-wide level.

The size of the challenge ahead is underlined by the fact that the first attempt to measure financial return at an aggregate level was only recently published.

The report by the Social Investment Research Council (2015) looked at the returns of three major lenders, finding an overall return of negative 9.2 per cent (2015, p. 7). This was an important first step for understanding levels of capital retention at major investors, but was still unrepresentative of the market as a whole and tells us nothing about the social returns secured.

> If measuring financial return at a market level is only in its infancy, then the challenge to measure the social value of the market remains substantial.

The *Oranges and Lemons* report (Moreau and Hornsby, 2015) found little standardisation between these funds and little or no pressure to harmonise approaches.

## The way forward

The size of the challenge is substantial, both in terms of enabling individual investors to increase their social impact through measurement and learning and developing a sector-wide understanding of the value of social investment.

However, many investors, funds and advisors are committed to developing and embedding impact practice (Hulme, 2016).

## Key next steps are for investors to

- **Step 1:** better understand the impact potential of investments at the fund-level;
- **Step 2:** build on the work of SIBs in developing outcomes-focused models; and
- **Step 3:** work towards shared measurement approaches, which help to foster standardisation in key market sub-sectors.

## Step 1: understanding impact potential/risk at fund-level

A lack of common metrics limits a comprehensive understanding of impact at the fund-level, particularly for investors with large portfolios spanning a range of thematic areas.

However, in the absence of common measures, investors can take steps to develop proxies for impact that can help guide decision-making.

One possible route is to look at the quality of evidence provided by investees as an indicator of the impact potential of investments, and aggregating these upwards. This is a logical first step and one often observed by impact analysts.

> Our experience of impact measurement in the charity sector over the last ten years [indicates that] a developed, intentional impact measurement process is likely to be associated with a greater focus on impact, and, by extension, an increased probability of impact.
>
> (Lomax *et al.*, 2015, p. 20)

**Bridges Fund Management** incorporates this approach into the pre-investment process through its IMPACT Radar, a tool to assess the impact risk/return profile of potential investments (Bridges Fund Management, 2014).

Target outcomes pre-investment are analysed using a theory of change approach, assessing the scale and depth of impact and potential for systemic change (so-called "impact return" for the investment and portfolio).

The level of impact risk (likelihood of no or negative impact) is assessed by reviewing the evidence base for the causal links in the theory of change.

The evidence bar is set relatively high, with investments required to have experimental studies demonstrating causality (Nesta 3 or above) to qualify as low risk (see Table 16.5).

Post-investment, the IMPACT Radar underpins a common set of key performance indicators (KPIs) developed with each investment to track performance. In this way, an understanding of impact risk/return at the fund-level enables a more tailored measurement of impact at the investment-level.

NPC working with the KL Felicitas Foundation (KLF) (Lomax *et al.*, 2015), uses a similar approach to audit its portfolio on the basis of the evidence reporting of investees. The "Impact Assurance Process" (Figure 16.5) assigns a score to each investment based on a review of impact data and processes around five components of good impact practice:

1   clarity of mission;
2   measurement of outputs;
3   use of standardised metrics (such as the Impact Reporting and Investing Standards, or IRIS);
4   data to show change; and
5   data to show additionality of investment (causality).

Investments are given an Impact Assurance Classification (Stage 1 to 4) on the basis of their overall score.

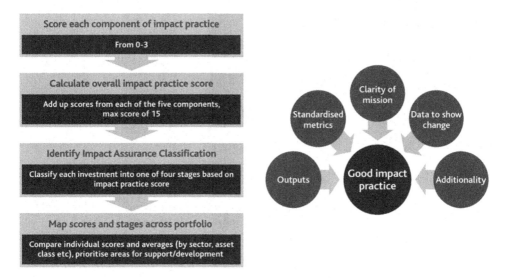

*Figure 16.5* KLF's Impact Assurance Process.
Source: Lomax *et al.* (2015).

The Impact Assurance Classification for each company or fund can be compared across different investments. It can also be monitored over time to see how an organisation develops its impact practice.

KLF can also monitor each component at the portfolio level to assess how impact practice (Figure 16.6) is developing across its investments.

## Step 2: developing outcomes-focused models

Arguably, the biggest innovation in social investment in recent years has been the development and propagation of social impact bonds (SIBs) as a specialist vehicle to deliver outcome-based contracts.

The first SIB was set up in 2010 by HMP Peterborough (David Ainsworth, 2017). While small in terms of sector penetration (GHK and BMG Research, 2013), SIBs have become a high-profile form of social investment, thanks largely to their aim of funding preventive measures and reducing costs to the public purse.

This key feature is based on funding models (Bridges Fund Management and BAML, 2014) which are intrinsically linked to the outcomes generated, with investors only being repaid if impact targets are met.

Rigorous monitoring of outcomes is, therefore, central to the functioning of SIBs. The higher the quality and standard of evidence produced, the more confident government or local authorities can be that target outcomes have been achieved and hence future savings assured.

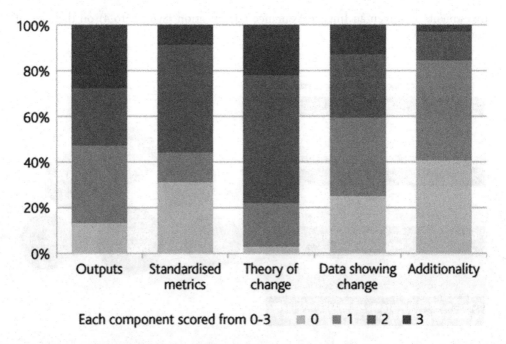

*Figure 16.6* Impact practice score by Impact Assurance component.

Source: Lomax *et al.* (2015).

The measurement frameworks supporting SIBs have, therefore, predominantly used (quasi-) experimental study designs.

In some SIBs, however, there has been a more recent trend of paying for outcomes on a per capita (rather than per cohort) basis, with accompanying monitoring systems not using counterfactual studies. For example, the UK Department for Work and Pensions' Innovation Fund SIBs and the Utah SIB (Tomkinson, 2015).

This is a pragmatic but troubling development.

> While the focus on evidence standards should not lead to a race among all investors to the higher-level approaches (Nesta 3+), it is particularly important for SIBs that measurement isolates the impact of the intervention.

Otherwise, there is a risk that public money pays for outcomes that would have happened anyway, as identified in *Lessons and Opportunities: Perspectives from Providers of Social Impact Bonds* (Rotheroe, 2014).

---

**The Arts Impact Fund (Nesta Arts Impact Fund, 2018)**

- A traditional form of social investment structured to better prioritise impact
- Aims to increase access to loan finance among UK arts organisations
- Places evidencing of social impact at the core of both the pre-investment process and post-investment monitoring
- Takes a "co-mingling" approach, providing other types of financial and non-financial support, to help develop investees' impact monitoring systems
- Contributes to evidence on social outcomes in the arts at the aggregate level.

---

## Step 3: enabling shared measurement

While the application of impact measurement and performance management is fragmented among different organisations, there is much overlap in the content and essential ideas at play.

Although tailored approaches are appropriate in certain circumstances, organisations risk wasting time and resources developing systems from scratch when similar frameworks are already in use.

One route to addressing this issue is shared measurement, an approach which "involves organisations working on similar issues developing a common understanding of what to measure and developing tools that can be used by charities, social enterprises and funders working towards similar goals" (Ní Ógáin *et al.*, 2013, p. 4).

> Developing shared measurement systems has the triple advantage of limiting duplicated effort, reducing barriers to entry for those looking to monitor their impact and contributing, at a sector-wide level, to a better understanding of what works.

A light-touch step towards this has been made through the development of common monitoring and reporting metrics with IRIS (2018).

---

**Impact Reporting and Investment Standards (IRIS) (IRIS, 2018)**

- Developed in 2008 as part of an initiative by the Rockefeller Foundation
- Subsequently a project of the Global Impact Investing Network (GIIN)
- Provides a catalogue of metrics which are predominantly quantitative and output-focused
- Investors can track progress at an individual investment or portfolio level.

---

This approach only gets us so far, however.

First, the large number of available metrics, spanning multiple thematic areas, means that, even if organisations are reporting on IRIS, it may be difficult to make comparisons.

Second, defining metrics only represents a small part of the Plan, Do, Assess, Review process. A more holistic approach to developing shared measurement models is needed to provide useable aggregate data and enable significant take-up by investors.

The **Inspiring Impact** programme (Inspiring Impact, 2018) – which aims to develop impact practice across the UK charity sector – has taken shared measurement one step further, by developing a measurement toolkit for organisations working to support youth employability.

The **Journey to Employment (JET) Framework** (Harries *et al.*, 2014) maps outcome areas, identifies relevant tools and provides measurement guidance to support improved impact practice among social sector organisations working in similar areas.

## A common language

A potential route to supporting the development of sub-sector investor/measurement communities is through the creation of recognised standards for measurement and reporting.

One resource that could be used as the basis for developing sub-sector standards is **Big Society Capital's Outcomes Matrix** (Good Finance, 2015)

This measurement tool – developed in collaboration with impact experts including the Good Analyst, New Philanthropy Capital, the SROI Network and Triangle Consulting – provides a series of outcomes mapped around nine thematic areas (such as employment, training and education, and housing and local facilities).

Within these outcome areas, the Matrix is designed to provide social investment market participants with access to tools and measures and to foster the development of "a common language regarding social investment and impact assessment" (Good Finance, 2015, p. 1).

## Combining top-down and bottom-up

A practical approach to taking this work forward may well be to combine top-down and bottom-up approaches to developing shared measurement.

As investors and investee organisations are often in the early stages of developing measurement frameworks, there's a clear need for guidance that helps them make these first steps confidently and constructively.

One option here is to build on the existing material in the Outcomes Matrix and develop slightly more detailed outcomes orientation packages in each of the outcomes areas or beneficiary groups. These could draw on the existing research literature and practitioner expertise and present users with:

- common theories of change in that area;
- suggested key outcomes in those theories of change; and
- suggested indicators and measurement tools for those outcomes.

This would help to encourage the development of measurement in the social investment field towards greater coherence, based on the most common theories of change.

At the same time, an ongoing programme of more in-depth work with subsector communities of interest could work towards standardisation around actual measurement tools and metrics.

## Final thoughts

It is both clear, and well-accepted, that impact measurement is integral to social investment. Progress has already been made, but renewed effort and commitment are needed from the social investment market to overcome the many challenges that remain.

As we make progress, the need to understand the balance between social and financial return will ultimately enable more informed capital allocation choices. This is essential, if social investment is to live up to its promise.

Although measurement can have multiple purposes, it must enable progress towards mission and learning and improvement within an organisation. If this purpose is not clear, there's a danger of measurement becoming a box to tick or a story to tell, and social investment being little more than financial investment with a feel-good factor.

While there are many ways to measure impact, the process of measurement can be mandated and standardised.

A Plan, Do, Assess, Review framework should be followed, in conjunction with the right measurement tools for the specific context. A mixed-method approach to measuring impact is recommended and there are multiple off-the-shelf tools that can be used.

There remain substantial challenges for measuring impact, including cultural barriers and the lack of standardised outcomes and metrics. These challenges are not insurmountable – they simply have not yet been tackled with the required combination of effort, resource and understanding.

Increasing standardisation and shared measurement will lead the way forward.

New approaches towards impact measurement are continually being developed. For example, at this stage in the market's development, innovation is important. But we should not be distracted by innovation for its own sake – innovation needs to be mirrored by investment in building infrastructure and developing the framework to deliver.

The social investment market needs to invest in the infrastructure for measurement – measurement capacity within investees and investors alike – and in the analysis and use of the data that results.

Ultimately, what we need is an ecosystem approach to impact measurement. That requires key players to have the vision to imagine and invest in that ecosystem and a culture of collaboration and partnership that can lead to such an ecosystem flourishing.

# References

Baumgartner, L., Kail, A. and Van Vliet, A. (2013), *Funding impact*, New Philanthropy Capital, accessed 20 January 2018, www.thinknpc.org/publications/funding-impact/.

Bridges Fund Management (2014), *Bridges Ventures unveils impact in its latest IMPACT Report*, accessed 20 October 2018, www.bridgesfundmanagement.com/bridges-ventures-unveils-impact-methodology-in-its-latest-impact-report/.

Bridges Fund Management and Bank of America Merrill Lynch (2014), *Choosing social impact bonds: A practitioner's guide*, accessed 20 October 2018, www.bridgesfundmanagement.com/publications/choosing-social-impact-bonds-practitioners-guide/.

Bull, D., Bagwell, S., Joy I. and Weston, A (2016), *Untapped potential: Bringing the voluntary sector's strengths to health and care transformation*, New Philanthropy Capital, accessed 20 October 2018, www.thinknpc.org/publications/untapped-potential/.

David Ainsworth (2017), *Peterborough social impact bond investors repaid in full*, accessed 20 October 2018, www.civilsociety.co.uk/news/peterborough-social-impact-bond-investors-repaid-in-full.html.

GHK and BMG Research (2013), *Growing the social investment market: The landscape and economic impact*, City of London Corporation.

Good Finance (2015), *Big Society Capital: Outcomes matrix full guidance*, accessed 20 October 2018, www.goodfinance.org.uk/sites/default/files/Outcomes%20Matrix%20Full%20Guidance_0.pdf.

Harries, E., Kail, A. and Ní Ógáin, E. (2014), *The Journey to Employment (JET) framework: Outcomes and tools to measure what happens on young people's journey to employment*, Inspiring Impact, accessed 20 October 2018, www.thinknpc.org/publications/the-journey-to-employment/.

Hulme, M. (2016), *Impact measurement in social investment*, Big Society Capital, accessed 20 October 2018, www.bigpotential.org.uk/sites/default/files/Social%20Impact%20Darlington%2010%2010%20Feb%202016.pdf.

Inspiring Impact (2018), *Inspiring impact*, accessed 20 October 2018, http://inspiringimpact.org/.

IRIS (2018), *IRIS*, accessed 20 October 2018, https://iris.thegiin.org/.

Kazimirski, A. and Prichard, D. (2014), *Building your measurement framework: NPC's four pillar approach*, New Philanthropy Capital, accessed 20 October 2018, www.thinknpc.org/publications/npcs-four-pillar-approach/.

Lomax, P., Rotheroe, A. and Harrison-Evans, P. (2015), *Investing for impact: Practical tools, lessons, and results*, New Philanthropy Capital, accessed 20 October 2018, www.thinknpc.org/publications/investing-for-impact-practical-tools-lessons-and-results/.

Moreau, S. and Hornsby, A. (2015), *Oranges and lemons: The state of play of impact measurement among UK SIFIs*, accessed 20 October 2018, www.bigsocietycapital.com/sites/default/files/attachments/Investing%20for%20Good%20-%20Oranges%20and%20Lemons.pdf.

Nesta Arts Impact Fund (2018), *Arts and culture finance*, accessed 20.10.2018, www.artsculturefinance.org/.

Ní Ógáin, E., Svistak, M. and de Las Casas, L. (2013), *Blueprint for share measurement: Developing, designing and implementing shared approaches to impact measurement*, Inspiring Impact, accessed 20 October 2018, www.thinknpc.org/wp-content/uploads/2018/07/Blueprint-for-shared-measurement1.pdf.

NPC (2012), *Making an impact*, by E. Ní Ógáin, D. Pritchard and T. Lumley, accessed 20 October 2018, www.thinknpc.org/resource-hub/making-an-impact/.

Puttick, R. and Ludlow, J. (2013), *Standards of evidence: An approach that balances the need for evidence with innovation*, Nesta, accessed 20 October 2018, www.nesta.org.uk/sites/default/files/standards_of_evidence.pdf.

REDF (2018), *SROI*, accessed 20 October 2018, www.redf.org/learn-category/sroi/.

Rotheroe, A. (2014), *Lessons and opportunities: Perspectives from providers of social impact bonds*, New Philanthropy Capital, accessed 20 October 2018, www.thinknpc.org/publications/lessons-and-opportunities/.

Rotheroe, A. and Joy, I. (2014), *Smart money: Understanding the impact of social investment*, New Philanthropy Capital, accessed 20 October 2018, www.thinknpc.org/publications/smart-money/.

Siddiqi, L. (2013), *Impact measurement: The faultlines*, Huffington Post, www.huffingtonpost.com/lutfey-siddiqi/impact-measurement-the-faultlines_b_4252539.html.

Social Impact Investment Taskforce (2014i), *Impact investment: The invisible heart of markets – Harnessing the power of entrepreneurship, innovation and capital for public good*, accessed 20 October 2018, www.gsgii.org/reports/impact-investment-the-invisible-heart-of-markets/.

Social Impact Investment Taskforce (2014ii), *Measuring impact: Subject paper of the Impact Measurement Working Group*, accessed 20 October 2018, www.gsgii.org/reports/measuring-impact/.

Social Investment Research Council (2015), *The social investment market through a data lens*, accessed 20 October 2018, www.oltreventure.com/wp-content/uploads/2015/06/SIRC_The_Social_Investment_Market_Through_a_Data_Lens_Report1.pdf.

Social Value International (2015), *The seven principles of social values*, accessed 20 October 2018, http://socialvalueuk.org/what-is-sroi/principles.

Svistak, M. and Pritchard, P. (2014), *Economic evaluation: What is it good for? A guide for deciding whether to conduct an economic evaluation*, New Philanthropy Capital, accessed 20 October 2018, www.thinknpc.org/publications/economic-analysis/.

Thorne, M. and Noble, J. (2016), *Stories and numbers: Collecting the right impact data*, New Philanthropy Capital, accessed 20 October 2018, www.thinknpc.org/publications/stories-and-numbers/.

Tomkinson, E. (2015), *What do we know about the Utah SIB results (without a counterfactual)?*, accessed 20 October 2018, www.emmatomkinson.com/2015/11/09/what-do-we-know-about-the-utah-sib-results-without-a-counterfactual/.

Vo, A. T. *et al.* (2015), *Understanding the measurement of social impact within the context of social investment: A descriptive study*, accessed 20 October 2018, Social Value International, www.socialvalueint.org/wp-content/uploads/2015/05/SIAA_Influencing-Impact-Report_April-2015.pdf.

# 16a Case study

## WSUP and Unilever – Clean Team Ghana

*Diane Chilangwa Farmer*

### Working with a corporate using social investment

An adaptation of a case study written by **Diane Chilangwa Farmer**, independent research professional, with quotes attributed to her interview with **Neil Jeffrey**, Chief Executive Officer at Water and Sanitation for the Urban Poor (WSUP).

### Introduction

Governments, scholars, the media and social purpose organisations increasingly recognise the importance of social entrepreneurial approaches and how they can help non-profit organisations operate in an innovative way (Christie and Honig, 2006; Hao Jiao, 2011). Stevens *et al.* (2015) add, the issue of sustainability is becoming more important for civil society as non-profits, NGOs and other civil society organisations (CSOs) face a variety of political, regulatory, organisational and financial challenges.

Within this context, Water and Sanitation for the Urban Poor (WSUP) worked with Unilever to create a new commercial sanitation business. It used the skills and resources of both parties to create something innovative and unique.

- Clean Team Ghana Limited is a wholly owned for-profit subsidiary of the non-profit company, Water and Sanitation for the Urban Poor (WSUP).
- Registered in 2012, the Clean Team business evolved from WSUP's Uniloo project – a collaborative venture between WSUP, Unilever and design consultants IDEO.
- The Clean Team business is aligned with Unilever's "Sustainable Living Plan", which aims to improve people's health, reduce environmental impact and enhance dignity and self-esteem (WSUP, 2011 and WSUP, 2016).
- The business focuses on low-income districts of Ghana's second largest city, Kumasi, where access to acceptable sanitation facilities remains extremely low for the two million people who live in this densely populated, unplanned urban sprawl.
- Many people in Kumasi have no household toilet, with an estimated 60 per cent of the population only having access to grossly unhygienic public toilet blocks.
- Clean Team Ghana and Unilever invested into this project.

**WSUP'S driving vision**

WSUP is a non-profit company with a mission to improve the lives of the urban poor in developing countries.

It does this by strengthening the capacity of service providers and others to provide sustainable water and sanitation services, promote good hygiene and raise the health and environmental standards of the community.

WSUP operates as a non-profit partnership and it is this structure that allows companies to become members (or shareholders).

This structure allows WSUP to qualify for a wide range of funding mechanisms, including NGO sources and those normally earmarked for private companies (WSUP, 2015).

WSUP is a non-profit that is structured differently from your traditional non-profit. It is not a charity. It sees itself, however, as a "non-profit" organisation.

WSUP has built long-term relationships with service providers from across the public and private sectors in six core country programmes: Bangladesh, Ghana, Kenya, Madagascar, Mozambique and Zambia (WSUP, 2015, p. 17).

## Clean Team Ghana and Unilever partnership

Unilever's initial investment in Clean Team was into the toilet mould business and in the creation of the Uniloo toilet. After this initial investment, most of the money for the business has been generated by WSUP through sales and marketing efforts.

According to Neil Jeffery, WSUP CEO, Clean Team was unique in WSUP's portfolio when it was established as a business and remains very different from what other charitable institutions are doing today. On the back of this experience WSUP has significantly expanded its work to support and promote other market-based sanitation services.

At present, no one is providing this type of toilet service (illustrated in Figure 16a.1) in Kumasi where its residents typically go to public toilets to buy sanitation facilities.

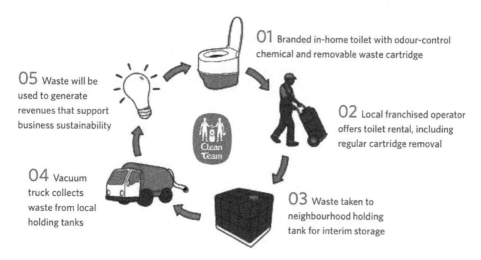

*Figure 16a.1* Figure showing the Uniloo concept in operation.
Source: WSUP (2011, p. 1).

People in Kumasi are used to paying for sanitation facilities, which works relatively well. What Clean Team's profitable social business now aims to do is to scale through the modest investment of social investment and return seeking capital (Clean Team, 2016). As Jeffrey explains,

> The existing facilities are relatively expensive, poor quality, fairly unhygienic, not great in terms of health, dignity and safety and very poor in terms of convenience. So Clean Team provides a toilet service in the home, which one can buy at a price point that is about a third of the public toilets – if you are thinking about a one-day use per family member over a period of time. It's significantly more convenient, because the waste is collected every two days and the odour of the waste is controlled.

The local government and Kumasi Municipal Authority are very supportive of Clean Team's efforts in that they allow them to transport their waste to their municipal site. This waste, as illustrated above, can be a useful way to generate energy for another business operation for Clean Team. Discussions on how to proceed in the long-term are still ongoing.

## Gross profit margins and reducing costs

The objective and interesting thing about Clean Team is that it is trying to create a business that generates a profit; and clearly, a whole lot of investment goes into that.

In 2015, Clean Team made an operating deficit which was underwritten by grant income from restricted funds provided for the purpose. But, ultimately, the organisation would like to get to the point where it can either raise its own debt or sell equity to advance the business. Neil Jeffery says,

> We are not at that point yet. If you look at the gross profit margin, it is still making a loss and we need to drive the business to a point where that growth margin zeros out and becomes a positive. That is where we need further investment to make that happen. We have a series of investors who are interested in pushing it over the line. It is not sustainable at the moment but certainly has the potential. We are selling into low income consumer settlements, so, depending on how the market will bear on the price, this clearly has a huge bearing on the ability of the business to sustain itself. At about $7 a month, it's an excellent price for the quality of the service. The equivalent competitor in the market would cost a family of a similar size probably about three times the price.

At the time of going to print gross margin for the business is approximately +30% and the significant further investment, both long term debt and technical assistance has been secured.

## Unilever's role

Unilever sells products like soap and detergents that people need to improve their health and hygiene and chemical fluid and detergents for use in their operations.

In an effort to help WSUP understand what the particular drivers are for its consumers, Unilever has a number of touch points with the organisation.

The company has worked closely with WSUP on segmenting this particular service unit. For example, collaborating on hygiene messaging. WSUP has a gender team which addresses how best to make service provision more appropriate to women in particular, as they remain key decision makers in most households.

Unilever have been working on how they can revolve business propositions and spin out businesses which could sell their products to low-income consumers. More long-term and sustainable business propositions include getting water supplies in slums so that people can then buy shampoo and soap.

> They [Unilever] have a whole series of different initiatives and they recognise that it is quite likely that many of them will not go to profitability, but it is about trying to understand how you can push forward service delivery in a bunch of different markets, so Clean Team is one of those.

## Conclusion

Since 2012, Clean Team has scaled up and grown to over 40 staff, 2,500 toilets, with approximately 17,500 consumers benefiting from in-home sanitation facilities (Clean Team, 2016).

Financial Auditors Ernst and Young (EY) recently looked at a number of different sanitation facility models. EY concluded that, even though Clean Team is still trying to get to the breakeven point, it is by far the most impressive operation that they have seen to date.

According to Neil Jeffery, this reflects not only how difficult it is to get such projects to function, but also the many advances the organisation has managed to make in that period.

## References and bibliography

Christie, M. J. and Honig, B. (2006), *Social entrepreneurship: New research findings, Journal of World Business*, 41 (1), pp. 1–5.

Clean Team (2016), *Our Model – Clean Team Ghana*, www.cleanteamtoilets.com/ [Accessed 20 October 2018].

Hao Jiao (2011), *A conceptual model for social entrepreneurship directed toward social impact on society*, *Social Enterprise Journal*, 7(2), pp. 130–149.

Stevens, R., Moray, N. and Bruneel, J. (2015), *The social and economic mission of social enterprises: Dimensions, measurement, validation, and relation, entrepreneurship Theory and Practice*, 39(5), pp. 1051–1082.

WSUP (2011), *Practice note, Clean Team, a human-centred approach to sanitation: initial trials in Ghana*, www.wsup.com/content/uploads/2017/08/PN008-ENGLISH-CleanTeam.pdf [Accessed 20 October 2018].

WSUP (2015), *Water and Sanitation for the Urban Poor, report and financial statements for year ended 31 March, 2015*, www.wsup.com/wp-content/uploads/2013/04/WSUP-2015-signed-accounts.pdf [Accessed 15 August 2016].

WSUP (2016), *Business plan 2016–2020*, www.wsup.com/content/uploads/2017/09/WSUP-Business-Plan-2016.pdf [Accessed 20 October 2018].

# 17 Can social investment become sustainable?

*Craig Dearden-Phillips*

**Craig Dearden-Phillips** is Managing Director of both Stepping Out and Social Club, which exist to help Third Sector organisations to grow their mission. He offers his personal perspective on social investment.

Quotes are attributed to informal conversations between Craig Dearden-Phillips and a wide range of individuals across the sector since 2016.

## Reality check

Anyone arriving in the UK charity sector in early 2017 could have been forgiven for thinking there was a revolution going on in the way charities and social enterprises were funded.

Following the election in 2015 of a new Conservative administration, the main thrust of government policy (and money) was focused on "payment against results" and social investment. This was mainly in the form of outcome-based funding, but also continued support for social impact bonds, social finance loans and quasi-equity investments in charities and social enterprises.

> Politicians talked up social investment as the big new solution in public services, a novel way of funding only "what works".

Headlines in 2016 (Guardian, 2016), read "in four years there will be no grants for charities – it will destroy communities". Roll forward several years to 2018 and the government is now reflecting on how important grants are to the continued sustainability of the sector. This has been led in part by the House of Lords report into civil society, *Stronger Charities for a Stronger Society*, a consideration of the work of the sector and its funding (House of Lords, 2018).

But has the rhetoric run ahead of the reality? How much social investment has really been going on? Could social finance *really* replace Boring-Old-Grants-and-Donations as the main source of charity and social enterprise finance? Or, is there something of the *Wizard of Oz* about it all, a lot of noise and light but no real substance?

# The UK social finance landscape

## *The early years: 2005–10*

Making sense of the changing social finance landscape isn't easy. Its big UK breakthrough came about a decade ago when private equity investor and philanthropist, Sir Ronald Cohen, convinced the Blair/Brown government that Third Sector bodies should borrow from socially motivated investors to scale up their best solutions.

Cohen's observation was that grants and donations represent only a fraction of the resources that could be made available to charities from "social investors" (The Lord Mayor's Charity Leadership Programme, 2014). The theory went that these individual investors and institutions are happy to forego a full return on their investment money for a "blended return", which combines verified social impact with modest levels of financial return on investment (Bugg-Levine and Emerson, 2011).

This idea is expressed in the simple graph shown in Figure 17.1. On the upward axis sit traditional grants, which look for a pure social return and nil financial return. On the horizontal axis sit ordinary investment, which is purely about financial return. And, in between them, sits "blended return", a coming together of financial and social outcome.

Successive governments bought into Cohen's idea of a new, untapped reservoir of social investment and have been highly active since in leading a market to try to make it happen. This really came to the fore in the UK's leadership of the G8 Task Force on Social Investment (G8 Social Impact Investment Taskforce, 2014)

To this end, the UK government has been the cornerstone investor of various pieces of social finance infrastructure. From 2005, a number of new funds were created, including *Futurebuilders* and *Communitybuilders* (SIB, 2018). For the first time, charities were encouraged to take on growth finance, mainly in the form of debt.

Repayment by these organisations would give mainstream investors the proof needed that social investment was, indeed, a safe place for their money. These funds, being government money, did actually permit the mix of grant funding with loans and found a market relatively quickly. Both funds were fully deployed, albeit with mixed results, as one would expect.

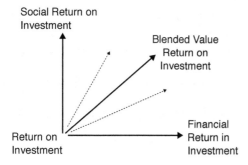

*Figure 17.1* Social investment ideal blended return.

Source: Bugg-Levine and Emerson (2011). Figure from Cass CCE Social Investment Toolkit (Cass CCE, 2016, p. 6).

## 2010–15: Big Society Capital (BSC) and the social finance intermediaries

But this was fairly small-scale experimentation. It wasn't until the formation of BSC, in 2012, that a serious attempt to create a national infrastructure for social finance was made.

Set up using £400 million from unclaimed redundant bank accounts, BSC was tasked by government to raise similar levels of funds from socially minded investors and institutions. Major investments have been made from four major high-street banks (Barclays, Lloyds, RBS and HSBC).

The idea of BSC was not to lend directly to the Third Sector, but to be a kind of Bank of England for social finance. Its role, therefore, was to channel "wholesale" funding to socially motivated "retail" banks like Charity Bank and new "social finance intermediaries" (SIFIs), such as Social and Sustainable Capital, Social Investment Business, Resonance and Big Issue Invest. In turn, these would put money to work in charities and social enterprises (Big Society Capital, 2018).

Big Society Capital and the SIFIs it works through have been held back by not being able to offer anything other than loans (or equity) funding to the social sector, and not to a wider commercial audience.

There has also been criticism of BSC about the amount of investment capital that has been deployed and the type of investment this has represented – mainly against property and assets and not genuine risk capital.

Post 2012, all that was on offer to charities and social enterprises was a group of debt-based products and services that looked very similar to those in a high-street bank (but more expensive and with the need to prove outcomes and social value created). They were being sold to those people from SIFIs fresh out of investment banking. The SIFIs on the one hand, and charities and social enterprises on the other, just weren't talking the same language. One focused on the social, the other on the financial. It just didn't work as expected – and the charity market, by and large, turned away.

Not only was the sales-pitch wrong, but the products were wrong for many organisations. One SIFI leader had this to say:

> The charity and social enterprise market typically seek loans of around £150,000 to £250,000, often to purchase an asset. But the new social investment market was set up on a cost-base that made this level of loan uneconomic. Only bigger investments of £1m plus actually allow the SIFIs to recover the set-up costs of the investment. So, we had a mismatch between the type of finance charities wanted (smaller simple, cheap loans) and the products being promoted to them (big complex, expensive financial instruments). Not a recipe for success.

It took several years for BSC to build a deeper understanding of the sector it was trying to serve. This changed in late 2015 with the appointment of a new CEO and several new executives with roots in the not-for-profit sector, who talked the language of the sector and understood their needs.

## 2015 and beyond: outcomes funding and social investment bonds

Following the Conservative general election victory in 2015 – and a renewed emphasis on fiscal austerity – there was, in parallel to continued support for BSC, a new drive towards "outcomes funding". This followed a couple of very early experiments from 2012 in the criminal justice sector in Peterborough, England (Civil Society, 2017). Facing fiscal austerity, the UK government became increasingly enthusiastic about the idea of only paying for what works – or "outcomes".

One of the main ways for enabling this has been the *social impact bond* (SIB). SIBs involve government letting social investors pay up front for charities to deliver the work and only paying back to investors, from the Outcomes Fund, for that work which delivers the desired result, or "outcome".

This leaves social investors to absorb losses on interventions that fail, with government funding held back for other schemes (those that work). SIBs encourage social investors, the thinking goes, to consider very carefully which operating models and partners they choose to deliver outcomes.

This has brought a new focus in the sector on impact, and organisations such as Impetus-PEF have focused on impact-led investments and impact systems. However, sometimes the sector has needed grants to be able to be sustainable and to learn what works in a supported and innovative way.

SIBs have brought flexibility of approach and new ways of bringing resources to help social causes.

---

**Ways to Wellness (2018)**

- A new social enterprise community interest company (CIC) set up in Newcastle-Upon-Tyne under a social impact bond
- Works with local charities to improve measurable health outcomes for local residents at risk of preventable long-term conditions
- The work was funded to £1.65 million by Bridges Ventures, a social investor
- If Ways to Wellness delivers its agreed targets, Bridges Ventures gets that money back with interest from the Newcastle Clinical Commissioning Group (CCG)
- If Ways to Wellness fails or falls short, the CCG does not pay, leaving Bridges Ventures to absorb the costs incurred by the failure as they will not be repaid.

(Ways to Wellness, 2015)

---

## Three key points

The social finance sector in the UK had its intellectual beginnings in the world of investment finance. Its steady progress over the last decade has made it the "funding mechanism of choice" for UK Governments as they engage with social enterprises and charities up to the 2020s.

Potentially, a set of ideas from a particular part of the commercial sector has been overlaid onto the charity and social enterprise sectors, reinforcing a widely observed adaptation of business and commercial concepts in these sectors over recent decades.

Let's look at this from three different angles:

### 1 Has social finance in the UK been hampered by a flawed Government strategy for roll-out?

This has potentially left a charities market yet to be impressed by what social finance can achieve. I see an overly commercial banking–dominated social investment market and an expensive at times social finance intermediary (SIFI) market which has often not listened, failing to convince enough charities that social finance can accelerate their purposes. However, this is now changing.

### 2 Despite this lost opportunity, there has been sufficient success to show that social finance in the UK has a valid and substantial future role to play in the finance of social purpose organisations

The successful deployment of social finance to a very wide variety of social problems – from children in the care system in Essex through to reducing obesity on Tyneside – has demonstrated *enough* early success to show that there is indeed genuine scope for greater use of social finance in the period to 2025. One we may safely assume will be characterised by continued fiscal constraint from government. Social investment continues to grow. Currently, there are around 4,000 separate social investments across the UK with an aggregate value of £2.3 billion (Big Society Capital, 2017).

### 3 For the future use of social finance to be optimised, there will need to be changes in the way it is promoted and operated in relation to the UK Third Sector

There is plenty of evidence to show that social finance – beyond relatively small, secured loans for assets like buildings – is commonly, and in some cases correctly, viewed as risky, expensive and overly complex. Charities have also made some very important and valid points about the appropriateness of debt-funding for certain types of charitable work. This often attracts a silent response from social investors who refuse to mix their loans with traditional grants, or see a reduction in market rates of return.

We are seeing this change with the Access Foundation and its ability to "blend" finance, mixing grants and loans to create something new and powerful for the sector. Salway (2017) highlights these shortcomings and asks that the social investment focuses on demand-led support and engages in creating bridges between investor and social purpose organisation over which capital can flow.

## How well is social finance working for the charity and social enterprise sector?

In truth, it has been a mixed story. The reality of the social finance roll-out has proved more complicated than first envisaged.

While the infrastructure put in place by government through BSC has provided a platform for growth, it has also suffered from structural and technical issues, as discussed so far in this chapter. However, we must also recognise that the anticipated demand from charities and social enterprises seeking investment has been far lower than expected.

Promising charities – particularly in a difficult economic period – do not necessarily behave in exactly the same way as growing businesses when faced with cheap debt and offers of help. They tend to be more risk averse. While the uptake of social finance is rising steadily (Big Society Capital, 2017), we are still in what social investors politely term an "early market".

So, why have things gone more slowly than predicted?

Three reasons stand out:

- the appetite in the charity and social enterprise sector for taking on large levels of debt finance was over-estimated – perhaps following the relative popularity of both *Futurebuilders* and *Communitybuilders* Funds
- there's a feeling in many charities and social enterprises that social finance – with its requirement for repayment – just isn't achievable for organisations dealing with genuine but intractable need
- the language, style and occasional brashness of the social finance camp has made selling the products much harder.

This mismatch between what charities want – smaller loans for assets – and what is being offered – large sums for growth – has been profound.

To the surprise of some in the investment market, trustee boards – while happy to borrow to buy tangible assets, like a building or a fleet of minibuses – were not at all comfortable to take £1 million plus of debt to spend on business development, or new R&D to accelerate the growth of their organisations. With this dynamic, it is critical to understand that much charitable activity is simply about offering care and compassion – a kindly conversation, a shoulder to cry on – not about getting a person from "A" to "B".

There is no "outcome" as such, merely the charitable action itself, which often alters nothing for the beneficiary beyond the moment of its discharge. There is no distance-travelled that can be measured, no evidence of success beyond, perhaps, a brief moment of comfort.

This isn't the natural territory of social investment. Or, as one senior charity executive put it,

> We're not making Innocent smoothies here, with a few nice social benefits on the side. We're dealing with hard-core social need, often with little to no visible progress. There's no financial return on that for anyone. Social investors need to get real.

Evidence of this antipathy is to be found in the pipeline for social investment deals. SIFIs – the middlemen of social finance – complain about "deal-flow" and a costly slog to find and cultivate uptake. This, in turn, makes social finance appear expensive and, to some, exploitative.

Then there is the downturn. Charities have, in effect, been in recession for the better part of a decade. Organisations large and small have been adjusting income expectations downwards as donated income has stagnated and margins on public service contracts have diminished.

Equally, many charities simply can't see beyond the grants and donations mind-set they are used to, lacking the confidence or impetus to change.

Charities also have the additional pressure of current and future unfunded pension deficits, which sit on the balance sheet of the organisation. Cumulatively, this has made charities cautious at just a time when a flood of new repayable funding was entering the market. As Stephen Bubb, the Chairman of Social Investment Business, said, as he was leaving the role, "These are hard years for charities. There is too little demand and far too much money, in far too large quantities, now being offered".

To try to make social finance more appealing, government has encouraged the creation of the Investment and Contract Readiness Fund (2013–15), Creating Better Outcomes Fund (2015–17), Big Potential (2015–17) and the Access Foundation (2016–), all designed to ease the path to social investment.

These funds are trying to get more charities and social enterprises to the point where they feel they can safely take on debt to grow their mission. Results so far have been mixed, but are helped, without doubt, by a realisation in BSC and the SIFI sector that their offerings have reflected the world many of them came from, not the charitable sector with whom they are now trying, and often failing, to engage.

> Then there's the cultural problem. On the social finance side sit bright young things fresh out of McKinsey or Deutsche Bank, with talk of "mezzanine finance" and "leverage". On the other stand are mostly older, battle-hardened stalwarts of the charity world. Although this is now changing.

This is changing, though. The relative success of intermediaries such as Resonance, Social and Sustainable Capital and Big Issue Invest – whose staff tend to come from, or have respect for, the Third Sector – demonstrates how important a connection to the sector can be when selling new ideas.

## What needs to change if social finance is to be a success?

It is clear to any business that, if the product is wrong, the price is wrong and your salesforce is wrong, you need to change things.

This seems to be where the government, BSC and the SIFIs found themselves in early 2017. New blood being brought into BSC (new CEO, new Strategy Director) and its rapid transformation to a convener of powerful conversations. Likewise, SIFIs have learned to be accessible, to speak the language of the sector they want to sell to.

More fundamentally, products and services have started to change, too. Charities and social enterprises are deeply intimidated by debt-only finance products that come in lumps of £500,000 or more (not less). But the history of *Futurebuilders* (still the biggest social investment fund ever created and deployed) suggests that the charity sector will embrace debt more readily when that debt comes alongside a grant that acknowledges, at product level, the mix of social and financial return being sought (Boston Consulting Group, 2015).

Will BSC and its paymaster, the UK government, let this happen? My hope is they do. More than any other thing, it will help unlock the charities sector to social financiers.

To get the market going, BSC and its SIFIs need to make some bold offer to charities and social enterprises willing to be the early pioneers of a move to a socially financed future.

If this involves grants as well as loans, so be it, in my view. Others will then follow.

## Successes

But, to write off social finance – even in its present, highly imperfect state – is, at best, premature, at worst, highly damaging. While it isn't always possible to use expensive, borrowed money to address all social problems, sometimes it is exactly the right thing to do.

- Midlands Together raised £3 million to buy houses for renovation by released offenders who are trained and then housed (Barrow Cadbury Trust, 2015)
- Unforgettable, a social enterprise tackling dementia, raised £750,000 to develop new products and services for those suffering with dementia (Unforgettable, 2018)
- K10 raised £800,000 to develop apprenticeships for marginalised young people (K10, 2018).

None of these organisations could exist or grow their impact without social investment.

The challenge now is to make the list a lot longer. These are mostly new organisations. We need older organisations to embrace the possibilities. Culturally, this is a challenge. Charity boards are notoriously conservative, often prioritising the existence of the organisation over the possibility of massively expanding its impact on beneficiaries.

While social finance organisations need to change, this is where charities and social enterprises have their role to play. It is high time that key leaders in the Third Sector came out and said this clearly.

The recent BSC initiative, Get Informed (2017), has enabled boards to have this critical conversation around social investment. It brings mentors and boards together in a learning environment.

## Learning

The learning from these successes contains the seeds of a wider adaptation of social finance as a means of increasing the pool of funding available to do good work in our society.

While it is always possible to say that there is no profit in helping people, we are consistently seeing social finance being used to develop organisations which do just that. The investment isn't necessarily targeted on paying for the activity of the organisation, but in facilitating the growth of the organisation itself, which then goes on to achieve social goals.

So, in the case of Midlands Together, social finance is used to provide working capital for the business and for development capital for them to buy and sell property. Without this capital, Midlands Together couldn't function in the way it does. Yes, it could obtain grants. But, as a start-up in a risky sector, with little track record, that would be quite difficult. And finding grant funding in the quantities needed at the time needed would be very difficult without social finance.

> It is important that we recognise the intellectual trap of believing that social finance doesn't necessarily have a role to play in addressing need.

The more valid point is that it has a limited role in funding an organisation's interventions when those interventions don't have fundable outcomes. But social finance *can* be used to help that same organisation to put itself on a path to growth – which, in turn, delivers on its mission, as long as this helps to generate the necessary income from whichever source is most suitable.

While social finance links best to outcomes, it has its uses beyond outcomes, as many of its recipients have found. Their organisation's ability to do good has been enhanced by it.

## Conclusion

So, what are we to make of social investment and social finance?

It is clear that its early advocates over-claimed its virtues without the examples of success to address the doubters. In turn, Big Society Capital has been a highly qualified success, as have the SIFIs. Large amounts of capital, however, have gone undeployed.

> The costs of social finance are still too high and need to be on a par with the high street for fuss-free, everyday finance.

And, yes, there are still a few people in Hugo Boss suits visiting community workers in Sunderland to talk about the need for "codified playbooks" and "verifiable metrics".

This aside, the charity sector has to be open-minded about social finance. Charity income is stagnant. Donations are levelling off. Grant funders are maxed out.

Sir Ronald Cohen, all those years ago, was right that the pool of money for good work isn't getting any bigger and our sector needs a reservoir of new money to tap into.

Sure, not all charities can or should pay money back. But, charities need to show that repayable money can be used in imaginative ways to extend their mission to larger numbers of beneficiaries.

So, it is time for both sides to step up. If the social finance sector cannot be flexible enough to meet its target market half-way, then it will fail. Capital will remain inside institutions, not working in charities achieving social good.

> If the Third Sector can't get its head around the possibilities opened up to them by social finance, it's hard to see how we can grow the sector's impact beyond the high-water mark of the pre-austerity years.

The core idea is easy enough to grasp. Social sector organisations can be invested in and create a "blended return" of social and financial outcomes for investors. The reality is proving far more complicated.

What this demonstrates is that there urgently needs to be change both in the way social investment and social finance is presented *and* in the way it works in relation to other, more traditional funding streams.

The charity and social enterprise sectors are and will probably remain financially conservative, partly grant-dependent and risk-averse compared to the mainstream businesses sector. Even promising charities do not necessarily behave the same way as upwardly mobile businesses.

It is to this reality that the social finance sector must accommodate itself.

# References

Barrow Cadbury Trust (2015), *Midlands Together: a "blindingly obvious" idea*, accessed 20 October 2018, www.barrowcadbury.org.uk/voices/midlands-together-a-blindingly-obvious-idea/.

Big Society Capital (2017), *Size of the social investment market*, accessed 20 October 2018, www.bigsocietycapital.com/home/about-us/size-social-investment-market.

Big Society Capital (2018), *Big Society Capital: about us*, accessed 20 October 2018, www.bigsocietycapital.com/about-us.

Boston Consulting Group (2015), *A tale of two funds: the management and performance of Futurebuilders England*, accessed 20 October 2018, www.sibgroup.org.uk/sites/default/files/files/Management and Performance of the Futurebuilders-England Fund.pdf.

Bugg-Levine, A. and Emerson, J. (2011), *Impact investing: transforming how we make money while making a difference*, Jossey-Bass (Wiley).

Cass CCE (2016), *Social investment tools for success: doing the right things and doing them right*, accessed 20 October 2018, www.cass.city.ac.uk/faculties-and-research/centres/cce/resources/tools-for-success.

Civil Society (2017), *Peterborough social impact bond investors repaid in full*, accessed 20 October 2018, www.civilsociety.co.uk/news/peterborough-social-impact-bond-investors-repaid-in-full.html.

G8 Social Impact Investment Taskforce (2014), *Impact investment: the hidden heart of markets*, accessed 20 October 2018, www.gsgii.org/reports/impact-investment-the-invisible-heart-of-markets/.

Get Informed (2017), *Social investment for boards*, accessed 20 October 2018, www.bigsocietycapital.com/get-informed.

Guardian (2016), *In four years there will be no grants for charities – it will destroy communities*, accessed 20 October 2018, www.theguardian.com/voluntary-sector-network/2016/feb/11/grants-local-charities-campaign-appeal-government-cuts.

House of Lords (2018), *Stronger charities for a stronger society*, accessed 20 October 2018, House of Lords, https://publications.parliament.uk/pa/ld201617/ldselect/ldchar/133/133.pdf.

K10 (2018), website, accessed 20 October 2018, www.k-10.co.uk/.

Salway, M. (2017), *Social investment as a new charity finance tool: using head and heart*, Cass Business School, Centre for Charity Effectiveness.

SIB (2018), *Futurebuilders and Communitybuilders*, accessed 20 October 2018, www.sibgroup.org.uk/.

The Lord Mayor's Charity Leadership Programme (2014), *Sir Ronald Cohen chair of the Social Impact Investment Taskforce established by the G8, The Mansion House*, accessed 20 October 2018, www.cass.city.ac.uk/__data/assets/pdf_file/0003/209775/LM-CLP_Sir-Ronald-Cohen-Jan-14.pdf.

Unforgettable (2018), website, accessed 20 October 2018, www.unforgettable.org/.

Ways to Wellness (2015), *Commissioning Better Outcomes Fund: Ways to Wellness evaluation report*, accessed 20 October 2018, www.waystowellness.org.uk/news/2015/07/commissioning-better-outcomes-fund-deep-dive-report/.

Ways to Wellness (2018), website, accessed 20.10.2018, https://waystowellness.org.uk/.

# 17a Case study

## Lendwithcare (www.lendwithcare.org)

*Tracey Horner and Mark Salway*

In this case study, **Tracey Horner,** Head of Lendwithcare, and **Mark Salway** look at the Lendwithcare microfinance initiative.

## Microfinance

---

### The concept

- Lendwithcare is a microfinance-lending website from the development charity CARE International UK
- Launched in September 2010, it allows individuals and groups in the Global North to make small loans to entrepreneurs in low-income countries, and help them work their way out of poverty
- It supports entrepreneurs across the world and in countries such as Ecuador, Occupied Palestinian Territories (OPT), Pakistan, Malawi and Zimbabwe through partner microfinance institutions (MFIs).

---

## Introduction

CARE International (CARE) is a global humanitarian and development organisation working to help the poorest across the world. It works in 90 countries (CARE International UK, 2018).

In 1972, CARE realised that it could help people out of the cycle of poverty and help build resilience for their communities through microfinance. Specifically, village savings and loan associations (VSLAs) were identified as a way that groups of women could come together to save and help each other.

From saving together the women could make loans to the community to set up micro-businesses: banana growing, pig farming and sewing, for example.

VSLAs were typically established by CARE directly or were established with the help of microfinance institutions (MFIs). At the same time CARE helped establish many of the MFIs that exist today. A USD96.6 billion gross loan portfolio was reported by MIXMarket at the end of the 2016 financial year (MIXMarket, 2019). The numbers are large.

Lendwithcare is enabling small value loans to be made to entrepreneurs in the Global South and is crowdfunding for capital. In turn, entrepreneurs make money and grow new businesses. It is this innovative social investment cycle that makes Lendwithcare special.

Lendwithcare also enables Sharia complaint loans to be made through Sharia complaint partners in Pakistan or the Palestinian Territories.

---

**What is microfinance?**

Microfinance refers to financial services for poor and low-income clients. Although most attention has been on the provision of small loans, microfinance also includes the provision of other basic financial services such as savings, money transfer and insurance.

---

## The background to Lendwithcare.org

In 2010 the biggest issue was that the general public were increasingly less likely to support international development organisations. Across many NGOs, the giving public in the UK were not able to see how their money was being used; people simply did not understand the nature of poverty and how difficult it is to work in many contexts. This was the social impact CARE wanted to achieve through Lendwithcare.

CARE also saw that peer-to-peer lending platforms, such as Kiva, were enabling new ways of crowdfunding money through online technology. It wanted to build financial inclusion for those in low-income countries, and find new sources of capital for its linked MFIs. Separately, it wanted to raise its brand profile to facilitate the flow of more funds and donations.

CARE had built its operational work through grants and contracts, but lacked the unrestricted and flexible funds to enable it to be innovative and learn. Donor pressure on funding and overheads was leading to less money being available for this; a vicious cycle (Bridgespan, 2009).

CARE International decided to do something about this. From an innovation fund of £75,000, it undertook a scoping exercise with Bluefrog, a specialist fundraising agency. After a successful pilot, the trustees invested £0.5 million of their reserves in developing, building and marketing the platform.

This was the initial investment that was provided to Lendwithcare.org to help it grow. By 30 June 2019 it had made £23.9 million of loans to economically active poor people, and had supported 116,181 entrepreneurs (CARE International UK, 2018). It has won several awards for innovation.

When Lendwithcare was launched the management and trustees were concerned that it would cannibalise income from existing donors and thereby erode CARE's regular giving portfolio. Instead, people have now learned more about how complex it is to work with poverty and have been incredibly supportive.

The internet is leading to a global pattern of innovation across the world, bringing communities together to help each other.

Lendwithcare was established not only as a powerful way of ensuring capital reaches economically active poor people, but also so lenders in the UK get to understand the stories and business dreams of the people they are supporting.

*Figure 17a.1* The Lendwithcare model.
Source: CARE International, reproduced with permission.

## How does it work?

Figure 17a.1 shows how Lendwithcare.org lending cycle takes place.
  It follows the following cycle (Lendwithcare, 2019):

**It starts with an idea:** Whether it's opening a market stall, or perhaps a small tailoring business, or diversifying the crops they grow, people across the developing world are bursting with business ideas – all they need is a helping hand to get started.

**The entrepreneur requests a loan:** Entrepreneurs approach a local Microfinance Institution (MFI) that is a Lendwithcare partner and, if their ideas show promise, they get the go-ahead for the loan they need to get their business going.

**You lend to an entrepreneur:** The MFI uploads the entrepreneur's profile to Lendwithcare. Lenders can see these in the Entrepreneurs section, where they can choose which promising business idea they'd like to support.

**The entrepreneur's business grows**: Entrepreneur profiles are updated so you can see how their business is transforming their lives.

**Your loan is repaid:** The entrepreneur pays back their loan in instalments to the MFI, which transfers these repayments to CARE International. We then credit the repayment to the lenders Lendwithcare account. It's as simple as that!

**The lender decides what happens next:** When the lender's loan is repaid they can withdraw it if they wish. They can also donate it to CARE International, or they can make another loan, helping more entrepreneurs turn their ideas and hopes for a better future into reality.

Lendwithcare's platform enables MFIs to work closely with communities to develop financial inclusion further. For example, MFIs are careful to help local communities learn how to budget and develop a business model. This enables entrepreneurs to develop real skills and develop sustainable businesses.

Lenders can browse the list of entrepreneurs on the website; read about their businesses; see the value of the loan they have requested; look at the percentage of the loan already provided by other lenders; and then choose an entrepreneur to lend to. It uses a website-based platform to innovate.

Lendwithcare can only continue if its operating costs are covered by donations from the general public, its lenders and its corporate and foundation donations. CARE asks for a voluntary top-up donation at the point loans are made to support this. CARE also makes unrestricted income from unredeemed gift vouchers and dormant accounts.

## In conclusion

Lendwithcare is a new breed of microfinance initiative using crowdfunding and peer-to-peer lending to enable funds to flow from the Global North to low-income countries.

Cutting-edge. Innovative. World-changing.

## References

Bridgespan (2009), *The nonprofit starvation cycle*, accessed 22 September 2018, www.bridgespan. org/insights/initiatives/pay-what-it-takes-philanthropy/the-nonprofit-starvation-cycle.

CARE International UK (2018), *CARE International UK annual report and accounts for the year ended 30 June 2018*, accessed 24 June 2019, www.careinternational.org.uk/sites/default/files/ CIUK-Annual-Report-and-Accounts-2018.pdf.

Lendwithcare (2019), website, https://lendwithcare.org/, accessed 24 June 2019.

MIXMarket (2019), *Data and intelligence for socially responsible investors*, accessed 24 June 2019, www.themix.org/mixmarket.

# 18 What about small charities and social investment?

*Leila Baker and Niamh Goggin*

**Leila Baker** and **Niamh Goggin** of the Institute for Voluntary Action Research, explore what small charities want from social investment and borrowing as they share their experience from recent research (IVAR, 2016, *Small Charities and Social Investment*; Baker and Goggin, 2013, *Charities and Social Investment*).

## The experience of 25

The Institute for Voluntary Action Research (IVAR) carried out a study (2015/16) of the experiences of 25 small English charities in seeking, receiving and managing social investment.

The research was funded by IVAR, The Barrow Cadbury Trust and Access – The Foundation for Social Investment, with the support of the Charity Commission.

There were three main reasons for concentrating on registered charities with an income under £1 million:

1   **Significant numbers.** Small and medium-sized voluntary organisations, including registered charities, total 62,789 in comparison to 4,273 large and major organisations in England (NCVO, 2016). Therefore, they merit consideration as a significant market segment in their own right.
2   **Absent voice.** Our review of the literature on social investment told us that the experience of large charities that receive social investment and of charities that make social investment is relatively better understood and more "visible" in debates about social investment. This gap in research means that the voice of small and medium-sized charities as potential investees is largely absent from discussions about their participation in the social investment market.
3   **Registered status.** We wanted to capture the voice of the "established" voluntary sector and their experience of social investment alongside grants, donations and public sector contracts. Concentrating on registered charities enabled us to do this.

A breakdown of the charities included by location and focus is shown in Tables 18.1 and 18.2.

The majority of the social investments were secured, one-off loans, relating to the purchase and/or refurbishment of property.

A small number of loans were for working capital, cash flow or new projects and most of these charities had borrowed more than once.

*Table 18.1* Distribution of charities by UK region

| Region | North East | North West | York & Humber | West Midlands | London | South East | South West |
|---|---|---|---|---|---|---|---|
| Number | 2 | 5 | 8 | 1 | 5 | 2 | 2 |

*Table 18.2* Distribution of charities by organisational focus

| Org. focus | Arts & culture | Community | Disability | Education | Families & children | Health |
|---|---|---|---|---|---|---|
| Number | 3 | 3 | 2 | 1 | 3 | 1 |

| Org. focus | Housing & homeless | Lesbian, gay, bisexual & trans | Social welfare | Women | Young people |
|---|---|---|---|---|---|
| Number | 4 | 1 | 2 | 1 | 4 |

Of the 36 loans made to the 20 borrowers (five organisations did not proceed with investment), five were grant/loan combinations.

## Insights from the literature

We reviewed the literature in the area of social investment in small and medium-sized charities and identified the landscape shown in Table 18.3.

## Key findings

This research draws attention to a range of common challenges for small and medium-sized charities seeking to address mainly social welfare needs in their communities of geography or communities of interest. A summary of key findings are as follows:

### Finding 1: The social investment journey

Understanding the social investment journey both from a charity and from an investor perspective could alleviate some of the difficulties that both parties experience in working together. Many of the problems that arise can be addressed through improved communication (most charities have never been through the process before and are essentially piloting it for their own organisation) and through deeper understanding of the drivers leading to charities engaging with social investment and the way charities experience investment.

*Table 18.3* Insights from literature

| | |
|---|---|
| **Charity voice** | • A gap in research means that the voice of small and medium-sized charities (those with a turnover of £10,000 to £1 million) is not being heard in the social investment debate.<br>• We found no material on charities that had been turned down for social investment. |
| • Small charities' effectiveness needs to be measured by their capacity to deliver on their mission, not their investment readiness.<br>• Some charities will never need to be investment-ready, as that status is not relevant to their capacity to deliver their mission.<br>• For others, investment readiness shows how they have opened up strategic and funding options and, thus, built their capacity to deliver.<br>• Investment readiness needs to be seen as related to mission, rather than a goal in itself. | **Mission** |
| **Capacity** | • Smaller organisations can find it difficult to dedicate time and resources for negotiating with third-party investors and generating the impact evidence that such investors require. This limits their access to finance (Moullin *et al.*, 2011; James, 2016).<br>• The Futurebuilders Fund learned that organisational size – along with its stage of development – was related to the likelihood that an organisation would default on its loan. Organisations that defaulted had an average turnover of "half the size of the rest of the closed portfolio"; and 67% of defaulters were "start-up"/growth investments, "compared to 30% in the rest of the portfolio, which was mainly composed of expansion investments" (Brown *et al.*, 2015, p. 25). |
| • NCVO acknowledges that the majority of charities are small and many are unincorporated, "meaning that the personal risk to the majority of Trustees in taking on debt would likely be considered unacceptable" (James *et al.*, 2016, p. 25).<br>• There's a potential demand for social finance in some smaller organisations (Ludlow, 2009) wanting to "scale up" in order to achieve greater impact and greater economies.<br>• Small and medium-sized charities are demanding smaller value, unsecured investments (Kane and Ravenscroft, 2016).<br>• There's a gap in the supply of the kind of higher risk investments that this would require – "builder finance" (Heap and Ravison, 2013).<br>• In order to make a surplus, there's an incentive for investors to concentrate on higher value transactions associated with larger, more mature organisations.<br>• Research from Cass Centre for Charity Effectiveness has found that 40% of charities feel that social investment will bring little or no change to their organisations, or are openly negative about it. However, 60% see social investment and borrowing as either positively changing their business models, or being transformational to them (Salway, 2017). | **Demand** |

## Finding 2: Mission-driven social investment

The aim of all social investments should be to leave an organisation in a stronger position, not only financially, but also in relation to its ability to pursue its mission. To do that requires:

- Broad assessments including, but not limited to, due diligence
- A willingness to engage with inexperienced charities to help them survive
- Alignment of mission and values
- Financial products and associated outreach and marketing tailored to charity need
- Recognition that not all social investment is impact investment
- Critical evaluation of property transactions

## Finding 3: Building good relationships

- Charities are driven by mission first and appreciate working with social investors whose values are aligned with their own
- Charities want to develop good relationships with social investors, rather than just experiencing a good transaction
- A good relationship between the CEO and chair is critical when dealing with social investment

## Finding 4: Suitable products and processes

- If the demand for social investment is driven by necessity, stability and development, then national and local outreach and marketing should reflect that reality, rather than focusing primarily on impact and scalability.
- Financial products, outreach and marketing should be driven by charity need, not investor market-building.

## Finding 5: Funding working capital and charity reserves

- Changes in local authority commissioning and contracting mean that many smaller charities find themselves at the end of long supply chains. This increases risk and requires the generation of surpluses to fund reserves and working capital.

We explore each of these findings in the remainder of this chapter.

Financial products, outreach and marketing should be driven by charity need not investor market-building.

# Finding 1: The social investment journey

---

### Three kinds of journey

We identified three kinds of organisational journey among the 25 charities: a highly stressful journey; a journey made with confidence; and, charities that chose to walk away.

---

### *Journey 1: A highly stressful journey*

These charities had little or no prior knowledge and experience of charity finance other than grants, donations and local authority contracts. Every aspect of the social investment experience was unfamiliar.

The application process was difficult to handle, not only because charities did not know how it worked, but also because lenders did not explain it.

These charities had not entered into social investment in a planned way. It was the only finance available at a time of urgent need. They did not see it as being a new way to finance their work, but instead had focused back on identifying independent funders for new grants.

### *Journey 2: A journey made with confidence*

While some charities did not take the decision to seek investment lightly, it was on a par with other major decisions that they had taken in the past. The experience may have been stressful at times, but it was manageable.

For several, the prospect of needing to generate an income and/or purchasing and managing property was not new to them and their track record gave them a degree of confidence.

A minority interviewed said they expected to take on further investment in the future. Most said that, while they would not rule it out altogether, there would need to be a strong business case for doing so and the finance would need to be something that the charity really needed to do.

### *Journey 3: Charities that chose to walk away*

These charities looked into the possibility of social investment because a trusted individual or advisor suggested investment in order to diversify their income. They withdrew from the process for three main reasons, the first one being dominant across all of the charities:

1   **Lack of alignment**
    Charities said investors did not understand and failed to take account of their social focus. They described investors as "well-meaning" but lacking understanding of charities and the idea of public benefit, as well as the nature of governance and leadership in small and medium-sized charities.
2   **Opaque process**
    Charities were honest about their own inexperience, which some said had probably not helped. Nonetheless, they felt that investors could do a lot more to explain their due diligence processes and were sceptical about some intermediary bodies who, they felt, appeared to be taking a "a big cut" without giving much back and lacked transparency.

3   **Organisation**
Some of the charities walked away due to a perceived weakness in their finances, their financial processes, governance or leadership.

## The influence of operating environment

**Four features** of the operating environment influenced the attitude of small charities to social investment:

1   **Local authority contracts and working capital**
Charities had lost contracts due to reductions in public expenditure, where services had been removed altogether or where smaller contracts had been combined into one large contract and awarded to a larger provider. Where they continued to provide services, some found themselves at the end of long supply chains, leading to delays in payment for completed work.
Second, they had been required to move to payment in arrears and to pay upfront for the resources they needed to deliver the contract.
These charities had a genuine need for working capital, without which they would have had to eat into carefully accumulated reserves, which are there to protect the organisation.
2   **Income diversification**
Charities aspired to move away from reliance on local authority contracts and to adjust the ratio of grants to contracts overall.
3   **Property investment**
Most of the loans were part of a larger capital and business development funding package, which the charities had assembled themselves. These comprised not only loans, but also multiple grants and contracts.
In many cases, the loans and other kinds of finance were inter-dependent, leading to a race to secure the loan in order not to lose a grant, or vice versa.
4   **Enterprise**
Most of the charities, with some exceptions, were sanguine about the extent to which they would be able to generate an income from the kinds of activities that support their mission. Rental income was modest, unpredictable and no basis for expansion.

A minority of charities saw enterprise or entrepreneurship as a philosophy because it had enabled them to move away from a service delivery model and adopt an approach where residents or volunteers were part of operating the charity. How this worked varied: running a shop or café; building resources for sale or operating a small-scale business from the site. However, these enterprises did not generate significant revenues and that was not their primary focus.

## Finding 2: Mission–driven social investment

In every case, the charities' application for social investment was mission-driven. However, despite this, some applications for social investment were not well thought through and this left those charities in difficulties.

Motivation for social investment among the charities was split roughly 50:50 between strategic opportunities and necessity or crisis.

### Strategic opportunities

These charities took social investment in a planned way, as part of their strategy to develop their organisation and/or protect themselves against changes in the operating environment, especially cuts to and reorganisation of local authority contracting.

A small number saw this as being explicitly about becoming independent, buying time to restructure or review their strategy, and highlighted the value of having unrestricted finance in the form of the loans.

### Necessity or crisis

Many of the charities needed funding fast, in order to cope with a cash flow problem created by their lack of working capital or the sudden need to move premises and/or to buy their own building because it was put up for sale.

## The role of trustees

All formal decisions to seek and take investment were made by trustees, but their role in the assessment of options was limited, as few options were considered.

In most cases, CEOs (perhaps supported by finance officers) discussed the borrowing proposal in advance with the chair and/or a committee of the board and then presented it to the full board for decision.

### Leading the decision-making

In some cases, the decision was strongly led by the CEO, a single trustee or a small group of trustees.

In other organisations, the CEO liaised with a board sub-committee that then reported to the board, or the CEO liaised with the chair and then took the proposal to the board.

In most cases, trustees took the decision seriously and brought in external advisors (accountants and solicitors).

> Having someone on the board, or available to trustees, capable of making "sound financial judgements" was important to trustees, who perceived a need for a bridge between the charity and the finance provider.

### Trustees' role and attitude

Most trustees took their role in agreeing social investment seriously and were serious through their review process. Some CEOs and trustees thought that trustees with business or finance experience were more comfortable with the prospect of a loan.

In a small number of cases, trustees opposed taking loans on "moral" grounds or felt that borrowing indicated that the charity was not a going concern, or were very anxious about liability and local reputation.

## Attitude to social investment now

Those who borrowed from necessity were wary of borrowing again for the same purpose.

There was a strong sentiment that the organisation would need to have moved on and strengthened its financial position.

Some organisations are very focused on "paying down the loan and getting out of debt".

Organisations with a working business model that requires further investment were more enthusiastic.

One organisation with multiple loans uses a hierarchy of tests to help decide whether to take a loan. Does it meet charitable aims? Is it an opportunity for profit or profile? How about strategic fit? And finally, interestingly, "is there a desire to do it" among staff and trustees?

## The application process

### Who did charities approach to borrow from?

The majority of newly borrowing charities only approached one social investor referred by one trusted advisor, mainly external to, but supportive of, the charity. One charity approached two social investors. Three charities contacted three or more potential lenders.

> There was little scoping or review of the market, which charities found to be opaque and confusing. They did not compare average loan sizes, interest rates, loan terms, lender experience in the sub-sector or track records of successful investing. Instead, they relied on their trusted advisors to direct them to the most appropriate lender for their purpose.

### Due diligence

Generally, due diligence refers to "the care a reasonable person should take before entering into an agreement or a transaction with another party" (Investopedia, 2018). To some extent, the term "due diligence" has become shorthand for the whole assessment process.

However, the assessment process also includes a focus on mission, governance, public benefit, non-financial risks and community engagement and empowerment.

> It might be helpful if the social investment sector explained the application, due diligence and assessment processes more clearly, so that charities could understand both what information is required, and how it will be interpreted. Charities may never have had explained to them, the shift in understanding from deficit-based funding to asset-based support that is integral to the change from grant assessment to social investment analysis.

Smaller charities may make many applications to a wide range of small and large grant funders, on the basis of identified need or deficit in their community. They may not have been questioned about their strategy for sustainability, the long-term viability of their charity or their capacity to trade and generate surpluses. This highlights the need for care in listening to potential borrowers and communicating how and why the process works, in terms that make sense to smaller charities.

## Using and managing the investment

### *What went well and what difficulties were encountered?*

✓

Most charities that received social investment took a secured loan to buy, redevelop or build a property.

These organisations had not encountered difficulties in making repayments and were conscious of the advantages of moving from paying rent to purchasing an asset. They were very positive about the outcomes.

Some other charities had borrowed, more recently, for working capital. While it was too early to say if the experience would be positive in the long term, one CEO identified immediate impact: "Everything we are doing now comes from [the social investment]. That's the impact, because without it, we wouldn't have survived" (IVAR, 2016, p. 45).

✗

A third of charities experienced difficulties or constraints following social investment.

At the lowest level, these charities included a number where awareness of the need to make loan repayments prevented the expansion of staff and services.

Other organisations' expansion or diversification plans failed, requiring renegotiation of loan repayments or a request for interest-only or repayment holidays.

In some cases, repeated refinancing and top-up loans have left charities in strategic, geographical or financial difficulties.

## Conclusions and implications

### *The social investment road and the journey itself*

One way of considering the experience of the two parties is to see social investors as building and equipping the "social investment road", while charities take a "journey" along that road.

The social investment road consists of:

- Outreach and marketing
- Capacity-building and investment readiness support
- Application, assessment and due diligence processes
- Investment offer, terms and conditions
- Take-up and use of social investment
- Loan repayment

Our research identified three experiences of that journey:

1   A stressful journey
2   A journey made with confidence
3   Charities that chose to walk away from the journey

Motivation of "drivers" for these journeys fell into two broad categories; "necessity" or "strategy".

Understanding the social investment journey from both a charity and from an investor perspective could alleviate some of the difficulties that both parties have experienced in working together.

Most charities have never been through the process before and are piloting it for their own organisation, so there's a need for significantly improved communication about the key components and requirements.

There is also a need for a deeper understanding of the drivers for charities to engage with social investment and the way charities experience investment.

It's important to note that we see the social investment journey as including, but not limited to, the due diligence stage in the wider process of thinking about, applying for, securing and then managing investment.

Typically, charities are more comfortable with the "thinking about" stage in this process, sometimes called "assessment" in grant making. In contrast, due diligence in social investment is less comfortable for them or entirely unfamiliar.

> Guidance on social investment tends to focus on investment readiness of the applicant, but is lacking on what happens once an application is submitted to a social investor. Mapping the full social investment journey would enable both parties to see where the charity is on this journey.

### Mission-first

While all the applications for social investment we looked at were mission-driven, some social investment purposes were not well thought through and led the charities into difficulties.

The aim of all social investments should be to leave an organisation in a stronger position not only financially, but also in relation to its ability to pursue its mission. To do that requires:

- **Broad assessments, including due diligence**
  Thorough assessment will enable investors to understand the social and financial potential of the charity applicants, including the role they play in their communities and the capacity of the investment to strengthen the charity's resilience and impact.
- **A willingness to engage with inexperienced charities to help them survive**
  Social investors could choose to support an application for social investment from a charity that is likely to struggle with the application process, but where investment will enable that charity to survive. The social impact would be "survival" and the investor would need to provide considerable support, possibly with a blend of grant, loan and mentoring. However, investor and charity alike would embark on the journey with their eyes wide-open to the challenges that lie ahead.
- **Alignment of mission and values**
  It's important for charities to know that their commitment to mission and values is understood and shared by their lenders. This means that charities should feel confident in sharing and discussing financial challenges in the context of what is right for the organisation's mission and beneficiaries, rather than what is most profitable.

For their part, it is commitment to mission and values that pulls charities through this challenging experience.

- **Financial products and associated outreach and marketing being tailored to charity need**
  Financial products need to be tailored to what charities need in order to fulfil their mission, rather than investor market-building.
- **Recognition that not all social investment is impact investment**
  Sometimes charities require the supply of a range of financial products and services similar to those provided by banks and other financial intermediaries to small businesses: overdrafts, working capital, leasing, factoring, commercial mortgages, etc.
- **Critical evaluation of property transactions**
  Most social investments taken by small and medium-sized charities are property-related. Often the property is hard to disentangle from mission, because the property itself is more than just a venue from which to deliver services, facilities and activities. It provides a space and a focus for community life itself.

  Some charities found themselves with depreciating and inappropriate assets – in some cases, in the wrong places or with the wrong facilities, hampering their capacity to deliver on their mission while drawing resources out of the organisation in loan repayments.

  Robust challenges by experienced social investors – as to whether particular property investments were the best option – could help relatively inexperienced charities make better strategic decisions.

## Finding 3: Building good relationships

Most investors wanted to have a good relationship with the charities they supported. Charities welcomed this but made two points about areas for improvement.

### *Lack of familiarity with charities*

Positive relationships can be undermined by lenders who quickly become anxious about charity finances, often unnecessarily, because they are unfamiliar with the state of uncertainty that is a daily reality for many small, local charities.

It takes experience for grant makers and lenders to be able to judge whether a charity is on the right side of financial uncertainty, given that most charities are living with a degree of instability in an operating environment that is continuing to change.

### *Distinction between good transactions and good relationships*

Some investors concentrate on good transactions; they build supportive, interested relationships around their social investment transactions over the short term. What charities mean by "good relationships" is an investor that understands and supports their social purpose and wants a long-term relationship that will focus on delivering on mission, as well as financial viability.

Having the support of an institution long-term was more important to the charities than having the same person to deal with during the transaction.

*Good governance equals confidence*

Governance is critical to the social investment journey, whether that's a confident journey, handling a stressful one or making the decision to walk away.

It is the trustee board that takes the decision to seek social investment and with which the formal transaction between charity and investor takes place.

Central to this is the relationship between a charity's chair and CEO. Where they work well together and have a shared vision for the organisation's direction, as well as mutual trust and confidence, then the charity is more likely to experience a confident journey.

Where we found that the relationship between chair and CEO was poor, often it was one "heroic" trustee or founder pushing through the investment with little challenge from other board members.

> The social investment process had given some charities the impetus to strengthen their Boards by refreshing membership where meetings had become stale and unproductive. They also looked at how the charity had changed and identified the kinds of new skills needed, particularly financial, legal and commercial.

## Finding 4: Suitable products and markets

*The opaque social investment market*

Within the literature there's a strong sense of a mismatch between the supply of and predicted demand for social investment. A lack of market segmentation reflects the distinction between the relatively few large and major organisations in the voluntary sector compared to the relatively greater number of small and medium-sized ones.

Our findings suggest that the social investment sector does not function as a market with charities under £1 million.

The social investment offer is opaque. Charities do not know – and it remains difficult to find out – the range and type of finance different lenders provide and therefore which to approach for particular needs and in particular circumstances.

Marketing and promotion by social investors is broad in its scope and makes it difficult for those approaching the market for the first time to differentiate between lenders, products and offers of support.

## Finding 5: Working capital

An emerging issue may be affecting the way small and medium-sized charities use social investment.

Many organisations have seen reduced local and central government funding and a switch to commissioning/output related funding. They are unlikely to be prime contractors and are often at the end of a long supply chain, which adds an extra level of risk to their funding. In the past, grant funding was often provided upfront, which removed the necessity for working capital. Now, organisations need to build both reserves and working capital.

Our findings are reflected in research across the wider voluntary and social enterprise sectors. Both this research, and a recent members' survey carried out by Social

Enterprise UK (2015), seem to indicate an increase in charity and social enterprise organisations needing to borrow for working capital, as a result of sub-contract work for the public sector.

In the words of one respondent, this means that organisations need "full, FULL cost recovery", covering not just direct and indirect costs, but the requirement to produce unrestricted surpluses to finance reserves, working capital and funds for innovation and development.

Most organisations are also attempting to diversify income by targeting major donors, trusts and foundations. A strategy that cannot work for all of them.

# References

Baker, L. and Goggin, N. (2013), *Charities and social investment: a study for the Charity Commission* London: IVAR.

Brown, A., Behrens, L. and Schuster, A. (2015), *A tale of two funds: the management and perform-ance of Futurebuilders England* London: The Boston Consulting Group, accessed 20 October 2018, www.sibgroup.org.uk/sites/default/files/files/Management and Performance of the Futurebuilders-England Fund.pdf.

Heap, H. and Ravison, R. (2013), *Financing social enterprise: the role of builder capital in funding innovation to address social need*, London: Seebohm Hill, accessed 20 October 2018, www.seebohmhill.com/blog-and-publications/helens-blog/25-financing-social-enterprise-the-role-of-builder-capital.

Investopedia (2018), *What is due diligence?*, accessed 20 October 2018, www.investopedia.com/terms/d/duediligence.asp.

IVAR (2016), *Small charities and social investment*, accessed 20 October 2018, www.ivar.org.uk/wp-content/uploads/2016/11/IVAR_Small-charities-and-social-investment-29    November 2016.pdf.

James, D., Kane, D. and Ravenscroft, C. (2016), *Understanding the capacity and need to take on investment within the social sector: summary report*, London: NCVO.

Ludlow, J. (2009), *Capitalising the voluntary and community sector: A review for the NCVO Funding Commission*, London: NCVO.

Moullin, S. and Shanmugalingam, C. with McNeil, B. (2011), *Growing interest? Mapping the market for social finance in the youth sector*, London: The Young Foundation, accessed 20 October 2018, www.issuu.com/youngfoundation/docs/growing-interest-august-2011.

NCVO (2016), *UK civil society almanac 2016*, London: NCVO, accessed 20 October 2018 www.data.ncvo.org.uk/a/almanac16/.

Salway, M. (2017), *Social investment as a new charity finance tool: using head and heart*, Cass Business School, Centre for Charity Effectiveness, accessed 20 October 2018, www.cass.city.ac.uk/__data/assets/pdf_file/0007/358864/CCE-Social-Investment-as-a-new-charity-finance-tool-using-both-head-and-heart-Report-May17.pdf.

Social Enterprise UK (2015), *State of Social Enterprise Survey: leading the world in social enterprise*, London: SEUK, accessed 20 October 2018, www.socialenterprise.org.uk/state-of-social-enterprise-report-2015.

# 18a Case study

## Oomph!

*Big Society Capital*

### Oomph!

Oomph! provides training to care home staff enabling them to deliver group-based exercise classes to their residents, ranging from chair cheerleading to sitting aerobics.

Nesta Impact Investments used funds invested by Big Society Capital, Nesta & Omidyar Network to help Oomph! grow from a small social business to a national one looking to expand even further.

> "Oomph! brings us all together, gets us out of our room. We mix and laugh and forget all of our troubles."
> Ronnie, Oomph! participant

| PHYSICAL HEALTH | MENTAL HEALTH AND WELLBEING |
|---|---|

### OOMPH!

**BIG SOCIETY CAPITAL**

### Problem
Regular exercise can improve the quality of life of older adults, yet it remains an unmet need for many of the 400,000 older people that live in care homes across the UK.

### Solution
Oomph! provides care home staff with the skills, training and props they need to deliver group-based exercises including chair cheerleading and sitting aerobics.

### Revenue Model
Oomph! used a capital investment to scale up its activity in return for a 17% stake in the company. The capital will be repaid through income from training services paid for by care homes.

### Impact
Oomph! exercise classes improve participants' mobility, mental stimulation and encourage greater social interaction.

| | | | |
|---|---|---|---|
| Invested | £200,000 | Cost of capital | Equity |
| Turnover | Not Disclosed | Duration of investment | Equity |

| **Organisational form** | **Investors** |
|---|---|
| Company Limited by Shares | Nesta Impact Investments |

**Other supporters**
UnLtd, Big Lottery Fund, Big Venture Challenge, Hogan Lovells, Deloitte, Nuffield Health

**www.oomph-wellness.org**

# NESTA IMPACT INVESTMENTS

Nesta Investment Management is the fund management arm of Nesta. It is the appointed fund manager of Nesta Impact Investments, which was launched in November 2012.

## Approach to investing

Nesta Impact Investments makes equity, quasi-equity and debt investments of £150,000 to £1 million in early-stage ventures supplying their products and services in the UK. It seeks innovations that have a positive impact on:

• the health and wellbeing of an ageing population

• the educational attainment and employability of children and young people

• the social and environmental sustainability of communities

It looks for organisations that have high potential social impact that can be evidenced and a financially viable business model capable of producing a return on our investment. It also seeks to improve the measurement of impact, providing support for all investees to develop their evaluation plan, structuring how they collect data and moving them through its established 'Standards of Evidence' framework.

## Why the investment was made into Oomph!

One of the biggest challenges for us as a society is how we provide good quality care to an increasingly ageing population against a backdrop of declining social care budgets. We were attracted to Oomph!'s approach of bringing health benefits to older people through interactive classes. Its potential for growth makes this a really exciting investment opportunity for our fund to create real and lasting impact in an area of relatively unmet need.
**Katie Mountain, Nesta Impact Investments**

## Key fund terms

| | | | |
|---|---|---|---|
| 🖊 Liquidity | NA | **Social issue** | Ageing / Education / Community |
| 🕐 Duration | 8 years | **Investment from Big Society Capital** | £8 million |
| 📊 Size | £17.6 million | **Big Society Capital strategy element** | Innovation |
| ❄ Product type | Equity venture fund | **Other investors** | Nesta, Omidyar Network |

**Accessible to**

| | |
|---|---|
| Institutional investors | ✔ |
| Professional individual investors | ✔ |
| Retail investors/depositors | ✘ |

**www.nestainvestments.org.uk**

# 19  What does the future of social investment look like?

*Cliff Prior, with Marcus Lees-Millais*

Eight questions posed to **Cliff Prior**, CEO of Big Society Capital. The interview and write-up are by **Marcus Lees-Millais**, Moore Kingston Smith and Cass CCE consultant.

## Big Society Capital and social investment

Big Society Capital (BSC) is a major institution in the social investment and social finance space. Its aim is to bring investment capital to a wide range of charities and social enterprises, enhanced by BSC's own expertise. Launched in 2012, it was the world's first social investment bank and was founded with the aim of building the social investment market in the UK.

Cliff Prior, CEO of Big Society Capital, is honest about the impact that BSC has had to date, but has great ambition. He is open that, in some ways, the uptake for social investment hasn't been as great as expected.

Big Society Capital published a large amount of raw data on social investment – on the assumption that academics would want to analyse it for their own publications; but that hasn't happened yet. This could well be because universities and other academic institutions want to publish new and interesting papers and social investment isn't seen as interesting enough without a specific focus or slant on it. Nonetheless, the data is out there showing that social investment can work for both investor and investee to deliver a financial and social return. One only has to see some of the BSC case studies included in the earlier chapters of this book to see the positive change it is having.

## Eight crucial questions for social investment

In November 2016, BSC published a document titled *UK Social Investment – Opportunities, Challenges and the "Critical Questions"* (Big Society Capital, 2016a). The aim of the document was to outline BSC's current views on social investment, but also to get people thinking about social investment through a set of questions that challenge the user to look to the future and examine it from the perspective of the different parties involved.

The eight questions are as follows:

1  What opportunity in social investment excites you the most? What challenge to social investment are you most concerned about?
2  Is there a limit to the amount of repayable investment needed in the regulated social sector; and if so, where do you think it is?

3    What kind of intermediation will be needed in the future and how will we get there?

4    What do most investors really want to invest in; and how many social investment opportunities would that include?

5    Which vehicles, in addition to the regulated social sector, will make a significant impact in the future – and are there any where there is a useful role for social investment?

6    How much do increasing awareness, understanding and demonstrating visible impact at scale matter to making social investment a success? And to whom?

7    Who should social impact ultimately be delivered for to make investment worthwhile?

8    Are we missing important questions or perspectives? If so, what are they?

## Question 1 – What opportunity in social investment excites you the most? What challenge to social investment are you most concerned about?

### *Opportunity*

Due to consumer demand, the mainstream investment market focus is rapidly switching to one of investing with an environmental, social and governance (so-called "ESG") focus. The funding potential for social investment on the back of this is enormous. One such example of this shift is Standard Life Investments (2017), whose new promotional video talks about investment "returns that broaden the definition of wealth to include prosperity for economies, society and our planet", rather than just positive, long-term financial returns.

Within this landscape, social investment is a specific opportunity for investors to offer a type of capital that really wants to create a social impact. While there is still a perceived divide between investment for social return and investments for financial return, ultimately there is no reason why an investment can't have both. There may well be trade-offs as we explore and develop this new capital, but there is real potential for future investments to have both. The market is also starting to develop solutions mixing grants and social investment (Access Foundation, 2019).

Cliff Prior is particularly interested in how this finance could help organisations and communities "do it themselves". What this means is that the investee gets to develop an income stream but also learns how to run a business, thus enabling them to implement their next idea too. "We have become obsessed with delivering impact like it is a bag of sugar without enabling the beneficiary to develop to win or make the next bag. Charity is necessary, but enterprise is far more honourable", Cliff says.

This hidden impact is grossly underrated and we can't just deliver impact from on high. France and the United States have developed a large number of cooperatives and community development agencies that are achieving this, but it has yet to happen in the UK to the same extent.

Social investment is also a great financial opportunity for investors. It is a chance for social mission organisations to be involved in a social idea right from inception through to IPO (initial public offering).

These kinds of opportunity are being taken in India where about $5.2 billion has been invested between 2010 and 2016 in social investment (McKinsey & Co, 2017), with some notable IPOs of social enterprises. In the UK, investees are hitting a wall when they need funding upwards of £10 million, as the UK social investors currently don't have that kind of firepower.

Social investment is a chance to offer social organisations a seamless pipeline of financial support and accompany them on their journey, enabling investees to maximise the impact that their organisations can have.

### Challenges

The challenges facing social investment are many. There's a whole host of reasons why social investment might not, or will not, work for a number of investors and investees. One of the key issues is that we forget about the charities and social organisations themselves when creating a social investment.

The main area of focus right now is on the investors and what finance models might achieve the best financial returns for them, while also having a social impact. The social organisations and their needs are coming second. We need to shift this focus from a top down – supply – view to a bottom up – demand – focus, in order for more social organisations to consider using social investment in the first place. We need to consider the requirements of both charities and social enterprises, and of investors; it's not one or the other but the matching of the two. We also need to develop capacity and training.

Social investment is in some ways constrained by some of its own early successes. When potential investors and investees look into social investment, they will naturally see the better known and publicised success stories, such as those included earlier in this book as case studies.

With examples like HCT, the Gym Group, Oomph!, Big White Wall and more, investors and investees can be forgiven for thinking that social investment is a simple process which naturally leads to a good financial return and an increase in social impact. However, that's not always the case.

Investors need to be realistic with their expected returns and be aware that they are dealing with organisations that may have no prior experience or knowledge about taking on investment.

Investees need to understand, first, that to gain investment in the first place will likely result in an organisation needing to provide detailed financial information and financial sensitivity planning it may not yet have. Second, that they will be dealing with organisations who are ultimately looking to make a *social* return from their investment as their primary motive; which may be different from their own primary motive.

The Big Society Capital blog titled *The Gritty Reality of Social Investment* (Big Society Capital, 2016b) shows how tough securing investment can be for a small organisation. As one anonymous social entrepreneur so honestly says, "it was confusing, draining and emotionally turbulent."

## Question 2 – Is there a limit to the amount of repayable investment needed in the regulated social sector, and if so, where do you think it is?

The current UK social investment market is around £2.3 billion (Big Society Capital, 2018) and is growing rapidly at 15–20 per cent a year. With the universe of potential investments being diverse (such as charities, housing and clean energy), this could top

£150 million, depending on how you measure it and what you include in the definition.

As 25 per cent of all UK stocks are now green or ESG, the appetite is clearly there. An estimated 25 per cent of new businesses start with a social mission. This is a figure that is rising rather than falling, with an increasing number of organisations having a social outlook. This is especially true of up and coming fintech and venture capital organisations.

There are around 250,000 regulated social purpose organisations in the UK with the vast majority being very small in size. In order for social investment to work, the organ-isation needs to be investible and a large number of the smaller social organisations simply never will be. That may be due to structure, business model, working on a voluntary basis, or simply lack of capacity to deal with the added level of internal reporting that social investment tends to bring. Once these are removed, you are left with a potential market of between thirty and forty thousand organisations for whom social investment could be a viable source of funding – and Big Society Capital estim-ated 15,000–26,000 in 2016 (Big Society Capital, 2016b), so that number and universe is growing. Of that number, only perhaps around 10,000 would consider taking on a non-asset-backed loan.

Given that 3,000 organisations have currently used, or are using, social investment, we can see the ceiling – but it's still far off. However, as social investment becomes more widely used and known, that 10,000 figure from the last paragraph is likely to rise. Added to that, there is the possibility of social organisations that have used social investment already – and have experienced its benefits – using it again for another round of funding or new and innovative projects.

## Question 3 – What kind of intermediation will be needed in the future – and how will we get there?

There has been concern about social investor intermediaries being fragile, whether financially or through team capacity. But, as the intermediation market establishes itself, plus the training and development activities underway, we should see that becoming less of a concern. Intermediaries are developing specialist areas of expertise and starting to get into second and further funds with more of a track record. The number of inter-mediaries with assets under management of £50 million or more has jumped from just one in 2012 to eight now.

Because of the complex and diverse nature of the social organisations looking for funding – and also the different investment methods available to them – most interme-diaries have chosen to be niche in their focus and expertise. This is a positive in many ways, as it means that the level of understanding achieved by these niche intermediaries is much higher and they are therefore able to use that knowledge to better serve both the investors and investees. However, that understanding is a double-edged sword, as it means that intermediaries can only really serve effectively their small area of expertise or focus. This gives rise to the need for much more collaboration between intermediaries to better serve the wide range of social organisations that they act on behalf of.

A wholesale institution with a market development remit as well as investing has more value than a pure fund-of-funds model (where that investor may not have a direct relationship with the final investee). This can help develop and build the social invest-ment market infrastructure. This was a key part of the original design of BSC. The development work on supporting intermediaries to build capacity is a strong example. However, some types of intermediaries have faced more difficult market conditions, particularly advisors and arrangers.

There is also the question of timing – for example, while it would be very useful for the market to have a relevant social stock exchange, we would need much larger social investment activity than at present to make that commercially viable as a standalone entity.

## Question 4 – What do most investors really want to invest in – and how many social investment opportunities would that include?

For the most part, investors tend to fall into two categories: those who are mission based and those who are more financially motivated. The former may be numerically in the majority, but it is the small number of big players who tend to be the most focused on finance-first and who make up a large part of available funding.

For example, if offered two investment opportunities, one creating a small social impact and a large financial return, and the other creating a large social impact but only a small financial return, almost all investors will pick the former. Cliff says that

> The supply is growing for mission focused investment but still not there yet. Trying to align the interests of investors and investees, so that both parties get what they want, is one of the biggest challenges faced by the social investment market currently.

Charities and social organisations need to get better at seeing social investors as on their side. There is a view that these investors are somehow exploiting social causes in order to make money and that they don't care about the social impact itself. If that were the case, those investors would simply invest their capital into financial investments rather than social ones. Investors and investees need to break down the barriers that lie between them and understand that they both, ultimately, want to create a positive, social impact.

Often, investors are given the brief by their ultimate funders that they want their money to do some good, but the funders aren't really interested in the detail of how this is done. They may be very particular about the area that they want their money to do good in, e.g. animal welfare, or a certain geographical region, but are less worried about the tool used to actually accomplish this.

We know that a high proportion of people say they would like to put some of their money into social investment and use it specifically for social purposes. There are also many regulatory and practical barriers to retail investors wanting to put money into social investment, but we are starting to see those barriers being addressed.

In the coming years, we will see how people's intentions turn into reality. We expect to see greater opportunities and easier pathways. We only need a small proportion of people to put money into the deep-impact areas; even a per cent or two of savings and investments would make a massive difference.

It is possible that the future may include blended funds, where a screened ESG fund also includes a small percentage of "deep" impact investment – allowing good financial returns and highly focused on social impact.

## Question 5 – Which vehicles, in addition to the regulated social sector, will make a significant impact in the future – and are there any where there is a useful role for social investment?

It is impossible to really know what lies around the corner. The ideas for the revolutions of tomorrow may not have even been conceived of yet, let alone developed and brought to market. However, there are vehicles that currently exist which could well have a significant impact on the social sector, particularly on social investment.

A good example of this is new fundraising platforms, such as crowdfunding, which could focus on social return. It's possible we'll see a split in platforms, in terms of what they are offering, depending on the investor's focus – social return or financial return. Regardless of their focus, such crowdfunding platforms are opening the way for non–high-net-worth individuals (HNWIs) to be more readily able to invest in social investment on an individually small scale, but with a large cumulative effect.

Ethex (www.ethex.org.uk) is one such platform that "makes positive investing easy to understand and do" (Ethex, 2019). Individuals can compare different "positive" investments and then choose those they would like to invest in. They can invest then and there on the Ethex website, track their investments there, too. It is a growing platform with a current tally of over 12,500 investors, raising £62 million for a variety of social organisations.

## Question 6 – How much does increasing awareness and understanding and demonstrating visible impact at scale matter to making social investment a success? And to whom?

BSC and the whole sector really struggled in the early days of social investment. For the most part, they thought that, if you build it, "they will come". They assumed they wouldn't have to go out hunting for clients, but that the lure of social investment would be such that clients would be coming to them. This was not the case and intermediaries have had to adapt and change their approach in order to survive.

Part of the reason for this initial lack of interest was that social investment was a new, unknown and untried tool. Organisations were scared to jump into this new pool of funding without knowing the depth of the water and strength of the currents. So, organisations dipped their toes in to test the water, if they did anything, with only a very few seeking to make the most of the opportunities that social investment presented. As time has gone by, those early pioneers of social investment have been able to share their stories, to show others that the waters are not as treacherous as first thought and to encourage others to use social investment themselves.

As charities and social organisations want to know that the tool they intend to use will work, such success stories are critical in attracting more of them to social investment. The more success stories, the more organisations thinking of it as a mainstream and ordinary form of funding for them. We are reaching the stage among social organisations now where, even if your organisation hasn't used social investment, you probably know someone who has. This is an exciting place to be, as it could start a snowball effect of more and more organisations taking the plunge and using social investment.

The need to create a better understanding of social investment is not consistent across different organisations, though:

- **Charities** – In a recent survey 69 per cent of respondent organisations said they did not understand social investment, with only 17 per cent feeling that their organisation understood social investment well (Salway, 2017).
- This is contrasted with **social enterprises** where a recent survey showed over 80 per cent of social enterprises confident that they understand social investment.

Cliff's hunch is that there is a much higher level of understanding among social enterprise than among charities – unsurprising as social enterprises start with an enterprise model, whereas many charities start with a donation or grant model.

For investors, a sector-wide increase in understanding should gain them more investment opportunities. For investees, the more that they know about the finance options available to them, the better equipped they are to make a decision on whether or not to use one of those options.

## Question 7 – Who should social impact ultimately be delivered for to make investment worthwhile?

This question seems simple. However, it is still worth answering it to make organisations take stock of their own situation and whether or not they are delivering the kind of impact that they want to.

One might think that social investment is a two-party process, the investor and the investee, but that leaves the most important party out of the picture. The beneficiary. Social organisations are social for a reason, to create a social impact. This social impact affects individuals, communities, environments and even landscapes. It is these parties that are the ultimate beneficiaries.

If social impact is not being delivered for the beneficiaries, then that begs the question who is it being delivered for? Social purpose organisations, such as charities, need to be clear about this and the social value created. This applies to social investors as well. If they are not investing to deliver social impact to beneficiaries, then they may as well undertake financial investments instead.

Given that the beneficiaries themselves are removed from the social investment process, it can be easy to lose sight of them and their needs. We need to find the sweet spot between investors, organisations and the ultimate beneficiaries. One way to assist with this is for all parties to be open and honest about what they want from social investment at the start of their conversations. Also, to build the beneficiary voice into the process.

One recent change is the rapid development of sets of principles and conduct rules for social investment.

One such example is the Alpbach declaration. Cliff Prior's blog (Prior, 2018) summarises the principles suggested by the Alpbach declaration as follows:

- Make explicit where you act in the impact investment field, using the Impact Management Project convention;
- Be clear where, when, how and with whom you are useful – or not – as an impact investor;
- Commit to respectful relationships across the system;
- Start with the social issue and end-user experience, rather than with the finance, using common standards such as the UN's Sustainable Development Goals framework;

- Engage with end-users in the impact investment process;
- Ensure that your investments add more value to end users than they extract;
- Balance risk and returns fairly among all stakeholders;
- Consider risk, return and impact in each of your investments;
- Measure and disclose unintended as well as intended consequences; and
- Report publicly and transparently against common impact standards.

Perhaps, within a year or two, we could expect social investors to sign up to these "rules of the road" in the same way that green investment and other sectors have.

## Question 8 – Are we missing important questions or perspectives? If so, what are they?

One aspect of social investment currently missing, or not as strong as it could be, is how to sense new opportunities and be able to move quickly to take those opportunities when they arise. This is in part due to the cautious and risk-averse nature of charities and social organisations; but is also due to potential investors not necessarily speaking the same language as the organisations. Investors need to be better at speaking in terms that a charity will understand, rather than using all of the technical investment jargon that so often leaves organisations put off from undertaking social investment at all.

An investor may have a fantastic social investment opportunity for an organisation, but if the organisation's decision makers doesn't understand it, they won't use it.

A question that needs answering is how to build demand for social investment from the investee rather than the investor side. This needs to be a balanced view, with both sides coming together with a common ambition and motivation.

> Rather than organisations being offered a type of social investment that the investor thinks would be good, we should encourage investors to really ask organisations what it is that they want and need and to build the investment around that so that the organisation can maximise the social impact that investment makes.
>
> (Cliff Prior)

### Institutional investors

Cliff has one final thought for the future. That is to open up the opportunities for social investment to retail investors. What needs to be made to work is how this can deliver both serious impact and decent financial returns for investors. That will be the future, one where BSC will no longer be the biggest investor in the social investment space, but a catalyst for much larger flows of capital for positive social impact.

So, the future requires other investors to join in – pension funds and banks. To get to scale, we need to bring in institutional investment and, if possible, retail, i.e. mass involvement. Most people's savings go via institutions and retail investors. People need their pensions to live on into old age – they need financial returns. This all needs to be figured out if social investment is to grow.

Some of the recent work on going "beyond the trade-offs" is useful in this space. It highlights that gains in momentum and impact investing's potential are hindered by this debate on trade-offs.

The reality, however, is far more nuanced. Even as the field continues to debate whether impact investing does or does not achieve market-rate returns at the sacrifice of social impact, we have found that leading practitioners have moved past this conversation to create highly nuanced and sophisticated portfolios of impact investments that target different levels of financial returns, different types of social impact, and a broad spectrum of risk profiles. This disconnect between the public debate and the actual diversity of investment opportunities available is creating confusion among existing, new, or potential impact investors, and may impede the healthy development of this market.

(FSG, 2018)

FSG partnered with the Omidyar Network to curate a new series, *Beyond Trade-offs: Investor Perspectives from across the Continuum of Impact Investing* (FSG, 2018), showcasing a set of examples from leading impact investors that illustrate the diversity of investment approaches helping to shift the debate and bringing new investors to the table.

Watch this space …

## Then, now and the future

The social investment market has come a long way from the days of the early pioneers.

As Cliff Prior so vividly explains, when social investment was first emerging, investors were wondering if there would be enough investment supply and demand to sustain a market and where the next social finance opportunity was going to come from.

Now, the social investment market has developed to the extent that it is no longer about creating opportunities, but about understanding how each social investment fits the need and opportunity and about matching investor and investee. However, social investment intermediaries need to be able to pool their specialist knowledge to best serve the market. Cliff is proud of BSC's goodfinance.org.uk website in this regard. We are starting to have "all of the information of a social investment Tripadvisor at our fingertips".

A lot of thought has been focused on whether or not social investment is working. Though the market clearly benefits from success stories, whether or not social investment is currently seen to be working or not doesn't change the fact that it is happening regardless. Investors are still being motivated to offer repayable financing to social organisations and those organisations are seeking new and innovative ways to maximise their impact with the funds available to them.

As social investment grows – and it is growing – and more and more success stories emerge, the market is going to be able to take more risks with the types of funding offered or the projects and organisations invested into. It will innovate and evolve. There is only really one way to know if an idea can be a success or not and that is to try it!

When a new trend developed of UK high streets becoming transformed by charity shops, it was the biggest and richest charities that were able to capitalise on that and cement their positions at the top of the pile. With the more recent change in funding from grants to contracts, the successful charities weren't necessarily the big ones. It was those organisations that were able to make the cultural and organisational shift. Which example will social investment be like? Will it be the large charities who are able to utilise it the most effectively, or will it be those charities, social enterprises and other social propose organisations that are able to be agile and adapt to changing times? Or, will it be something different altogether?

## References

Access Foundation (2019), *Access: the foundation for social investment*, accessed 29 July 2019, https://access-socialinvestment.org.uk/.

Big Society Capital (2016a), *UK social investment: opportunities, challenges and the "critical" questions*, accessed 20 October 2018, www.bigsocietycapital.com/sites/default/files/UK Social Investment – Opportunities, Challenges, and Critical Questions.pdf.

Big Society Capital (2016b), *The gritty reality of social investment*, blog, accessed 20 October 2018, www.bigsocietycapital.com/latest/type/blog/gritty-reality-social-investment.

Big Society Capital (2018), *Size of the social investment market*, accessed 20 October 2018, www.bigsocietycapital.com/home/about-us/size-social-investment-market.

Ethex (2019), *Ethex: make money do good*, accessed 6 August 2019, www.ethex.org.uk/.

FSG (2018), *Moving beyond trade-offs in impact investing*, accessed 6 August 2019, www.fsg.org/blog/moving-beyond-trade-offs-impact-investing.

McKinsey & Co. (2017), *Impact investing finds its place in India*, accessed 19 July 2019, www.mckinsey.com/industries/private-equity-and-principal-investors/our-insights/impact-investing-finds-its-place-in-india.

Prior, C. (2018), *Alpbach fundamentals: ten principles to help bring clarity to impact investing*, blog, accessed 4 August 2019, https://impactalpha.com/alpbach-fundamentals-ten-principles-to-help-bring-clarity-to-impact-investing/.

Salway, M. (2017), *Social investment as a new charity finance tool: using head and heart*, Cass Business School, Centre for Charity Effectiveness.

Standard Life Investments (2017), *Impact investing promotional video*, accessed 20 October 2018, www.europe.standardlifeinvestments.com/institutional/funds/focus_on_funds/impact_fund.html.

# Doing social investment

# 20 The purpose of this section

## Doing social investment

*Jim Clifford*

The following chapters have been written by **Jim Clifford** OBE MSc FCA ATII CF MCSI MEWI FRSA DChA, Founder and CEO of Sonnet Advisory & Impact CIC, formerly the Advisory & Impact division at Bates Wells, and Visiting Research Fellow at Cass Centre for Charity Effectiveness.

### An in-depth guide to doing social investment

We have written this book so that readers can step into different sections and learn a little, or a lot, about social investment. This depends on their needs.

The chapters that follow in this section of the book aim to create an in-depth guide of *how* to do social investment. It is detailed, because it needs to be.

**This section provides the foundations for actually bringing social investments into existence.**

- Chapter 21, **A practical outline**, starts by taking the reader through what is involved in social investment. This takes a look at the strategic need for funding, different kinds of funding instrument and the sources of funding. It explores the pros and cons of each. It then explores what investors want and looks in overview at how to approach them.
- Chapter 21 also touches on **social impact bonds**. Whilst they involve elements of social investment they are not primarily investment instruments and are included here so the reader can understand the distinction and why they are important.
- Chapter 22, **Finding the right funding**, looks at how to match funding to need and identify sources for it. It takes a detailed look at the process of fundraising, including the legal and regulatory environment.
- We then look in Chapter 23 at **Structuring the deal** and the best way to handle inwards investment to your organisation. We consider legal forms, governance and control structures, funds flow and ongoing management.
- Chapter 24 considers the **importance of due diligence** and how both sides can build confidence before entering into an investment agreement. We look at the types of due diligence, how to structure it and how to select and commission external support.
- Chapter 25 looks at **accounting for social investment**, before Chapter 26 takes a deeper dive into **reporting impact, and good data management**. This chapter builds on the reporting theme, looking at the measurement of social impact and the gathering and management of data to accompany this.

- Finally, Chapter 27 considers **Governance aspects of social investment** and how trustees and managers can provide effective oversight and governance of social investment, whether as investee or investor.

We hope these chapters provide a deep reference guide so that students can dip in and out of what it means actually to deliver and "do" social investment. For the advanced student, the section provides a detailed step-by-step guide to help you think and build your confidence about what this entails.

These chapters also take a technical look at social impact and its definitions through the lens of the published European standards, developed by the GECES (Clifford *et al.*, 2014).

We hope this gives all the tools you need to help you grow and deliver social investments.

## Reference

Clifford, J., Hehenberger, L. and Fantini, M. (2014), *Proposed approaches to social impact measurement in European Commission legislation and in practice relating to EuSEFs and the EaSI*, report by GECES (Groupe d'experts de la Commission sur l'entrepreneuriat social) subgroup on impact measurement, accessed 15 October 2018, www.ec.europa.eu/social/main.jsp?catId=738&langId=en&pubId=7735&type=2&furtherPubs=yes.

# 21 Social investment

## A practical outline

*Jim Clifford*

How can you think strategically using your funding models? What kind of funding is available? What do investors want and how can you access investment?

Over the next seven chapters, **Jim Clifford** OBE, Founder and CEO of Sonnet Advisory & Impact CIC, and Visiting Research Fellow, Cass Centre for Charity Effectiveness, takes the reader through the technical aspects of developing social investment from strategic intent, to finding funds, through structuring the deal and finally managing the money.

This chapter focuses on deciding to use social investment and finding funds.

## What is a strategic funding approach and why take one?

Your charity is, quite rightly, focused on delivering impact for its beneficiaries. It needs to use all of its assets effectively and efficiently to deliver that, whether they be financial or non-financial ones.

In taking this wide view, the charity should consider first what impact it wishes to create, for whom and how. That, in turn, demands decisions as to whether the impact will be achieved:

- By **direct delivery** from the charity's resources and activity.
- By **leading other organisations** to do likewise out of their own resources and from their activities.
- By **influencing others** to recognise the need and take action of their own accord.

Having covered that, the charity can consider how to resource the activities it needs to undertake, so considering all main classes of assets it can harness to create impact:

- **Funds:** what cash funds can be brought in to support the development and delivery of services, whether as donation, contract or grant (for example, to support research and development), or as an investment.
- **Know-how and other intellectual property:** what can be brought to bear in developing new or improved methodologies for delivering outcomes? This may be written material, knowledge amongst staff, websites and other market access, contact lists and agreements, formulae or working methods, among others.
- **Real assets:** what property, vehicles, plant and equipment does the organisation hold, and what can usefully be harnessed for service delivery?

- **Influence and network:** the wider contacts the organisation has, and can marshal for good, including its ability to influence third parties and partner organisations, including funders, commissioners, volunteers and others, the greater its impact can potentially be.

To take a strategic funding approach is to look at how much investment funding is really needed, as well as how funding may be structured, raised and used to enhance long-term service delivery which underpins the charity's mission.

Social investment is a powerful tool which can be used to maximise the charity or nonprofit's work. This fits into the list of resources above, but when used also changes the dynamics of the organisation. From the point that you use social investment in your charity or nonprofit onwards you'll be managing it in an organisational context. The organisation will be affected by it and this will bring about change.

So a charity must understand and manage how the social investment interacts with other aspects of its operations. This brings with it great opportunities and challenges, both positive and negative. Four areas are of particular importance and are as follows:

> **Effects on business models.** Social investment could change your business model or it may open opportunities or increase competitiveness in certain markets, e.g. by investing in a new service to take to market.
>
> **Impact on donors.** Using social investment, the relationship with any particular donor may change. A former donor may choose to invest as an alternative to giving a donation. Equally, the donor might approach their investment and donation from different "pockets" of money, sometimes blending grant and investment together. An investment may lead someone to an engagement with the charity which develops into donation, or alternatively some form of outcomes-based payment.
>
> **Encouraging and discouraging grants.** Again, a grant-maker can also be a potential investor, but may be unwilling, or more willing, to do both. Social investment may encourage or discourage grant-makers and may lead to a different relationship in future.
>
> **Members and existing supporters.** These give an obvious pool of potential social investors. However, with some investing and some not, a two-tier membership can arise which may not be helpful to ongoing relationships. On the other hand, a new deeper engagement with members may be achieved, particularly valuable for "destination" charities such as gardens, historical sites and arts venues.

## Trustees

For social investment of any real size to be taken on, the trustees' consent is almost invariably required. There are frequently heard concerns about trustees being too risk averse and social investment is a prime potential area for seeing this get in the way.

It's reasonable for the trustees to consider the risk involved. However, objecting wholesale to social investment on the grounds of risk – and so failing to deliver the optimal social outcomes for a charity's work – is not a tenable position to take, especially with the scale of social need that exists in most arenas.

The board should take steps to educate themselves about the options and the real risks involved, and take professional advice rather than failing to consider the opportunities.

## For what can social investment funds be used?

Social investment covers four purposes, with direct and obvious parallels in the commercial markets. This comparability is hardly surprising, since both finance business operations.

It is worth noting that social investment involves borrowing money, which must be paid back (or the capital released in another way), potentially with interest. As such, this is a different funding model from grants or donations and relies on revenue-generating activities, or alternatively savings to the organisation, to pay for capital repayment and a financial return.

The four purposes to which social investment can be applied are:

- **Working capital,** which funds timing differences between the work to be done, or value generated, and it being billed and paid by the end customer.
- **Fixed capital,** which funds the underlying permanent assets of the business. These may be properties, machinery, equipment and vehicles, or intangibles, such as know-how, trademarks and licences, and the building of customer bases, websites, systems; and the other myriad requirements of a modern business.
- **Research & development,** which encompasses the wider research necessary to get a business started, to develop new products and services, and to establish new markets, collaborations and outreach.
- **Broader risk sharing,** which is an area in which new business models are created or an investor helps to develop an existing product or service. It is similar to many venture capital arrangements in the private sector, but is increasingly being talked about in the area of social investment, not least in the context of the funding of pay-for-success (payment by results) contracts. It also fits neatly with the development of trading activities and social enterprise models.

    An example of broader risk sharing could equally be with a charity or nonprofit developing a social enterprise. Investment would be needed to capitalise and fund this, and may be used to share risk as well.

## Five types of funding instrument

Social investment works through contracts that set out how funding is provided, detailing the risk (to capital and return) and reward (pricing) profiles associated with them.

We talk about five principal types of funding instrument:

1 **Senior debt** – loan capital often secured on property or trading assets, it's the capital most frequently provided by high-street banks and asset-based lenders. With its fixed repayment terms, security and sometimes fluctuating interest rates, it generally carries the lowest risk to the funder and a correspondingly higher risk to the borrower.
2 **Junior or mezzanine debt** – a broad category covering most other repayable capital. Often unsecured, it can carry higher, or fixed, percentage interest rates over longer periods than for senior debt.
3 **Quasi-equity** – although it's a loan instrument, quasi-equity has the risk profile and the return (yield) characteristics of equity. It typically pays yields varying with the volume or success of operations, such as a profit share (with some restrictions if the investee is a charity – see Chapter 23), a percentage of turnover, or bonuses.

The capital may be repayable, or semi-permanent (locked in for an extended period, perhaps 25 years or more).

4  **Equity** – share capital, carrying a yield in dividends or premia on redemption. It also allows investor and borrower to share in the upside and downside of returns.

5  **Guarantees and derivatives** – these are funding instruments which underpin other investment forms, often used to support investment by third parties, such as lease contracts for motor vehicles or plant. A derivative may appear in the form of an interest rate swap, or another risk management contract. Underwriting agreements are a particular form that is likely to grow in popularity, in which some of the risk of loss for an investor is taken by a third party.

An example of this is a local authority or clinical commissioning group (CCG) which may underwrite a loan and guarantee it in the event of default by a provider charity or social enterprise.

There has been considerable recent conversation in social investment circles about the need for longer-term patient capital. Social ideas often take longer to develop and bring to fruition than more commercial projects, given the inherent complexity of having to deliver both financial and social return. As such, we may need patient longer-term or even evergreen funding (this is discussed early in the Bridges case study, Chapter 8a).

## Seven sources of funding

If many different contractual structures for investment exist, there are even more sources of investment capital. We're looking here at seven different types of funding sources, each with its own rationale for investment and approaches to making and managing investments:

1  **Conventional institutional sources.** These span from clearing banks to social banks, and venture capitalists to private equity providers. Social banks, such as Charity Bank, Unity Trust and Triodos, are a major source of debt finance for charities and social enterprise. They will evaluate an investment prospect on the same criteria as for private sector lending, focusing on ability to service the debt (interest and capital payments) and a risk profile leaving minimal or negligible capital risk but adding a social impact "gateway" or minimum criterion.

Venture capitalists and private equity providers are generally willing to provide funding to a higher risk and higher return model than banks, often operating through a corporate or partnership structure, and investing their own and other investors' funds.

2  **Social Institutions and funds.** Social funds may sacrifice some financial return in recognition of the social impact being achieved, such as Impetus-PEF and Nesta Impact Investments. There is a debate around the extent to which such funders are willing to accept lower returns. For some, it may mean no real difference in yield, but a flexibility in terms instead.

3  **Grant-makers and charitable foundations.** A number of grant-making and charitable foundations have entered the social investment market as direct funders, investors in managed funds and leaders of managed social funds – the Esmée Fairbairn Foundation and Tudor Trust, for example. Some have allocated sections of their endowments to be applied and managed in this field. Others are approaching this as part of their existing investment management strategy.

Changes in the Charity Commission guidance on investment assets which created new classifications of mixed motive investment were designed both to clarify and stimulate this activity (Charity Commission, 2016).

4 **Other charities.** Investment by one charity in the operational activity of another has existed for many years, but is perhaps taking on a new lease of life with a wider range of cross-investment. This may be as an investment in its own right, evaluated against normal investment principles, or as a primary purpose of the charity, better to deliver its charitable purpose. Alternatively, it may be as a mixed motive investment, blending both elements.

5 **Private individuals.** This source of capital for social enterprise has existed for many years, but only in certain areas (such as housing, through housing bonds and capital projects for schools and nurseries). Over the last decade it has developed more widely, with the advent of crowdfunding and direct investment by high-net-worth individuals.

6 **Private corporates.** Similarly, this area has existed for many years in the form of joint venture capital, where a private sector provider is working with one in the social sector. There is some evidence that corporates are now being sought to invest in social impact bonds (SIBs – explained later in this chapter). They may invest for philanthropic reasons, as an investment prospect or for development reasons around their own businesses, perhaps in public service arenas. In addition the corporate venturing arena is developing to embrace social investment so private corporates are seen investing in social projects incidental to their wider business development and stimulus of new markets (Love *et al.*, 2017).

7 **Public bodies.** This may be through public sector pension schemes, local authorities or others investing in social investment as part of their investment fund or treasury management. It could be as transitional capital in a transaction, such as a mutualisation of a public service operation, or as a strategic investment in a public service delivery body or project.

## What do investors want from their investment?

The reasons why investors are interested in social investment vary to a degree between individual investors within each category, but common themes include:

a   A desire for a financial return;

b   A desire for repayment of capital after a period (which demands an underpinning sustainability in the nonprofit organisation);

c   Placing their investment into a venture that can deliver social outcomes generally, and the extent of those;

d   Aligning to the specific mission or area of social interest of the funder;

e   Placing their money in a way that will enable an outcome that otherwise would not happen (known generally as "additionality");

f   An investment which is well governed and accountable;

g   Gaining tax reliefs;

h   Backing and developing something that will have a longer-term or system-changing social effect; and

i   Profile development by association with a good, and high impact, social prospect (a form of "affinity" or "brand halo" marketing).

Table 21.1 matches those themes against the seven investor types in the previous section, indicating both themes that are relevant (ticks) and those that may be relevant to a degree (the bracketed ticks).

## Approaching investors

Before looking to approach investors, it's clearly important to match your funding purpose to the interest and scope of the proposed funder. The funders existing within each category vary over time. So, to achieve a well-priced and aligned funding relationship, do some sound research and get informed advice, as to which might best meet your needs.

With your research done and advice to hand, there are three broad approaches you can take to presenting an opportunity to an investor and arousing their interest.

| Via direct placement | To existing funders and stakeholders | Accessing lists |
|---|---|---|
| • Direct approaches to a list of investors in a category<br>• Often through an intermediary: professional investment broker<br>• With restrictions: to some overseas funders and private individuals | • Going back to the audience who knows you best<br>• Finding a new dialogue<br><br>• Offering the right to invest before going to outsiders | • Issuing bonds on general stock markets<br>• Accessing a wide range of investors<br><br>• Advantage of liquidity for investors |

The third of these areas, "accessing lists", involves going to a stock market or general issue. In the UK, there are three main types of list-based access points:

1 **General markets,** including the Full List of the London Stock Exchange; Alternative Investment Market (AIM), ICAP Securities and Derivatives Exchange (ISDX, now the NEX exchange) and overseas stock exchanges. The social purpose organisation would develop an offering and launch this in their own name.

2 **Allia RCB and other managed intermediary platforms,** in which a Third Sector organisation issues securities into the retail bond market, offering a lower cost, standardised approach to issuing listed securities. In this case, the borrower would raise funds through Allia RCB or other similar organisations.

3 **Social Stock Exchange (SSX),** developed in London, but with regional exchanges intended to be opened in other cities around the UK. It is a platform developed specifically for social purpose organisations to raise capital and funds, and does have a profile-raising aspect and a following of investors, but obtains its trading aspects through listing on a regular exchange such as AIM or NEX.

**EXAMPLES**

| | |
|---|---|
| In 2012, the charity, Scope, issued a bond which was listed on the Luxembourg Exchange. This is a general market offer. | Golden Lane Housing has securities listed on the Social Stock Exchange (SSX) and on Allia's RCB. |

*Table 21.1* Typical reasons for investment by investor groups

| | (a) Financial return | (b) Capital return | (c) Social outcomes | (d) Aligned to mission | (e) Additionality | (f) Good governance | (g) Tax reliefs | (h) Systemic change | (i) Affinity |
|---|---|---|---|---|---|---|---|---|---|
| 1 Conventional institutions | ✓ | ✓ | (✓) | | | ✓ | | | (✓) |
| 2 Social institutions | (✓) | (✓) | ✓ | ✓ | (✓) | (✓) | | ✓ | (✓) |
| 3 Grantmakers and foundations | (✓) | (✓) | ✓ | ✓ | | (✓) | | ✓ | |
| 4 Other charities | (✓) | (✓) | ✓ | ✓ | ✓ | (✓)(✓) | | (✓)(✓) | |
| 5 Private individuals | ✓ | ✓ | ✓ | (✓) | | (✓)(✓) | ✓ | (✓)(✓) | |
| 6 Private corporates | (✓) | ✓ | ✓ | ✓ | (✓) | (✓) | | (✓) | ✓ |

Source: reproduced with permission from Jim Clifford OBE.

## Social impact bonds (SIBs) – the non-financial instrument

A social impact bond – often confused with the wider term "social investment", or a bond raised as a debt instrument for social purposes (sometimes called a "social investment bond") – is not really a financial instrument. It can be defined (Rotheroe, 2014, p. 3) as:

A contract between a commissioner and a separate delivery agency

- In which the latter delivers defined social outcome or outcomes, for which the commissioner will pay if it is delivered
- With at least one investor which is neither the delivery agency nor the commissioner
- With that investor taking some element of risk.

It is part of the payment by results (pay-for-success) arena, rather than an investment. The SIB does, however, present a finance opportunity with a distinct investment profile. So, the financial instrument element within it needs to be recognised within the whole social investment market.

The finance element is generally to provide working capital for the delivery contract and fixed capital where infrastructure and other assets are required for the delivery of the contract by the delivery agency.

Effectively, the delivery agency delivers social outcomes, against which the commissioner pays the investor if outcomes are achieved. The charity (delivery agency) gets the money it needs from the investor as working capital, and the investor gets paid its capital plus risk premium and return if the outcomes are achieved.

This type of model will typically be operated through a special purpose vehicle (SPV), set up and established specifically to manage the flow of funds and payments and to allow all parties to contract with each other. This is explained in Figure 21.1. Further details of this and the other two main models ("Direct", and "Managed" or "Networked") can be found below.

## Who's involved in a SIB?

It's useful to get to know the stakeholders involved in SIBs. Specific parties include:

- **Commissioner:** the purchaser of the services or service outcomes. It could be a local authority, or CCG, a housing association, or a private corporate philanthropist or interested party. None are investors, as they provide revenue funding to the scheme: they pay for the impacts achieved.
- **Funder/investor:** supplier of the external capital investment in accordance with an investment agreement.
- **Provider/delivery agency:** in addition to receiving funding through the investment element of the SIB, this stakeholder may be both investing some of its own funds in infrastructure and delivery capacity, or even alongside the outside funders, as well as shouldering some element of financial risk in connection with the delivery, while receiving some form of reward in return. A provider may also be an internal funder.
- **Coordinator:** the stakeholder coordinating the services – and may also be investing its own resources in infrastructure, or again in parallel with the outside investors.

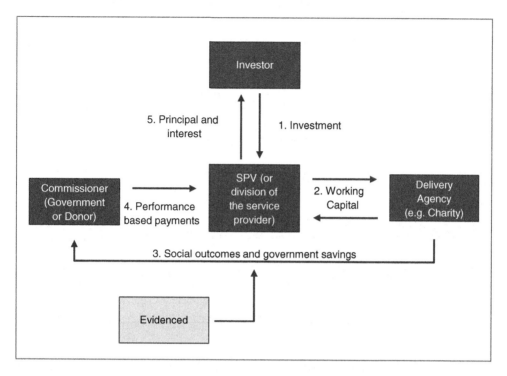

*Figure 21.1* SIB funding flows ("Classic" or "intermediated" model).
Source: Mark Salway and Jim Clifford OBE.

- **SPV:** special purpose vehicle (legal vehicle or company) established for the purpose of managing the parties to a SIB or enabling its delivery. Note that not all SIBs use one of these (see below).
- **Service-user:** for whom there is an emerging possibility of either acting as a commissioner or co-commissioner, or indeed as investor. This provides new possibilities for engagement with beneficiaries.

## Considering the appropriate vehicle for investment for a SIB

Three types of SIB investment structures have emerged to date (Clifford and Jung, 2016, p. 171):

1   **Special purpose vehicle (SPV – the "intermediated" model):** the traditional model for a SIB, it's a company formed specifically to take the contract, then subcontracting the services to the (social sector) delivery agency.
2   **Single provider, directly funded:** here, the delivery agency itself is directly invested in, taking on the contracts in its own name.
3   **"Networked" or "Managed" bond:** whereby a standalone fund serves a network of multiple delivery agencies coordinated by a central management company (which may be one of the delivery agencies, a sector body or an SPV). This invests in the SIB.

These models are considered in more detail in Clifford and Jung (2016)

---

**EXAMPLES**

---

In 2013, It's All About Me, the UK adoption bond, was the first to be established with this networked model.

(Big Society Capital, 2018a)

The Children's Investment Fund Foundation for the Education of Girls in Rajasthan, a philanthropic foundation, is a typical commissioner of a development impact bond (DIB), an emerging form of SIB. The provider is Educate Girls and investor Optimus Foundation from UBS.

(CIFF, 2016)

---

SIBs are seen by government as a way to involve investors and spread risk.

In 2018, there were 32 SIBs in the UK (Big Society Capital, 2018b), tackling a range of issues including homelessness, youth unemployment, children in or at the edge of care and many others. Most national SIBs have a contract duration of three to seven years. Some of them have funded new innovations, with many using the mechanism to scale evidenced alternative approaches. The contract value is typically £1 million to £10 million, with investment requirement usually under £2 million. (Big Society Capital, 2018b).

---

**In this chapter, we introduced:**

The strategic need for funding
The different kinds of funding instrument
Various sources of funding
Understanding why investors want to invest
How to approach investors
Social impact bonds – the "not an investment" bond – and the people involved in them

---

**In the next chapter, we'll explore:**

The importance of an organised approach to investment raising
Balancing own capital with that raised from third parties
The pros and cons of each of the main sources of investment
The process of fundraising for social investment
Regulated approaches to fundraising
Engaging advisors and intermediaries to find funding

---

# References

Big Society Capital (2018a), *Adoption social impact bond*, accessed 24 September 2018, www.big societycapital.com/what-we-do/investor/investments/adoption-social-impact-bond.

Big Society Capital (2018b), *Outcomes contracts and social impact bonds*, accessed 24 September 2018, www.bigsocietycapital.com/what-we-do/current-projects/public-service-reform/outcomes-contracts-social-impact-bonds.

Charity Commission (2016), *Charities and investment matters: a guide for trustees*, accessed 24 September 2018, www.gov.uk/government/publications/charities-and-investment-matters-a-guide-for-trustees-cc14.

CIFF, Children's Investment Fund Foundation (2016), *World's first development impact bond on track to deliver social impact and financial returns*, accessed 24 September 2018, www.ciff.org/news/worlds-first-development-impact-bond-track-deliver-social-impact-and-financial-returns/.

Clifford, J. and Jung, T. (2016), *Social Impact Bonds: exploring and understanding an emerging funding approach*, p. 171 in Lothmar, O. (Ed.), *Routledge handbook of social and sustainable finance*, London, Routledge.

Love, C., Rebholz, J. and Feldman, A.. (2017), *The practitioner's guide: steps to corporate investment, innovation and collaboration: a practical guide to creating positive outcomes*, accessed 22 April 2019, www.bigsocietycapital.com/sites/default/files/attachments/The%20Practitioner%27s%20Guide%20-%20Steps%20to%20Corporate%20Investment%2C%20Innovation%20and%20Collaboration.pdf.

Rotheroe, A. (2014), *Lessons and opportunities: perspectives from providers of social impact bonds*, accessed 24 September 2018, www.thinknpc.org/wp-content/uploads/2018/07/Lessons-and-opportunities-perspectives-from-providers-of-SIBS.pdf.

# 22 Finding the right funding

*Jim Clifford*

## What are the resources you need and where can you find them? How do you approach investors for these?

In the last chapter, we started looking at "doing" social investment and what this means in practice. This chapter takes the reader on to consider how practically to find the right funding, and how to approach investors.

## Good planning for good results

What does it take to find and raise the right funding? The answer is simple – planning, sourcing and process. Nothing less than careful planning and an organised approach, with advisory support at appropriate stages, will enable you to get the funding you need. ***Many charities simply underestimate the change and effort this involves.***

You will benefit from appropriate and focused help and guidance in this. You're looking to bring experience as to what will interest an investor and help them to engage quickly and simply. Remember that legal compliance comes into it here, too (see the next chapter, "Structuring the Deal", for more details about this).

---

### Examples

---

The English RFU has issued live venue debentures over many years to fund the construction of its stands, giving the holder the right to buy tickets for rugby games at the Twickenham stadium.

(Rugby Football Union, 2017)

Retail chain Hotel Chocolat has engaged in debt fundraising from current and potential customers by paying interest in chocolate. Intentionally, this encourages the investor to engage better with the investee's product, so has marketing benefits.

(Financial Times, 2018)

---

### Crafting the plan for social investment

A charity has to raise funds in a way that best suits its needs. This requires planning.

Fundraising for social investment without proper planning will either fail, be more expensive than it needs to be (to do, or in use), or can even cause knock-on problems that are unforeseen. For example, investment not properly planned may come with constraints that are too rigid, preventing necessary flexing of the charity's delivery of services as service-user needs or commissioner demands change. This demands foresight and upfront negotiation.

Ten key considerations when planning to take on social investment are as follows:

1  **Purpose: for what will the funds be used?** This affects sourcing, the structure and required terms of the investment, and how easy it will be to find funding that fits. It can be used to align the motivation of social investor and recipient charity. It also links into more contextual aspects of fundraising, such as how it can be used to enhance the charity's profile, or introduce potential customers to services.
2  **Funds needed: what funds do you really need to raise?** This demands a thorough review of the project cash flows and working capital. It may also involve the construction or development of new fixed assets.

   •  Avoid under-budgeting for funding requirements (raising too little – so, running out) and over-budgeting (raising too much, thereby incurring expensive servicing investment you don't need).
   •  Regular areas in which mis-budgeting arises include: under- or over-estimating VAT; not allowing for sensitivities in income levels, or the timings of customer or supplier payments; not allowing for delayed starts on projects; or the time and cost of staffing up.

3  **Time period: over what period is the finance to be drawn down and used?** Due consideration must be given to how long it will take to create both financial returns and the social outcomes which are expected to flow from the investment. Separately, any plan will need clarity on the length of time funds will be needed before repayment or refinancing from another source.
4  **Risk profile: what are the risks involved in delivery, in the business model and in financing?** Think about how these risks will be managed, mitigated and monitored. Also, consider how they'll be shared between stakeholders. For risk management to be at its most effective, the risks should be shared between the parties on the basis of what each can best afford, or best manage (sometimes referred to as "risk arbitrage").
5  **Yield: what return to investors is appropriate and under what circumstances?** Consider whether it is to be a fixed annual yield, a variable one or part and part. This in turn links to the source and structure of funding as not all sources offer all options.
6  **Funding type: is this debt, equity or a hybrid?** Compare the different types of funding mechanism you could use to raise funds, noting that it is the repayment of the capital and the risk accepted by the investor on capital and yield that are in question here. Further discussion of these is in Chapter 23.
7  **Simplicity: how can the fundraising be simplified?** Think about simplicity in application of funds, investment structure and in key terms and conditions.
8  **Liquidity: how will the investors gain repayment of their capital at the end of the term?** How will this be achieved and to what extent do the investors need to be able to release capital early? Recent conversations have focused on patient long-term capital and evergreen capital, which will stay with a recipient organisation for the long-term; but, even here, it is right to consider how long term is "long term": rarely does it mean "forever".
9  **Redemption or repayment: in what way is the capital to be repaid or released on maturity?** Weigh up different ways to release capital – by redemption of shares or debt out of surpluses, by refinancing through a renewed or new issue; or by another means.

10 **Ownership and structure?** It will be important to consider who owns the capital, their expectations and likely behaviours in the future. How are these, and the purpose and terms of application of the money within the charity reflected in the legal and governance structure of the investment vehicle and contract?

Your charity or nonprofit will need to have answers to the above questions. It will also need to develop an operating and financial model whereby the investment can be paid back (both capital and interest). This is not the same as the model if being funded by grants and donations, and nonprofit organisations often forget this difference.

## Whose resources?

We need to consider from where and from whom investment resources will come. The resources that may be considered, brought to bear and invested, fall into four main headings:

1   **The charity's own funds and resources** – held and managed by it and invested as such.
2   **The charity's own resources, leveraged with others' resources.** Here, the charity invests, but adds outside investment from third parties to stand alongside its own. Banks have traditionally been involved. Now, other types of investor are getting involved. The charity augments the funds it manages and applies these to its mission in this way.
3   **Others' funds, managed or co-managed.** In this case, the charity holds and controls third-party funding, but does not match with any of the charity's own.
4   **Others' funds through influence.** Here, it does not control the third-party investment, but influences how it's applied.

## Sources of funds

There are three main sources, each of which needs a different approach (more details of approaches are shown in Chapter 23 on "Structuring the Deal").

| Existing funders | Engaged sources | New sources |
|---|---|---|
| • the starting point for further investment | • beyond existing funders come other stakeholders | • after existing and engaged sources come wider sources |
| • could even have first rights to invest | • perhaps members of a body who have not yet been involved at an investor level | • important to plan an investment approach for the long-term |
| • easiest group to identify and ask | • or volunteers or associated organisations | **But …** |
| • interested in, and informed about, your field of operation, objects and approach | • opportunity to change the relationship positively | • assess whether the potential investor is not only likely to invest, but whether they may invest on subsequent occasions |
| • may already be a "converted" audience | **But …** | • identify whether the relationship can develop in a wider sense for the benefit of all |
| **But …** | • may take some change in mindset to see you as an investment prospect | |
| • may not have the resources for further investment | • take care to avoid adversely changing the relationship with them | • in particular, is this a sufficient alignment of approach that you can work with them through both good, and maybe bad, times |
| • may not be interested in the particular focus of the investment | | |

## Creating an investment pack

> An investment pack will need to be developed to take to potential investors. It will need sufficient background and details of the requirements for the investor to easily understand the needs.
>
> Cass CCE Social Investment Toolkit (Cass CCE, 2016)

The process of completing an investment pack can also be valuable in itself, crystallising intent and aligning management teams and boards around investment plans.

The investment pack should be direct and concise but provide sufficient information to enable the investor to get an idea of the organisation and how it intends to achieve financial and social returns, together with a clear view of the "ask" from the investor.

A sample investment pack might contain the elements shown in Table 22.1.

*Table 22.1* A simple investment pack

| Section | Contents the investors want to see |
| --- | --- |
| **Executive summary** | |
| Overview of the proposition | • No more than 2–3 pages containing the key points |
| **Introduction** | |
| Purpose of the investment pack | • Make this clear<br>• What is required from the investor (what is the "ask")? |
| Background and introduction | • Explanation of the organisation's vision, mission and strategy<br>• Some context on recent year's history, operations etc. |
| Management and governance | • Details of those who control and run the organisation (board of trustees and key management staff)<br>• Current structure, and legal entity details |
| **Current operations and future outlook** | |
| Current operations | • Business segments, activities, locations, customers and funders<br>• Current projects and priorities<br>• Potential market – size, segment, value, opportunities<br>• Competitors – who else is in the market? What are their strengths against yours? |
| Impact | • How the non-profit's work will lead to measurable outcomes and short- and long-term impact |
| Future outlook | • Current outlook of the organisation – where does it see itself going and plans |
| **Social impact overview** | |
| Social impact | • Full explanation of planned social impact and how this is created, including overview of the context for the generation of impact (i.e. what is the social need, the outcomes expected, and do these manifest themselves in the local area)<br>• How data is regularly collected, analysed and used within the organisation<br>• Historical trends<br>• Reference to any external reports and evaluative studies<br>• Examples of any internal impact reporting used for communications with staff or the board<br>• How the impact can be measured (cost-effectively and proportionately) – explained further in Chapter 26 |

| Section | Contents the investors want to see |
| --- | --- |
| **Financial overview** | |
| Historical financial summary | • Define and describe each area of income and expenditure |
| | • Provide summary financials for previous years, highlighting key trends and large or unusual items |
| Current year | • Breakdown of current year budget, key insights and risks, including current year forecast and cashflow |
| Balance sheet | • Current year balance sheet with key insights |
| Loans and banking facilities | • Detail current loans and any facilities held with banks, as well as any existing social or other investment |
| **Risk analysis** | |
| Risk analysis and management plan | • Outline of key risks, explaining likelihood and effect |
| | • Plan for monitoring, management and mitigation |
| | Note that this should include impact risk: the risk of not delivering the intended impact, or delivering a negative consequence |
| **Request for investment** | |
| Request for investment | • Summary of what the key request is and what this will be used for (linked to the introductory section) |
| | • This should include full details of financial and social return on investment |
| Long-term financial illustrations | • Five-year plan for income & expenditure and cashflow (longer for longer maturity projects such as phased construction) |
| | • Explanation of key assumptions |
| | • Sensitivity analysis: how does the ability to service investment change as risks manifest themselves? |

Source: Cass CCE Social Investment Toolkit (Cass CCE, 2016).

The content of the investment pack will vary depending on the size of the organisation, the complexity of any investment "ask", as well as the type of investor that is being approached (commercial banks, charity banks, high-net-worth individuals etc.). It is important to seek advice (professionally and/or from the investor) as to what they need and expect.

The investment pack may also be supplemented by:

- Financial reports and accounts, and management accounts
- Product/services brochures
- Valuation of assets (where applicable)
- Impact reporting material
- Regulator and other third-party reports.

## The process of raising social investment

The previous section talked about how to pull together an investment pack to approach investors. This section considers two approaches to doing just that.

The key to achieving the right investment from the right investor is to follow an organised process, ensuring that the approach, engagement and closure of a deal works for both parties.

There are two separate investor processes to consider, each applying in certain circumstances:

- an approach to an institutional funder (already authorised for social investment business)
- a regulated approach to certain categories of retail investor (and private individuals).

## Staged approach to an institutional funder or fund

There are three main types of institutional investor you might want to approach:

1  venture capital–type funds (typically experienced, professional investors co-managing a portfolio of investments)
2  funds managed by a third party, professional, investment manager
3  foundations and endowed funds managing their investment portfolios to include social enterprises and charities.

All three have their own processes, which follow a broadly similar pattern.

First, an approach is made to the potential investor by the organisation hoping to find social investment ("the investee"). This will often be supported by an investment flyer: a short summary document. Initial discussions between the nonprofit and investor take place, and this typically leads to some type of presentation of the investment pack and accompanying material. The investor often prepares an expression of interest (EOI) as its initial response to the application. Further review leads to a formal application by the nonprofit to the investor.

Following a process of initial fact-finding, the application is considered by the investor's investment committee (IC). If a "yes" is given, a more detailed financial and social due diligence is carried out including a detailed review of the financial statements, intended delivery of social impact, budgets, cashflow, use of profits, constitution and governance and understanding of the risks and levers of the business.

The investor will often visit to meet key personnel including the executive team and sometimes the audit committee and members of the board.

Once this has been completed, a report is provided to the investor's investment or credit committee for initial sanction of funds. If it gets a positive response, the formal legal, financial and operational due diligence process commences as well as negotiation of terms. If still positive this will lead to terms being finalised and the funds being provided to the organisation.

The diagram (at Figure 22.1) shows the main steps as a flow chart:

- The box on the left shows the series of documents that a funder will generally expect to see from the investee.
- The centre features the flow (from top to bottom) of the investor's internal processes. The "I.C." refers to the investor's investment committee, which approves the investment.
- To the right are the key exchanges between the investor and the investee (as explained above).

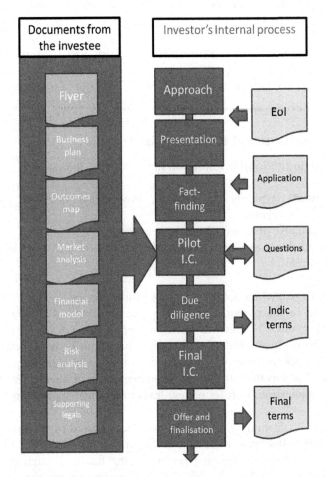

*Figure 22.1* Social investment fundraising: the process.

Source: reproduced with permission from Jim Clifford OBE.

This process may take longer than negotiating a grant, but moves very rapidly towards the end. Equally, investors will want to see that a nonprofit is ready to go and get on with implementing the business plans.

` Often in the nonprofit world there is a delay between getting funds and starting work. It is critical to minimise this in order to avoid costly delay (since a cost of funding may have to be paid even though the supported project hasn't yet started) and to build investor confidence in its new relationship.

## Regulated approaches to funders

Encouraging individuals to invest in financial securities (a collective term for debt and equity instruments) is regulated in law. This applies throughout Europe and in many other jurisdictions.

The subject of the regulation is generally the act of "promotion", which is "an invitation or inducement to engage in investment activity" (s.21 Financial Services and Markets Act 2000).

Simply put, it's an approach by one person to another to ask them to invest in the securities of a business. Here's an overview of the regulations affecting this approach.

**Financial Services and Markets Act 2000 (FSMA) – requirements and exemptions.** Unless exempt, a financial promotion requires approval by an authorised individual – a professional broker, fund manager, accountant or lawyer, or similar, holding the relevant authorisations under the Act, overseen by the Financial Conduct Authority (FCA).

**When does a financial promotion begin?** At initiation of contact, when the subject is broached, it's a promotion from the promoter to the potential investor. That said, a request for information, initiated by the potential investor, and the response to it, are generally not promotions, although the request for information may have been prompted by a promotion in the first place. Financial promotions are either real time (generally conversational or through spoken word) or non–real time (written down as a hard copy or on social or other electronic media). This is shown in more detail in the flowchart at Figure 22.2.

---

**Real time financial promotions**

- the wording must be pre-approved
- the authorised person has to take steps to ensure that the individual making the promotion (perhaps the CEO or chair of the charity) sticks to the script
- approval focuses on whether the promotion is fair and does not include misleading information
- it's a review to ensure the authorised person understands the securities to be promoted, has carefully considered the wording, validated key facts and disclosed testing of key opinions.

---

**What if I fail to meet requirements and issue the promotion anyway?** Failing to meet the requirements of FSMA 2000 and issuing financial promotions without proper authority can result in the individual responsible being liable to fines and imprisonment. Second, the investor can renounce the investment agreement, making it ineffective.

**What about the exemptions?** The main exemptions are for:

- approaches to high-net-worth individuals (HNWI), who certify themselves as such; or to sophisticated investors (so designated because of their prior experience)
- transactions in securities that represent more than a 50 per cent interest in the equity of a company, effectively conferring day-to-day control
- an approach to an authorised investment intermediary, such as an investment fund manager, or authorised person.

**EU Prospectus Directive – requirements and exemptions.** The other main area of regulation affecting the sale of securities is the EU Prospectus Directive (European Union, 2003). This governs the forms of documentation required to promote public issues to larger numbers of individuals.

Its provisions apply where more than €5 million of securities are issued by an organisation within a 12-month period. In this case, you have to produce a particular form of document (a prospectus) containing a specified range of information, subject to professional checking and approval.

The main exemptions are for cases where:

- it's a promotion to fewer than 150 individuals in any one EU member state – remembering that that is the number of people to whom it is promoted, not who invest
- the minimum subscription, or the minimum purchase price of a single share or security, is at least €100,000
- the total issue value is no more than €100,000
- it's an offer to a qualified investor.

The flowcharts in Figures 22.2 and 22.3 show the decisions to determine the need for approval of a financial promotion.

**Tip:** Be sure to take advice about the status of a promotion you're considering and the limits and exemptions applying at the time.

## Working with advisors and intermediaries

It's important to realise that the skills and knowledge in your charity may well be insufficient to achieve investment fundraising in an efficient and effective way. You may well need to add the expertise of advisors and intermediaries to help the process along and, crucially, to ensure that you get the best deal, with the right flexibility and fit to meet your future plans. The level of any outside support and when to use this is a key part of any planning.

The principal types of professional advice to seek in relation to fundraising are: legal and financial; brokerage; social and impact advisory and reporting; and resourcing the development, including leadership. The principal areas covered by each are outlined in Table 22.2.

### Big Society Capital's role as an investor

There are around 4,000 separate social investments across the UK with an aggregate value of £2.3 billion, according to recent figures from Big Society Capital (2018a).

Big Society Capital (BSC) (as a wholesaler of investment funds) does not invest directly but places capital with certain social investment financial intermediaries (SIFIs) to build the social investment market on their behalf. A SIFI is "an organisation that provides, facilitates or structures financial investments for social sector organisations and/or provides investment-focussed business support to social sector organisations" (Big Society Capital, 2018b). The SIFI market continues to develop and is now much more able to meet the needs of the charity sector, in terms of both capacity and understanding.

BSC has placed funds with SIFIs focused on a wide range of themes, ranging from ex-offenders, adoption and rough-sleepers to health and ageing. There are many fund-holding SIFIs, such as Social and Sustainable Capital, Social Investment Business, Resonance and Social Finance, as well as specialist advisors.

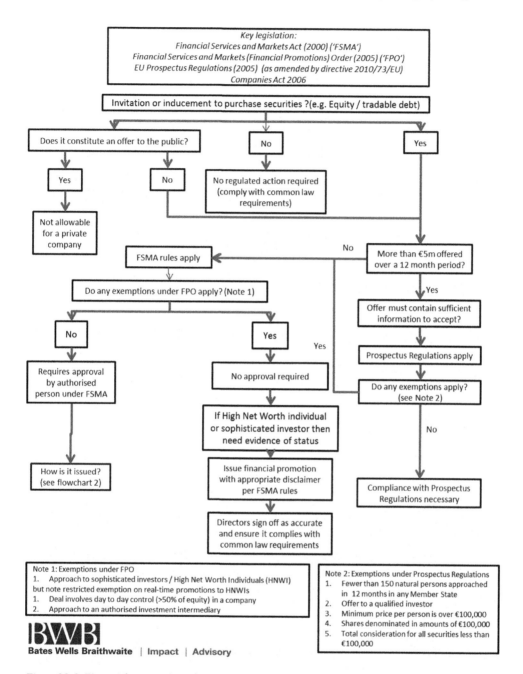

*Figure 22.2* Financial promotions: key requirements.

Source: reproduced with permission from Jim Clifford OBE and Bates Wells.

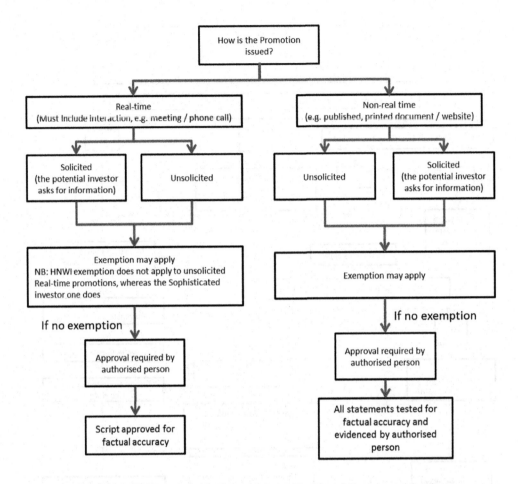

**Note:** This paper is intended as general guidance, but it should not be relied-upon as total guidance on the compliance of a particular set of actions in a fundraising activity. Appropriate advice should be taken. In particular a promotion which may not fall within these two sets of regulations may be subject to the provisions regarding Unregulated Collective Investment Schemes.

**ALSO:** further advice is needed if the promotion (whether exempt under this paper or not, is being made to non-Europeans or those not resident in Europe.

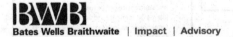

*Figure 22.3* Financial promotions: key requirements (2).

Source: reproduced with permission from Jim Clifford OBE and Bates Wells.

*Table 22.2* Forms of professional advice

| | |
|---|---|
| **Legal and financial** | This is obtained from professional firms or qualified individuals and covers six main areas: |

- **Compliance:** Advice and the preparation of documentation to ensure compliance with both legislation (e.g. FSMA 2000 or the Charities Act 2011) and best practice standards.
- **Reporting:** Where some form of reporting is necessary in the context of the transaction concerned (e.g. the requirement, under s.124 Charities Act 2011, for advice by a financially skilled person, before creating a changeover property).
- **Regulated functions:** Certain functions in connection with fundraising can only be performed by authorised individuals (e.g. contact with individual investors and the management of collective funds on their behalf).
- **Advice:** Access to a range of experience in technical areas and also the practice, conventions and behaviours necessary to bring fundraising to fruition. Includes improving not only the way of doing what is necessary and best, but identifying and managing more effectively the risks involved.
- **Document drafting:** There's a frequent need for a range of legal documents to be drafted. There may also be reports and promotional investment documents requiring financial and other input.
- **Management of process and negotiation support:** An advisor who has delivered successful fundraising can support the charity in managing an effective and efficient process. They may also bring considerable experience in advising on, or leading, negotiation with investors.
- **Due diligence and inward investment advice:** Legal and financial advice are also useful to the investor. Including advice about the benefits and risks of making the investment, how it will be controlled and managed and the documents needed for it. Also, due diligence: specific review and reporting on the risks and benefits of the investment and the investee – see Chapter 24.

| | |
|---|---|
| **Brokerage** | Taking the investment prospect to market and finding the parties to invest in the securities.<br>This is best done by those who know the relevant markets, who are recognised and respected by the investors and who can best deliver the relationships and dialogues that will make for an effective and supportive investor base. Some considerations include: |

- practical aspects (e.g. finding and contacting investors)
- advisory aspects (e.g. how to present the investment prospect in an engaging but fair way).

Where the chosen investor market is already known to the charity (e.g. a re-issue to existing investors), the practical aspects may be less important than the management and advisory ones.

| | |
|---|---|
| **Social and impact advisory and reporting** | Approaching markets that formally require this level of accountability (such as the Social Stock Exchange), or other investors who will be encouraged to invest when they know about the social impact. It may require formal research, validation and reporting. A charity could use explanations such as a theory of change to explain the social case.<br>Practical guidance is available from a number of sources, including the EU's standards, which include a section on forms of independent or internal validation and audit and when to use it. (Clifford *et al.*, 2014) |
| **Resourcing the development, including leadership** | Using the investment to deliver the development that will pay for the yield on it.<br>As well as growing the wider mission of the charity, this may require additional staff, management and leadership resources, some of them specialist. It's important to plan in resources so that they're there when needed. A project that's under-resourced at the outset may cost the organisation considerably as it grows. |

## Tax relief as an incentive

The introduction of the Social Investment Tax Relief (SITR) is also likely to encourage more people to use social investment as a tool. Some small-scale direct investments have benefitted from this; UBS released the first SITR fund in 2015 and others look set to follow. This is discussed further in Chapter 23.

---

**In this chapter, we thought about:**

Taking an organised approach to investment raising – planning and resourcing
The pros and cons of approaching each main sources of investment
The process of fundraising for social investment
Regulated approaches to fundraising
Engaging advisors and intermediaries to find funding

---

**In the next chapter, we'll explore:**

The most appropriate investment structures
A charity's important considerations when choosing a legal form for investment
Accountability to investors through corporate structure and investment vehicles
Selecting structural forms to receive and manage investment
The pros and cons of corporate vehicles for charities and social enterprises seeking investment

---

# References

Big Society Capital (2018a), *The size and composition of social investment in the UK*, Social Investment Insight Series, accessed 30 September 2018, www.bigsocietycapital.com/latest/type/research/size-and-composition-social-investment-uk.

Big Society Capital (2018b), *Big Society Capital Glossary*, accessed 30 September 2018, www.bigsocietycapital.com/glossary/.

Cass CCE (2016), *Social investment tools for success: doing the right things and doing them right*, Cass CCE, accessed 30 September 2018, www.cass.city.ac.uk/__data/assets/pdf_file/0007/358864/CCE-Social-Investment-as-a-new-charity-finance-tool-using-both-head-and-heart-Report-May17.pdf.

Clifford, J., Hehenberger, L., and Fantini, M. (2014), *Proposed approaches to social impact measurement in European Commission legislation and in practice relating to EuSEFs and the EaSI*, report by GECES (Groupe d'experts de la Commission sur l'entrepreneuriat social) subgroup on impact measurement, accessed 15 October 2018, www.ec.europa.eu/social/main.jsp?catId=738&langId=en&pubId=7735&type=2&furtherPubs=yes..

European Union. (2003), Directive 2003/71/EC, as amended 2010 and 2017, accessed 30 June 2019, https://ec.europa.eu/info/law/prospectus-directive-2003-71-ec/law-details_en.

Financial Services and Markets Act 2000 (2000), *Financial Services and Markets Act s21*, accessed 30 September 2018, www.legislation.gov.uk/ukpga/2000/8/section/21.

Financial Times (2018), *Hotel Chocolat to repay "mini bonds"*, accessed 22/01/2019. www.ft.com/content/dc4cf35a-67be-11e8-b6eb-4acfcfb08c11.

Rugby Football Union (2017), *75 year debentures*, accessed 22 January 2019, www.englandrugby.com/mm/Document/General/General/01/31/99/80/DebentureTermsandConditions-2017SeriesFINAL_English.pdf.

# 23 Structuring the deal

*Jim Clifford*

How does a charity's legal structure affect social investment as an opportunity? What will investors think about in this dynamic?

What is the best method to handle social investment funds coming into a charity – through the charity itself or through a separate entity set up for the purpose? What legal form will this take?

In the last chapter we talked about where to find investors and how to engage with them. In this chapter we think about legal forms and their pros and cons. We also think about the best way to take social investment into your organisation and how to structure the deal.

## What are the principal legal and corporate forms for organisations in the UK?

The UK offers a bewildering range of corporate and legal forms for commercial businesses, charities and social enterprises. This chapter takes a deeper dive into that analysis. As charities have two levels of regulatory compliance – corporate; and charitable compliance through the Charity Commission – we focus specifically on charities later in this chapter.

Table 23.1 summarises the main legal forms for corporate organisations in the UK.

Other incorporated forms include: charter bodies; industrial and provident societies; and cooperatives of various types. Together with non-UK corporate forms, these are beyond the scope of this book, as are unincorporated associations such as English and Welsh, and Scottish, limited partnerships. Professional advice should be sought if these are to be considered.

Let us consider first the charity's perspective, and then the investors', before moving onto some practicalities about fund flow.

## Step one: the charity's perspective

### Main corporate forms for charities

A charity is defined as such by its constitution. Charities typically take one of two main corporate forms (see also Table 23.2):

- A company limited by guarantee (CLG); or, more unusually,
- A company limited by shares (CLS).

*Table 23.1* Main legal forms of corporate organisations in the UK

| Company Limited by Shares (CLS) | |
|---|---|
| | • the simplest, most widespread company form |
| | • each owning party owns a "share" in the assets and liabilities of the company, with that share determined by the rights attaching to "shares" in the company's articles of association |
| | • confers limited liability for the company's debts on shareholders |
| | • governed by a board of directors appointed by shareholders |
| | • cannot issue shares to public or have shares or securities traded on a public exchange |
| | • without its shares being both numerous and listed, its shares are relatively illiquid: there may be limited means for realising investor's capital quickly |
| | • a frequently used form for charity subsidiaries, SPVs and joint venture vehicles |
| • has all the benefits of a CLS | **Public Limited Company (PLC)** |
| • can issue shares or securities to the public, with trading allowed on a public exchange | |
| • advent of Social Stock Exchange and listed charity bonds has promoted its use as an intermediary vehicle for issuing shares or bonds to the public | |
| • the PLC may be a charity subsidiary or an independent vehicle (such as Allia's "RCB plc") | |
| • CLS can convert to a PLC, but CLG without shares cannot | |
| **Company Limited by Guarantee (CLG)** | • confers limited liability on owners and investors |
| | • limited by amount members promise to pay in the event of a wind-up, rather than nominal value of the shares (guarantee – generally £1 each) |
| | • except for the very rare CLG with shares (formed as such), a CLG cannot issue shares; therefore would receive inward investment in the form of debt |
| | • a CLG cannot convert into a CLS, or vice versa |
| | • traditional form for a charity |

*continued*

*Table 23.1  Continued*

| | **Community Interest Company (CIC)** |
|---|---|
| • regulated by the Office of the Regulator of Community Interest Companies<br>• this is a CLS or CLG that is not a charity, but whose founders wish it to apply an 'asset lock', thereby locking an appreciable proportion of its assets and profits into delivering for public benefit rather than personal gain<br>• has ability to pay out up to 35% of annual surpluses in profits as dividends<br>• can carry many of the benefits in terms of access to capital of a simple CLS or CLG non-charity, while retaining degree of protection against for-profit exploitation<br>• makes a useful joint venture vehicle, or trading entity operating as a social enterprise<br>• subject to corporation tax in the UK<br>• a charity can be a member of, or invest in, a CIC | |
| **Limited Liability Partnership (LLP)** | • gives investors (owners) the protection of limited liability, while being tax-transparent<br>• as a partnership, it's not a taxable entity under UK legislation, so profits are subject to tax or not based on the investors or owners to whom they are attributable<br>• useful where investors and owners are a mixture of taxable and non-taxable (e.g. charity) entities<br>• managed by a board similar to corporates<br>• can be used as vehicles for pooled investment funds from multiple investors<br>• can constitute a collective investment scheme, requiring a regulated fund manager to run them<br>• a charity can be a member of (or investor in) an LLP |

*Table 23.2* Main legal forms of charities and what this means for social investment

| Company legal form | Key concerns |
|---|---|
| **Company Limited by Guarantee (CLG)** | • the principal charity form<br>• cannot issue shares, unless it is a CLG with share capital (investment as an equity holding is therefore not possible)<br>• investment by way of debt instrument only |
| **Company Limited by Shares (CLS)** | • CLS as a registered charity is rare, but possible<br>• more usually found among community interest companies (CICs)<br>• can raise social investment, with some restrictions<br>• popular form as an investment vehicle for a charity subsidiary (although other forms are possible for this) |

Charities must also be registered with the Charity Commission: in England and Wales, if operating there; separately in Scotland, if operating there. A charity operating in both locations needs dual registration.

In 2013, the charitable incorporated organisation (CIO) was introduced. Its intention is to reduce bureaucracy, allowing a company to be formed as a charity directly by registration with the Charity Commission, rather than having to form a company with the Registrar of Companies and apply separately for registration as a charity. It is aimed primarily at smaller charities and to reduce the burden of red tape. As it has certain shortcomings if intended to be used for larger or more widely trading entities, professional advice should be taken if it is to be considered for all but the smallest of entities.

### What do charities need to consider regarding social investment?

As a registered charity, you've a number of statutory, regulatory and practical aspects affecting your ability to raise investment capital. These are not insurmountable problems, by any means – but considerations you must address. They cover both your relationship with inward investors and the approach to your investing in others.

Bear in mind that they may limit your options to some degree, compared to the options open to other legal forms or structures, such as community interest companies (CICs), PLCs and corporate forms.

1   **Ability to distribute profits**
    By definition, a charity must only exist for charitable purposes (Charity Commission, 2013). So, there's a general prohibition on charities distributing their profits (because this would be for the personal benefit of its shareholders). In social investment, this potentially precludes paying a yield (return) on equity instruments (shares) to an investor, since this is a distribution of profits and potentially outside the charity's objectives. Equally, redeeming the shares at a premium could become problematic.
    *Exception*: The prohibition can be lifted for specific cases with the consent of the Charity Commission.
    *Alternative*: Link variable returns to something other than profits. This opens the possibility of having outcomes-linked, or volume-linked or turnover-linked returns on social value created. Assess each case on its merits.

2   **Ability to raise debt**
    Most charities do have the power to raise debt, as long as it's in proper pursuance of their objects. In most charities, this would be found in their articles of association, or founding deed.
    *Action*: A careful review of the charity's constitution is required before debt is raised. This applies not just to debt in the form of a bond issue, or from investment institutions, but also debt from supporters, or taking on debt or loans from traditional clearing banks.

3   **Granting security**
    Most charities have the power to charge their assets, in other words to grant security over such things as buildings to secure borrowing or other financial obligations. This involves following the due process for creating the security – assessing whether it's in the interests of the charity's mission and taking relevant financial advice, in the case of land and buildings, following ss.124–126 Charities Act 2011.

**Action**: Check whether this power exists and take advice to confirm it and any restrictions to it.

4 **Primary purpose trading**

A charity is exempt from tax on surpluses (profits) it makes on its activities (i.e. from trading), provided that trading is part of the primary charitable purpose and helps it. Even if there's a small element of non-primary purpose trading, the exemption may still apply if the trading turnover is small, both in absolute terms and in relation to the charity's gross annual income.

*Alternative*: Where non-primary purpose trading turnover exceeds 25 per cent, the most usual approach is to form a subsidiary company – normally limited by shares (see below) – and to put the non-exempt activities into that.

**Action**: There are further details and guidance in the Charity Commission publication CC35 (2017).

5 **Mixed motive investment**

Just as programme-related investment (PRI) demonstrating social returns can be recognised as social investment, so a further category of authorised investment activity was introduced for charities in 2011. Full details are provided in the Charity Commission guidance CC14: *Charities and Investment Matters: A Guide for Trustees*.

In a mixed motive investment (MMI), both financial investment and PRI characteristics (social returns) are present, but the investment cannot be wholly justified as either. It therefore is deemed "mixed motive".

*Action:* Take professional advice. Check whether the investment can be justified by the dual nature of the return – part financial and part PRI. Assess whether there might be an impediment to making the investment (e.g. private benefits to trustees or non-incidental private benefit to others).

More guidance can be found at Big Society Capital's website; Good Finance (2018): *Understand Social Investment*, www.goodfinance.org.uk; or from government guidance at Gov.UK (2016a, 2016b, 2017).

### *Sometimes charities encounter internal objections to social investment*

Some charities find their trustees, key management, grant funders or backing philanthropists raising objections to social investment on ethical grounds, or through a feeling of being conflicted by making "profit" through a charity (essentially a "nonprofit" vehicle).

This is rarely a legal problem (which would arise for a constitutional restriction or lack of power), but one of perception, mixing charity with investment, which is often seen as a more commercial way of undertaking business.

An alternative impediment may be encountered if particular structures of return on investment (for example in Islamic finance) or levels of return may be unacceptable to key stakeholders or under the charity's constitution.

It is important to highlight, discuss and clarify any such cultural or ethical objections with trustees, management or other key stakeholders before pursuing a social investment strategy.

## Step two: the investor's perspective

In terms of corporate form and the structure and type of investment instrument, the investor looks for something familiar and understood; a reasonable level of control; accountability; flexibility and agility. As different investors will have different expectations and responses (especially if plans change), it is important that these are understood and confirmed at the outset as something with which the charity can live in the future.

It's important for a charity to plan for all these investor expectations, considering how they enable or restrict what the parties can do in future. Discuss and agree them at the outset, leaving nothing uncertain or open to later interpretation and dispute.

1   **Reasons to invest**
These may be: alignment with the vision and mission of the charity; the outcomes it intends to deliver; the investment return and risk profile; the tax reliefs available; or all of these. The investor wants to see these areas of interest reflected appropriately in the legal structure, as well as the softer areas of governance and accountability.

*Action:* Clarify these points with the potential investor at the outset, explaining why you may not be able fully to address them, then negotiate an alternative. The potential investment may concern a wider group, making individual dialogues impractical. When you consider listed investments, some discussion with selected current or potential investors or their advisors may add some clarity to this. However, take care about this drifting into pre-publicising an issue of securities and affecting the market, which may be unhelpful or even illegal.

2   **Control and influence**
Some investors require it, others desire it. Some prefer to sit back and watch. However active or inactive, some degree of control will be there: appropriate to investors' needs and hopefully negotiated to something that is practical and workable.

*Action:* Ensure you have an appropriate level of management and oversight in these discussions. However, too much pushback against an investor's involvement may disadvantage the charity, as the investor could bring new skills to your organisation (for example, Impetus-PEF are among a number of social investors careful to help improve a charity's impact measurement skill base, aiming to build capacity in this way).

An investor may look for control in the following ways:

- **Voting control** – embedded in share or debt rights and exercised by votes in general meetings, or debt-holders' meetings.
- **Board membership** – giving a right to attend and be heard and perhaps to vote at board level on operational and strategic matters. Both board and member voting may be subject to tailored arrangements, allowing one or more parties to exert additional control in specified circumstances.
- **Contractual control** – the relationship with the investor may be further controlled under the terms of a contract between them and the other investors, between them and the charity or both.

3   **Investor obligations and expectations**
Be aware that the investor has certain obligations under their terms of investment, their company's articles, as well as company law under which they also operate.

Consider abiding by any voting protocols the investor may have. Also, discuss investor expectations such as responses to future funding rounds or events (e.g. sales of business operations or changes in strategy) and how they will behave in board meetings and other engagements with the charity.

*Action:* Clarify and document investor obligations and expectations in advance.

4    **Protecting investor rights**

The investor will be investing subject to: the charity's constitution and charity and company law as it affects it, overlaid with the contents of any investment agreements. For example, all companies are under an obligation not to act in a way that is prejudicial to a minority. They have a duty to take care of the investor's interests and try to make the desired (financial or social) return on their investment. A charity must pursue its charitable objectives. Don't forget the need to communicate and be accountable, to listen and respond to concerns and comments. The greater the investor's commitment to the investee, the more they will be likely to seek clarity around their rights and how the investee will protect them.

*Action:* When mapping investor needs, think about how you might respond to them in the future, taking into account flexibility and agility as conditions change.

5    **Accountability**

Scrutiny, transparency and involvement are all of interest to the investor. Properly thought through, these can lead to engaged and supportive investors. **Account-ability** is your acknowledgement that the charity owes duties to provide information and explanation to the investor. **Transparency** is the provision of information to meet that obligation: information that is helpful and relevant, appropriately selected and explained and not just data in raw form. **Involvement** is you making clear the channels through which the investor can raise comment and query and through which and how the charity will respond. You will also have to be transparent about social investments in your reports and accounts and discuss this with investors in advance.

*Action:* Plan how you will address accountability, transparency and involvement in advance, thinking about what is necessary, useful and practical. Document that appropriately, taking advice as necessary.

**Accountability** is discussed further in Chapter 27 "Governance aspects of social investment".

6    **Tax Reliefs**

Since the introduction of Social Investment Tax Relief (Sch. 11 and 12 Finance Act 2014), the incentives afforded to investors in private sector SMEs have largely been available to those investing in social enterprise undertaken by charities. Social Investment Tax Relief (SITR) can be claimed by individuals investing in charities, CICs and community benefit societies carrying out a qualifying trade. It's not available for large social enterprises: those with more than 500 employees or with gross assets of more than £15 million. It provides the individual with income tax relief of 30 per cent of the amount invested in the year of investment. Financial limits apply to investor and investee, which are subject to change as the legislation gains full approval and implementation.

*Action:* Due to the range of detailed rules, taking professional advice is recommended. So is carrying out further detailed review before developing SITR-qualifying securities. Understand the limits to investment and also how it relates to social impact bonds and social venture capital trusts.

## Thinking about how the funds will flow into the organisation

Having found an investor and agreed terms, funding is now available to deliver against your charity's objectives. The investment can happen in one of four ways:

**Method 1: Directly into the charity.** In which the investment is made directly into the main charity or social enterprise. The charity needs to have the power to issue the relevant securities, which will mostly be structured as debt.

- Check your constitution and governing documents for any restrictions which would stop you doing this.
- The structure and terms of the financial instrument will need to work with the general prohibition on a charity distributing its profits (so-called "asset lock"). This can be achieved either by linking returns to another factor (such as service-user volumes in a project) or by obtaining the consent of the Charity Commission. Equally, the terms of the investment may be set to limit the risk to the charity's wider work by linking them specifically to the delivery and success of a project.
- Many charities are companies limited by guarantee (with no share capital) and therefore can only receive debt finance and not equity funding. However, raising debt is still a route that is simple and direct. HCT is an example of a charity that has grown its work through social investment in the form of debt (HCT Group, 2018). If the purpose of the investment does not generate sufficient return, servicing it may come from the wider organisation.
- Where the main entity is a company limited by shares (e.g. a CIC limited by shares), the investment can be by way of share capital.

**Method 2: Indirectly into the charity.** In which the investment is made through an investment vehicle, which then onward-lends to the charity, or invests in the main entity or project vehicle.

**Method 3: Through a special purpose vehicle (SPV).** The project and its inward investment are focused in a separate corporate vehicle. This has long been an approach used for specific projects. Charities have formed subsidiaries to ring-fence risks and allow third-party interests to be focused on the relevant area of the operations. It also appears in the traditional form of SIB as the prime contracting vehicle (see Chapter 21 for further details).

- This form of inward investment feeds directly into an SPV, which is typically a subsidiary of the charity.
- SPVs are also used as conduits for investment in circumstances where there is a restriction on direct investment into a charity in the governing documents.
- Shares in an SPV will also potentially allow an equity stake to be taken in an investment.

**Method 4: Through a managed, tied fund.** Rather like the SPV in corporate structure and purpose, this is focused on a joint project or trading. However, unlike the SPV, the joint venture (JV) vehicle often comprises multiple interests and levels of interest, conferring different control rights and rights to return on investment and capital returns or gains.

- Here, the investors jointly contribute to a standalone fund. This may also include funds co-invested from the charity or social enterprise itself.
- This separate fund lends, or invests, onward, with drawdowns that match the charity's needs.
- Such funds may be investor-managed and may require independent Financial Conduct Authority (FCA) regulated management, if they rank as certain types of collective investment scheme (FCA, 2018).

---

**EXAMPLES**

---

The Allia bond issuance platform uses an SPV to issue bonds into the London Retail Bond Market. Operating for Allia, Retail Charity Bonds PLC raises the investment on the basis and lends on to the charity for the disclosed purpose.

(Allia, 2018)

A well-publicised example of a managed, tied fund is used in connection with "It's All About Me", a UK-based adoption bond raised to help hard to place children. This is a subsidiary of the charity, the Consortium of Voluntary Adoption Agencies.

(Home for Good, 2018)

---

## Keeping the funds flowing

With the management of investor money comes an obligation and an accountability that demand their own data gathering and management.

1  **Managing, applying and repaying the capital.** As the capital has been invested for a particular use, you should be able to prove it's been properly applied. Good capital management could mean keeping funds segregated, often in accordance with the investment agreement. Repayments may be periodic, variable, payable on certain key events or achievements, or repayable at a given date (requiring that the investee plans ahead for that repayment).

2  **Calculating and paying the return on investment**. The calculation may call for a fixed or variable rate of interest on outstanding capital, or even as well as, a share of a surplus, which may or may not be the surplus for the whole organisation. That calculation must be done promptly, carefully and accurately and the data retained to support the calculation.

3  **Meeting financial and other covenants.** As with conventional bank debt, some social investments may include financial covenants as a means of the investor monitoring their investment risk. Conventional debt will measure interest cover (cash generated or **e**arnings **b**efore **i**nterest, **t**ax, **d**epreciation and **a**mortisation – EBITDA – divided by interest payable on unrestricted funds); and debt service (EBITDA divided by interest plus repayments on unrestricted funds) for a rolling 12-month period at quarterly or annual intervals. Other covenants may apply, such as the surplus or income being generated from the project being invested in.

4  **Reporting results.** Almost invariably, there's a requirement for reporting financial results to investors. Wherever possible, this should be agreed in line with existing annual or management reporting, to avoid additional calculation and reporting. Depending on the purpose and focus of the investment, this may not be acceptable. A notable exception to the general need to report results to investors is for listed retail debt instruments. Here, a certificate of compliance with payment obligations is normally the only thing required to be sent to them.

## Other things to consider

Other strategic considerations before taking on social investment are as follows:

**The finance director's role is key.** The finance director has to: analyse the opportunity and the risks; support the financial aspects of negotiating the arrangement; liaise with advisors; and advise the trustees. More than that, the role calls for managing and reporting upon the project, the return on investment and the capital. This requires a different skill set from that possessed by most charity finance directors. We must be careful to train and mentor staff, so they have the necessary skills.

**Don't forget to benchmark.** Before accepting, a charity should always benchmark the investment offered against what is available in the market. That may be done through the expertise of the advisor or intermediary or, better if larger, by market-testing. Alongside this – except where precluded by confidentiality obligations – it may be useful to outline particulars of the investment publicly available at an early stage. This often helps develop the market data from which others can benchmark their own facilities.

This benchmarking covers more than just commercial terms and covenants. Each investment depends for its terms on the investment source, risk profile, sector and the social impact being targeted and achieved.

**Branding, positioning and partnering.** Good branding gains the confidence and engagement of service-users, partners and other stakeholders. It also enhances the investor's view of the charity.

Then there's the "affinity effect". A brand may be enhanced, changed or be heavily damaged by an association with another which is perceived differently. Charities should think carefully about their choice of lender or funder, because of their possible association with unfair practices.

**Review and update the measurement, too.** Social investment relies on impact measurement to evaluate the social impact created. As such, it takes on a much wider importance in partnering and in coordinating multiple interventions to achieve complex, multi-faceted change for individuals, families, communities and the state. To encourage continuous improvement, impact measures must themselves be tested, challenged and developed (Clifford *et al.*, 2014).

**Stakeholders have even more control and influence now.** The introduction of social investment gives an additional area for control and influence by stakeholders. The investors exert an additional form of control through their investment agreement. From the charity's point of view, it's important to balance that control to ensure it does not adversely affect it or constrain its activities or delivery of outcomes. However, through that involvement, the charity can also influence the investment policy of the investor and the overall balance of the investment portfolio. It may also gain new valuable skills.

**Stay flexible and agile.** The final thought is perhaps the most important of all in the recipe for success. The contractual arrangements, the financial ones, the way in which the investment backs the delivery of social outcomes – all must be structured to be flexible and agile.

Flexibility is the ability to adjust to accommodate the ebb and flow of operations, needs and circumstances and the changes that occur in the natural course of events. Agility is the ability to cope with and work around wider changes in the policy and operating environment.

Investors will often look at the investment in terms of the social hurdle (the social value created), the team, the business model and the financial plans. However, the biggest element of this is the team.

Think big, start small, learn fast …

(Chunka Mui, 2018)

---

**In this chapter, we've looked in some detail into:**

A charity's important considerations when choosing the legal form for social investment

Accountability to investors through corporate structure and investment vehicles

The most appropriate inward investment structures

Selecting legal and structural forms to receive and manage inward investment

The pros and cons of different corporate and legal forms for charities and social enterprises seeking investment

Some other considerations around agility, the finance director and the brand of the charity

---

**In the next chapter, we'll explore:**

The use of due diligence as part of your decision-making process

What due diligence is, and when might you expect to use it

Types of due diligence, and the balance between internal and external review

---

# References

Allia (2018), *Retail charity bonds*, accessed 14 October 2018, www.allia.org.uk/social-finance/retail-charity-bonds.

CC14 (2011), *Charities and investment matters: a guide for trustees (CC14)*, accessed 14 October 2018, www.gov.uk/government/publications/charities-and-investment-matters-a-guide-for-trustees-cc14.

CC35 (2017), *Trustees, trading and tax: how charities may lawfully trade*, accessed 14 October 2018, https://assets.publishing.service.gov.uk/government/uploads/system/uploads/attachment_data/file/592404/CC35.pdf.

Charities Act 2011 (2011), *Charities Act 2011*, accessed 14 October 2018, www.legislation.gov.uk/ukpga/2011/25/pdfs/ukpga_20110025_en.pdf.

Charity Commission (2013), *Charitable purposes and public benefit*, accessed 14 October 2018, www.gov.uk/government/collections/charitable-purposes-and-public-benefit.

Chunka Mui (2018), *Think big, start small, learn fast*, accessed 14 October 2018, www.forbes.com.

Clifford, J., Hehenberger, L. and Fantini, M. (2014). *Proposed approaches to social impact measurement in European Commission legislation and in practice relating to EuSEFs and the EaSI*, report by GECES (Groupe d'experts de la Commission sur l'entrepreneuriat social) subgroup on impact measurement, accessed 15 October 2018, www.ec.europa.eu/social/main.jsp?catId=738&langId=en&pubId=7735&type=2&furtherPubs=yes.

FCA (2018), *Unregulated collective investment schemes*, accessed 14 October 2018, www.fca.org.uk/consumers/unregulated-collective-investment-schemes.

Finance Act 2014 (2014), *Finance Act 2014*, accessed 14 October 2018, www.legislation.gov.uk/ukpga/2014/26/introduction.

Good Finance (2018), *Understand social investment*, accessed 14 October 2018, www.goodfinance.org.uk.

Gov.UK (2016a), *Charities (Protection and Social Investment) Act 2016*, accessed 14 October 2018, www.legislation.gov.uk/ukpga/2016/4/section/15/enacted   and   www.legislation.gov.uk/ukpga/2014/26/schedule/11/enacted.

Gov.UK (2016b), *Guidance: trustees trading and tax: how charities may lawfully trade*, www.gov.uk/government/publications/trustees-trading-and-tax-how-charities-may-lawfully-trade-cc35/trustees-trading-and-tax-how-charities-may-lawfully-trade#trading-by-charities.

Gov.UK (2017), *Guidance: social impact bonds*, accessed 14 October 2018, https://data.gov.uk/sib_knowledge_box/node/183.

HCT Group, website, accessed 14 October 2018, www.hctgroup.org.

Home For Good, *It's All About Me*, accessed 14 October 2018, www.homeforgood.org.uk/adopt/its-all-about-me.

# 24 The importance of due diligence

*Jim Clifford*

## What is due diligence and what does it involve?

In the last chapter we looked at how a charity's legal structure affects how social investment is raised and the possible corporate structures for funding. We also considered how both the charity's and the investor's needs can be aligned and met.

This chapter looks at how plans and proposals should be tested using good due diligence. It considers three questions:

1   What is due diligence and what does it involve?
2   Why do it and on what should you focus?
3   What types of due diligence are there and who should do it?

## What is due diligence and what does it involve?

### What is it?

The Cambridge Dictionary defines due diligence as the "action that is considered reasonable for people to be expected to take in order to keep themselves or others and their property safe", and again in a business and finance sense, "the detailed examination of a company and its financial records, done before becoming involved in a business arrangement with it" (Cambridge English Dictionary, 2019).

Prior to entering into a social investment contract, it is incumbent on each party to consider carefully whether that can deliver what it is seeking and whether it carries the value that is being offered. This is appropriate due diligence.

The different parties to the social investment should document this, using it as a foundation for their decision-making and also to inform the ongoing management of their relationship. It is a fundamental part of a contractual arrangement that one party cannot rely on the other to make its decision for it: it must take responsibility for its own side of the deal.

At its simplest, due diligence for a charity is the trustees' duty to take care of the assets of the charity. Contractual due diligence is a key part of doing so.

There are two key elements to the phrase "due diligence", namely:

- **Due** – meaning as needed, matched to its purpose and proportionate to it; and
- **Diligence** – meaning care and focus: a review of relevant, reliable information to enable the person undertaking the enquiry to form a view.

*What does it involve?*

Due diligence requires four key elements:

1   **Understanding the project plan and intended investment**
    Both parties will aim to make the project or investment a success, so due diligence must be set in that context. It follows that any due diligence must start with the investment and project plan, meaning care should be taken to ensure that there is a common understanding of what success looks like, before the work starts.
        All key terms of the investment deal need to be understood, as this may affect performance and delivery. This understanding needs to be drawn out carefully as each party (investor or investee) may embrace success differently: through financial, social or other factors.

2   **Identifying the critical success factors and key assumptions**
    From this initial understanding, the parties should develop critical success factors (CSFs): those events, terms, resources or actions that are key to delivering a successful project. As these may be different for the investor and investee, the focus of due diligence may be different for the two parties.
    This should embrace the obvious, but should also seek out the less obvious items as a key part of the work. It may be beneficial here and in other areas to draw on the experience of others who have undertaken similar projects, or have undertaken due diligence on them.
        In addition to the CSFs, the project will be based on certain key assumptions, which should be arrived at reasonably and with sound underpinning argument or evidence, but which, if incorrect, would result in the project or investment failing to deliver.

3   **Testing these**
    The CSFs and key assumptions are then tested. This involves answering three questions for each:

    • What is the reasoning behind each CSF and assumption; is it sound; and appropriately evidenced?
    • What will happen if it is not true, or not met?
    • How likely is that to happen; and how can the risk of it happening (or the impact of this) be reduced?

This is a risk-based due diligence approach that avoids a checklist-driven series of enquiries that would waste money and time in chasing irrelevant and immaterial items. Analysing first what matters and why from a risk perspective usually works best, followed by developing a tailored work programme and testing those elements.
    Techniques that are used to do this include:

    • **Testing against past experience** – often used in looking at forecasts of growth or future business predictions
    • **Testing against third-party experience** – where the organisation is seeking to replicate and develop what has been done elsewhere
    • **Management enquiry** – asking management their plans and the reason why they believe in them
    • **Reviewing supplementary evidence** – checking against academic research sources (if relevant) and documentary and legislative sources

- **Financial and impact scenario modelling** – modelling scenarios to outline what might be achieved if the operating circumstances change; and
- **Risk planning** – planning how risks can be managed, monitored and their impact mitigated.

4 **Concluding and taking action**
Once this has been done, action is needed. There is no point undertaking due diligence unless:

- You are prepared to walk away from the deal if the due diligence indicates you should
- You are prepared to act to cover risks and ensure that the deal works around problems if they arise.

The conclusions must be reported back to the trustees and the decision taken by them. The report to them should be in writing and the decision recorded in the minutes.

Trustees should be given sufficient time not just to make their decision, reading and understanding the due diligence and its messages, but also to ask for further and better particulars. This requires planning and timetabling the trustees' decision and it is usually better if they, or a trustee subgroup, can see the due diligence findings as they are emerging and have the chance to steer the line of enquiry, if necessary.

Finally, decisions should be captured in writing to reflect the process undertaken, demonstrating that due care and attention was taken in reaching a decision.

## Why do due diligence and on what should you focus?

### *Why do it?*

At the beginning of this chapter, due diligence was introduced as a form of "look before you leap" analysis. Taking due diligence to a deeper level, it brings four key benefits:

1 **To challenge the social investment plan and challenge assumptions underpinning it**
This brings an *objective* review of the plans; and from an independent viewpoint. It enables views not to be over-ridden, but to be tested and challenged, positively and helpfully. It draws out risks that may be too close to see and asks important questions that may have been missed. It may find benefits and solutions that have been overlooked, just as it can spot problems.

It also enables the plan to be adapted and changed to make it more robust and sustainable.

2 **To inform the structuring and pricing and approach to the transaction**
The review will also enable the social investment to be better priced and structured.

For example, a proposed structure may result in a VAT "loss", or a set of covenants being used by a lender to control and monitor its perceived risk may be focused on the wrong items, creating an inflexibility that compromises future success. Either can probably be catered for by restructuring the deal at the outset. Similarly, if better understood by all parties, it may be possible to mitigate a source of risk that the lender has recognised with a higher contract price, thus lowering the cost of capital to the borrower.

3   **To underpin the decision**

The due diligence provides a sound and tested information pack from which the trustees can take a decision. While not making their decision for them, it can give a strong guide towards that.

4   **To ensure delivery and monitoring of the intended results**

It can also set a framework of factors which can be monitored in future, enabling strategies and tactics to be followed that make success more achievable.

### On what do you focus?

When undertaking due diligence, it is possible to look from a number of different angles. In its simplest form, we could look at both investor and investee (as entities) and also the project itself. Due diligence could then take the following basic forms:

- **For the investor on the investee**

  The investor will want to assess whether the investee can: service the investment; pay the yield and pay back the capital when applicable; and do so while delivering the intended social impact. It will also want to know about the investee's capacity and powers to accept and manage the investment, as well as the governance and management processes upon which the investor is going to rely.

- **For the investee on the investor**

  The investee will also want to assess the investor and whether they can deliver what the project needs. This will cover such aspects as the longevity of underlying funds' availability (for example, a ten-year investment requirement supported by funds with only five years' supply has an inherent problem at the outset); the management style of the funder, its reputation and profile; the real cost of capital it is offering; and the risks inherent in the pricing approach.

- **For the investee on the underlying project**

  The underlying project, its purpose, risks and funding needs, are an area where the investor's and investee's interest in due diligence most closely match. The project itself is subject to risks and assumptions and these need to be understood, worked around and managed. Above all, it is essential that the investment matches the project being funded: in funding requirement, in serviceability, in flexibility and agility for the future.

## What types of due diligence are there and who should do it?

### What types of due diligence are typically considered?

Whether it is focused on the project, or on the investment in the provider charity, there are typically six broad types of due diligence that are undertaken.

Each of the six areas and their corresponding focus is explained in Table 24.1, with a note as to the key skills needed to be able to address each.

In some lists you may find only the first three (legal, financial and commercial), with operational and regulatory combined with commercial and financial (or legal)

*Table 24.1* Six core areas of due diligence

| Legal | **Focus:** The constitutional ability of the charity to take on the social investment; and the terms of the investment itself. For example, can the charity enter into the funding arrangement? Do the governing documents allow this? Are the terms clear, certain and practical? Are the terms in the investment agreement carefully drafted? Does the charity have appropriate title to the assets it needs for the project? And are legal aspects of governance for the project and investment workable and clear? |
| --- | --- |
| | **Key Skills:** technical legal knowledge covering charities; the project or operational area where investment will be made (which may include real estate); and social investment knowledge. |
| **Focus:** The sustainability of financial and operating arrangements: income and expenditure; cashflow; and working capital requirements. Is the funding being raised sufficient and sustainable? Are management information systems up to the job and reliable? Can the charity sustain the reporting the investor requires? Will money be paid back; and is the interest affordable? | **Financial** |
| **Key skills:** technical financial knowledge of charity finance and accounting; social investment; management information systems and reporting. | |
| **Commercial** | **Focus:** Commercial due diligence considers the charity's project and the commercial arrangements that this entails with third parties. These may be customers, service-users, and key suppliers. Due diligence recognises a level of competition and the market as relevant. |
| | **Key skills:** understanding of necessary commercial relationships; and relevant competition. |

*continued*

*Table 24.1* Six core areas of due diligence (Continued)

| | |
|---|---|
| **Focus:** The external commercial arrangements are only part of the story. For example, a charity operating as a social enterprise has many operational practicalities to manage; it may be regulated, not just by the Charity Commission, but by the Care Quality Commission, Ofsted, or others. An example is an independent living service offered by a charity focused on older people, where such help may need to be regulated.<br><br>Key questions focus on how this service is regulated and operations run and managed. Are they compliant with regulatory standards and best practice? Can growth be sustained? How is marketing for this service taking place?<br><br>**Key skills:** understanding the operational side of the enterprise and how it works in practice; understanding regulatory position and requirements; staffing; management controls; and how growth can be achieved. | **Operational and regulatory** |
| **Impact** | **Focus:** This involves understanding the theory of change (how relevant outcomes will be delivered for beneficiaries); and how the impacts are measured. It needs to be based on understanding the beneficiaries and their lives, both with and without the intervention planned. To produce an overall, integrated picture, this should link back to the resources needed, how and when they are used, including the financial flows from them. The level of detail required depends on the interest and focus of the audience for the review and the purpose to which the information will be put.<br><br>**Key skills:** understanding the cohort of clients or beneficiaries; and the intervention; fluency with impact planning and measurement; understanding research evidence, as opposed to audit-type evidence. |
| **Focus:** The association between investor and investee will last for a period of time and be public. The cultural and relationship side will affect how well it works. The association between the organisations will have an effect on public perception, either positive or negative. Just as it is usual to do some research on the background and associations of a new executive or trustee, so similar checks should be done on the counterparty in a funding arrangement. Will that association enhance or harm other funding and partnering relationships? Or enable or impede access to future contracts or opportunities?<br><br>**Key skills:** market knowledge; fluency with social media and web-based searches; interview skills; understanding of reputational risk. | **Reputation and public profile** |

respectively. However, these two areas do bear separate scrutiny, requiring a distinct knowledge and skill base to address them.

The final two areas (impact and reputation) are key areas in the context of charity projects and social investments.

### The soft side of contracting: personalities, the team, agility and working together

While perhaps not a matter for formal due diligence – and one for internal assessment rather than external advice in most cases – the soft side of contracting also needs a similar level of test and critical challenge.

Sources of testing this information may be drawn from meetings, review of papers, web searches, references (especially speaking to others who have worked with the parties in similar circumstances before) and perhaps more formal assessments. Areas that can usefully be covered include:

#### On an investee

- Who leads the organisation, what is their operating style and how do they work with their team?
- How stable is the team? How long have key personnel been in office?
- How do they deal with disagreement and conflict both internally and externally?
- How well does the organisation work with partners and other investors?
- How does the dynamic between management and trustees work?
- Have there been any breakdowns of relationships and why did they happen?
- How does the organisation deal with change, either regular or major?
- What are the positives and concerns arising from the introduction and negotiation experience?

#### On an investor

- What is the investor's mission and how does that balance between supporting its investees and leading or controlling them?
- Who are the decision-makers and how do they sit with the relationship-holder? What is the investee's access to the decision-makers?
- What does the investor believe it brings to the relationship and how does that match to the investee's needs and expectations?
- How flexible and agile will the investor need to be? Or will they remain passive?
- What information does the contract require and how regularly? What will the investor do with it?
- How does the organisation deal with disagreement and conflict?
- What are the positives and concerns arising from the introduction and negotiation experience?

This area should not be treated as the poor relative of the formal financial, legal and other due diligence. It should be the subject of a report to the trustees (or investment committee of the investor), with executive input, referred to in their decision.

### Should due diligence be done by an internal team, or sourced externally?

There is no hard and fast rule to this. Rather, it should be done properly, which in practice means whoever is doing it must exhibit the relevant:

- Skills, knowledge and experience to do it
- Objectivity to provide test and challenge to those that developed the plans, together with the standing to be able to report independently and without conflicts of interest
- Capacity and focus to get the work done, within the timetables required
- Ability to communicate findings in writing and verbally to enable the decision-makers to understand them clearly
- Willingness to give an opinion and not "sit on the fence".

Any one or more of these points can tip the decision towards internal or external providers.

The final factor that can tip the balance is risk. The riskier the item being investigated, the more important it becomes to have a detailed appraisal and probably an independent view on it. This means that best practice for a due diligence review will involve an early risk assessment and then using that to highlight the key elements that may need further external review. The external reviewer should liaise with the internal reviewers, so that their findings can fit together to create a total picture, meaning any apparent differences of view can be explored and explained.

### Finding an external partner

With a bewildering array of potential providers, particularly in the financial and legal arenas, whittling these down to find those best suited to your needs is key. When doing that and selecting those with whom you want to work, take into account that you want someone who:

- You like enough to listen to, but who will tell you frankly if you are about to make a mistake
- Knows what you are trying to do and understands the context and risks
- Shares enough of your ethos and interest to be able to understand your needs and intentions
- Has real experience
- Can see and explain the whole process of the transaction and what needs to get done, but is happy to play their part and not second-guess others' input unnecessarily
- Will focus their work and deliver soundly and quickly what is needed
- Is cost-effective, taking into account what needs to be done (which doesn't mean taking the cheapest quote as the sole criterion for assessment)
- Has the professional approach, appropriate regulatory status and (if necessary) professional indemnity insurance to cover the work being done.

---

**In this chapter, we've taken a look at:**

The use of due diligence as part of your decision-making process
What due diligence is and when you might expect to use it
Types of due diligence and the balance between internal and external review

---

---

**In the next chapter, we'll explore accounting for social investment, including:**

Accounting for social investment, in both the investor's and the investee's accounts
Common UK accounting principles for inward investment
Reflecting social investment in the balance sheet and SoFA

---

## Reference

Cambridge English Dictionary (2019), dictionary definition of *due diligence*, accessed 22 April 2019, https://dictionary.cambridge.org/dictionary/english/due-diligence.

# 25 Accounting for social investment

*Jim Clifford*

How do we account for social investment? What does it look like on the balance sheet and in the statement of financial activities (SoFA) of your charity?

## UK accounting approaches for social investment

Considering how accounting for investment in charities and social enterprises is a standard reporting requirement, it's surprising how little the subject is discussed in the press or social investment commentaries. Here, however, we're going to explore how the common accounting approaches in the UK are applied to social investment – in charities, social enterprises or joint ventures and SPVs.

Accounting for UK charities and social enterprises is governed by three main sets of standards:

- **UK-GAAP** (Generally Accepted Accounting Principles): Financial Reporting Council (2015)
- **IFRS** (International Financial Reporting Standards): IFRS (2018)
- **Charities SORP (FRS102)** (Accounting and Reporting by Charities: Statement of recommended practice aplicable to charities): Charities SORP (FRS102) (2015).

By far the most applicable to social investment in charities is the Charities SORP s.21 (FRS102) (2015). This explains how social investment, programme-related investments (PRI) and mixed motive investments (MMI) should be treated in the trustees annual report, the statement of financial activities (SoFA), balance sheet and notes to the accounts.

Whilst quite technical, SORP (FRS102) (2015) explains simply how this should be done and the rest of this chapter summarises this discussion.

It is worth noting that, strictly, SORP also applies to organisations run as charities even if not registered as such. For small enterprises, the Financial Reporting Standard for Small Enterprises (FRSSE, pronounced "frizzy") applied for a short period between 2015 and 2016, limiting some of the more detailed disclosures in the accounts under UK-GAAP. For periods beginning on or after 1 January 2016, the relevant standard is FRS102. For small charities, a cash flow statement is not required. The third main approach is IFRS. This has been compulsory (under EU legislation) since 2005 for all companies issuing securities traded on an EU-recognised public exchange – including the Social Stock Exchange, which is linked for trading purposes to the NEX market – and optional for any other UK-registered company. The test of compulsory or optional adoption applies separately to the consolidated accounts and the individual company accounts.

## How the SORP defines social investment

The following text is taken directly from s.21 SORP (FRS102) (2015) with section numbers included:

> 21.6.   The SORP uses the term "social investment" to describe programme related investments and mixed motive investments.

### Programme related investments
> 21.9.   A programme-related investment is an asset held by a charity that provides investment funding to individuals or organisations in order to directly further the charitable purposes of the investing charity; any financial return obtained is not a primary reason for making the investment.
> 21.10. A programme-related investment is made exclusively to further the charitable aims of the investing charity by funding specific activities or related tangible fixed assets of a third party which, in turn, contribute to the investor's own charitable purposes.

### Mixed motive (mixed purpose) investments
> 21.11. A mixed motive (or mixed purpose) investment is an asset held by a charity that provides funding to individuals or organisations in order to generate a financial return for the investing charity and it also contributes to the investing charity's purposes through the activities or related tangible fixed assets funded by the investment.
> 21.12. A mixed motive investment can be distinguished from a programme related investment in that the investment is not made wholly to further the investing charity's charitable purposes. The investment is deemed to be "mixed motive" as neither the investment return nor the contribution to the investing charity's purposes is sufficient on its own to justify the investment decision. The investment is not justified wholly by either the financial return or by the contribution it makes to the investing charity's aims but by the combination of the two.

Social investment has two sides to the investment – the investor and recipient organisation. As such, we need to consider both in our accounting.

We deal first with the investor's accounting.

## The investing organisation

The accounting for the investment by the investor will depend on the accounting principles and processes applying to it – because of its constitution and country of jurisdiction. In this section, we focus on charity investors.

If you are a charity making a social investment, you need to show the social investment you have made in your charity's accounts. Turning to SORP s.21 (FRS102) (2015), we see the following:

21.21. Programme related investments must be disclosed either as a separate line on the face of the balance sheet or identified as a separate class of investment in the notes to the accounts, depending on the materiality of the holding.

21.22. Mixed motive investments must be disclosed either as a separate line on the face of the balance sheet or identified as a separate class of investment in the notes to the accounts, depending on the materiality of the holding.

Along with these disclosures will come the notes to the accounts, where any social investment must be explained. If it's sizeable, the trustees should also make reference to the nature of the social investment in their TAR (trustees annual report).

Programme-related investments (PRIs) are shown at fair value on a separate line in the balance sheet. Mixed motive investments (MMIs) are similarly valued and disclosed on a separate line. This is substantially based on the economic value and returns, with the social aspects defining whether the investment continues to be categorised as PRI or MMI.

If unlisted investments cannot be reliably valued, they are retained at cost less impairments (a writing down of cost to reflect a loss of value through the using up of the asset, the effects of time on it, or of market forces).

For details of further accounting, please refer to SORP s.21 (FRS102) (2015) for a charity or Financial Reporting Council (2015), and IFRS (2018) for commercial organisations, and PLCs.

### Income and gains

These are recognised in the SoFA when the charity becomes entitled to them, it is probable they will arise and they are able to be measured (s.5, SORP – FRS102, 2015).

So, this deals with the investing organisation. What about the recipient organisation?

## The recipient organisation

Social investment must be recognised in the recipient organisation in several places: the balance sheet, the income and expenditure statement, the trustees annual report (TAR) and the notes to the accounts.

We assume in this section that the charity or social purpose organisation is taking on social investment, as inward investment. It will therefore have to account for the following:

- the way it financed the investment, either as debt or as equity (in the latter case as "shares")
- the associated asset (typically cash) and liabilities (loan or debt)
- the onward application for the project purpose it was raised to meet and the social impact it creates.

### How the investment is financed

**Debt or loan:** This is treated as a liability and shown as a long- or short-term liability on the balance sheet, based on the extent to which it is repayable within one year of the balance sheet date, or longer.

**Equity and quasi-equity:** Generally speaking, shares, together with any premium payable on issue, are shown as equity and loans as debt. However, take care around lower-risk shares (such as preference shares). These may pass the tests for being treated as debt – especially under IFRS (2018). Also bear in mind that loans carrying quasi-equity rights and obligations could, in theory, be treated as "equity interests" – even in a CLG which doesn't issue shares.

In both cases, we must show the picture on the balance sheet and also in the reserves of the charity – restricted or unrestricted.

### *How are the associated assets and liabilities disclosed?*

**How do we treat assets**? Where social investment helps the purchase of an asset, these are usually operating assets (e.g. premises, plant and equipment or working capital), so they appear in the balance sheet in line with normal accounting principles. Fixed asset investments are recognised at cost or fair market value. Investment properties are similarly treated. General working capital would be reflected in cash and debtors net of creditors, if held for short-term operational purposes.

**What do we do with liabilities**? These will include liabilities associated with the investment, such as capital repayable once debt or equity becomes due to be repaid to investors. Also, they include any yield on that investment due but not yet paid. The invested-in assets may also have liabilities (e.g. leases) associated with them.

Such liabilities are treated as long- or short-term in line with normal accounting principles. Where a liability will be settled in future periods, the future sums should be discounted to present value and the discount unwound over the period to which they apply, as a financing cost under the appropriate expenditure heading.

## Reflecting social investment in the statement of financial activities

Formerly the income and expenditure account, the charity statement of financial activities (SoFA) aligns with normal accounting approaches, except in a few key respects:

### *Income recognition*

For charitable entities, we look towards sections 5.1 to 5.59 of the Charity SORP (2015). The main paragraph is s.5.8, which states income can only be recognised in the SoFA if:

- **Entitlement** – control over the rights or other access to the economic benefit has passed to the charity.
- **Probable** – it is more likely than not that the economic benefits associated with the transaction or gift will flow to the charity.
- **Measurement** – the monetary value or amount of the income can be measured reliably and the costs incurred for the transaction and the costs to complete the transaction can be measured reliably.

If entitlement to income is subject to fulfilling performance-related conditions, the income is recognised as and when those conditions are achieved (when, and to the extent, entitlement arises).

In the case of social investment, this means we have to consider when the charity is entitled to funds, when performance has been completed to draw down tranches of funds and when we can measure this with certainty.

## Cost recognition

As indicated under the above section on liabilities, costs are recognised when all of the following criteria are met (per Charity SORP (2015) s.7.5):

- **Obligation** – a present legal or constructive obligation exists at the reporting date as a result of a past event.
- **Probable** – it is more likely than not that a transfer of economic benefits, often cash, will be required in settlement.
- **Measurement** – the amount of the obligation can be measured or estimated reliably.

Effectively, expenditure is recognised when incurred – when the obligation arises. Separately, we do not match expenditure and income, rather income is recognised when entitlement is achieved. Many organisations try to match income and expenditure – this is not correct and is different from commercial accounting rules under FRS (2018).

Where this results in income being recognised ahead of associated costs – with the result that net surpluses or deficits appear better than if they were matched – some charities, in the interests of transparency, are seeking to explain the mismatch in the TAR.

## Fund accounting

We must also consider whether the social investment should be treated as restricted or unrestricted funds – see Charity SORP (2015) section 2.

Where interest or other costs relate to income earned within a restricted fund, the finance costs would also be attributable to that restricted fund.

## Netting off: when is it appropriate?

Netting off occurs when income is offset against expenditure and the 'net' position recorded in accounting records, rather than the income and expenditure being separately and distinctly recorded. This can sometimes distort the underlying financial picture.

Income and costs should not be netted off. There are similar prohibitions on netting off deferred costs of fundraising against the related liability, even where they are to be set off in the course of settlement. If these arise, advice should be taken on the treatment, which may vary depending on the specific circumstances.

## Consolidation: the control puzzle

When to consolidate? That is, to produce group accounts for a group of companies? The principles are the same as for non-charities. In essence, the parent charity:

- exercises control – the power to govern financial and operating policies of the subsidiary
- obtains benefits (economic, social or environmental) from its activities.

If an investing entity passes this control test regarding a charity or other investee enterprise, it may need to prepare consolidated accounts. It is beyond the scope of this section to describe the full detail of accounting for consolidated entities – we leave the interested reader to pursue this through the references to SORP (2015), Financial Reporting Council (2015) and IFRS (2018).

## Reporting on the social impact created

Finally, we must explain the social impact created by the social investment. SORP (2015) s.21 says:

> 21.39. This SORP requires that larger charities that are subject to statutory audit must include an explanation of the charity's policy for the use of programme related investments and mixed motive investments in the trustees' annual report when such holdings are material. The report must also explain the investment's performance in relation to the objectives set by the trustees.

Charities using social investment should also explain the nature of the social investment and the social returns it creates: specifically, they should

> include an explanation of the use the charity makes of the following:

> Social investment, when this forms a material part of its charitable and investment activities. In particular, the report must provide an explanation of its social investment policies and explain how any programme related investments contributed to the achievement of its aims and objectives.

This does not specifically extend to explaining strategy and the outputs, outcomes and impact that arise or are intended to arise from the use of the investment. However, while accepting that an explanation can be descriptive and not necessarily include quantification of impacts, it is probably helpful to explain "the achievement of its aims and objectives" in those terms. The trustees should explain this in the TAR.

We consider the measurement and reporting of social impact further in the next chapter, Chapter 26.

---

**In this chapter, we've taken a look at:**

> Accounting for social investment, in both the investor's and the investee's accounts
> Common UK accounting principles for inward investment
> Reflecting social investment in the balance sheet and SoFA

---

**In the next chapter, we'll explore some further aspects, including:**

> Impact measurement, and why it's needed in social investment
> The different perspectives of investor and investee
> A brief walk through how to measure impact
> Aspects of data management and confidentiality

## References

Charities SORP (2015), *Charities SORP FRSSE*, accessed 23 January 2019, www.charitysorp. org/choose-sorp-modules/charities-sorp-frsse/.

Charities SORP s.21 (FRS102) (2015), *Charities SORP FRS102*, accessed 14 October 2018, www.charitysorp.org/media/619101/frs102_complete.pdf.

Financial Reporting Council (2015), *Latest Editions: FRS 100, FRS 101, FRS 102, FRS 103, FRS 104, FRS 105*, accessed 14 October 2018, www.frc.org.uk/Our-Work/Codes-Standards/Accounting-and-Reporting-Policy/Standards-in-Issue/FRS-102-The-Financial-Reporting-Standard-applicabl.aspx.

IFRS (2018), *List of IFRS Standards*, accessed 14 October 2018, www.ifrs.org/issued-standards/list-of-standards.

# 26 Reporting on impact, and the importance of good data management

*Jim Clifford*

How should you report impact in a social investment agreement and to whom? What data do you need to retain and why? How do you manage it?

In the last chapter, we looked at accounting for the social investment in both the investor's and the investee's accounting records, picking up on social impact reporting for charities in the trustees' annual report. This chapter builds on that theme, looking at the measurement of social impact and the gathering and management of data to accompany this.

## Introduction

Part of "doing" social investment is to ensure we deliver the outcomes we set out to achieve. We must be able to measure these and be held accountable. In some cases, such as outcome-based funding, our funding terms will also be linked to what we deliver and how well we do this.

This section looks at three aspects: (i) impact measurement and how it links into and supports social investment; (ii) data gathering, and validation, and its use in contract measures; and finally (iii) some thoughts about data maintenance, management and confidentiality, largely within the investee, but reflecting on the investor too. Through these three key aspects, we'll look at how we:

- assess what data we need
- gather it
- store it
- report it
- audit or validate it.

## Impact measurement for social investment

### Why measure social impact?

The purpose of social investment is to deliver a financial return *and* social impact. There are two actions implied here, to which impact measurement can contribute:

- **Transactional** – To make decisions to invest in delivering that impact; to choose the impact to deliver; to get third parties to pay for the impacts; and to plan which resources to use – **essentially a transactional set of decisions**; and

- **Performance management** – To manage performance to ensure that it achieves impact; and to build in continuous improvement to that process.

There are then two further reasons for measuring impact, both relating to relationships with third parties and the opportunity to influence others:

- To **engage meaningfully** with beneficiaries, delivery partners and others involved in the intervention that is intended to deliver the impact
- To **report more widely**, to influence others and to engage with a wider public.

These are shown in Figure 26.1.

Impact measurement should focus on what is relevant, simple and needs to be known – valuing the things that matter (Clifford *et al.*, 2014; Social Impact Investment Taskforce, 2014; Social Value International, 2019). The eight characteristics of good measurement, including "relevance" and "simplicity" from the work of the GECES are shown in Table 26.1.

With impact measurement, the purpose to which the measurement is to be put by the relevant stakeholder needs to be understood before the measurement is designed and made. In practice, that may mean that measurement in relation to a particular project or intervention takes on different forms for different purposes.

In the case of It's All About Me (an adoption bond), for example, the measurements for *the commissioners* in paying for the service were based on: adoption being successful; whether the parents had been trained to parent therapeutically; and whether the child

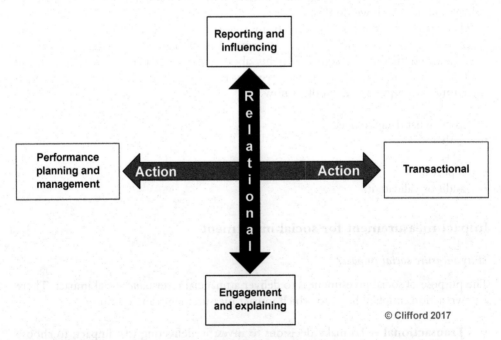

*Figure 26.1* Why measure: an action–relational perspective.

Source: reproduced by permission of Jim Clifford OBE.

*Table 26.1* The eight characteristics of good measurement

| For measurement to be effective, it must be: | |
| --- | --- |
| **Relevant** | related to and arising from the outcomes it is measuring |
| **Helpful** | in meeting the needs of stakeholders, both internal and external |
| **Simple** | both in how the measurement is made and in how it is presented |
| **Natural** | arising from the normal flow of activity to outcome |
| **Certain** | both in how it is derived and in how it is presented |
| **Understood and accepted** | by all relevant stakeholders |
| **Transparent and well-explained** | so that the method by which the measurement is made – and how that relates to the services and outcomes concerned – is clear |
| **Founded on evidence** | so that it can be tested, validated and form the grounds for continuous improvement |

Source: GECES, in Clifford *et al.* (2014).

had moved in and stayed there. That was a good indicator of savings to the commissioning local authority (Government Outcomes Lab, 2019).

The project was also used for research by South London and Maudesley NHS doctors and staff. As a different stakeholder to the project, they considered broader measurement for *the service delivery organisation*. They used these for performance management; and for a broad range of psychological, developmental and social work measures.

### What to measure, and how we report it

Arguably, social investors, recipient charities and social purpose organisations using social investment are united over two things: the desire to deliver impact and the keenness to make the investment relationship work.

As investors need to understand impact and outcomes effectively to fulfil promises to their board and investors, so charities and social enterprises need to pay attention to what they achieve through delivery. Creating social value and creating social change sits at the heart of their legitimacy to exist.

### What do we mean by outputs, outcomes and impact?

The terms outputs, outcomes and impact were defined by the GECES subgroup, for the European Union. This was endorsed in the subsequent work of the Social Impact Taskforce, formed under the UK's period of leadership of the G8 (Clifford *et al.*, 2014; Social Impact Investment Taskforce, 2014).

An **output** is "how that activity touches the intended beneficiaries ... effectively the points at which the services delivered enter the lives of those affected by them" (Clifford *et al.*, 2014, p6 and p12).

An **outcome** is a "change in the lives of those affected" (Clifford *et al.*, 2014, p6).

An **impact** is "the extent to which that change is caused by the intervention" (Clifford *et al.*, 2014, p6).

We take an illustration of this from HCT's travel training social impact bond (HCT, 2019), which seeks to help young people with learning difficulties become more able to travel on public transport independently:

- The **outputs** are the young people's attendance (successfully) on the training programmes
- The **outcomes** are that these young people can travel independently; that they grow in confidence; that the local authority support for travel to and from schools and education can be reduced; and that their dependency on their family's support can change and develop
- The **impact** is that the training programme and the support given to parents and wider family acts as a catalyst for change, with the family, school and others (including the young people themselves) helping to achieve the change.

The GECES standards include further worked examples (Clifford *et al.*, 2014).

### Why investors need impact measurement

Investors need impact measurement for their own purposes, as well as to encourage more investment to their funds.

Their interest falls into four main headings:

- **Boundary criteria for their fund.** Whether formally set when raising investments, or simply a matter of personal investor preference, social investors typically have preferred areas of focus in which to invest. They will look to measurement to help "prove" they are adhering to these and what they are achieving in these areas.
- **Investment decisions.** The point of social investment is to secure a return, part of which is determined in terms of social (or environmental) impact. This will need to be demonstrated as a deliverable for the investor to approve the investment. It does not necessarily mean it should have been delivered and measured in the past, but that it is likely to result from the project in future. Measuring social impact is key to that.
- **For control and delivery.** Investors are keen to see that the targeted impact they expected is actually achieved.
- **For fund reporting.** In funds which are set up with a social impact purpose, investors will want to deliver that to their investors. It will also be useful for their profile and development. As they will usually be expected to report regularly on social impact, they will have to gather impact data from their onward investments to fulfil that need.

Investors will naturally be monitoring financial returns and will seek to relate them to the details of social return created.

## A brief summary of how to measure impact

A wide variety of published materials gives guidance on how to measure impact, not least the GECES standards (Clifford *et al.*, 2014) and the EVPA Impact Management Project (EVPA, 2019), referenced by the GECES publication, now in updated form

The Impact Management Project (2018) has worked to bring consensus among investors, practitioners and others at a higher and global level, building on the work of the GECES, the Social Impact Investment Taskforce (2014) and others. It has published this in the form of its five dimensions of impact, shown in Figure 26.2.

At the core of measuring impact, we are trying to get an account of a story of changed lives, environments or circumstances. The word "story" is key here. A story can be evidenced, challenged and underpinned. But, to give a good account of an impact, the story must shine through. Measurement must be of the relevant aspects of that story and the story should always come first; before the measurement.

From the GECES, EVPA, and the Impact Management Project (2018), and from various other practical sources, a simple six-stage framework for developing a theory of change and delivering impact measurement emerges. This is shown in Figure 26.3.

The framework breaks down into the following six steps:

- **Step 1: define your cohort** – on whom or on what (in the case of an environmental impact) are you focusing? You should develop an understanding of the situation and social, economic and environmental setting.
- **Step 2: understand their needs** – both from the outsider's perspective and, most particularly, from their own. This may require you to look at their ideal state and to assess their current situation against that, or it may be possible to look directly at a group of identifiable needs.
- **Step 3: identify the outcomes needed** – if their needs were met, what change would you and they see?

What tells us what outcomes the enterprise is contributing to and how important the outcomes are to stakeholders.

Who tells us which stakeholders are experiencing the outcome and how underserved they were prior to the enterprise's effect.

How Much tells us how many stakeholders experienced the outcome, what degree of change they experienced, and how long they experienced the outcome for.

Contribution tells us whether an enterprise's and/or investor's efforts resulted in outcomes that were likely better than what would have occurred otherwise.

Risk tells us the likelihood that impact will be different than expected.

The IMP reached global consensus that impact can be measured across five dimensions: What, Who, How Much, Contribution and Risk

| Impact dimension | Impact questions each dimension seeks to answer |
|---|---|
| ☐ **What** | •What outcome is occurring in the period?<br>•Is the outcome positive or negative?<br>•How important is the outcome to the people (or planet) experiencing them? |
| ○ **Who** | •Who experiences the outcome?<br>•How underserved are the affected stakeholders in relation to the outcome? |
| ☰ **How Much** | •How much of the outcome is occurring - across scale, depth and duration? |
| + **Contribution** | •Would this change likely have happened anyway? |
| △ **Risk** | •What is the risk to people and planet that impact does not occur as expected? |

Source: Impact Management Project

*Figure 26.2* The Impact Management Project's five dimensions of impact and its key questions.
Source: Impact Management Project (2018).

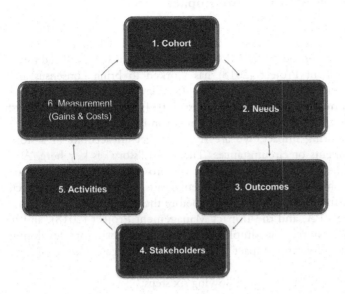

*Figure 26.3* A simple six stage framework for developing a theory of change and impact measurement.

- **Step 4: focus on stakeholder's interests** – Who are the stakeholders in the outcomes to be delivered and what is the nature of their interest? What aspects of outcomes are they interested in?
- **Step 5: what activities can deliver those outcomes and using what resources?** – Some of those you will deliver and for some you will secure other organisations to help you deliver. You will need to focus on how you get them to do so and coordinate their effort with yours.
- **Step 6: measuring outcomes** – How will we measure the outcomes, in order to engage appropriately with the relevant audience of stakeholders? Think about how easily and reliably that can be done (taking into account the eight aspects of good measurement from GECES in Table 26.1 earlier in this chapter).

When looking at this framework, it will help to recognise that there are two ecosystems (or "worlds") at play here. To ignore either could lead to a poorly defined measurement framework.

The first is the world in which the beneficiaries live; some of this you can change and some you cannot. Equally, some of the dynamics will prove helpful and some will not. This will change and develop over time, so your solution and your measurement needs to respond to that.

The second world or ecosystem in which you are delivering and measuring the effect of that delivery is a complex one. We should recognise this. This world will offer a wide range of influences on and partners in your delivery and its impact.

Ideally, we can focus on measuring the actual outcomes and those directly related to the project or social investment's work. However, some outcomes may be so far in the future that the measurement for purposes, such as payment for outcomes, cannot wait that long. When we don't achieve the actual outcome in the short term, we can use a measurable milestone on the route to that outcome (Clifford and Jung, 2017). Alternatively, we may pick a parallel event arising at the same time as a proxy.

Having briefly looked at impact measurement, we now move on to look at data gathering and data management.

## Data gathering for impact measurement

The principles for data gathering, interpretation and validation come from social research. Care must be taken that: the data is gathered with appropriate objectivity; it is not compromised as to its validity; and it does fairly relate to the relevant subject being measured, both cohort and the intervention or project. Methods that are used include:

* questionnaires
* interviews
* methods of self-assessment
* workshops and groups
* storytelling and dialogue
* action research and continual enquiry methods, often from professional researchers as observers.

### Validation and assurance

The GECES standards (Clifford *et al.*, 2014) have a specific comment on this subject. This is shown verbatim in Table 26.2. It explains that the underlying processes of data gathering and its use should build in appropriate tests of validity, albeit managed internally by the organisation. There is a place for external independent review and, indeed, assurance – in practice under International Standards on Assurance Engagements (ISAE) 3000 (IFAC, 2019) around systems and data testing, and allied to internal audit processes. However, both should be focused and used only where necessary.

Reference should also be made to the sections of the GECES on proportionality, which emphasise that the amount of effort and cost put into measurement should match the reliance to be placed on the figures and data and the actions that may come from them. An enthusiasm to measure what doesn't really matter should be avoided.

### Payment measures for contracts

Just as a business selling goods should retain proof of delivery and evidence of the quality of product, so an organisation delivering services of a social nature should maintain evidence that the provider has delivered the contracted services or outcomes.

There are broadly four types of payment measures for contracts, each of which requires evidence to be recorded and retained to support invoicing:

1  **Service-defined contracts.** Where the contract is for defined delivery of a service against quality, style, reach and other standards:
    * a very traditional style of publicly funded contract
    * payments may be under block or cohort arrangements for defined groups of beneficiaries
    * there may be reductions for short or sub-standard delivery.

*Table 26.2* Extract from Chapter 4 of the GECES standards, on validation, independent review or audit assurance

---

**Validation, independent review or audit assurance**

4.20.  Evidential underpinning is important. With a form of measurement that is based upon social and management research principles, this is implicit. How this is done is a matter of balancing the needs of stakeholders, the use to which the measurement is to be put, and the costs.

4.21.  The SE and its stakeholders will choose between three options:

  4.21.1.  **Validation:** This is part of the normal research process. Either completed internally within the SE or Fund, or as part of an externally-sourced piece of research, it demands that appropriate supporting evidence is sought and disclosed for all materials matters.

  4.21.2.  **Independent review:** This requires an independent party reviewing the measurement process and findings and commenting upon their completeness and the underlying logic for the conclusions. It is essentially a report on method and evidence: on process and documentation of findings.

  4.21.3.  **Audit assurance:** This is a more formalised approach requiring the issuing of a pre-worded opinion similar to a "true and fair" opinion on financial accounts. It requires the reviewer to consider not just whether the researched findings are sound in themselves, but also whether they give a complete and accurate view, appropriate to their purpose. It generally requires the reviewer to consider the purpose to which the reported information will be put by relevant stakeholders.

4.22.  The first is most widely used, since it is implicit in all social impact measurement. Coupled with proper disclosure of the evidential underpinning for the measurement, it may be both necessary in all, and sufficient in many, situations, as is the case in much good quality research. The second and third are in use to varying degrees, and in each case will be sought by one or more stakeholders, possibly when the researchers are less experienced, or when the measurement may have less credibility because they are insiders. Where the second and third are done, it is essential that those people doing the review or audit understand the intervention and its impacts.

---

Source: Clifford *et al.* (2014, p37).

2  **Output-defined.** In this case, the contract payments are made based on the engagement points between intervention and beneficiary:

- an example would be a health trust remunerated on surgical procedures completed
- education achievements measured by attendance on courses is perhaps another example.

3  **Outcome-defined.** The payment is made based on measured outcomes:

- usually attached to those relevant to the payor, which are easily measured with a good degree of certainty, without too much additional effort
- good proxies are simple events or documents produced in parallel with, or as a by-product of, the achievement of the outcome
- these may not concern all outcomes
- examples would be reducing the percentage of a whole cohort of former offenders from reoffending; or reducing the chaos in the lives of women working with community projects, so that they can engage with health services and get into sustainable regular employment.

4  **Use of outcomes milestones, or "informed outputs", as proxies.** Where the true outcome is not achieved for many years, but where a clear pathway to these exists, we can use proxies instead. These are measures which stakeholders can all recognise, along with milestones to be achieved:

- an example would be finding satisfactory therapeutic adoptive families for harder-to-place children in an adoption bond; with survival in placement for at least two years being the accepted milestone, en route to achieving an effective and engaged adulthood for those children.

---

**Measuring impact: a summary**

In summary, some golden rules and final thoughts stand out:

- Tell the story and then measure it
- Agree up front what will be reported, when and how, together with rights to test and challenge information and validation or assurance processes
- Think about proportionality and what is "relevant and helpful"
- Allow for the resources and costs needed to measure
- Think about what follows if expectations are not met, just as for other covenants
- Build in flexibility and agility
- Develop attribution: an understanding of who and what is actually causing the outcome
- Understand that there is no such thing as "do no harm" – outcomes can be negative as well as positive, so think about them in your planning and your measurement.

---

## Good data management

### Data systems and storage

In addition to the points around gathering data with integrity discussed earlier in this chapter, the organisation (indeed both investee and investor) will need to consider:

- **Safe storage for data** – ensuring that the data is appropriately encrypted, can't be corrupted, but also that old data will not be lost or become inaccessible through technological updates and obsolescence.
- **Data security processes** – how is data maintained and validated from an electronic perspective?
- **Is data storage resilient** – how are back-ups managed and what happens in the event of systems failure?
- **Integrated collection mechanics** – can data collection be appropriately automated, thinking about web-enabled or app-enabled collection and similar?

### Confidentiality issues

The final area to consider on data management is that of confidentiality. The sort of data covered may be personal, commercial, or in relation to know-how and intellectual property. The interest being protected may be that of the charity, a contractual counterparty, an investor, a beneficiary or another party.

- **Protection of the organisation's data**: Data must be stored securely. If sensitive, it must be encrypted or locked away. Follow appropriate procedures (and GDPR) to protect against loss of data.

- **Contractual confidentiality**. There may be obligations of confidentiality under funding, service or other agreements that must be met. Be sure to manage the underlying data to ensure that the organisation can prove they have been met.
- **Title to data**. Data should only be stored if owned by the organisation, or if it has the permission of the owner to store it. If you do this, hold proof of it.
- **Regulated data**. Personal data and much information about children and vulnerable adults bring specific confidentiality requirements under statute. This covers how the data is gathered and stored, who has access to it and how it is used.
- **Consent and use**. With the exception of statutory protection – where often the individual cannot contract out of their protection – a consent to use of data may permit its use. Consents should be gained in writing. It's generally appropriate to take legal advice before doing so. The consents should be for a long enough period and be wide enough to cover the particular use of the data. Keep the consents for at least six years beyond the expiration of the obligation.
- **Protection of personal confidentiality.** Over and above the statutory obligations to keep personal data confidential, it should be recognised that funders will not necessarily be entitled to access to all the data the organisation has even if they are taking some of the risk of non-delivery of outcomes. A variety of other factors – including the protection of children and vulnerable adults – comes into play and open access should be resisted.
- **Data sharing boundaries**. Be careful what you share with the investors. The consents and, indeed, the need are unlikely to justify access to care files and individuals' data.

---

**In this section, we've taken a look at:**

Impact measurement, and why it's needed in social investment situations
The different perspectives of investor and investee
A brief walk through how to measure impact
Measurement in delivery contracts
Aspects of data management and confidentiality

**In the final section we will look at good governance around managing social investments, from the perspectives of both investee and investor.**

---

# References

Clifford, J., Hehenberger, L. and Fantini, M. (2014), *Proposed approaches to social impact measurement in European Commission legislation and in practice relating to EuSEFs and the EaSI*, report by GECES (Groupe d'experts de la Commission sur l'entrepreneuriat social) subgroup on impact measurement, accessed 15 October 2018, www.ec.europa.eu/social/main.jsp?catId=738&langId=en&pubId=7735&type=2&furtherPubs=yes.

Clifford, J. and Jung, T. (2017), *Social impact bonds: exploring and understanding an emerging funding approach*, Ch.10 in Lehner, O. (Ed.), *Routledge Handbook of Social and Sustainable Finance*, Abingdon, Routledge.

EVPA. (2019), *Measuring and managing impact: a practical guide*, Brussels, European Venture Philanthropy Association, accessed 16 May 2019, https://evpa.eu.com/knowledge-centre/publications/measuring-and-managing-impact-a-practical-guide.

Government Outcomes Lab (2019), *Case studies: It's All About Me*, accessed 16 May 2019, https://golab.bsg.ox.ac.uk/knowledge/case-studies/its-all-about-me/.

HCT (2019), *Independent travel training: the programme*, London, HCT, accessed 18 May 2019, www.travel-training.org/independent_travel_training/the_programme__4.

IFAC International Federation of Accountants (2019), *International Standard on Assurance Engagements (ISAE) 3000 revised, assurance engagements other than audits or reviews of historical financial information*, accessed 8 June 2019, www.ifac.org/publications-resources/international-standard-assurance-engagements-isae-3000-revised-assurance-enga.

Impact Management Project. (2018), *What is Impact?*, London, IMP, accessed 16 May 2019, https://impactmanagementproject.com/impact-management/what-is-impact/.

Social Impact Investment Taskforce (2014), *Measuring impact: subject paper of the Impact Measurement Working Group*, accessed 2 October 2018, https://iris.thegiin.org/research/measuring-impact-subject-paper-of-the-impact-measurement-working-group/summary

Social Value International (2019), *The seven principles of social value*, accessed 16 May 2019. https://socialvalueint.org/social-value/principles-of-social-value/

# 27 Governance aspects of social investment

*Jim Clifford*

What is good governance in the context of social investment decisions and management?

In the last chapter, we looked at impact measurement, then at the maintenance and management of non-financial data. This chapter looks at the whole social investment transaction and relationships from a good governance perspective. It picks up both the investor's and the investee's governance.

## What do we mean by "governance"?

Acknowledging that there are academic and political debates and varied viewpoints on it, The Canadian Institute of Governance defines governance as "how society or groups within it organize to make decisions" (Institute of Governance, 2019). It incorporates three key elements: **authority, decision-making and accountability.**

Governance's importance is reflected on an international scale too. For the World Economic Forum, "the word governance is usually applied to laws and standards that pertain to the global community, and the ways in which transnational bodies, governments and corporations implement them" (World Economic Forum, 2016).

The Australian Governance Institute observes that "Governance encompasses the system by which an organisation is controlled and operates, and the mechanisms by which it, and its people, are held to account. Ethics, risk management, compliance and administration are all elements of governance" (Governance Institute of Australia, 2019).

In the context of corporate governance, which underpins the governance of many charities and social investment funds, the Cadbury Report's explanation of governance still stands sound, nearly 30 years on:

> Corporate governance is the system by which companies are directed and controlled. Boards of directors are responsible for the governance of their companies. The shareholders' role in governance is to appoint the directors and the auditors and to satisfy themselves that an appropriate governance structure is in place. The responsibilities of the board include setting the company's strategic aims, providing the leadership to put them into effect, supervising the management of the business and reporting to shareholders on their stewardship. The board's actions are subject to laws, regulations, and the shareholders in general meeting.
>
> (Cadbury, 1992)

Those principles are most recently stated in the FRC's updated UK Corporate Governance Code, but the themes remain substantially unchanged from the 1992 version (Financial Reporting Council, 2018).

In social investment, then, "governance" is approached from two perspectives:

- **That of the investee,** acting through its board of directors or trustees; accountable to its members, beneficiaries and other stakeholders for its decision-making to seek and take on the inward investment; and applying it in line with its constitution and wider accountabilities; and
- **That of the investor,** again acting through its board; accountable to *its* investors and wider stakeholders for its decision-making in deciding on whether to invest, and the terms to apply in doing so. It brings in aspects such as risk, financial and social impact evaluation.

The investor, of course, may be a charity in its own right, so may have that additional set of constraints around what it can and cannot do. In which case, these require good governance processes to recognise and address them.

Rabindrakumar (2016), writing on behalf of Big Society Capital, identifies four common themes of governance in social investment which need to be addressed across big as well as small organisations:

- The shared ambition between the board and management team to grow their impact
- Getting the right mix of skills and experience on the board in the first place
- The board's role in embracing risk and opportunity to deliver mission in additional ways and being able to ask the right questions to protect the organisation's assets
- The underlying trust between executive and board.

We pick up on each of these points at various stages through the detailed text below.

## What are the key reference documents to consider in an organisation's governance structure?

Whether for the investee or the investor, there are three main source documents to consider when looking at governance:

- **General governing law** – around the company, unincorporated fund or charity.
- **Governing documents and constitution** – the articles of association and memorandum of incorporation for the company, agreements for the unincorporated fund, and the charitable objects for the charity.
- **Best practice standards** – from a variety of sources, driven in part by regulators, and in part by the developing needs of stakeholders and their relationships with the organisation. These are brought together at various intervals in such reports as Cadbury (Cadbury, 1992) and codes such as the Charity Governance Code (Good Governance Steering Group, 2017).

The Charity Governance Code is the third generation of the work originally started by NCVO (the National Council of Voluntary Organisations), ACEVO (the

Association of Chief Executives in Voluntary Organisations) and the Cass Business School's project "Know-how-non-profit". Developing from various sources – including Cadbury and the Charity Commission publication *The Essential Trustee* (Charity Commission, 2018) – it outlines seven principles of good governance applying to charities.

They are worth repeating here verbatim (Good Governance Steering Group, 2017, p4):

1 **Organisational purpose** – The board is clear about the charity's aims and ensures that these are being delivered effectively and sustainably.
2 **Leadership** – Every charity is led by an effective board that provides strategic leadership in line with the charity's aims and values.
3 **Integrity** – The board acts with integrity, adopting values and creating a culture which help achieve the organisation's charitable purposes. The board is aware of the importance of the public's confidence and trust in charities, and trustees undertake their duties accordingly.
4 **Decision-making, risk and control** – The board makes sure that its decision-making processes are informed, rigorous and timely and that effective delegation, control and risk assessment and management systems are set up and monitored.
5 **Board effectiveness** – The board works as an effective team, using the appropriate balance of skills, experience, backgrounds and knowledge to make informed decisions.
6 **Diversity** – The board's approach to diversity supports its effectiveness, leadership and decision-making.
7 **Openness and accountability** – The board leads the organisation in being transparent and accountable. The charity is open in its work, unless there is good reason for it not to be.

## What does a well governed charity look like?

Drawing from these sources, we can see a clear framework for an effectively governed charity. We can express this in a 3x3 matrix, taking the three elements of the operations (board; organisation; resources and activities) and recognising that, in each, there are characteristics which identify each, how it behaves and what it achieves. This is shown in Table 27.1.

This is the framework into which we place decisions about social investment, its effective application and how it should be monitored once taken on. There are many aspects of this table that also apply to the social investor, albeit they are delivering and managing investments rather than services and the "beneficiary" for the most part is the investee charity.

The organisation will set up a governance structure for decision-making and monitoring and for accountability. The main decisions will be made by the trustees or directors, who will receive the information from the executive and management to enable them to do that effectively.

*Table 27.1* The characteristics of a well governed charity

|  | Board | Organisation and resources | Activities |
|---|---|---|---|
| **Who we are and how we relate** | • Right skills and experience<br>• Making time available | • Well-resourced<br>• Right people<br>• Right support structures | • Delivering sound and effective services<br>• Delivered to beneficiary need |
| **How we behave** | • Bring all skills and experience to the table<br>• Work efficiently<br>• Work as a team | • With integrity, focus and cohesion<br>• Risk-focused<br>• Efficient | • Engaged, open<br>• Accountable, responsive<br>• Efficient |
| **What we do and how we deliver** | • Focus on objects<br>• Focus on public benefit<br>• Focus strategically and with view to future needs<br>• Focus generatively, with future innovation and new ideas to help beneficiaries | • Run effectively and efficiently<br>• Led well<br>• Cohesive<br>• Open to external scrutiny<br>• Taking note of value for money | • Run programmes and work efficiently and effectively<br>• Develop continuously to meet current and future beneficiary needs |

## Relating this to social investment

What does good governance over social investment involve? Four aspects are relevant:

- **Making good decisions** – The decision to be made must be understood and made by the right body – the board – acting together, well chaired and having a voice and an opinion. Understanding the decision means the alternatives must be known and all possible impacts of the decision considered. The board should seek advice on any aspects on which they are unsure.
- **For the right reasons** – This is about having the right information on which to base the decisions and both understanding and using it. It is also about the logical underpinning of the decision. It includes testing and challenging that information, but also the scope of the decision itself, to ensure that the implications and options are understood well. Implicit in this is a risk–benefit analysis, with conditions around the decision and a risk strategy that will follow into the delivery stage.
- **Delivering the results and outcomes** – Apart from getting the decision-making right, there is an obligation to deliver the results of that decision and to pursue the targeted outcomes. Four elements of this stand out as important:
    - Monitoring actual delivery and outcomes and comparing to the original intention decided upon by the board.
    - Acting appropriately to improve and re-focus delivery, if it starts to veer off from what was intended or becomes harder to deliver, or if it is realised that something else is needed.

- Putting in place risk processes: assessing and planning for risk at the outset, in terms of financial, operational, delivery risk (not achieving the targeted impact, or causing something unintended); and governance (losing appropriate control, or its vesting in the wrong people); then monitoring to spot problems; and acting in line with the plan to address them.
- Ongoing test and challenge, as without going into the sort of continuous soul-searching that never gets anything delivered, it's important to occasionally revisit certain aspects: whether what is being delivered is meeting the needs of the beneficiaries; whether something else is needed; and whether it could be delivered in another, better, more efficient or more effective, way.

- **Engaging with and informing stakeholders**
  In addition to the beneficiaries, a range of other stakeholders is involved. They need to be kept informed and engaged so that they:
  - can understand and support service delivery
  - can know how to engage with it
  - want to put their resources behind it
  - can act to support the wider mission (for whole system change, changed behaviours, policy, or something else) the charity is pursuing.

## Good governance needs controls – but by whom and for what purpose?

Looking back at the grid in Table 27.1, the characteristics of the organisation and its activities mean that the board will need controls in place to ensure that these happen as planned. Also, that they can be reliably reported upon, first internally and later to external stakeholders.

The board should put in place control systems that cover the key risks and areas of delivery, but remain proportionate to them. An over-complicated system, with controls over things that don't actually matter, is as much a waste of charitable resources as a system which doesn't control what it should.

It is beyond the scope of this chapter to develop a detailed exposition of control environments in organisations – other authors have done that. Systems inevitably need tailoring to the circumstances, which means that detailed suggestions here are not likely to be useful. However, some key focus points in those control systems can be summarised as an outline structure for addressing this. These are shown in Table 27.2, split between controls applying to investors and investees. These areas of interest for social investment should be integrated with the organisation's own, wider control systems. This does not replace those.

### Scrutiny and effective challenge are key

The board is involved not just in decision-making, but in looking into, testing and challenging the information coming from the organisation's delivery team, whether that is the investee or the investor. This demands thinking about three elements:

1   **What's done**
    Information coming to the board needs to be complete, relevant and accurate. How will the board test that that is so and ensure that it understands it? It can use a mixture of four methods:

*Table 27.2* Outline structure for developing controls in social investment

| Area for control | High level control questions | |
|---|---|---|
| | Investor | Investee |
| **Financial** | 1  Is the investment drawn down and applied for the agreed purpose? <br> 2  Are sound financial controls in place in the investee? <br> 3  Are sound financial controls in place in the investor? | 1  Is the investment drawn down and applied for the agreed purpose? <br> 2  Are sound financial controls in place? <br> 3  Are obligations to the investor monitored and met? |
| **Operational** | 4  Are appropriate operational controls in place in the investee? | 4  Are operational controls appropriate to delivery? |
| **Impact** | 5  Will it achieve its targeted impact? | 5  Will it achieve its targeted impact? <br> 6  Will it avoid unintended adverse effects? |
| **Risk** | 6  Are all material risks identified and planned for? | 7  Are all material risks identified and planned for? <br> 8  Are risk-monitoring systems in place and fit-for-purpose? <br> 9  Are we able to take appropriate action to mitigate risk? |
| **Future planning and sustainability** | 7  How will the funding be repaid? <br> 8  Will this have an adverse effect on the long-term viability of the investee? | 10  How will the funding be repaid? <br> 11  How will long-term sustainability be achieved after initial capital is repaid? |
| **Constitution and objectives** | 9  Is the investment in line with the investor's focus and objectives? <br> 10  Is investment decision-making appropriate? | 12  Is the investment in line with the organisation's powers and constitution? <br> 13  Is fund-raising decision-making appropriate? <br> 14  Are terms of funding best value and appropriate to the organisation's needs? |
| **Stakeholder engagement** | 11  Have stakeholders been identified? <br> 12  Is an engagement plan in place and effectively delivered? | 15  Have stakeholders been identified? <br> 16  Is an engagement plan in place and effectively delivered? |
| **Documentation and reporting** | 13  Is documentation maintained for all key decisions, and monitoring? <br> 14  Where this relies on documentation from investee or others, is this timely and accurate? <br> 15  Is internal and external reporting appropriate and responsive to stakeholders? | 17  Is documentation maintained for all key decisions and monitoring? <br> 18  Where this relies on documentation form third parties, is this timely and accurate? <br> 19  Is internal and external reporting appropriate and responsive to stakeholders? |
| **Beneficiaries** | 16  Are we appropriately meeting the needs of beneficiaries and listening to their voice? | 20  Are we appropriately meeting the needs of beneficiaries and listening to their voice? |

- Read and interpret in the context of what it already knows, but using the evidence that is in the document in front of it
- Request further supporting evidence, including due diligence, which was discussed in Chapter 24
- Verbal challenge and enquiry of the person who has prepared the document
- Analytical review – testing what is being presented against previous expectations, against evidence from other sources (sometimes described as "triangulation" in a research context) and forms of overall "sense-checking".

2   **How it's done**

There needs to be an atmosphere of positive and supportive enquiry: robust and methodical, but respectful and not unnecessarily combative. This means that the relationships between board members and between board members and those reporting to the board need to be worked upon. The chair will need to lead this aspect.

3   **How it's recorded**

Scrutiny in public sector contexts tends to be the subject of detailed notes, in a question and answer format. This is likely to be helpful only on rare occasions in the context of social investment decisions and governance. The focus is likely to be better if it recognises and records in minutes:

- Who was there and that they made enquiry
- The key elements that were discovered that are pertinent to the decision or its follow-through.

It may be that some of the matters discussed and minuted are commercially sensitive or confidential and so should be kept in a confidential "second part" of the minutes, which are not published in the way that may be the norm for general board minutes.

## Ensuring the assets of the organisation aren't put at undue risk

This is an underpinning theme for both investor and investee. However, the focus on risk must support the investment and not drive it. The governance approach and processes must help the organisation stay in that middle ground between headlong, mission-driven enthusiasm and risk-focused immobility.

Any activity will put assets at risk: that is the nature of running an organisation which is trying to achieve something, especially social change. The focus needs to be on understanding the risk, working out which risks are acceptable and to whom and how they can mitigate or accept them.

## Engaging stakeholders: a key, and developing, area of governance

The Centre for Public Scrutiny, noting that scrutiny needs to embrace all involved in public service (so including charities, and social investors) suggests that accountability, good communication and a relationship underpinned by transparency, and an open dialogue are key (Centre for Public Scrutiny, 2019; Bullivant and Gilling, 2017). These are described elsewhere as accountability, transparency and involvement (or participation).

Understanding these three elements gives a useful foundation to the stakeholder engagement side of good governance, and stakeholders are interested in the social investment interaction just as they are in the work that is delivered. Looking at those three:

- **Accountability**
  This is a recognition by one party that they are responsible to stakeholders for their actions and the success of these. It embodies recognising who is interested, the nature of that interest, and the responsibility to them, and then communicating that to them as the foundation of the relationship.

  In an investor–investee relationship it is, at least in part, communicated in the funding agreement, but it should be reflected in other formats, both private and for publication.
- **Transparency**
  It is unhelpful to see this as a drive to make everything public. At best unstructured publication of data without explanation is not helpful, and at worst it may be damaging commercially, or to mission. What is needed is a helpful, open, communication of what is being done, how, why, and the impact that is expected, together with enough to gain a useful understanding of risks and uncertainties.

  There will be constraints around this, on the one hand to protect third parties' privacy and interests, and on the other driven by statutory and contractual requirements (e.g. publication of accounts and reports, regulatory scrutiny or the requirements of the Freedom of Information Act 2000).
- **Involvement, or participation**
  The relationship with stakeholders needs to be open to a dialogue: a two-way conversation. So whilst the organisation should communicate clearly and transparently, and acknowledge its accountability, it should also support and respond to feedback from stakeholders.

Receiving feedback from beneficiaries and listening to their needs carefully, will enable the social investment to be a powerful change tool. It will also lead to a greater chance of success.

## Understanding and getting to know your stakeholders

Running through all of this has been the theme of stakeholders and engagement with them. It is probably helpful to draw those various aspects together in one place, to examine how good governance demands we deal with them, including some actions we can take. This can be done in five headings:

- **Who are they?**
  This is clearly the starting point. That list should be put together at the outset, regularly developed and updated. Some suggestions, in no particular order and split between investor and investee, are shown in Table 27.3.
- **Staying aware ... staying balanced ...**
  Times and events mean change and the list changes, too. Pressures from particular stakeholders may tend to skew attention away from others, so this must be monitored and guarded against. These pressures may cause behaviour and relationships to change, meaning these need to be recognised and dealt with before they compromise success.

*Table 27.3* Some likely stakeholders

| Investor | Investee |
| --- | --- |
| Investee | Investor |
| Project beneficiaries | Other investors |
| Investors (where it is a fund) | Funders |
| Founders and other backers | Commissioners and other customers |
| Investees on other projects | Beneficiaries |
| Board | Trustees and committee members |
| Staff and management | Staff and management |
| Regulators | Regulators |
| Government | Government and local government |
| The wider public | The wider public |
| The environment | The environment |
| | Other charities and social purpose organisations |

- **Understanding their interest and their need to know**
  Each stakeholder's interest should be understood and, wherever possible, looked at from their particular perspective. This leads naturally into an understanding of what they need to know about the project and its operation and success, either to satisfy or to develop that interest. The best way to know is to ask. So, where practical, ask.
  The best way to success is to understand each party's motivation for engaging in the social investment and mapping these out in advance. By taking on this dynamic, we can understand what each party brings and what success looks like. This can be brought into the planning and social investment structure.
- **Engaging with them**
  Given who your stakeholders are and their level and focus of interest, plan how to engage with them. This should span the three elements of accountability, transparency, and participation or involvement. How will you get them to realise you are seeking to engage with them? How do you open the channels for them to respond?
- **Reporting to them**
  Reporting needs to be relevant, timely and presented in a way that is interesting to stakeholders. The eight characteristics of meaningful impact measurement – while focused just on one area of reporting – remain a helpful checklist here – see Table 26.1 (Clifford *et al.*, 2014, p. 33). The reports also need to get to stakeholders in a conveniently accessible form. Consider choice of media, format of document and the use of presentational tools, such as infographics, picture and video or audio.

## Making social investment governance a success

As a final word, we turn to Rabindrakumar (2016) in the Social Investment Insight series for Big Society Capital. She asks, "what do Trustees think needs to improve if social investment is going to be more readily used as a tool to deliver impact?"

Rabindrakumar (2016, p1) identifies the following:

- Strengthening boards by the private sector and other agencies potentially playing a role in finding trustees with necessary skills, while still maintaining focus on mission and impact.

- Providing information for trustees, to help them make sense of the funding landscape and enabling more informed decisions.
- Encouraging more discussion around the opportunities and risks of social investment at board level earlier in their thinking around strategy, rather than when looking to fund a specific project.
- Demystifying common questions around risks and responsibilities which can raise red flags – by sharing stories and learnings and reaching more trustees and non-executive directors.

---

**In this chapter we've taken a look at:**

The nature of good governance, highlighting some of the sources of guidance on that
Making and delivering social investment decisions
Scrutiny of social investment decisions
Engaging with stakeholders as a key element of good governance

**We hope you have learned through the *doing* section what needs to be thought about and delivered when using social investment.**

---

## References

Bullivant, J. and Gilling, T. (2017), *Scrutiny: the new assurance? A good governance discussion document*, London, The Good Governance Institute and CfPS, accessed 16 May 2019, www.good governance.org.uk/wp-content/uploads/2017/09/Scrutiny-report-A-Good-Governance-Discussion-Document-3.pdf.

Cadbury, A. (Chair) (1992), *Committee on the Financial Aspects of Corporate Governance: report*, London, Gee & Co., para. 2.5, accessed 16 May 2019,https://ecgi.global/sites/default/files//codes/documents/cadbury.pdf.

Centre for Public Scrutiny (2019), *Scrutiny frontiers 2019: experiences from the scrutiny frontline*, London, CfPS, accessed 19 May 2019, www.cfps.org.uk/wp-content/uploads/CfPS-Scrutiny-Frontiers-2019-v3-WEB-SINGLE-PAGES.pdf.

Charity Commission. (2018), *The essential trustee*, publication CC3, London, the Charity Commission, accessed 16 May 2019, www.gov.uk/government/publications/the-essential-trustee-what-you-need-to-know-cc3.

Clifford, J., Hehenberger, L. and Fantini, M. (2014), *Proposed approaches to social impact measurement in European Commission legislation and in practice relating to EuSEFs and the EaSI*, report by GECES (Groupe d'experts de la Commission sur l'entrepreneuriat social) subgroup on impact measurement, accessed 15 October 2018, www.ec.europa.eu/social/main.jsp?catId=738&langId=en&pubId=7735&type=2&furtherPubs=yes.

Financial Reporting Council, FRC (2018), *The UK corporate governance code*, accessed 16 May 2019, www.frc.org.uk/getattachment/88bd8c45-50ea-4841-95b0-d2f4f48069a2/2018-UK-Corporate-Governance-Code-FINAL.PDF.

Good Governance Steering Group (2017), *Charity governance code for larger charities*, London, accessed 18 May 2019, www.charitygovernancecode.org/en/pdf.

Governance Institute of Australia (2019), *What is governance?*, accessed 16 May 2019, www.governanceinstitute.com.au/resources/what-is-governance/.

Institute of Governance (2019), *What is Governance?*, accessed 16 May 2019. www.iog.ca/what-is-governance/.

Rabindrakumar, G. (2016), *Governance and social investment: exploring the experiences of charity and social enterprise boards with social investment*, Social Investments Insights Series, July 2016,

London, Big Society Capital, accessed 16 May 2019, www.bigsocietycapital.com/sites/default/files/attachments/Social%20Investment%20Insights%20-%20Governance%20July%202016.pdf.

World Economic Forum (2016), *What do we mean by governance?*, edited by Bruce-Lockhart, A, accessed 16 May 2019, www.weforum.org/agenda/2016/02/what-is-governance-and-why-does-it-matter/.

# Appendices

# Appendix 1

## 28 questions for social investment success

## A diagnostic tool

Social investment can:

| ensure your organisation's sustainability and viability by diversifying funding streams | provide funding for infrastructure to provide a platform from which your work can be scaled up or replicated | increase the impact of your organisation by ensuring sufficient funds to expand your reach |
|---|---|---|

Use the diagnostic tool in Table Appendix 1.1 to help you think about:

*   whether social investment is right for your organisation
*   whether your organisation is ready to consider and use social investment
*   what type of social investment product could best help your organisation.

Answer all 28 questions "Yes" or "No".
The completed questionnaire will highlight strengths (Yes) and weaknesses (No).

*Table Appendix 1.1* Table to help consider preparedness for social investment

*Strategic fit and understanding social investment*

**General questions**

| | | |
|---|---|---|
| **Question 1** | Are planned activities and the impact from social investment in line with charitable articles/objects? | Yes/No |
| | AND | |
| | Do you have a clear intention to create social impact with these funds? | Yes/No |
| **Question 2** | Does your organisation understand social investment (and is there a cultural fit)? | Yes/No |

**Governance considerations**

| | | |
|---|---|---|
| **Question 3** | Is your board engaged? | Yes/No |
| **Question 4** | Have you considered the financial risks of taking on repayable finance, including any impact on your reserves policy? | Yes/No |

**Commercial model**

| | | |
|---|---|---|
| **Question 5** | Do you have a clear commercial proposition for the social activities and clarity about the business model for this? | Yes/No |
| **Question 6** | Are you clear about the selling proposition and the customers – is there a compelling rationale why customers will choose you if trading? | Yes/No |

*continued*

*Table Appendix 1.1* Continued

| | | |
|---|---|---|
| **Question 7** | Will the pricing model deliver strong investment returns? | Yes/No |
| **Question 8** | Do you have a track record of delivering activities in this area? | Yes/No |
| **Question 9** | If not focused on trading, can the investment lead to savings or revenue for the public purse? | Yes/No |
| **Question 10** | If used for building infrastructure, can you identify the savings to your business from this investment? | Yes/No |
| **Business plans** | | |
| **Question 11** | Are your business plans robust and do they clearly articulate the use of social investment? | Yes/No |
| **Question 12** | Have you reworked funding models for the organisation so that it is clear that repayments can be made? | Yes/No |
| **Question 13** | Does the business plan discuss sustainability of the activities, their impact and how they may be replicated or grown? | Yes/No |
| **Question 14** | Do the business plans break down growth into different stages so that the organisation can think carefully about innovation, proof of concept and scaling this effectively? | Yes/No |
| **Question 15** | If the new activities involve trading and social investment, have you considered the legal and tax issues and any concerns over control? | Yes/No |
| **Investment readiness and finding funds** | | |
| **Question 16** | Have you identified the type of social investment that fits your need? | Yes/No |
| **Question 17** | Are the reporting, evaluation and management processes in place to take on social investment? | Yes/No |
| **Question 18** | Have you created an investment pack? (Note this is different from the business plans above) | Yes/No |
| **Question 19** | Can you find funds and do you have good links to funders and SIFIs (social investment financial intermediaries)? | Yes/No |
| **Question 20** | Can you negotiate effectively with investors to get a good deal? | Yes/No |
| **Infrastructure and implementation** | | |
| **Question 21** | Do you have robust implementation plans so you can hit the ground running from day one? | Yes/No |
| **Question 22** | Are the marketing and sales plans ready to go? | Yes/No |
| **Question 23** | Do you have the entrepreneurial skills, supporting culture and key relationships in place to deliver the activities? | Yes/No |
| **Question 24** | Do you have support functions in place to handle social investment? This includes being able to receive funds, account for this correctly and manage the change in activities. | Yes/No |
| **Impact reporting and evaluation** | | |
| **Question 25** | Have you established appropriate data and management systems? | Yes/No |
| **Question 26** | Can you demonstrate and report effectively on outputs, outcomes and impact? | Yes/No |
| **Question 27** | Are you able to effectively attribute the impact to your activities, and have you planned to evaluate your work? | Yes/No |
| **Starting** | | |
| **Question 28** | Are you ready to go and have you targeted enough resources for a successful implementation? | Yes/No |

Source: Cass CCE Social Investment Toolkit (Cass CCE, 2016).

# Reference

Cass CCE (2016), *Social investment tools for success: doing the right things and doing them right*, Cass CCE, Accessed 30 September 2018, www.cass.city.ac.uk/__data/assets/pdf_file/0007/358864/CCE-Social-Investment-as-a-new-charity-finance-tool-using-both-head-and-heart-Report-May17.pdf.

# Appendix 2

## The language, terminology and nomenclature of social finance and social investment

### Introduction

What do we call investments that have the intent and motivation to create financial as well as social returns? The full discussion of definitions occurs in Chapter 5, but we summarise this here.

### Impact investments

Bugg-Levine and Emerson (2011) use the term **"impact investments"**. They state, "impact investing recognizes that investments can pursue financial returns while also addressing social and environmental challenges".

Similarly, the Global Impact Investing Network (GIIN, 2018) has authority in this space. It often refers to the term "impact investments". "Impact investments are investments made into companies, organizations, and funds with the intention to generate social and environmental impact alongside a financial return."

Impact investment perhaps tends to refer to the entire universe of investments that create both financial and social returns.

### Social impact investment

The G8 Social Impact Investment Taskforce – established by former prime minister David Cameron in 2014 under the UK Presidency of the G8 – was set up to review the landscape for social investment.

The Taskforce referred to **"social impact investments"** as "those that intentionally target specific social objectives along with a financial return and measure the achievement of both" (G8 Social Impact Investment Taskforce, 2014, p1).

### Social finance

The umbrella term **"social finance"** further confuses the landscape, with Nicholls, Paton and Emerson (2015) identifying that investments are only one type of funding instrument. They focus on the "the broad term *social finance_*rather than the narrower alternative *social investment*" (p2).

A simple example highlights the reason why. If an investment tool blends both grants and investment together, what is this called? They argue only the umbrella term **social finance** caters for this.

*Social investment*

The term **"social investment"** is used by Big Society Capital, the organisation established to promote these types of investments. It states that "Social investment is the use of repayable finance to achieve a social as well as a financial return" (Big Society Capital, 2018).

This term has been preferred by Daggers and Nicholls (2016) in their work reviewing the academic landscape relating to investments which create both a social and financial return. They identify that "the providers of capital are motivated to create social or environmental impact" (2016, p6). Again, they talk about motivation as being a key requisite for social investment.

## Conclusions

With such diversity of terms and complexity, it is therefore perhaps not surprising that Floyd *et al.* (2015) conclude that "social investment has come to be seen as something to do with finance for the social sector" (2015, p22).

In this book, we use a slightly modified definition:

> Social investments have the intent and motivation of generating a social or environmental impact as well as financial return on investment. They aim to measure both the social and financial value they create and be held accountable for this.
>
> (Salway, 2017, p. 9)

## References

Big Society Capital (2018), *What is Social Investment?*, accessed 20 October 2018, www.bigsociety capital.com/.

Bugg-Levine, A. and Emerson, J. (2011), *Impact investing: transforming how we make money while making a difference*, Jossey-Bass (Wiley).

Daggers, J and Nicholls, A. (2016), *The landscape of social impact investment research: trends and opportunities*, University of Oxford.

Floyd *et al.* (2015), *After the gold rush: the report of the Alternative Commission on Social Investment*, accessed 20 October 2018, www.socinvalternativecommission.org.uk/wp-content/uploads/2015/03/SS_SocialInvest_WebVersion_3.pdf.

G8 Social Impact Investment Taskforce (2014), *Impact investment: the hidden heart of markets*, accessed 20 October 2018, www.gsgii.org/reports/impact-investment-the-invisible-heart-of-markets/.

GIIN (2018), *Global Impact Investment Network*, accessed 20 October 2018, www.thegiin.org/impact-investing/need-to-know/#what-is-impact-investing.

Nicholls, A., Paton, R. and Emerson, J. (2015), *Social finance*, Oxford University Press.

Salway, M. (2017), *Social investment as a new charity finance tool: using head and heart*, Cass Business School, Centre for Charity Effectiveness.

# Glossary

**Asset**   Any resource owned by an organisation (either tangible or intangible) that can be used to produce financial or social value.

**Blended value**   A blend of financial and social returns.

**Bond**   A fixed income financial instrument that represents a loan made by an investor to a borrower.

**Borrowing**   When a borrower approaches a lender to obtains funds. Common forms of borrowing include mortgages and loans.

**Bridging loan**   A loan to assist daily activities as working capital for an organisation waiting for other funds to arrive.

**BSC**   Big Society Capital.

**Business model**   A plan for the successful operation of a business, identifying sources of revenue; the intended customer base; products; and details of financing.

**CAF**   Charities Aid Foundation.

**CDFIs   Community development finance institutions**   Institutions lending money to businesses and people who struggle to get finance from high-street banks. They support local communities.

**Charity**   Defined in the UK by the Charity Commission (and regulated as such) are organisations "set up with purposes which are exclusively charitable and for the public benefit."

**Charity bond**   A formal debt instrument issued by a charity, usually at a fixed rate of interest, as an alternative to borrowing from a bank.

**CIC   Community interest companies**   CICs are a type of limited company for people wishing to establish businesses which trade with a social purpose or to carry on other activities for the benefit of the community. CICs limit the distribution of profits and are clear about maintaining assets for the social good in the event of a wind-up.

**CLG   Company limited by guarantee**   A company which confers limited liability on owners and investors. Limited by amount members promise to pay in the event of a wind-up, rather than nominal value of the shares (guarantee – generally £1 each).

**CLS   Company limited by shares**   Each owning party owns a "share" in the assets and liabilities of the company, with that share determined by the rights attaching to "shares" in the company's articles of association.

**Counterfactual**   An estimate of what would have happened in the absence of the intervention, service or organisation.

**Crowdfunding**   Funding a project or venture by raising money from a large number of people, who each contribute a relatively small amount, typically via the Internet.

**CSR**   Corporate social responsibility.

**Debt finance**   Investment with the expectation of repayment. Usually takes the form of loans, both secured and unsecured, as well as overdrafts. Generally, these require a borrower to repay the amount borrowed, along with some form of interest and sometimes an arrangement fee.

**DIB**   Development impact bond.

**Equity**   An investment in exchange for a stake in an organisation, usually in the form of shares. Each share represents ownership of a proportion of the value of the company. Equity investors expect to receive dividends paid out of the organisation's earnings and/or capital gain on the sale of the organisation, or on selling their shares to other investors.

**FCA**   Financial Conduct Authority.

**Finance-first**   A social investment focused on generating financial returns over social returns.

**Financial returns**   The surplus generated by an organisation that can be used for the benefit of an investor or shareholder, or be reinvested back into the business for more social value.

**Financing**   Financing is the process of providing funds for business activities, making purchases or investing.

**Fixed costs**   A fixed cost is a cost that does not change with an increase or decrease in the amount of services delivered.

**Funding**   Funding is the money that lenders and equity holders provide to a business for daily and long-term needs.

**HNWIs**   High-net-worth individuals.

**IFRS**   International Financial Reporting Standards.

**Impact**   The extent to which that change is caused by the intervention.

**Interest**   The charge for the risk of borrowing money.

**Junior debt or Junior mezzanine debt**   A broad category covering most other repayable capital. Often unsecured, it can carry higher, or fixed, percentage interest rates over longer periods than for senior debt.

**Liability**   A company's legal financial debts, or obligations that arise during the course of business operations.

**Loan**   A sum of money that is borrowed and expected to be repaid with interest.

**Microfinance**   A type of banking service provided to low-income individuals or groups which otherwise would have no other access to financial services.

**Mission-driven**   A social investment focused on generating social returns over financial returns.

**MMI   Mixed motive investment**   A mixed motive (or mixed purpose) investment is an asset held by a charity that provides funding to individuals or organisations, in order to generate a financial return for the investing charity. It also contributes to the investing charity's purposes, through the activities or related tangible fixed assets funded by the investment.

   An investment is deemed to be "mixed motive" as neither the investment return nor the contribution to the investing charity's purposes is sufficient on its own to justify the investment decision.

**Outcomes**   The change in the lives of those affected.

**Outputs**   How the activity touches the intended beneficiaries – effectively the points at which the services delivered enter the lives of those affected by them.

**Patient capital**   Long-term capital.

**PBR**   Payment by results.

**PRI**   A programme-related investment is made exclusively to further the charitable aims of the investing charity, by funding specific activities or related tangible fixed assets of a third party which, in turn, contribute to the investor's own charitable purposes.

**Quasi-equities**   A category of debt taken on by a company that has some traits of equity, such as having flexible repayment options, or being unsecured.

**ROI**   Return on investment.

**Secured loan**   A loan in which the borrower pledges some asset (e.g. property) as collateral for the loan in the event of default.

**Senior debt**   Loan capital often secured on property or trading assets.

**SIB**   Social impact bond.

**SIFI**   Social investment finance intermediary.

**SITR**   Social Investment Tax Relief.

**Social enterprises**   Defined by the trade organisation for social enterprises, Social Enterprise UK, as businesses that:

• have a clear social and/or environmental mission set out in their governing documents

• generate the majority of their income through trade

• reinvest the majority of their profits

• are autonomous of the state

• are majority-controlled in the interests of the social mission

• are accountable and transparent.

**Social finance**   An umbrella term for all finance and funding that creates a financial as well as a social return on investment (see also Appendix 2 and Chapter 5).

**Social investment**   Social investments have the intent and motivation of generating a social or environmental impact as well as financial return on investment. They aim to measure both the social and financial value they create and be held accountable for this (see also Appendix 2 and Chapter 5).

**Social returns**   The benefits to society generated by actions, activities or investments.

**SORP   Statement of recommended practice**   The Charities SORP is a statement of recommended practice, which sets out how charities should prepare their annual accounts and report on their finances.

**SPV**   Social purpose vehicle.

**SROI**   Social return on investment.

**Unsecured loan**   Where no collateral is pledged against the loan in the event of default.

**Variable costs**   A variable cost is an expense that changes in proportion to the level of services or outcomes delivered.

**VCSE**   Voluntary, community and social enterprise.

**Venture capital**   A venture capitalist is a private provider of investment capital, often operating through a corporate or partnership structure and investing their own and other investors' funds.

**Working capital**   The funds used in an organisation's day-to day operations.

# Index

Printed in the United States
By Bookmasters